THE CERTIFIED QUALITY MANAGER HANDBOOK

Also Available from ASQ Quality Press:

Success through Quality: Support Guide for the Journey to Continuous Improvement
Timothy J. Clark

Managing Quality Fads: How American Business Learned to Play the Quality Game
Robert C. Cole

The Toolbox for the Mind: Finding and Implementing Creative Solutions in the Workplace
D. Keith Denton with Rebecca A. Denton

Critical SHIFT: The Future of Quality in Organizational Performance
Lori Silverman with Annabeth L. Propst

Juran's Quality Handbook, Fifth Edition
J.M. Juran , editor-in-chief, and A. Blanton Godfrey, associate editor

Principles and Practices of Organizational Performance Excellence
Thomas J. Cartin

Perspectives in Total Quality
Michael J. Stahl, editor

The Quality Toolbox
Nancy R. Tague

Quality Problem Solving
Gerald F. Smith

Business Process Improvement Toolbox
Bjørn Andersen

To request a complimentary catalog of ASQ Quality Press publications, call
800-248-1946.

THE CERTIFIED QUALITY MANAGER HANDBOOK

Quality Management Division
American Society for Quality

ASQ Quality Press
Milwaukee, Wisconsin

The Certified Quality Manager Handbook, 1/e
Quality Management Division
American Society for Quality

Library of Congress Cataloging–in–Publication Data

The certified quality manager handbook / ASQ Quality Management
 Division.
   p.   cm.
  Includes index.
  ISBN 0-87389-387-5
  1. Total quality management—Handbooks, manuals, etc.
 I. American Society for Quality.   Quality Management Division.
 HD62.15.C43   1999
 658.4'013—dc21   99-22702
                                                        CIP

10 9 8 7 6 5 4 3 2

ISBN 0-87389-387-5

Acquisitions Editor: Ken Zielske
Project Editor: Annemieke Koudstaal
Production Administrator: Shawn Dohogne

ASQ Mission: The American Society for Quality advances individual and organizational performance excellence worldwide by providing opportunities for learning, quality improvement, and knowledge exchange.

Attention: Bookstores, Wholesalers, Schools and Corporations:
ASQ Quality Press books, videotapes, audiotapes, and software are available at quantity discounts with bulk purchases for business, educational, or instructional use. For information, please contact ASQ Quality Press at 800-248-1946, or write to ASQ Quality Press, P.O. Box 3005, Milwaukee, WI 53201-3005.

To place orders or to request a free copy of the ASQ Quality Press Publications Catalog, including ASQ membership information, call 800-248-1946. Visit our web site at http://www.asq.org.

Printed in the United States of America

∞ Printed on acid-free paper

American Society for Quality

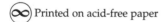

ASQ

Quality Press
611 East Wisconsin Avenue
Milwaukee, Wisconsin 53202
Call toll free 800-248-1946
http://www.asq.org
http://standardsgroup.asq.org

Contents

❖ **Part 5**
Project Management **259**

❖◆❖

List of Figures and Tables

Preface

When you purchased this handbook, you entered into a select group of individuals who will sit for the Certified Quality Manager's Examination. This exam was several years in the making; since its development and implementation, several thousand individuals have passed it and are now certified quality managers.

This exam was developed because the Quality Management Division of the American Society for Quality saw a huge void in other, more topical exams. Several hundred quality professionals participated in the development and review of the CQM Body of Knowledge. Several hundred more have participated in the development of the exam and the grading of the constructed response questions.

This handbook is not the first, but it is one of the most comprehensive collections based on this Body of Knowledge. Although no book can ensure your success in passing this exam, we are proud to say that many leading quality practitioners volunteered their time and energy to what we believe is a very important cause: creating this work to assist others in preparing for the Certified Quality Manager's Examination. I urge you to use this work beyond the purpose of attaining an award or certification to any quality system. This handbook will enhance your ability to perform your job, challenge what you do on a daily basis, and, it is hoped, inspire you to lead your organization on the ultimate quality journey.

To those of you undertaking the exam, I say good luck! To those of you who have contributed time and energy to the *Certified Quality Manager Handbook* development process, I say thank you!

> *Rickey Bowen*
> *Chair, Quality Management Division*
> *American Society for Quality*

Notes to the Reader

DISCLAIMER

The Body of Knowledge (BOK) for quality manager certification (see Appendix A) is largely based on conceptual ideas and models rather than on exact mathematical formulas or tangible items that can be held up as "correct." For some of the areas of the BOK, there may be multiple "correct" views because of differences in industry, organizational maturity, geographic location, competitors' strategies, and so on. Even the "gurus" of quality (see Appendix B) differ in their philosophies, priorities, and approaches to quality. Furthermore, ASQ policy maintains a strict separation between people who prepare the examination and people who present material for candidates. Success as a quality manager requires experience and a mature understanding of the various concepts as well as the specific knowledge obtained from this or any other source.

DESIGNING THE HANDBOOK CONTENT

This handbook was designed as a study aid for those preparing to take the Certified Quality Manager Examination administered by the American Society for Quality (ASQ). Therefore, the subject matter is aligned with the Certified Quality Manager BOK, published by ASQ.

The supplementary section of this handbook contains sample test questions, both multiple choice and constructed response, similar in structure to those on the examination.

Early in the design phase of this handbook, like publications were compared and customer satisfaction levels researched. From this, it was learned that readers preparing for the examination considered the applicability and the depth of most of the topics covered inadequate. Specific feedback suggested that material presented in like publications was reflective of the knowledge base and skills required for a quality engineer, with an emphasis on the tactical and technical requirements for performing quality engineering types of tasks. Missing were the critical-thinking elements associated with strategic, managerial types of decision-making activities that a quality manager would be expected to perform and that are the focus of the examination.

Keeping these factors in mind, the authors of each BOK subject area researched and collected information to describe the following:

- historical perspectives relating to the evolution of a particular aspect of quality management, including recognized experts and their contributions
- key concepts or terminology relevant in providing quality leadership, applying quality management principles, and communicating quality needs and results

◆ benefits associated with the application of key concepts and quality management principles

◆ best practices describing recognized approaches for good quality management

◆ barriers to success, including common problems that the quality manager might experience when designing and implementing a quality management system and insights as to why some quality initiatives fail

The Certified Quality Manager Study Guide Committee and the contributing authors have strived to provide readers with a more holistic perspective of the quality manager's role within the context of the subject matter specified in the BOK. Not every quality manager possesses expertise in each subject area, so the content of this handbook can be used to help readers properly direct their study efforts.

THINKING LIKE A QUALITY MANAGER

The roles and responsibilities of the quality manager and approaches toward quality management vary, depending on the type of industry or the size of the business entity. The BOK is a product of inputs from all these sources and reflects areas of common interest and importance. The development of actual examination questions is intended to measure the level of knowledge and skill that a person possesses relative to each area of the BOK, regardless of individual job design, industry practice, or company culture.

For individuals planning to take the ASQ Certified Quality Manager Examination, getting into the mind-set of the role for which the certification was designed can be key to a successful outcome. Some recommendations for establishing the proper mindset in using this study guide and preparing for the examination include:

1. *Think of yourself as a corporate director of quality for a multiplant business entity.*

In businesses in which products and services are not highly regulated by government legislation and in smaller business enterprises, the quality manager is less likely to have a support staff to perform quality engineering-related tasks and make day-to-day quality decisions. As a result, he or she might spend the majority of his or her time acting in the capacity of an engineer and carry that mind-set in studying for and taking the Examination.

Individuals taking the Certified Quality Manager Examination need to place themselves in the context of having to think strategically. After placing yourself in the role of a corporate director of quality for a multiplant business, envision addressing such questions as "What can the quality function do to help the company identify or implement new initiatives that will enable it to break into new markets?"

2. *Think of yourself as having to integrate the needs of the quality assurance function with the needs of the management team.*

In addition to managing the quality department, the quality manager's role includes facilitating deployment of quality approaches in other functional areas, including supplier quality in purchasing and customer satisfaction in marketing/sales.

❖❖❖

3. *Always think Plan-Do-Check-Act.*

Constructed response questions are purposely designed to assess the ability of the test taker to integrate elements of the body of knowledge. Therefore, using Plan-Do-Check-Act (PDCA) to structure responses will help ensure more complete answers to the described situations.

The role of the test taker in answering the problem statements described in the constructed response questions is not to solve the problem but to define a process on the basis of the principles of continuous improvement that would be appropriate to diagnose and correct the problem. The planning step of the PDCA cycle often involves assessing the current situation as well as past efforts to identify and eliminate the root cause.

4. *Develop an understanding of how all the elements of the BOK are interrelated.*

A good way to practice the use of critical-thinking skills that will further aid in answering constructed response questions is to select two elements or subelements of the BOK and consider how they are related, such as the linkages between quality standards and project management.

A linkage in one direction is that the quality of how a project has been managed could be evaluated on the basis of a standard, such as the design of a new product. Viewed from another direction, when implementing a new quality standard, it is evident that project management will be a key tool for successful planning and deployment.

Throughout this handbook, similar linkages are described in the course of addressing the key requirements associated with good quality management practices for each specific part of the BOK.

Acknowledgments

◆◆

This project was several years in the making and is the result of a truly outstanding team effort on the part of many. Initially, volunteers contributed articles on sections of the Body of Knowledge; this material was supplemented by information obtained from phone interviews with quality professionals.

As the project began to take shape with the assistance of a professional writer, many individuals reviewed drafts of the manuscript; their comments and suggestions greatly enhanced the final output. In the end, a small group of volunteers dedicated themselves to the task of improving and, where necessary, rewriting sections of manuscript. This publication is the result of their exceptional effort.

Because it is impossible to compare the significance of one individual's contribution to another's, the following listing is strictly alphabetical and in no way indicates the size or value of that individual's contribution to the project.

Judith J. Akers
Ronald L. Akers
Reggie Audibert
Bill Baker
Roger W. Berger
Milton Boyd
Gautam Brahma
Eliot M. Dratch
Richard Edelen
Traci V. A. Edwards
Richard A. Gould
William V. Harper
Missy Hartman
Lynda J. Hunn
Jeff T. Israel
Ruby Ivens
Terry Johnston
Tim King
Sylvia J. Makowski
Brenda Malony
Cindy Lee Miller
Wayland Moore

Sandy Mundis

K. A. Muralikrishnan

Phil Mustaphi

Earl E. (Ed) Nelson

Duke W. Okes

Oksana R. Orel

John Pappachan

Tom Peterdy

Janet Raddatz

Terry Regel

John L. Schlafer

James P. Schlichting

Thomas I. Schoenfeldt

John C. Schottmiller

William J. Smith

Daniel M. Stowell

Josh Tye

Krishna Uppugonduri

Raymond E. Urgo

James E. Walters

Russell T. Westcott

Timothy Wiedman

Many others might not have made a tangible contribution to the project but were actively involved in the planning stage or were invaluable to the project because of their support throughout its development. This is a very large group, so it is impossible to recognize these individuals by name.

The project team would like to thank ASQ author Thomas Cartin for permitting the modification and use of a draft of his glossary from *Principles and Practices of Organizational Performance Excellence*. Also, ASQ member Thomas Pyzdek was actively involved in the planning of this project and graciously provided many original pieces of artwork for inclusion in this handbook. We were also fortunate to have a competent and dedicated technical writer in Janice Smith, whose professionalism was indispensable to this project.

It has been a difficult and very unique challenge to manage this project and to avoid conflict of interest for all concerned. We have taken great pains to keep the group who contributed to the development of the exam separate from the people who contributed to this book's content. We are happy to report that we have been successful. As far as determining the value of this book, we will let you, our customer, be the final judge!

Arvind Tripathi
Vice-Chair, Quality Management
Technology
Quality Management Division
American Society for Quality

Part 1
Quality Standards

Chapter 1

Total Quality Management

❖ *This chapter should help you*

- ◆ Define Total Quality Management (TQM) and list its benefits
- ◆ Describe and differentiate between Deming's, Juran's, Feigenbaum's, and Crosby's approaches to total quality
- ◆ Understand the Japanese model of quality improvement
- ◆ Understand barriers to the successful implementation of TQM

WHAT IS TOTAL QUALITY MANAGEMENT (TQM)?

Total quality management (TQM), a term initially coined by the Naval Air Systems Command to describe its Japanese-style management approach to quality improvement, "is a customer driven, process improvement approach to management."[1] A holistic approach to management, TQM "involves a knowledge of the principles and techniques of the behavioral sciences, quantitative and nonquantitative analysis, economics, and system analysis to continuously improve the quality of all activities and relationships."[2] When understood clearly and applied properly, TQM results in many benefits. Before discussing the key concepts of TQM and the resulting benefits, it is necessary to examine the evolution of TQM and the changes that have influenced it.

Evolution of TQM

The first seeds of quality management were planted in the 1920s, when the principles of scientific management were applied wholesale in U.S. industry. At that time, union opposition arose because Taylorism[3] had deprived workers of a voice in the conditions and functions of their work.

Elton Mayo's Hawthorne experiments from 1927 to 1932 (see Chapter 12) showed the positive effects of worker participation on productivity. As a participatory management system continued to evolve during the period of automation in the 1930s, Walter Shewhart used probability mathematics to develop the concept of statistical analysis for quality control in industries. In the 1950s, W. Edwards Deming taught these new methods to Japanese engineers and executives. Joseph M. Juran brought quality management and the concept of management breakthrough to Japan in 1950. Like Deming, Juran is considered one of the architects of the quality revolution in Japan.

Armand V. Feigenbaum's *Total Quality Control,* written in the 1950s, is a forerunner for the present understanding of TQM. According to Feigenbaum, *total quality control* is "an effective system for integrating the quality-development, quality-maintenance, and quality-improvement efforts of the various groups in an organization so as to enable marketing, engineering, production, and service at the most economical levels which allow for full customer satisfaction."[4] Likewise, Philip B. Crosby's four absolutes of quality management paved the way for many companies to improve their quality. Appendix B lists the basic tenets and briefly describes the philosophies of Deming, Juran, Feigenbaum, and Crosby as well as those of other leading contributors to the quality field (Ishikawa, Shewhart, and Taguchi).

The Japanese approach toward quality management, started in 1949 and influenced by Deming, Juran, and Feigenbaum, was promoted under several names: integrated quality control, total quality control, and so on. In 1968, the Japanese agreed to call their approach to total quality control "Company-Wide Quality Control."[5] Kaoru Ishikawa's synthesis of a company-wide quality control philosophy contributed to Japan's ascendency as the quality leader of the world.

Today, TQM is the popular name for the philosophy of encompassing a company-wide approach to managing quality. Well-known standards, such as the ISO 9000 series as well as the criteria for the Malcolm Baldrige National Quality Award (MBNQA), Deming Prize, and other national and state quality award programs, specify the processes that contribute to the implementation of TQM in an organization.

Many others have contributed to the total quality philosophy, its awareness, and its methodology, and these numbers continue to soar. As research on quality and its impact on business continues, changes to the existing tenets and their applications will be inevitable.

Key Concepts of TQM

To analyze and apply TQM, a few popular definitions need to be examined. Several are listed here:

- "TQM is a structured system for meeting and exceeding customer needs and expectations by creating organization-wide participation in the planning and implementation of breakthrough and continuous improvement process."[6]
- "TQM is the system of activities directed at achieving delighted customers, empowered employees, higher revenues, and lower costs."[7]
- "TQM is a customer-focused strategic systematic approach to continuous performance improvement."[8]
- "TQM is a management approach of an organization, centered on quality with a global strategy, based on the participation of all its members and aimed at long-term profitability through customer satisfaction, including benefits to the members of the organization and to society."[9]

All these definitions of TQM all reflect several key concepts, which are discussed in the following.

THE PRIMARY ELEMENTS OF TQM

The primary elements of TQM philosophy can be summarized as follows. TQM is customer focused, requires total employee involvement (commitment at all levels), and is organization centered with the goal being continuous improvement in all aspects of the organization. Additionally, TQM is a complex, integrating system that uses strategic approach, process improvement, and effective communication to change the traditions, attitudes, and activities of the entire organization. Decisions and changes must be fact based so that continuous improvement can be measured and to avoid "change for the sake of change."

Customer Focused

"The customer defines the quality."[10] No matter what a company does to foster quality improvement—training employees, integrating quality into the design process, upgrading computers or software, or buying new measuring tools—the customer ultimately determines whether the efforts were worthwhile. No matter what a company puts into its product or service, if the customer does not purchase or use it, nothing is gained.[11] Chapter 5 discusses different facets of customer service, and Part 4 is devoted to customer satisfaction and focus. These sections will help you understand more about customer focus.

Total Employee Involvement

Total employee involvement refers to employee participation at all levels in working toward common goals. Regardless of the excellence of a company's documentation, data and change control systems, or management's dictums and edicts, effort exerted and money invested will be wasted if employees are not committed to the fostering of TQM. Employee commitment can be obtained only after fear has been driven from the workplace, when empowerment (see chapter 42) has taken place, and when management has provided the proper environment. High-performance work systems must be put into place to help drive the continuous improvement effort resulting from employee involvement. Using self-managed work teams (see chapter 43) that have the power to make changes is one way to do this.

Organization Centered

A company's organization profoundly affects all the other linking elements of TQM. Organization is the infrastructure on which the entire management system depends for efficient operation.[12] At a minimum, the organizational philosophy must be based on mutual trust, confidence and reliability, fairness and justice, recognition of the values of individuals, and openness, with freedom from fear and central decree.[13]

Integrating System

Some business improvement experts believe that employee satisfaction equals customer satisfaction. For this to happen, clear links must exist across the organization. Employees must clearly establish and understand the mission, vision, and guiding principles as well as the quality policies, goals, objectives, and critical processes of the organization. Most important, all aspects of communication must be established and validated continuously. A fine integrating system can be modeled after the MBNQA criteria or the ISO 9000 series standards. Chapter 6 discusses these quality awards and standards.

Every company has a unique work culture, and no organization can succeed without a good quality culture. It is virtually impossible for a company to achieve excellence in its products and services unless a good quality culture has been fostered. Thus, an integrating system connects business improvement elements in an attempt to continuously improve and exceed the expectations of customers, employees, and other stakeholders.

Strategic and Systematic Approach. A critical part of the management of quality is the strategic and systematic approach to achieving its vision, mission, and goals. This process, popularly called *strategic planning*, includes the formulation of both an overall strategic plan and a quality plan. Chapter 14 discusses this formulation process and describes the linkages that exist at all levels of an organization. Although specific approaches to strategic planning continue to evolve, several common elements have emerged.

◆   Customer needs are the focus of strategic planning.

◆   Upper management leads in the development of quality goals and strategies.

◆   Strategies are translated into annual business plans.

◆   Line management implements the actions instead of relying on the quality function to do so.

Process Improvement. A major thrust in TQM is process improvement. Continuous process improvement is discussed in chapter 2, and in Part 6.

Communications. During the change management process, effective communications play a large part in maintaining morale and in motivating employees at all levels. Communications involve strategies, method, and timeliness. Chapter 10 discusses communications within the organization.

BENEFITS OF TQM

TQM improves the efficiency and effectiveness of the supply chain and subsequently improves the service or product. Numerous direct and indirect benefits—to the organization, its employees, and other stakeholders—result when an organization adopts a TQM philosophy. These benefits might include the following:

◆   strengthened competitive position

◆   adaptability to changing or emerging market conditions and to environmental and other government regulations

◆   higher productivity

◆   enhanced market image

◆   elimination of defects and waste

◆   reduced costs and better cost management

◆ higher profitability

◆ improved customer focus and satisfaction

◆ increased customer loyalty and retention

◆ increased job security

◆ improved employee morale

◆ enhanced shareholder and stakeholder value

◆ improved and innovated processes

APPROACHES FOR TQM PLANNING AND IMPLEMENTATION

No one solution is effective for TQM planning and implementation in all situations. Each enterprise is unique in terms of the quality culture, guiding principles, management practices, and the processes used to create and deliver its products and services, so the strategic approach will vary from company to company. The key concepts listed above will be present in whatever models or strategies a company develops or chooses to follow. Several elements and tools required to effectively plan and implement TQM are mentioned in the model described in this section. This model consists of the following steps:

1. Top management decides and commits to TQM.

2. The company identifies and prioritizes customer demands and then aligns products and services to meet those demands.

3. Management lists and identifies the vital processes through which the organization meets its customers' needs on a consistent basis.

4. Management oversees the formation of teams and examines the implications of TQM for the organization.

5. A TQM master plan is developed on the basis of steps 2, 3, and 4.

6. The momentum of the TQM effort is managed by the steering committee.

7. Managers contribute individually to the effort through hoshin planning or other methods.

8. Daily process management and standardization take place.

9. The improvement efforts begun in step 4 are continued through new functional and cross-functional teams.

10. Progress is evaluated and the plan is revised as needed.

11. Constant employee awareness and feedback on status are provided and a reward/recognition process is established.

The five strategies outlined here are followed commonly by U.S. industries and are often applied internationally as well.

Strategy #1: The TQM Element Approach
The TQM element approach takes key business processes or systems and/or organization units and uses the tools of TQM to foster improvements. This method was widely used in the early 1980s by companies trying to implement parts of TQM as

❖❖

they learned them. Examples of this approach include quality circles, statistical process control, Taguchi methods, and quality function deployment.

Strategy #2: The Guru Approach
The guru approach uses the teachings and writings of any one of several leading quality thinkers as a benchmark against which to determine where the organization has deficiencies and then makes appropriate changes to remedy those deficiencies. For example, managers would attend Deming's courses and study his 14 points and seven deadly diseases or would attend the Crosby College. They would then work on implementing the approach learned.

Strategy #3: The Company Model Approach
In the company model approach, individuals or organizational teams visit companies taking a leadership role in TQM and determine their degree of and reasons for success. The individuals or teams then integrate these ideas with their own ideas to develop an organizational model adapted for their specific organization. This method was used widely in the late 1980s and is exemplified by the initial winners of the MBNQA.

Strategy #4: The Japanese Total Quality Approach
Organizations using the Japanese total quality approach examine the detailed implementation techniques and strategies employed by Deming Prize–winning companies and use this experience to develop a five-year master plan for in-house use. This approach was used by Florida Power and Light—among others—to implement TQM and to compete for the Deming Prize.

Strategy #5: The Prize Criteria Award
When using this model, an organization uses the criteria of a quality award, for example, the Deming Prize, the European Quality Award, or the MBNQA, to identify areas for improvement. Under this approach, TQM implementation focuses on meeting specific award criteria. Although some argue that this is not an appropriate use of award criteria, it is recognized that some organizations do use this approach and that it can result in improvements.

COMMON MISTAKES AND BARRIERS TO SUCCESS IN TQM IMPLEMENTATION

A poorly implemented TQM process can cause substantial damage to company morale. A failed effort to introduce TQM can result in a high level of cynicism among management, and this attitude will permeate the entire work force. Top managers in companies with failed TQM programs are less committed to optimizing working conditions, are less likely to provide job performance feedback, and often do not ensure good two-way communication with employees. They are less loyal to the company, more likely to be passive (or passive aggressive) when they encounter wrongdoing, and are less likely to maintain high ethical standards.[14]

In the sense that the word is used here, a *barrier* is anything that blocks or filters the implementation or realization of continuous improvement. All companies must examine systematically what constitutes barriers for them. Such barriers can be cultural, environmental, management or stakeholder related, or employee effected. To reduce or eliminate barriers, the company must examine its communications links, decide what drives the corporate climate (for example, profits or customers), determine the degree of disparity between the salaries of top executives and lower-level employees, and promote mutual trust and respect among all employees. Although mistakes in the implementation of TQM vary from company to company, some of the most commonly encountered problems are listed here.

Lack of Management Commitment

When top management and other company leaders verbally support TQM implementation but their actions fail to confirm this support, the quality program will suffer. If employees see discrepancies between what management says and what it actually does, the resulting cynicism and mistrust can damage the company's growth, performance, and general well-being. For successful implementation, the administrative team must have a clearly communicated purpose for adopting TQM, be consistent in its application of TQM principles, and not treat it as the latest management fad. In addition, TQM will not succeed if upper management is motivated only by external pressures, such as pleasing the board of directors or seeking accreditation.[15]

Inability to Change Organizational Culture

Changing an organization's culture to reflect TQM is difficult and requires time. Fear of change must be removed, poor labor-management relations must be resolved, and the company's focus must change from the status quo.[16] Employees should be convinced of the benefits that a TQM program will provide and should "buy in" to the changes. However, this might mean that employees need to change their behaviors or perform tasks in a different manner. If motivation and enthusiasm for the changes are lacking, frustration and job stress can result.

Plan Implementation Problems

If the implementation plan is unclear or if the plan is not communicated among participants, problems can result. Before implementing TQM, management should (1) obtain a company-wide commitment to the process; (2) communicate the company's vision, mission, and goals; and (3) provide open communication about the company's new focus.[17]

Ineffective Measurement Techniques or Misinterpretation of Data

Data are critical to informed decision making in a TQM environment. Thus, lacking system understanding, having no measurement process, relying on ineffective measurement techniques, lacking statistical understanding, failing to maintain accurate and reliable data, and failing to provide sufficient access to data can lead to TQM's failure. For TQM to succeed, data must be credible and reliable, the measurement process must be consistent, and data retrieval methods should be efficient. Finally, decision makers must be trained in data analysis and interpretation.[18]

Other Common Problems

Additionally, the following mistakes often contribute to difficulties in the implementation of TQM:

◆ lack of cooperation and teamwork (not necessarily a lack of teams) among different work or task groups

◆ a failure to understand what teamwork entails

◆ focus on short-term profits rather than on long-term goals

◆ insufficient resources

◆ lack of continuous training and education

◆ failure to focus on customers' needs and expectations

◆ lack of mutual trust and respect among levels of employees

◆ lack of shared vision, mission, or guiding principles

◆ lack of strategic direction

◆ management's failure to recognize or reward achievements

Management must be aware that barriers such as these exist. Recognition of these barriers should exist during the planning and early implementation phases of TQM. Even organizations that have been involved in TQM for some time can evaluate the program's progress and improve existing systems after studying these reasons for failure. Training in TQM concepts and methods should emphasize these barriers to promote awareness and understanding of the reasons that TQM fails; only then can plans be made to counter them.[19]

🏛 Additional Readings 🏛

Bhote, Keki R. 1991.*World Class Quality—Using Design of Experiments to Make It Happen.* New York: AMACOM.

Cartin, Thomas J. 1999. *Principles and Practices of Organizational Performance Excellence.* Milwaukee: ASQ Quality Press.

Cartin, Thomas J., and Donald J. Jacoby. 1997. *A Review of Managing Quality and a Primer for the Certified Quality Manager Exam.* Milwaukee: ASQ Quality Press.

Creech, Bill. 1994. *The Five Pillars of TQM—How to Make Total Quality Management Work for You.* New York: Truman Tally Books/Dutton.

Crosby, Philip B. 1988. *The Eternally Successful Organization.* New York: McGraw-Hill.

Feigenbaum, Armand V. 1991. *Total Quality Control.* 3rd ed. New York: McGraw-Hill.

Gee, Glen, Wes Richardson, and Bill Wortman. 1996. *The Quality Manager Primer.* West Terre Haute Quality Council of Indiana.

GOAL/QPC Research Committee. 1990. *Total Quality Management Master Plan—an Implementation Strategy.* Methuen, Mass: GOAL/PPC.

Hyde, A. C. 1994. "Barriers in Implementing Quality Management." *The Public Manager* (spring) Vol. 93, No. 1: pp. 33–37.

Ishikawa, Kaoru. 1985. *What Is Total Quality Control? The Japanese Way.* Trans. David J. Lu. Englewood Cliffs, N.J.: Prentice Hall.

❖❖❖

Jacob, Rahul. 1993."TQM—More Than a Dying Fad?" *Fortune,* October 18, pp. 66–72.

Jacques, Elliot, and Stephen D. Clement. 1994. *Executive Leadership—a Practical Guide to Managing Complexity.* Malden, Mass.: Basil Blackwell and Caston Hall & Co.

Johnson, Richard S. 1993. *TQM: Leadership for the Quality Transformation.* Milwaukee: ASQC Quality Press.

Juran, Joseph M., and Frank M. Gryna. 1993. *Quality Planning and Analysis.* 3rd ed. New York: McGraw-Hill.

Ladner, Robert A. 1994."Avoiding Fallout from TQM Failure: Measure Twice, Cut Once." *American Business Challenges,* July, pp. 1–6.

Litsikas, Mary. 1995. "No One Can Afford to Buy Cheap Any More—An Exclusive Interview with A. Feigenbaum." *Quality,* June, pp. 37–39.

Long, Carl, and Mary Vickers-Koch. 1995. "Is It Process Management and, with, or instead of TQM?" *Journal for Quality and Participation,* Vol. 18 No. 3: pp. 70–74.

Marash, Stanley A. 1993. "The Key to TQM and World-Class Competitiveness." *Quality,* September, pp. 37–39.

Masters, Robert J. 1996. "Overcoming the Barriers to TQM's Success." *Quality Progress,* May, pp. 53–55.

McArthur, C. Dan, and Larry Womeck. 1995. *Outcome Management—Redesigning Your Business Systems to Achieve Your Vision.* New York: Quality Resources.

Parr, Gary L. 1995. "The Customer Is Still the Final Test." *Quality,* March, p. 4.

Poirier, Charles C., and Steven J. Tokarz. 1996. *Avoiding the Pitfalls of Total Quality.* Milwaukee: ASQC Quality Press.

Stevens, David P. 1993. "Avoiding Failure with Total Quality." *Quality,* December, pp. 18–22.

Walton, Mary. 1990. *Deming Management at Work.* Milwaukee: ASQC Quality Press.

Weaver, Charles N. 1995. *Managing the Four Stages of TQM.* Milwaukee: ASQC Quality Press.

___. 1991. *TQM: A Step-by-Step Guide to Implementation.* Milwaukee: ASQC Quality Press.

Whalen, M. J., and M. A. Rahim. 1994. "Common Barriers to Implementation and Development of a TQM Program." *Total Quality Management* (March/April): 19–21.

Chapter 2

Continuous Process Improvement

❖ *This chapter should help you*
  ◆ Describe the key historical players and their major contributions to process improvement
  ◆ Describe Deming's nonstatistical contributions to process improvement
  ◆ Become familiar with key concepts and benefits of continuous improvement
  ◆ Understand some of the typical barriers to successful continuous improvement efforts

WHAT IS CONTINUOUS PROCESS IMPROVEMENT (CPI)?

A process can be viewed as a collection of activities that results in an output. *Continuous process improvement* (CPI), also called *continuous improvement* or *process improvement*, is the improvement of processes continuously by eliminating waste so that all processes operate at the most efficient and effective level. Process improvement is characterized by the identification and redesign of an organization's business processes. It can be applied to various processes within an organization, from micro processes, such as the final assembly of a product or the grinding process of a shaft, to macro processes, such as the process for strategic planning or the process for new product development and market introduction. Continuous improvement is linked to two key issues: increasing customer value (which should result in increased profits) and reducing all sources of waste.

In the past, problems often were blamed on employees, who were characterized as lazy, unintelligent, unmotivated, and so on. W. Edwards Deming asserted that most problems (an estimated 94 percent) were a result of poorly planned and operated business processes. Deming's contributions to the quality arena included the concept that employees do not cause most problems; rather, most problems stem from the poor design and functioning of processes. In *Out of the Crisis* and *The New Economics,* Deming cites numerous examples of significant improvements made in business operations when the focus shifted from employees to processes. Deming is just one of many pioneering individuals who focused attention on the need for process improvement.

The Shewhart cycle (named after Walter Shewhart) of Plan-Do-Check-Act (sometimes called the Deming cycle of Plan-Do-Study-Act, as Deming modified it and

❖❖

made it well known) was an elementary but important approach to process improvement because it shows the need for continual process improvement.

The Japanese industrial engineer Shigeo Shingo, a driving force in the Toyota quality improvement program, studied industrial processes and found ways to make improvements and reduce defects. His ingenious ideas for process improvement did not involve the now-popular process maps. Instead, he focused on removing the possibility of making errors that could result in defects. Some of his most interesting work dealt with zero quality control based on source inspection and poka-yoke (mistake proofing). Shingo also introduced vertical (controlling the upstream process) and horizontal (detecting defect sources within the process) source inspections, self-check inspections, and successive check informative inspections (next-person check). His book *Zero Quality Control: Source Inspection and the Poke-yoke System* includes many examples of his efforts in this area and also points out some limitations of reducing defects based solely on statistical process control.

Brian Joiner continues to be influential in the process improvement movement. He has educated many on how to focus improvement efforts and how to implement aspects of team building, all the while emphasizing the need for continuous improvement. Peter Scholtes, a former Joiner employee, authored perhaps the most well-known text on teams (*The Team Handbook*) and has written numerous articles on systems and teams. Additionally, Scholtes has been one of the most vocal advocates of eliminating the typical employee performance appraisal.

Eli Goldratt developed the Theory of Constraints, a methodology for ongoing improvement of systems. Goldratt has focused attention on the possible suboptimization of a system or enterprise by organizations that focus on optimizing each subcomponent. This results in a set of local maxima that does not provide the systemwide global optimum. Two of his most popular books, *The Goal* and *It's Not Luck,* introduce his philosophies of continual improvement along with another Goldratt innovation called the "Thinking Process."

Michael Hammer and James Champy, coauthors of the best-selling *Reengineering the Corporation,* are not considered to be quality pioneers. However, they have stimulated the process improvement movement tremendously. Their business process reengineering (BPR) efforts show that their main concern is process improvement. Their approach might seem radical to some, but they have revitalized the quality area. In *Reengineering the Corporation,* the authors state that TQM is for small, ongoing process improvement, whereas BPR creates major breakthrough process changes. Many dissenters in the quality area feel that TQM provides the mechanism for both major and minor process enhancements.

More recently, Michael Hammer's *Beyond Reengineering* focuses on process-centered organizations. Hammer confesses that *Reengineering the Corporation* emphasized too strongly *radical* change and that he now realizes that the key word in the reengineering definition should be *process.*

KEY CONCEPTS OF CPI

At the most basic level, the product manufacturing process consists of design, material procurement, and manufacturing activities. If the process is expanded to the customer, then additional activities, such as shipping to the distributor, sales promotion, and the actual sale, become a part of the process. Each activity is a separate process that consists of various activities. Activities that do not add value to the process waste resources, so a process is optimized by eliminating non-value-added activities. For example, a process that uses an operator to count parts can be improved by automating or eliminating that task (e.g., by taking advantage of bar-coded inventory systems). When all such activities are removed, the process operates at its optimum with no wasted resources. However, processes must be improved on a continuous basis to ensure that resources are used for activities that add value. Doing the right things in the right manner is the underlying principle of CPI.

The concepts of cycle time reduction and employee involvement are central to CPI.

Cycle Time Reduction

Cycle time reduction is one of the most important goals of CPI. When a given process works at its best, with no waste, the cost and cycle time of the process are greatly reduced because unnecessary activities in a process add cost and time. Thus, implementing CPI results in the elimination of non-value-added activities and the subsequent reductions in cycle time; these help contain costs and improve productivity. Customer satisfaction is improved when cycle times in that area improve. Likewise, cycle time reduction in product development cycles results in faster response to market needs and helps improve revenues. See Chapter 3 for an in-depth discussion of cycle time reduction.

Employee Involvement

CPI programs are highly successful when they receive management support. When top management completely supports CPI projects, adequate resources are allocated to the projects, and employee morale is boosted. The success of CPI also depends heavily on employee involvement because such involvement boosts employee morale and thereby creates a better work environment.

CPI is cross-functional; dealing with work processes, business processes, and manufacturing processes across department boundaries. Cross-functional project teams, called *process improvement teams*, are typically formed to analyze a process in need of improvement. Those who work closely with and have the best knowledge of the process, (e.g., in the case of shop floor improvement projects, the operators and technical personnel who work regularly with the equipment and processes) need to be involved in improvement efforts. If their input is not considered and a team formed solely of people who are not directly involved with the process attempt to improve it, a less-than-optimum or even a negative improvement process can result. However, team members should also come from other areas of the company, as the resulting improvements often benefit more than one department. A cross-functional team approach to process improvement usually yields better results than an approach that focuses on a project in isolation.

The CPI team members might perform different roles. For example, the team leader helps members understand how to work as a team and may train others in how to perform as facilitators. Other team members may be assigned the duties of scribe or timekeeper. Often, the CPI team is a group of five to eight employees who are changed out annually. Regardless of the composition of the CPI team, members are representatives who can solicit input from other employees and thus receive even greater input into the improvement process.

Project leaders, team members, and other employees in the company should receive appropriate training so that they have a better understanding of the improvement process. Clear and measurable goals should be established; management and the team must communicate that these are understood and agreed on.

REENGINEERING

In recent years, many companies have used the practice of reengineering to achieve improvement. Reengineering is the critical thinking and redesign of processes, systems, and functions of the organization to improve its performance. Reengineering assumes that a process (or system or function) has been improved to its maximum and that it is time to revolutionize its design because of diminishing returns.[1] Although both CPI and reengineering result in increased efficiency and effectiveness of processes, various experts have differing opinions as to whether reengineering actually constitutes CPI. It is generally agreed, however, that whether or not reengineering is regarded as *continuous* process improvement, it does result in improvement and so is a tool for achieving improvement.

CPI is the philosophy of continuous, incremental improvement; it refers to small, ongoing changes in day-to-day activities. CPI usually does not result in a radical, new system in a short time, and the process must be measured regularly to identify the need for improvement. In contrast, reengineering involves the rethinking of the functions within an organization; it refers to overnight, or breakthrough, revolutions. An organization begins the reengineering process by looking at the desired end result or benefit of the product or service and working backward to achieve the desired result. (This often requires throwing out the old ways and starting over. Once re-engineering occurs, a whole new measurement process is needed to validate the improvement.) Without a measurement, it is difficult to identify the need for further improvement, so this would not constitute continuous improvement.

Finally, from a training standpoint, CPI is a fairly easy concept for most people to understand. Reengineering, on the other hand, is a complex process that might require formal, professional facilitation.

COMMON BARRIERS TO SUCCESSFUL CPI

CPI can fail for many reasons, some of which are listed here.

Lack of Management Support

Lack of management support is one of the major reasons that improvement efforts fail. Continuous process improvement must be an expectation of management and needs to be demonstrated in an ongoing, tangible way that all employees can recognize. Management can indicate its involvement by helping to identify improvement needs or opportunities, making adequate resources (people, time, and equipment) and training available, monitoring progress, and rewarding improvement efforts and results. Management needs to implement continuous improvement on a daily basis rather than having it viewed as a special activity that takes place in addition to "our normal jobs."

Fear of Change

Fear is a real and often valid concern in any continuous improvement effort. People are afraid of change because of its potential impact on them. Corporate downsizing has forced many people to seek new employment, and improvement efforts are often blamed for job losses. To overcome fear as much as possible, it is important that the vision of the corporate future be well communicated and that jobs be protected when feasible. Ongoing and open communication during any change process is paramount. Although these will not totally remove fear, they can remove some of the uncertainty of not knowing the direction in which the organization is headed.

Change is inevitable. Organizations that direct changes to improve their processes will have a higher probability of success than those that change only in a reactionary mode. Those companies with the foresight to fix and continually improve their processes will find that they are considerably more fortunate than those that stagnate.

This chapter introduced the concept of continuous process improvement. Part 6 deals further with the subject, and Chapter 35 offers specific guidelines for planning and implementing process improvement in an organization.

🏮 Additional Readings 🏮

Deming, W. Edwards. 1994. *The New Economics.* 2nd ed. Cambridge: Massachusetts Institute of Technology, Center for Advanced Engineering Study.

Dettmer, H. William. 1997. *Goldratt's Theory of Constraints: A Systems Approach to Continuous Improvement.* Milwaukee: ASQ Quality Press.

___. 1995. "Quality and the Theory of Constraints." *Quality Progress,* April, pp. 77–81.

Goldratt, Eliyahu M. 1992. *The Goal.* 2nd ed. Great Barrington, Mass: North River Press.

___. 1994. *It's Not Luck.* Great Barrington, Mass: North River Press.

Hammer, Michael. 1996. *Beyond Reengineering.* New York: HarperBusiness.

Hammer, Michael, and James Champy. 1993. *Reengineering the Corporation: A Manifesto for Business Revolution.* New York: HarperBusiness.

Harrington, H. James. 1991. *Business Process Improvement: The Breakthrough Strategy for Total Quality, Productivity, and Competitiveness.* San Francisco: Ernst & Young.

Kelada, Joseph N. 1996. *Integrating Reengineering with Total Quality.* Milwaukee: ASQC Quality Press.

Lowenthal, Jeffrey N. 1994. *Reengineering the Organization: A Step-by-Step Approach to Corporate Revitalization.* Milwaukee: ASQC Quality Press.

Lowerre, J. 1994."Training for Effective Continuous Quality Improvement." *Quality Progress,* December, pp. 57–61.

Roberts, Lon. 1994. *Process Reengineering: The Key to Achieving Breakthrough Success.* Milwaukee: ASQC Quality Press.

Scholtes, Peter R. 1988. *The Team Handbook.* Madison, Wis.: Joiner Associates.

Shingo, Shigeo. 1986. *Zero Quality Control: Source Inspection and the Poke-yoke System.* Portland, Ore. Productivity Press.

Stamatis, D. H. 1997. *TQM Engineering Handbook.* New York: Marcel Dekker.

Trischler, William E. 1996. *Understanding and Applying Value-Added Assessment: Eliminating Business Process Waste.* Milwaukee: ASQC Quality Press.

Chapter 3

Cycle Time Reduction

❖ *This chapter should help you*

- ◆ Understand the concept of cycle time reduction and how it is implemented
- ◆ Understand common mistakes or barriers to successful implementation of cycle time reduction

---

WHAT IS CYCLE TIME REDUCTION?

Cycle time reduction has its roots in the concepts developed by Frederick W. Taylor for his scientific management theory. Taylor was the first to use time values to design and improve the method of performing a task. Frank and Lillian Gilbreth subsequently developed a system of basic motions that are common to most repetitive tasks. As these concepts were built on by others, the discipline of industrial engineering emerged, with "methods analysis" as a subset.

Between 1898 and 1928, industrial engineering concepts were used by several pioneering companies, (e.g., Armstrong Cork Company, Dow Chemical Company, Eastman Kodak Company, Eli Lilly and Company, and Western Electric Company) to improve cycle time and productivity.[1] In fact, Henry Ford revolutionized manufacturing processes with his automotive assembly line for Ford Motor Company's Model T automobile. With complete vertical integration and application of industrial engineering techniques, Ford claimed that the process of producing an automobile would take only 81 hours from the time an ore boat docked and unloaded until an automobile made from the steel of that ore rolled off the assembly line.[2] However, this was probably a theoretical estimate consisting only of the processing time and not the modern throughput definition, which would include all storage and delays in the overall time calculation.

During the 1980s American industry began to investigate and study the Japanese techniques of total quality control and productivity methods. Of particular interest was the Toyota Production System, which emphasized "just-in-time" (JIT) production and Kanban inventory control systems. This approach was necessary because of Toyota's need to produce diverse products that could be delivered quickly. Because the traditional American manufacturing model using economies of scale to reduce cost did not fit their needs, the Japanese applied classic industrial engineering techniques in nontraditional ways. Most previous American methods

❖❖❖

analysis had focused on direct labor and the methods of actually producing a part, with the output being increased production rates (pieces per hour). The Japanese applied these concepts to nontraditional operations (such as setup) that caused the failure to improve throughput and caused a buildup of inventory rather than just-in-time flow of the product. For example, they concentrated on the time it took to change a die in a stamping operation, as a long die change time meant that a longer production run would be required to amortize the downtime caused by setup. Because the Japanese had a goal of reducing inventory costs by producing only what was required, when it was required, they studied the operations that prevented this from happening and then applied the classic industrial engineering methods analysis techniques. When this technique was given a catchy name, "single minute exchange of die" (SMED), the concept was adopted by American industry on a large scale. Rates to change dies in stamping operations were dramatically reduced, as die changes that had required 12 to 24 hours to accomplish were completed in a matter of minutes.

IDENTIFYING OPPORTUNITIES AND IMPLEMENTING CYCLE TIME REDUCTION

Cycle time is "the total amount of time required to complete the process, from boundary to boundary; one measure of productivity."[3] One of the keys to reducing cycle time is to define the system and the parameters that require improvement. Many times the system can be represented as a network of nodes and arcs connected to the nodes. These networks are also used in project planning models, such as the critical path method (CPM) or the project evaluation and review technique (PERT). Most systems can be modeled as charts to track either product or material flow improvement, personnel activity improvement, or events occurring on a particular piece of equipment or group of equipment (e.g., a manufacturing cell).[4]

For plantwide or department analysis, it is sometimes possible to develop process maps directly on the plant layout chart. The information normally contained in these illustrations includes the following:

- ❖ an operation in which some value-adding activity is taking place
- ❖ transportation from one location to another either for an operation or for storage
- ❖ quality verification of critical product or process characteristics, such as inspection or statistical process control
- ❖ a delay when the product or person is waiting for another scheduled activity
- ❖ storage when a part is assigned to a specified area and protected against unauthorized removal

To perform a cycle time reduction analysis, tasks first must be characterized as they relate to the parameters requiring improvement (such as value-added or non-value-added tasks or tasks that must be done internal to a machine cycle and those that can be done external to a machine cycle, preferably while the required internal tasks are occurring). Internal tasks are those that are part of the process done in series, whereas external tasks are done while an internal task is taking place.

Once the network and current sequence of tasks have been established, times are assigned to each task. The critical path—the path that controls overall system performance—should be established to determine which part of the system requires analysis and cycle time reduction. Cycle time reduction analysis must be applied to the portion of the system that controls overall system performance if several flow lines are in parallel. In other words, if the network consists of several parallel pathways, the critical path is the element of the system that should be studied and improved.

After the critical path has been identified, goals for cycle time reduction should be determined. The tasks should be reordered in a manner that minimizes the undesirable parameter and maximizes the desirable parameter, that is, that decreases the time spent on non-value-added tasks to increase the overall percentage of time spent on value-added tasks. For maximum efficiency, internal activities should be rearranged so that they can be done external to the value-added operation. The activity should be improved so that there is less chance for error, decreased travel times, less storage, and so on.

In implementing change, four basic principles are recommended for improving housekeeping: a requirement for effective cycle time reduction. The four principles are as follows:

"*Simplify* means to identify needed tools, parts, etc., and remove everything else from the work area. The operator should sort through then sort out.

Organize means to designate locations for everything and set quantity limits. Locations should be designated with the objective of minimizing material handling, distance traveled, and unnecessary work.

Participate means to involve the local operator in determining what he/she needs to do a better job, and then meeting those needs.

Discipline means developing standard operating procedures and sticking to them. This provides the basis for not only reducing changeover times but also for performing changeovers to achieve consistent, stable, results."[5]

Implementing cycle time reduction can reduce work-in-process and finished goods inventories, shorten production runs, decrease lead times for production, and increase throughput (decrease overall time from start to finish). Improvement opportunities exist at both the macro and the micro levels. At the macro level, opportunities can be identified through benchmarking with industry leaders. For example, it might take a competitor one and a half years to introduce a new product to the marketplace. If it takes another company four years to do the same thing (product development), a cycle time reduction opportunity exists. An internal analysis can point out bottlenecks and delays that demand attention. Because many opportunities might be identified, a Pareto analysis (discussed in Chapter 33) can be performed to decide which factors demand immediate attention. Some problems might be fixed easily in minutes; whereas others might require the establishment of a process improvement team and take many months to correct.

❖❖❖

TRACKING AND REPORTING CYCLE TIME REDUCTION PERFORMANCE

Once a change has been implemented, someone should be responsible for verifying that the expected improvement has occurred. If improvement has been accomplished, the system should be reanalyzed to determine whether a new critical path has been formed. If the expected improvement has not occurred, the analysis should be continued.

Cycle time can be measured by the actual time it takes for something to happen. An expectation must be established, and then elements of the project are lined up so that their completion can be measured against the expected time factor. If differences exist between what one actually sees and what one expected to see, the expected benefits might not be taking place, and a reanalysis of conditions might have to take place to identify why.

Cycle time must be continually measured and monitored. Run charts are an effective tool for doing this. When problems are noticed, they must be investigated and causes assigned.

COMMON MISTAKES AND BARRIERS TO SUCCESS IN ACHIEVING CYCLE TIME REDUCTION

The problems listed in the following sometimes occur when cycle time reduction is attempted.

Creation of a Bottleneck

The most common mistake in attempting to achieve cycle time reduction is to sub-optimize a portion of the system that is not on the critical path. Bottleneck operations in a production process have long been recognized. Prior to the Toyota Production System, manufacturers tended to work on improvement of the bottleneck of the process without regard to the contribution of the process to the overall manufacturing system. Substantial improvement to the process might not produce any savings and might actually increase costs if the result is increased inventory and storage of product components when they must be held until components from another, less efficient process are completed and ready for final product assembly.

Inattention to Other Issues

Cycle time reduction cannot be performed in a vacuum. In itself, cycle time reduction might not result in an improved product or service; it must be studied to ensure that it does not adversely affect the quality of resources or other items devoted to it. Any change in the production cycle may cause a new problem. Expectations need to be examined to determine whether they are realistic. For example, the importance of a deadline might be diminished if it is impossible to achieve the desired result in the specified time frame.

Absence or Misinterpretation of Data

Making decisions without data or misinterpreting data can lead to unexpected results. Establishing times for and determining the true sequence of events is very important to the improvement process. Videotaping activities for review by the cycle time improvement team is an excellent technique for doing this.

Additional Readings

Bockerstette, J. A., and R. L. Shell. 1993. *Time Based Manufacturing.* New York, NY: Industrial Engineering and Management Press and McGraw-Hill.

Emerson, H. P., and D. C. E. Naehring. 1988. *Origins of Industrial Engineering.* New York, NY: Industrial Engineering and Management Press.

Ford, Henry. 1926. *Today and Tomorrow.* New York, NY: Doubleday Page.

Galloway, Dianne. 1994. *Mapping Work Processes.* Milwaukee: ASQC Quality Press.

Lu, D. J. 1986. *Kanban—Just-in-Time at Toyota.* Portland, Ore.: Productivity Press.

Ohno, T. 1988. *Toyota Production System—Beyond Large Scale Production.* Portland, Ore.: Productivity Press.

Salvendy, Gavriel, ed. 1982. *Handbook of Industrial Engineering.* New York, NY: John Wiley & Sons.

Shingo, Shigeo. 1985. *A Revolution in Manufacturing: The SMED System.* Portland, Ore.: Productivity Press.

Thomas, P. R. 1990. *Competitiveness through Cycle Time.* New York, NY.: McGraw-Hill.

Chapter 4

Supplier Management

❖ *This chapter should help you*
- ◆ Understand the steps involved in supplier selection
- ◆ Understand the benefits of supplier certification
- ◆ Understand how indices and other quality tools can be used to develop a supplier rating system
- ◆ Realize the benefits that result when the customer and supplier have established a good relationship

MANAGING SUPPLIER QUALITY

Supplier management is a broad term that encompasses supplier selection, supplier certification, and customer–supplier relationships. The selection, certification, and management of suppliers has a tremendous effect on the amount of variation that enters a process, thus creating an enormous impact on the quality of the finished product.

The need for ensuring supplier quality began during the industrial era as production lines and mass production became commonplace. Companies involved in business on a global scale have discovered the importance of removing variation from their systems while emphasizing quality. Today an increasing number of companies are requiring their suppliers to become certified to quality standards. Two such standards, the ISO 9000 series standards and QS-9000, are discussed in Chapter 6.

SUPPLIER SELECTION

The fourth of Deming's 14 points for management is "End the practice of awarding business on the basis of price tag alone."[1] Total cost, not price, is the more important measure when selecting a supplier. Total cost includes the cost of incoming inspection, the cost of managing defective product (e.g., the cost of rework, reinspection, or scrap), and the cost of material of unknown variability entering the buyer's processes and products (e.g., the cost of delays).[2] Total cost should also take into account the level of service offered by a supplier. The supplier that best meets these factors while offering the most customer value should be selected.

All variables are the same in the two columns in Table 4.1 except that in Case 2 the cost of raw materials has been reduced by 5 percent. This reduction results in an additional $35,000 profit—illustrating the need for a buyer to exercise good supplier selection and management practices. In Table 4.1, the largest cost (70 percent of the

❖❖

◆ TABLE 4.1. Cost Comparison		
	Case 1	**Case 2**
Sales dollars	$1,000,000	$1,000,000
Raw materials	700,000	665,000
Overhead costs	250,000	250,000
Total cost	950,000	915,000
Profit	$50,000	$85,000

total cost) is the cost of materials, and this holds true in most manufacturing environments. With a 5 percent reduction in raw material costs, a 70 percent increase in profit is realized. Companies that want to remain competitive must develop a quality system and a supplier base that allows them to lower their total cost, thereby increasing profit.

Alternatively, the savings in Table 4.1 could be obtained through a low-price bidding process, but such a method will not produce long-term results. Low-price bidding tends to drive suppliers away from a business or force them completely out of business. If an organization and its key supplier work together, both companies might realize increased levels of profit. Table 4.1 shows only one business transaction and the resulting financial impact. Consistent, long-term savings usually result when an organization builds relationships with its key suppliers and accordingly shrinks its supply base.

Developing Supplier Criteria

The modern approach to quality management includes selecting suppliers on the basis of predetermined selection criteria that examine all aspects of a supplier's business, not just the cost of materials. A cross-functional team can be formed to develop criteria to be used in the evaluation and selection of the best supplier for a particular product group. The criteria should include proposed material specifications along with their related test and sampling methods. The criteria should also include needs specific to the company or industry, for example, required registration of products with a government agency in the case of medical devices.

Identifying Prospective Suppliers

Prospective suppliers can be identified from suppliers used in the past, from resource books that list suppliers, or from suppliers contacted through sales calls. Prospective suppliers are then provided with the previously described criteria so that they can formulate questions for discussion and present a proposal. The supplier's quality system and any other areas of concern about a product group and its special supply requirements should also be discussed in detail. In the case of just-in-time inventory systems, the supplier's history of on-time delivery is usually reviewed. The supplier's credit ratings or previous credit history might also be considered.

Assessing Supplier Capabilities

The supplier's quality systems can be closely scrutinized through a survey so that the supplier's capability to provide product that meets the specified requirements can be accurately assessed and verified statistically. On the basis of the results of the survey, a supplier audit might be required to verify and clarify statements from the survey. Audit results should satisfy the customer that a quality system is in place and functioning or include recommendations for areas of improvement when problems are detected. All problems should be resolved to both parties' satisfaction before the business relationship continues. Once a supplier has been tentatively selected, representative samples can be requested and evaluated for conformance with specifications and for stability. The samples can be tested in a lab-scale manufacturing process to see how well they perform. Following laboratory evaluation of the samples, larger quantities of material might be required for pilot or extended plant trials to make sure that the material will work correctly in the finished product.

Approving a Supplier

Once a supplier has been approved, a long-term contract with the customer, or a customer–supplier agreement, can be signed. As the business grows, targets and limits can be redefined so that processes operate at the optimal efficiency. Managing the customer–supplier relationship is the topic of Chapter 25.

Finally, the customer should be aware of the many benefits associated with supply base reduction, that is, using one or a few key suppliers to meet all needs. However, because a different set of criteria might be important for each product group within a company, the supplier of another product group or the largest producer of a product is not necessarily the best supplier in all cases.

SUPPLIER CERTIFICATION

Supplier quality management (SQM) is the next generation of supplier certification; it incorporates business objectives and performance with quality tools. Successful, quality-focused relationships with suppliers are key to efficient product or service providers. Supplier selection and certification are actually subsets of SQM—outcomes, not the objectives. The objective of an SQM program is to reduce the total cost of purchased goods or services by improving the supply chain in time, dollars, and quality.

Objectives and Benefits of Supplier Certification

Objectives of supplier certification include the development of a long-term relationship between the buyer and supplier, ensuring the supplier's capability of meeting the customer's needs in all areas and fostering a desire for continuous process and system improvement. Suppliers meeting these objectives will be rewarded with a higher level of certification and as a result will be given more business.

Certification benefits both the supplier and the customer and strengthens the win-win relationship being developed. A good supplier certification system improves product quality through the control and analysis of the production process, thereby increasing productivity. Quality, cost, and service should improve concurrently.

In an effectively functioning quality system that monitors and measures performance and provides feedback on a timely basis, problems are recognized quickly and can be corrected before a company's reputation is damaged or costly corrective action is needed. Lean manufacturing methods determine the production requirements, not inventory. Equipment setup and changeover will be done easily and efficiently, and traditional performance measurements will no longer be needed. Business volumes should be awarded on the basis of the lowest total cost rather than on the lowest initial cost. With the push to reduce costs comes the need to reduce inspection costs, which in turn results in reduced inspection or no inspection, supplier certification, and product acceptance on a certificate of analysis.

Supplier Rating System

An effective supplier certification system will have a three- or four-tier rating classification. Typical ratings, in ascending order, are qualified (sometimes subdivided as restricted and conditional), preferred, and certified. This type of system allows the supplier to climb from one classification level to the next and helps the customer determine which suppliers are most likely to meet their requirements.

A supplier's performance should be evaluated periodically to determine that progress is being made as well as to verify that the supplier should remain certified at the current level. Indices developed for the critical materials that a customer is concerned with are a good tool to use when developing a supplier rating system to support supplier certification. Some examples of indices follow.

Past performance index (PPI). This index can be based both on quality and/or delivery and/or best value measures as the index is calculated. This index is used primarily for individual materials and can be calculated for each supplier that provides this material. Suppliers can be compared easily using this index.

Supplier performance index (SPI). This index can also include both quality and/or delivery measures as the index is calculated. This index tracks the different materials provided by a supplier in order to yield performance trends.

Commodity performance index (CPI). This index, often used when there is no past performance history, is a more general category used to determine trends and evaluate performance.

Quality performance index (QPI). This index can be organized by product or by supplier and takes into account things such as floor failures (manufacturing problems), scrap, supplier corrective action, and failures at receiving inspection.

Delivery performance index (DPI). This index can be organized by product or by supplier and shows delivery trends. Late, early, and on-time deliveries are considered on the basis of requested delivery dates.

Chip Long of World Class Consulting describes the formula that applies for all these indices as follows:

Performance Index (PI) = (Purchased Costs + Nonproductive Costs)/(Purchased Costs)[3]

Nonproductive costs include material rejected at the supplier by a second source inspection and material returned to the supplier. If nonconforming material is accepted by the recommendation of a material review board or if the material must be reworked, the associated costs are nonproductive. Late deliveries and incorrect quantities delivered are also nonproductive costs. All these areas need to be considered when selecting the index that will best monitor the area critical to the business.

All indices represent a ratio of the total costs of ownership compared to the price of the product. For example, an index of 1.85 means that every dollar spent with a supplier costs the customer a total of $1.85. The lower the index, the better.

Suppliers also can be rated and analyzed using quality tools such as Pareto analysis, process capability, and control charts. These methods help identify the best supplier in a particular area and also help that supplier improve as the information is shared and acted on.

CUSTOMER-SUPPLIER RELATIONSHIPS

Historically, the role of purchasing has been to procure materials at the lowest cost. Companies purchased from multiple suppliers, and the purchaser sometimes received incentives to use a certain supplier. Although some of the incentives were legitimate, many had little to do with product quality. The practice of accepting "gifts" from suppliers is no longer considered ethical at most companies in the United States; however, it is an acceptable practice in many other cultures.

Supplier management has changed. In the past, purchasing departments were often told, "Keep manufacturing running. Do not let it run out of anything." This common practice caused purchasing departments to use multiple suppliers to guarantee a continuous supply of needed materials. This approach also worked counter to building relationships with suppliers. Today quality-oriented companies recognize that supplier management is largely based on relationships and that both parties benefit when they cooperate to ensure that an excellent product results. The recent trend toward "lean manufacturing" has increased the importance of supply chain management. Lean manufacturing, also called lean production or the Toyota Production System, is the concept of making what one needs when one needs it. Because it relies on a system of management/production that is totally responsive, it is a system that contains very little waste. Waste includes the following:

◆ overproduction (making more than is needed, which means time and equipment are not available to produce what is actually needed)

◆ inventory (materials that could be used to produce something that is currently desired by a customer and that occupy space)

◆ transportation (putting effort into moving things around, such as from one storage area to another, rather than minimizing unnecessary movement)

◆ movement (having to reach for something rather than having it located right where it is needed, requiring wasted time and effort to get it)

In lean manufacturing, the manufacturing process begins only after an order has been placed; in other words, no inventory exists. Benefits of lean manufacturing include the need for significantly less warehouse space for both incoming and outgoing materials, higher quality of finished goods, smaller manufacturing areas, more satisfied work-force, and higher productivity. Because of the risks involved in having no safety stock, lean manufacturing can be a consideration only when strong customer-supplier relationships based on open communications exist.

Most recently the move has been to work with suppliers to develop relationships, open communications, and so on. These relationships encourage sole sourcing or single-source supply, the selection of one supplier as the provider for a particular material. Sole sourcing reduces variation, especially if that supplier has the quality systems in place to permit certification and eliminate incoming inspection.

A current trend is supply base reduction, in which the number of suppliers is significantly decreased (sometimes by 75 percent to 80 percent). With fewer suppliers the job of managing them becomes easier. Long-term strategic alliances or partnerships with single-source suppliers are developed and nurtured as companies realize that buying from a large number of suppliers does not result in the lowest total cost. Partnerships and strategic alliances between customers and suppliers is the topic of Chapter 27.

The reverse of supply base reduction is customer base reduction. This occurs when a supplier partners with only its best customers. All the previously listed factors for supply base reduction also apply to customer base reduction.

A supplier management system must be supported by the upper management of both companies if it is to function successfully to realize the maximum possible benefits. Money spent initially to build relationships and become better acquainted will be justified through later savings. Successfully building a solid, trusting relationship will guarantee business for both parties on an ongoing basis.

Creative approaches need to be used in relationships to help both businesses benefit. The total cost of doing business needs to be evaluated to determine which supplier might be best. "What else can this supplier do for me?" is a question that needs to be asked, with answers being sought from both parties. Openness to change will help the process and make the relationship stronger at greater savings to both companies. In a good relationship both companies' processes and the largest cost-adding steps need to be analyzed to see whether they are really necessary and how they could be modified to reduce costs. Very unusual ideas can save a tremendous amount of money when applied to the proper areas.

A customer–supplier relationship should be based on mutual trust; it takes an investment of time and money to really reap the benefits of a good relationship. What one party does should not add costs to the supplier's process. An inflexible attitude on the part of either company can increase the costs incurred at the supplier.

A customer does not have to be a major portion of a supplier's business for a good relationship to work. In fact, a good rule of thumb is that requirements should not exceed 30 percent of the supplier's total sales, as a supplier should not be so reliant on one customer that it cannot stay in business if the customer's needs change significantly or if the customer experiences difficulties. An excellent supplier is developed, not found.

⛩ Additional Readings ⛩

Quality Assurance for the Chemical and Process Industries: A Manual of Good Practices. 2nd ed. ASQ Chemical and Process Industries Division. Chemical Interest Committee. 1999. Milwaukee: ASQ Quality Press.

Bossert, James L., ed. 1994. *Supplier Management Handbook.* Milwaukee: ASQC Quality Press.

Brandt, David, and Robert Kriegel. 1996. *Sacred Cows Make the Best Burgers.* New York: Warner Books.

Burt, David N., and Richard L. Pinkerton. 1996. *A Purchasing Manager's Guide to Strategic Proactive Procurement.* Milwaukee: ASQC Quality Press.

Copacino, William C. 1997. *Supply Chain Management: The Basics and Beyond.* Boca Raton, Fla.: St. Lucie Press.

Fernandez, Ricardo R. 1995. *Total Quality in Purchasing and Supplier Management.* Delray Beach, Fla.: St. Lucie Press.

Long, Chip. 1995. *Advanced Supplier Certification.* Seal Beach, Calif.: World Class Consulting Group.

___. 1995. *Supplier Certification.* Seal Beach, Calif.: World Class Consulting Group.

Maass, Richard A., John O. Brown, and James L. Bossert. 1990. *Supplier Certification: A Continuous Improvement Strategy.* Milwaukee: ASQC Quality Press.

Rackman, N., L. Friedman, and R. Ruff. 1995 *Getting Partnership Right: How Market Leaders Are Creating Long-Term Competitive Advantage.* New York: McGraw-Hill.

Schoenfeldt, Thomas I. 1998. *Effective Supplier Relationships.* Presented to Automotive Division Conference in Dearborn, Michigan (June), and Kitchener, Ontario (November). Published in the proceedings of the conferences.

___. 1997. *Supplier Relationships—the New Role.* Presented at the Customer-Supplier Division Conference of ASQ (November). Published in the proceedings of the conference.

___. 1998. *A Supplier Selection Workshop.* Presented at the Customer-Supplier Division Conference of ASQ (November). Published in the proceedings of the conference.

Van Mieghem, Timothy. 1995. *Implementing Supplier Partnerships: How to Lower Costs and Improve Service.* Milwaukee: ASQC Quality Press.

Weber, Richard T., and Ross H. Johnson. 1993. *Buying and Supplying Quality.* Milwaukee: ASQC Quality Press.

Windham, J. 1995. "Implementing Deming's Fourth Point." *Quality Progress,* December, p. 43.

Womak, James, and Daniel T. Jones. 1996. *Lean Thinking.* New York: Simon & Schuster.

Chapter 5

Customer Service

❖ *This chapter should help you*

◆ Become familiar with concepts and philosophies for managing customer service

◆ Become familiar with approaches for fostering good customer service

◆ Understand common mistakes or barriers to success in servicing customers

WHAT IS CUSTOMER SERVICE?

Customer service can be loosely defined as the way in which an organization interacts with its customers. However, customer service goes far beyond the manner in which organizations relate to their customers in day-to-day interactions. To achieve high performance in the area of customer service, the attitudes and values held by employees and promoted by the overall organization must focus consistently and continuously on the customer.

Prior to World War II, manufacturing a good product was the chief concern of most companies. As the postwar economic boom brought about increased competition, the marketing and delivering of goods and services that satisfied the needs and wants of the marketplace received more attention. However, even with the advent of the "Marketing Concept,"[1] customer service usually was relegated to a backroom operation. At best, complaint departments were often viewed as a necessary evil. Unfortunately, some organizations' cultures still tend to minimize the importance of offering good customer service.

In the past few decades, some companies have succeeded in differentiating themselves from their competitors by the level of service they provide. As service leaders, these organizations not only excel in customer retention but also have succeeded in leveraging their service as a means to win customers from the competition.[2] Service leaders enjoy preference (and often legendary status), in the minds of the consumers of their industry sector, promulgated through positive word of mouth (e.g., Nordstrom's mythology).

Today, as organizations are increasingly affected by the global economy, effective customer service procedures and processes are becoming paramount in many economic sectors. Once the basis of differentiation, good customer service is often a requirement just to survive. In some industries high levels of customer service have become the norm, with competitors trying to gain on the early service leaders.

Organizations face a daunting challenge as customer expectations for good service are rising faster than actual performance is being improved. Many organizations have elevated their customer service functions to the forefront of their mission and culture. Additionally, the proliferation of customer service literature in the past decade has been overwhelming. Several experts who have made significant contributions to the topic are discussed here.

Jan Carlzon's contributions are noteworthy in two particular areas. First, he coined the phrase "moments of truth" to represent the collective interactions that customers experience while using a company's services or products. The outcomes of these interactions define the level of each customer's satisfaction. Second, while president of Scandinavian Airlines System (SAS), Carlzon modeled effective leadership in creating a culture for customer service. His constancy in communicating the vision for SAS to become a leading service provider in the airlines industry is an inspiration to any leader.

Karl Albrecht is a noted author in the customer service arena whose best-known books include *Service America* and *At America's Service*. Albrecht's works have blazed new territory in many areas. His messages challenge organizations and their leaders to shift from old ways of thinking to new, customer-focused paradigms.

One of Albrecht's key concepts, the "inverted pyramid," encourages leaders to turn their organization chart upside down. By placing customers at the top of the organization chart, he suggests that the organization's collective actions must support the customer's needs and expectations. Frontline employees are identified as key individuals in the organization, as customer satisfaction is a direct outcome of their performance in each and every "moment of truth" that customers experience. Managers and supervisors serve as coaches and enablers, supporting frontline workers in satisfying the customer. Leaders constantly communicate the vision of customer focus and assist managers in effectively enabling frontline employees to succeed.

A frequent quote in Albrecht's work is "If you're not serving the customer, you better be serving someone who is."[3] Albrecht's point is that good customer service is not just the responsibility of the frontline employees with day-to-day customer contact. Everyone in the organization has a customer (whether internal or external), and all activities must be aligned with how they support the external customer's satisfaction.

John Goodman of Technical Assistance Research Program (TARP) is well known for his role in studies titled *Consumer Complaint Handling in America*. The 1986 study describes practices of American companies in handling customer complaints and is a rich source of ideas for those creating or improving customer contact management systems. In addition, Goodman has published a large number of articles and technical papers, including some that address his "market damage model."[4] Market damage is the cost (in lost sales or profits) stemming from preventable problems that lead to customer defections. The model helps estimate the monetary value of a customer and then looks at the relative impact of various problems on customer loyalty and ultimately on sales and profits. Ranking problems and assessing the likely gains or return on investment (ROI) of various improvement initiatives helps decision makers quantify the financial impact of customer service improvement initiatives.

KEY CONCEPTS OF CUSTOMER SERVICE

Best-in-class service organizations are distinguished from others by their ability to listen to customers and make modifications to meet customers' needs and desires. Companies are able to achieve a culture focused on serving the customer when management says, "This is something we're committed to doing." Such an organization often knows enough about its customers to give them something before they ask for it.

A key measure of customer service performance is "What do the customers think of your product?" To achieve customer satisfaction, a company needs to collect information from customers and evaluate their responses. A company might be willing to satisfy customers, but without the capability of collecting and interpreting that information, satisfaction will not result.

Organizations need to go beyond providing fundamental training on effective customer service techniques (sometimes referred to as smile training). In addition, organizations must deploy service improvement initiatives at a systems level to be effective. Some of the key concepts of good customer service are discussed here.

Create a Climate for Service

Organizations need to create a "climate for service." This requires transformation at each level in the organization. An organization must strive for alignment of related groups of stakeholders.

Frontline Employees Are Key

These owners of all "moments of truth" that customers experience need the rest of the organization behind them. Leaders and managers need to engage employees in their work and enable them to succeed in satisfying customers, often removing and minimizing barriers that prevent success.

The Manager Is a Coach

The role of the manager in high-performing organizations has evolved from that of directing/controlling to coaching/supporting their workers.

Everyone Serves the Customer

Everyone serves the customer or supports someone who does. It is important that all stakeholders in the organization understand the needs of their customers (internal or external) and focus on serving the external customer.

Complaints Are Good

Every complaint is painful, but customers should be thanked for taking the initiative in communicating their problems. If complaints are resolved quickly and well, customer loyalty will likely remain high. The customer who has had a bad experience and who does not complain is the customer least likely to return and most likely to spread negative word of mouth.

Not All Customers Are Equal

Some organizations try to provide high levels of performance to all customer groups. Sometimes the company spends too many resources serving marginal (secondary) customers; this can dilute service provided to customers who are of strategic importance (primary customers). The Pareto principle can be applied here: An organization's primary customers are generally the 20 percent who account for 80 percent of current sales and future profits. An organization should focus on the needs and expectations of these customers.

Do Not Argue with the Customer

The customer is always right! Customer expectations and requirements must be managed appropriately, taking into account that they sometimes change over time. The customer is the one who pays the bills!

Keep Score on Actual Performance

Satisfaction surveys should be conducted periodically to ask customers about performance and to gather suggestions on how to improve satisfaction. Complaints should be tracked, and root causes for frequently occurring problems should be identified. The ordering patterns of customers must be tracked also so that any changes can be detected and discussed with the customer. Resolving complaints might not necessarily bring about customer satisfaction. Many times customers do not complain—they just change suppliers.

BENEFITS OF GOOD CUSTOMER SERVICE

Some of the frequently cited benefits of good customer service include the following:

- building loyalty from existing customers, improving retention, and profits
- generating positive word of mouth, promulgated by highly satisfied customers
- winning market share away from competitors
- higher levels of employee satisfaction, which leads to higher levels of retention

In some industries, superior customer service is a source of competitive advantage because it positions one company above its competitors. However, in industries in which high levels of customer service are the norm, competitors are fighting for market share with each trying to hold on to what it has. Lagging behind the service levels offered by competitors can be tenuous because customer loyalty is always at risk to those who provide higher service levels.

Satisfied customers are more likely to be repeat purchasers. The value of these customers over the lifetime of their relationship with the organization can be quite significant. In fact, Carl Sewell, a well-known Cadillac dealer from Texas, has estimated his typical customer's lifetime purchases to be worth $332,000.[5] In addition to direct revenues, satisfied customers are the most likely to spread positive word of mouth. In some cases these customers go out of their way to sing an organization's praises to other potential customers.

In contrast, dissatisfied customers can cause much damage to an organization's reputation. Not only does the organization lose the customer to competitors, but often the customer spreads negative word of mouth. This is compounded by the fact that at least half of customers are unlikely to complain. Often it is beneficial to make it easier for a customer to voice complaints. This can be accomplished by setting up and publicizing a toll-free phone number and by providing the resources needed to handle questions and complaints.

A key to maximizing profitability and revenue growth lies in facilitating internal service quality. The "Service-Profit Chain"[6] shows the linkages that result from facilitating employees' work. The first benefit is increased employee satisfaction, which drives both employee productivity and employee retention. These in turn drive customer loyalty, which in turn drives both revenue growth and profitability.

HOW IS GOOD CUSTOMER SERVICE FOSTERED?

Good customer service can be fostered in many ways. Some of the most effective elements for achieving it are by creating a culture for service, creating a service strategy, and applying a systems approach to service.

Create Culture for Service

Organizations need an imperative to create a culture for service. This is usually embodied in the mission statement of the organization. If not, it might be time to update these cornerstones of the organization. Leaders are accountable for overcoming inertia (resistance) and for building support and commitment throughout the organization.

Treating employees well is important to generating support and energizing transformations. Hal Rosenbluth of Rosenbluth Travel provides many examples of how leaders can build a strong service culture from within the organization.[7]

Create Service Strategy

Most organizations have a strategic plan and a marketing strategy, but few have a service strategy. Because the goal of marketing is to attract and retain customers, it stands to reason that the service strategy (how one will build customer loyalty; i.e., improve retention) should be integrated with the marketing strategy.

Apply Systems Approach to Service

Davidow and Uttal present a comprehensive six-step plan in *Total Customer Service*. A simpler systems-based approach to high-performance customer service might include leadership, service capability, service delivery process, and measurement and customer data.

Leadership. As discussed earlier, strong leadership is absolutely necessary for an organization to excel in customer service. The leader needs to be perceived as a staunch supporter for customer satisfaction and good customer service. The leader not only needs to convey the vision for excellent customer service but also needs to act accordingly. The leader's personal involvement in special task forces and unwavering support to work through difficult issues will demonstrate to employees that the commitment to service is genuine.

Service Capability. Service capability refers to the resources available to serve the customer in general. These resources include frontline employees, training systems and funding, and infrastructure (phone and computer systems as well as other capital-intensive tools and systems). Many organizations see expenditures in this area only as costs, but in reality these are investments in competitiveness, employee development, and customer loyalty.

Service Delivery Process. Historically, process mapping has been used as a tool to identify steps and improvement opportunities in manufacturing processes. Process mapping is a valuable way to describe the ways by which service is delivered as well. One way to construct this type of process map is to document the way the customer views service. What are the steps that the customer experiences, and what are the customer's expectations in the resulting moments of truth? Who are the frontline employees who "own" the moments of truth, and what is the organization doing to assist these workers in satisfying customers? A good reference for charting the service delivery process is "Staple Yourself to an Order."[8]

Stakeholder alignment (within the service delivery process) is possible once stakeholders have been identified and collective customer service objectives and initiatives are agreed on by each stakeholder group. The outcome of having stakeholders in alignment is synergy and high-performance service levels.

Measurement and Customer Data. The organization needs to systematically gather, process, and act on data to support high performance in customer service. Implicit in this data gathering is soliciting feedback from external customers.[9]

"Voice of the customer" feedback systems have become popular and might include customer satisfaction surveys, complaint data, warranty and returns claims, customer databases, and field sales reports. These data sources can be helpful in identifying areas for improvement, whether in process or service capability. Internal barrier surveys and climate surveys can help the organization identify opportunities for improvement in leadership and management areas.

COMMON MISTAKES AND BARRIERS TO SUCCESS IN SERVICING CUSTOMERS

Customer service initiatives fail to get off the ground or achieve their full potential for many reasons. Some of the more prevalent problems follow.

Lack of Management Commitment

The first critical hurdle is the strength of convictions about the role of customer service at the top of the organization. Although many leaders "talk the talk," their actions might fall short of the single-minded tenacity required to stay the course, overcome inertia, and energize a customer-focused transformation. The difficulty can be magnified in organizations with a history of decisions based on day-to-day financial results.

Lack of Employee Buy-In

New initiatives can encounter apathy or lack of buy-in by employees for a variety of reasons. Employees might resist further changes as a result of downsizing or even because of evolving cynicism about management's adventures with new improvement initiatives (reflected by the employee attitude "This too shall pass"). In some organizations, significant internal barriers to high performance might exist, such as a lack of trust between workers and managers or limited cooperation between departments.

Failure to Create a Service Strategy

Organizations need to move past reactive customer service. Creating systems to handle complaints is a reactive approach. Creating voice-of-the-customer processes and placing an emphasis on customer service through the creation of a service strategy reflect proactive approaches to effective customer service.

The service strategy should fit within the context of marketing and product development strategies and should be incorporated in the organization's overall strategic plan. Of vital importance is attaining a clear focus on the primary customers of the organization as well as an accurate idea of the needs and expectations of these customers.

Lack of Management-by-Fact-Processes

Data-based decision making is a key to improving service delivery processes, and service capability and for addressing cultural issues that might be impeding progress to the desired levels of service performance. Metrics for each of these areas should be established, and the data should be provided to the stakeholders who are in the best position to implement improvements.

Inadequate Resources

Obviously, to achieve high levels of customer service an organization needs to have appropriate levels of staff. In addition, these employees need to enjoy the respect and support of their non-front-line counterparts. They must be properly trained to do their jobs effectively, and also should have access to the right tools and equipment to perform at the desired level.

📖 Additional Readings 📖

Albrecht, Karl. 1988. *At America's Service*. New York: Dow Jones-Irwin.

___. *Service America*. New York: Warner Books.

American Customer Satisfaction Index. Milwaukee: ASQ Quality Press.

Carlzon, Jan. 1987. *Moments of Truth*. New York: Harper & Row.

Davidow, William H., and Bro Uttal. 1989. *Total Customer Service—the Ultimate Weapon*. New York: Harper & Row.

Goodman, John, Scott M. Broetzmann, and Colin Adamson. 1992. "Ineffective—That's the Problem with Customer Satisfaction Surveys." *Quality Progress*, May, pp. 37–38.

Hays, Richard D. 1996. *Internal Service Excellence: A Manager's Guide to Building World Class Internal Service Unit Performance*. Milwaukee: ASQC Quality Press.

❖❖❖

Heskett, James L., et al. 1994. "Putting the Service-Profit Chain to Work." *Harvard Business Review* (March/April): 164–74.

LoSardo, Mary M., and Norma M. Rossi. 1993. *At the Service Quality Frontier.* Milwaukee: ASQC Quality Press.

Peters, T., and R. Waterman. 1982. *In Search of Excellence.* New York: Harper & Row.

Rosenbluth, Hal F., and Diane McFerrin Peters. 1992. *The Customer Comes Second and Other Secrets of Exceptional Service.* New York: William Morrow.

Sewell, Carl, and Paul B. Brown. 1990. *Customers for Life—How to Turn That One-Time Buyer into a Lifetime Customer.* New York: Doubleday/Currency.

Shapiro, Benson P., V. Kasturi Rangan, and John J. Sviolka. 1992. "Staple Yourself to an Order." *Harvard Business Review* (July/August): 113–22.

TARP (Technical Assistance Research Programs). 1985–86. *Consumer Complaint Handling in America—an Update Study, Parts I and II.* Washington, D.C.: U.S. Office of Consumer Affairs and TARP.

Wing, Michael J. 1993. *Talking with Your Customers—What They Will Tell You about Your Business When You Ask the Right Questions.* Chicago: Dearborn Financial.

Chapter 6

Quality Awards/ Quality Standards Criteria

❖ *This chapter should help you*

♦ Recognize the similarities and differences between ISO series quality standards requirements and the Malcolm Baldrige National Quality Award criteria

♦ Understand the benefits that are realized when companies seek registration or recognition or when quality award and quality standard frameworks are used for self-assessment

MODELS FOR ASSESSING QUALITY

Earlier chapters have presented many important principles of total quality that provide the foundation for achieving customer satisfaction. Armand Feigenbaum, who pioneered the concept of total quality, recognized that an organization needs a precise, well-structured system that identifies, documents, coordinates, and maintains all the key quality-related activities throughout all relevant company and plant operations. He defined a total quality system as "the agreed company-wide and plantwide operating work structure, documented in effective, integrated technical and managerial procedures, for guiding the coordinated actions of the work force, the machines, and the information of the company and plant in the best and most practical ways to assure customer quality satisfaction and economical costs of quality."[1]

A company needs both a model for guiding all employees' quality-related actions and a means of assessing how well these actions are carried out, especially as they relate to the firm's competitors or world-class standards. Awards and certifications provide tested business models as well as a basis for assessing progress, achievement, and conformance. The most widely used models for quality management are the United States' Malcolm Baldrige National Quality Award (MBNQA), Japan's Deming Prize, and the worldwide ISO 9000 series standards. In addition, many states, municipalities, industry groups, and even large corporations have developed significant quality awards, thereby widening the range of organizations eligible for recognition.

ISO 9000 SERIES QUALITY STANDARDS

To satisfy the emerging need for quality systems standards, initially in European markets, the International Organization for Standardization (ISO), with representatives from the national standards bodies of 91 nations, adopted the ISO 9000 series of standards in 1987. The standards were adopted in the United States by the American National Standards Institute (ANSI) on June 8, 1987, with the endorsement and cooperation of the American Society for Quality Control (ASQC), now the American Society for Quality (ASQ). The series was updated in 1994 to the ANSI/ISO/ASQC Q9000-1994 series. The standards are becoming recognized throughout the world. In some foreign markets, companies will not buy from noncertified suppliers. Thus, meeting these standards is becoming a requirement for many organizations desiring to be internationally competitive.

Purpose of ISO Standards

The ISO series of standards are different from the traditional notion of a standard, (e.g., engineering standards for measurement, terminology, test methods, or product specifications). Rather, they are quality system guidelines and models that assist an organization in developing, implementing, registering, and sustaining an appropriate quality management system. They are based on the premise that a well-designed and carefully managed quality system can provide confidence that the product or service produced by the quality management system will meet customer expectations and requirements. Importantly, an ISO 9000 certification does not certify or guarantee the quality of the product or service produced.

Accordingly an organization should:

1. achieve, maintain, and seek to improve continuously the quality of its products in relationship to the requirements for quality;
2. improve the quality of its own operations, so as to meet continually all customers' and other stakeholders' stated and implied needs;
3. provide confidence to its internal management and other employees that the requirements for quality are being fulfilled and maintained, and that quality improvement is taking place;
4. provide confidence to the customers and other stakeholders that the requirements for quality are being, or will be achieved in the delivered product;
5. provide confidence that quality-system requirements are fulfilled."[2]

The complete set of ANSI/ISO/ASQC Q9000 and related standards can be purchased through the American Society for Quality, P.O. Box 3005, Milwaukee, WI 53201-3005; ASQ's toll-free phone number is 1-800-248-1946.

Summary of ISO 9000 and Related Standards

The performance of an organization is judged by the quality of the goods and/or services it produces. To meet the trend of increasing worldwide quality expectations, the ISO 9000 series has evolved. The basic series consists of ISO 9000-1, 9001, 9002, 9003, and 9004-1, which have U.S. technical equivalents named ANSI/ISO/ASQC

❖❖❖

Q9000, Q9001, Q9002, Q9003, and Q9004-1994 standards. Additional supporting standards include ANSI/ISO/ASQC A8402-1994 and ANSI/ISO/ASQC Q10011 series. These documents are summarized here.

A8402-1994 ANSI/ISO/ ASQC	Quality Management and Quality Assurance—Vocabulary Defines the fundamental terms relating to quality concepts, as they apply to all areas, for the preparation and use of quality management and assurance standards.
ISO 9000 Q9001-1-1994	*Guidelines* for selection and use of the quality management and quality assurance standards (used to determine which standard—ISO 9001, 9002, or 9003—is most applicable).
ISO 9001 Q91-1994 (standard)	Quality Systems—Model for Quality Assurance in Design, Development, Production, Installation, and Servicing. For use when conformance to specified requirements is to be assured by the supplier (your organization) during several stages, including design/development, production, installation, and servicing.
ISO 9002 Q9002-1994 (standard)	Quality Systems—*Model* for Quality Assurance in Production, Installation, and Servicing. For use when conformance to specified requirements is to be assured by the supplier during production, installation, and servicing, excluding design.
ISO 9003 Q9003-1994 (standard)	Quality Systems—*Model* for Quality Assurance in Final Inspection and Test. For use when conformance to specified requirements is to be assured by the supplier solely at final inspection and test.
ISO 9004 Q9004-1-1994	Quality Management and Quality System Elements—*Guidelines*. Provides guidelines on the technical, administrative, and human factors affecting the quality of products and services. The guideline lists the essential elements that make up a quality assurance system with some detail, including management's responsibilities. Sections cover each major aspect of a quality system, (i.e., marketing, design, procurement, production, measurement, post production, materials control, documentation, safety, and statistical methods). ISO 9004 should be viewed as part of the basic criteria for implementing a quality management system and continuous improvement process.

❖❖

ISO 9000-3 Q9000-3-1991	*Guidelines* for the application of ISO 9001 to the Development, Supply, and Maintenance of software.
ISO9004-2 Q9004-2-1991	*Guidelines* for Services-type organizations.
ISO9004-4 Q9004-4-1993	*Guidelines* for Quality Improvement.
QSO10011-1 Q10011-1-1994	*Guidelines* for auditing quality systems.
ISO10011-2 Q10011-2-1994	*Guidelines*—Qualification criteria for Quality System Auditors.
ISO10011-3 Q10011-3-1994	*Guidelines* for auditing quality systems—Management of Audit Programs.
Q10013-1995	*Guidelines* for Developing Quality Manuals.

ISO 9000 standards lay out requirements in broad, general terms. Each company must professionally interpret them within the context of its own business and write its own procedures to comply. An outline of the requirements of the key 20 elements of the ISO 9001 standard as follows:

1. Management Responsibility
   - documented and communicated mission, plans, and policy for quality
   - organization and assignment of responsibilities for key elements in the quality system, including a management representative
   - adequate resources
   - periodic review of the quality system with corrective action as needed
2. Quality System
   - structured and documented system of procedures ensuring that activities, products, and services conform to requirements
   - quality planning process
3. Contract Review
   - procedure to ensure that each contract (order) is reviewed to ensure that customer requirements are thoroughly understood and that the capability exists to meet the specified requirements
   - amendments to the contract are controlled and documented and records kept
4. Design Control (not required by ISO 9002 or 9003)
   - procedures to ensure that engineering and/or design produce: a design plan that is complete, all customer's requirements are addressed, and there is reasonable assurance that if the final product is produced to specifications, it will meet customer requirements
   - design changes controlled and documented

5. Document and Data Control
   ◆ to ensure that all quality system documents are the correct documents to be used

6. Purchasing
   ◆ procedure to ensure that subcontractors are properly assessed for their ability to meet quality requirements, purchasing data are clear and accurate, and purchased products and services are properly verified for fitness for use

7. Control of Customer Supplier Product
   ◆ procedure to ensure verification, storage, and maintenance of products and supplies provided by the customer for use or inclusion in the delivered product and service

8. Product Identification and Traceability
   ◆ procedure to ensure that, where appropriate, product is properly marked and controlled

9. Process Control
   ◆ procedures to ensure that the production, installation and servicing processes are capable and carried out under controlled conditions
   ◆ workers must use approved equipment and follow specified criteria for workmanship

10. Inspection and Testing
   ◆ system and procedures for inspecting and testing, as appropriate, at receiving, in process, and at final inspection; ensuring that no product is dispatched until all activities specified in the quality plan have been carried out and that the results meet specified requirements and maintaining inspection and test records

11. Control of Inspection, Measuring and Test Equipment
   ◆ system and procedures for the control, calibration, maintenance, and use of inspection, measuring, and test equipment

12. Inspection and Test Status
   ◆ procedures for the identification and control of the test status of products

13. Control of Nonconforming Product
   ◆ procedures to ensure that any product that does not conform to specified requirements is prevented from unintended use or installation
   ◆ procedures for segregation, review, and disposition of nonconforming product

14. Corrective and Preventive Action
   ◆ system and procedures for investigating and eliminating causes of nonconforming product, handling of customer complaints, and review of actions taken

❖❖❖

15. Handling, Storage, Packaging, Preservation, and Delivery
    ◆ procedures for preventing damage or deterioration in handling, storage, packaging, preservation, and delivery
16. Control of Quality Records
    ◆ system and procedures for identifying, collecting, indexing, accessing, filing, storing, maintaining, and disposing of quality records
17. Internal Quality Audits
    ◆ system and procedures for planned and documented internal audits of the quality system by qualified auditors independent of the area audited
18. Training
    ◆ system and procedures for identifying and documenting the need for training of personnel in all activities affecting quality
    ◆ training records
19. Servicing
    ◆ procedures for performing, verifying, and reporting that servicing meets the specified requirements
20. Statistical Techniques
    ◆ procedures for determining the need for and control and application of statistical techniques required for establishing, controlling, and verifying process capability and product characteristics

Note that the requirements of ISO 9003 are contained within ISO 9002, and the requirements of ISO 9002 are contained within ISO 9001.

When reviewing a business system, management generally should consider the following factors when evaluating quality management effectiveness:

◆ handling of nonconforming product
◆ impact of quality methods on actual results
◆ management effectiveness
◆ product defects and irregularities
◆ results of statistical scorekeeping tools
◆ solutions to quality problems
◆ successful implementation of past solutions
◆ the results of internal quality audits[3]

The Registration Process

The ISO 9001, 9002, and 9003 standards provide the requirements for companies who want their quality management system certified (registered) through a third-party auditor (registrar). Both the registered organization and its customers might benefit in that the registrar's initial and subsequent surveillance audits might preclude the need for customer audits.

The registration process includes (1) optional preassessment (by a consultant, but usually by the registrar) to identify potential noncompliances in the quality system, including its documentation; (2) document review (by the registrar) of the quality system manual and procedures to confirm compliance with the applicable standard; (3) assessment (by a team of auditors from the registrar) of the conformance of the quality system in operation to the documented system, including the resulting records; and (4) periodic surveillance audits to verify conformity with the practices and systems registered. Recertification is usually required every three years. Because all costs are borne by the applicant, the process can be expensive.

Many companies seek certification to the ISO 9000 standards for the following reasons:

◆   For improving internal operations, the standards provide a set of good common practices for quality assurance systems and are an excellent starting point for companies with no formal quality assurance program.

◆   For companies in the early stages of formal quality programs, the standards enforce the discipline of control that is necessary before they can seriously pursue continuous improvement. The requirements of periodic audits reinforce the stated quality system until it becomes ingrained in the company way of doing business.

◆   For meeting contractual obligations, some customers now require certification of all their suppliers. Thus, suppliers that do not pursue registration can eventually lose customers.

◆   For meeting trade regulations, many products sold in Europe require product certifications to ensure safety. Often ISO certification is necessary to obtain product certification.

◆   For marketing goods in Europe, ISO 9000 is widely accepted within the European Community. It is fast becoming a de facto requirement for doing business within the trading region.

◆   For gaining a competitive advantage, many customers use ISO registration as a basis for supplier selection. Companies without it might be at a market disadvantage.

◆   The standards are intended to apply to all types of businesses, including electronics and chemicals, and to services such as health care, banking, and transportation.

Using ISO 9000 as a basis for a quality system can improve productivity, decrease costs, and increase customer satisfaction. At Dupont, ISO 9000 has been credited with increasing on-time delivery from 70 percent to 90 percent, decreasing cycle time from 15 days to 1.5 days, increasing first pass yields from 72 percent to 92 percent, and reducing the number of test procedures by one-third. In Canada, Toronto Plastics, Ltd., reduced defects per million from 150,000 to 15,000 after one year of ISO implementation.[4]

Common Criticisms of ISO 9000 Standards

Some criticisms of the ISO 9000 standards include the following:

◆ fall short of the quality that world-class corporations demand of themselves and their suppliers.

◆ extremely narrow focus on quality assurance, which is mainly in the area of documentation

◆ make no demands or assurances about a company's products

◆ ignore the formula of modern quality management that there is no mandate to reduce cycle time, cut inventories, speed up deliveries, and increase customer satisfaction.

◆ not a legal requirement for doing business in the European Community

◆ too vague to be of significant value to high-tech industries

◆ concern manufacturers that the certification base costs of registration fees might run over $50,000. (expenses for consultants, employee time, and documentation can drive the total cost to more than $200,000.)

◆ auto industry giants (General Motors, Ford, and Daimler-Chrysler) require those who are ISO 9000 registered to also become QS-9000 registered.[5]

Myths Surrounding ISO 9000 Standards

There are some myths surrounding ISO 9000 that, once clarified, should not prevent an organization from pursuing registration.

Myth #1:
There is an ISO 9000 requirement to which all companies trading outside their borders must respond. Actually, registration is voluntary; however, customers might require their subcontractors/vendors to be registered to ISO 9001, 9002, 9003, or QS-9000.

Myth #2:
One must be a specialist in a particular industry to implement the ISO 9000 series in that industry. Actually, the underlying quality control and quality assurance model is sufficiently generic to fit almost all enterprises.

Myth #3:
The ISO 9000 series applies primarily to companies that export to Europe. Not true. The series applies to virtually any type of organization in any part of the world. For certain products imported to certain countries, the marketplace might demand registration to an ISO 9000 standard.

Myth #4:
Every operating procedure must be documented to satisfy ISO 9000 series registration requirements. ISO 9000 standards do require documented procedures, for applicable elements of the standard, for those processes and practices which have an impact on the quality of the products and services delivered. For example, many companies do not service their products after initial delivery (element 19), so no procedure is required.

❖❖

Myth #5:
It is difficult (and costly) to get ISO registration. The costs of designing, documenting, implementing, and registering a quality system is dependent on: size of the organization, the extent of the existing quality system, the complexity of the products and services delivered, customer requirements, resources available, level of outside assistance needed, the applicable ISO 9000 standard, urgency of any customer mandates, time frame to completion, and the registrar chosen.

Myth #6:
ISO 9000 does not apply to nonmanufacturing organizations. The ISO 9000 model has been successfully implemented in schools, health care organizations, government entities, consulting firms, financial services, and so on.

Myth #7:
There is only one way to achieve registration, and that is through ISO itself. Registration is obtained through an accredited registrar, not IOS (International Organization for Standardization). There are a sizable number of accredited registrars available.

MALCOLM BALDRIGE NATIONAL QUALITY AWARD (MBNQA)

In October 1982, recognizing that U.S. productivity was declining, President Ronald Reagan signed legislation mandating a national study/conference on productivity. The American Productivity Center (now the American Productivity and Quality Center) sponsored seven computer networking conferences in 1983 to prepare for an upcoming White House Conference on Productivity. The final report from these conferences recommended that "a National Quality Award, similar to the Deming Prize in Japan, be awarded annually to those firms that successfully challenge and meet the award requirements." The Malcolm Baldrige National Quality Award (MBNQA) was signed into law (Public Law 100-107) on August 20, 1987. The award is named after President Reagan's secretary of commerce, who was killed in an accident shortly before the Senate acted on the legislation.

A total quality management (TQM) business approach is the basis for the MBNQA; an annual award to recognize U.S. companies for business excellence. This award promotes an understanding of the requirements for performance excellence. It fosters sharing information about successful performance strategies and the benefits derived from using these strategies. The Baldrige criteria are presented from a systems perspective in Figure 6.1, which shows the interrelationship of each of the seven categories. Customer- and market-focused strategy and action plans serve as the "umbrella."

MBNQA: Award Structure

Building active partnering in the private sector and between the private sector and all levels of government is fundamental to the success of the MBNQA program in improving national competitiveness. Support by the private sector for the program in the form of funds, volunteer efforts, and participation in information transfer

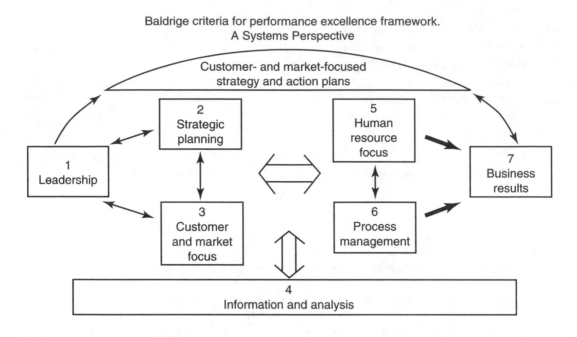

Baldrige criteria for performance excellence framework.
A Systems Perspective

Figure 6.1.   Baldrige criteria for performance excellence framework.

continues to grow. To ensure the spread and success of the MBNQA program, each of the following organizations plays an important role:

◆ U.S. Congress passed Public Law 100-107 on August 20, 1987, creating the MBNQA program.

◆ The Foundation for the Malcolm Baldrige National Quality Award was created to foster the success of the program, with the main objective being to raise funds to permanently endow the award program. Prominent leaders from U.S. organizations serve as foundation trustees to ensure that the foundation's objectives are accomplished. Donor organizations vary in size and type and represent many kinds of businesses.

◆ The Department of Commerce has the assigned responsibility for the award program.

◆ The National Institute of Standards and Technology (NIST), an agency of the Department of Commerce's Technology Administration, manages the award program.

◆ The American Society for Quality (ASQ), a professional organization furthering improvement through quality, assists in administering the award program under contract to the NIST.

◆ The board of overseers is the award's advisory organization to the Department of Commerce. The board is appointed by the secretary of commerce and consists of distinguished leaders from all sectors of the U.S. economy.

◆ The board of examiners evaluates award applications and prepares feedback reports. The board's panel of judges makes award recommendations to the director of the NIST. The board consists of leading U.S. business, health care, and education experts. These volunteer members are selected by the NIST through a competitive application process. All members of the board take part in an examiner preparation course.

MBNQA: Award Process

The application process for the MBNQA is described here.

Award Eligibility. The award has five eligibility categories: manufacturing companies, service companies, small businesses, education institutions, and health care organizations. Organizations participating in the award process are required to submit application packages that include responses to the award criteria. A maximum of three awards may be given in each category each year. Award recipients may publicize and advertise their awards. Recipients are required to share nonproprietary information about their successful performance strategies with other U.S. organizations at the annual Quest for Excellence Conference and are encouraged to further share information on a voluntary basis.

Award Criteria. The award is based on criteria for performance excellence. Separate criteria are used in the business, education, and health care categories. In responding to these criteria, each applicant is expected to provide information and data on the organization's key processes and results. Information and data submitted must be adequate to demonstrate that the applicant's approaches are effective and yield desired outcomes. In addition, the award criteria are designed not only to serve as a reliable basis for making awards but also as an assessment tool for each applicant to use in assessing their overall performance management system.

Application Requirements. Applicants must submit a three-part application package that includes (1) an eligibility determination form showing that eligibility has been approved, (2) a completed application form, and (3) an application report consisting of a business overview and responses to the award criteria. The business overview is a five-section outline of the applicant's business, addressing what is most important to the business, the key factors that influence how the business operates, and where the business is headed. These sections provide information on (1) a basic description of the company, (2) customer requirements, (3) supplier relationships, (4) competitive factors, and (5) other factors important to the applicant's business.

When completing an application for the award in the business categories, a company must respond in 70 or fewer pages to the requirements of the seven award criteria and more specifically to the 19 criteria items, which are worth a total of 1,000 points for the near perfectly managed business. Table 6.1 lists the 1999 Award Criteria for Business applicants. Each item is further detailed by at least one clarification requirement called "Areas to Address," which is intended to help the applicant's report better address the item's conditions. In total there are 27 Areas to Address that clarify the 19 items that specifically meet the seven award criteria categories. For additional details, see *The Malcolm Baldrige National Quality Award 1999 Criteria for Performance Excellence* booklet. A single free copy can be obtained

◆◆

◆ TABLE 6.1.   1999 MBNQA Criteria Categories and Point Values (Business)

1999 Categories/Items	Point Values
1 Leadership	**125**
1.1 Organizational leadership	85
1.2 Public responsibility and citizenship	40
2 Strategic Planning	**85**
2.1 Strategy development	40
2.2 Strategy deployment	45
3 Customer and Market Focus	**85**
3.1 Customer and market knowledge	40
3.2 Customer satisfaction and relationships	45
4 Information and Analysis	**85**
4.1 Measurement of organizational performance	40
4.2 Analysis of organizational performance	45
5 Human Resource Focus	**85**
5.1 Work systems	35
5.2 Employee education, training, and development	25
5.3 Employee well-being and satisfaction	25
6 Process Management	**85**
6.1 Product and service processes	55
6.2 Support processes	15
6.3 Supplier and partnering processes	15
7 Business Results	**450**
7.1 Customer-focused results	115
7.2 Financial and market results	115
7.3 Human resource results	80
7.4 Supplier and partner results	25
7.5 Organizational effectiveness results	115
Total Points	**1,000**

from the NIST: U.S. Department of Commerce, Technology Administration, National Institute of Standards and Technology, National Quality Program, Route 270 and Quince Orchard Road, Administration Building, Room A635, Gaithersburg, MD 20899-0001; 301-975-2036 (phone); 301-948-3716 (fax); nqp@nist.gov (e-mail); http://www.quality.nist.gov (Web site).

A general description of each of the seven award criteria categories pertaining to business applicants is shown in the following:

1. The *Leadership Category* examines senior executives' personal leadership and involvement in creating and sustaining a customer focus, clear values and expectations, and a leadership system that promotes performance excellence. Also examined is how the values and expectations are integrated into the company's management system, including how the company addresses its public responsibilities and corporate citizenship.

2. The *Strategic Planning category* examines how the company sets strategic directions and determines key plan requirements. Also examined is how the plan requirements are translated into an effective performance management system.

3. The *Customer and Market Focus category* examines the company's systems for customer learning and for building and maintaining customer relationships. Also examined are levels and trends in key measures of business success: customer satisfaction and retention, market share, and satisfaction relative to competitors.

4. The *Information and Analysis category* examines the management and effectiveness of the use of data and information to support customer-driven performance excellence and marketplace success.

5. The *Human Resource Focus category* examines how the workforce is enabled to develop and utilize its full potential, aligned with the company's performance objectives. Also examined are the company's efforts to build and maintain an environment conducive to performance excellence, full participation, and personal and organizational growth.

6. The *Process Management category* examines the key aspects of process management, including customer-focused design, product, service, and delivery processes; support services; and supply management involving all work units, including research and development. The category examines how key processes are designed, effectively managed, and improved to achieve higher performance levels.

7. The *Business Results category* examines the company's performance and improvement in key business areas—product and service quality, productivity and operational effectiveness, supply quality, and financial performance indicators linked to these areas. Also examined are performance levels relative to competitors.

Scoring System. The system for scoring applicant responses and for developing feedback is based on three evaluation dimensions: (1) approach, (2) deployment, and (3) results. "Approach" refers to how the applicant addresses the item requirements, that is, the method(s) used. "Deployment" refers to the extent to which the applicant's approach is applied to all requirements of the item throughout the organization.

❖❖❖

"Results" refers to outcomes achieved. The examiners use tables (published in the MBNQA criteria booklet) to develop the applicant's score.

Application Review. Applications are reviewed and evaluated by members of the board of examiners in a four-stage process as follows:

Stage 1: Independent review and evaluation by at least five members of the board of examiners

Stage 2: Consensus review and evaluation for applications that score well in stage 1

Stage 3: Site visits to applicants that score well in stage 2

Stage 4: Judges' review and recommendations of award recipients

Board members (volunteers, and trained examiners) are assigned to applications, taking into account the nature of the applicants' businesses and the expertise of the examiners. Strict rules govern examiner assignment to avoid conflicts of interest.

Feedback to Applicants. Each award applicant receives a feedback report at the conclusion of the review process. The feedback is based on the applicant's responses to the award criteria. In the most competitive business sectors, world-class organizations are able to achieve and maintain a score above 70% percent. However, a score of about 25 percent would be far more typical for most organizations. Even if an organization does not apply, the completion of its self-assessment to determine how well it measures up on the award's scoring scale is worthwhile for self-improvement and competitive purposes.

Benefits of Applying for the MBNQA

Over the years, award applicants have reported numerous benefits. Commonly cited benefits are the following:

◆ Responding to the criteria forces a realistic self-assessment from an external point of view. This self-assessment, when combined with the comprehensive feedback report received from the award's board of examiners, targets key gaps and priorities for improvement. The overall assessment also recognizes and reinforces company strengths.

◆ The pace of performance improvement is accelerated.

◆ The knowledge gained from assessment and feedback teaches new and better ways to evaluate suppliers, customers, partners, and even competitors.

◆ Use of the award criteria in assessment leads to the integration and alignment of numerous activities that previously were loosely connected. The assessment provides an effective means to measure progress and to focus everyone in the company on the same goals.

◆ Use of the award criteria helps organizations understand, select, and integrate appropriate management tools such as reengineering, ISO 9000, total quality management, activity-based costing, just-in-time production, lean manufacturing, flexible manufacturing, benchmarking, and high-performance workforce practices.

◆ The award criteria and scoring system provide a clear perspective on the distinction between typical performance and world-class performance.

◆ Participation frequently leads to companies' attending information-sharing meetings and joining sharing networks, where it is often possible to obtain free or inexpensive advice and help from other business leaders. One networking opportunity is the annual Quest for Excellence Conference.

Negative press has been generated regarding well-known quality failures. For example, Deming Prize winner Florida Power and Light subsequently dismantled much of what had been established to win the award. Wallace, Inc., an MBNQA winner, filed for chapter 11 bankruptcy protection. In response, the NIST conducted an investment experiment. A hypothetical sum was invested in each publicly traded winning company's common stock on the first business day in April of the year that it won the Baldrige Award (or the date when it began public trading, if later). One thousand dollars was invested in each whole company, and for subsidiaries the sum invested was $1,000 times the percentage of the whole company's employee base that the subunit represented. The same total dollar amount was also invested in the Standard & Poor's (S&P) 500 on the same day. Adjusting for stock splits and/or stock dividends, the value on August 1, 1995, was calculated. The 14 publicly traded winners outperformed the S&P 500 by over four to one, achieving a 248.7 percent return compared to a 58.8 percent return for the S&P 500. The five whole-company winners outperformed the S&P 500 by greater than five to one, achieving a 279.8 percent return compared to a 55.7 percent return for the S&P 500.

Criticisms of the MBNQA

The Baldrige Award has been subject to some criticisms, including the following:

◆ Winners have not necessarily solved all their business problems and gone to capitalist heaven.

◆ The award does not guarantee that a winning company's products are superior. At Cadillac-GMC the judges judged the quality management system, not the product.

◆ Applicants have found that the award process is an ordeal that can eat up management time and cost hundreds of thousands or even millions of dollars.

◆ As with any corporate push, bureaucracy can creep in—jobs and procedures can sap productivity and eventually have to be discarded.

◆ With the increasing visibility of the award, there is a growing misunderstanding. The goal of winning can appear to displace the goal of achieving real performance excellence.

❖❖❖

ISO 9000 AND THE BALDRIGE AWARD

With all the publicity surrounding the Baldrige Award and ISO 9000, many misconceptions about them have risen. Two common misconceptions are that the Baldrige Award and ISO 9000 requirements cover similar requirements and that both address improvement in end results. In reality, the Baldrige Award and ISO 9000 have distinctly different purposes and approaches; however, they can be mutually reinforcing when properly used. Table 6.2 contrasts the key differences between them. ISO 9000 could be considered a minor subset of the Baldrige Award criteria. The Baldrige criteria encompass the whole organization and its stakeholders as a total system, and the MBNQA is a business model for achieving world-class excellence. ISO 9000 focuses on the minimum requirements for a quality system needed to produce products and services that meet customer requirements. Many organizations are using both the Baldrige Award criteria and the ISO 9000 series standards in achieving their business strategic plans and goals. Organizations obtaining the best results are usually those that approach award programs and ISO 9000 standards as complementary, not competitive, methods for achieving their business goals, including improved quality and customer satisfaction.

Because of the growing focus on ISO 9000 as well as the many emerging state- and municipal-level quality awards, applications for the Baldrige Award have declined from a peak of 106 in 1991. However, thousands of the Baldrige criteria booklets are distributed by the NIST each year. Although the MBNQA applications have declined, the number of state- and municipal-level award programs and internal company assessments patterned after the Baldrige Award have increased. Many state award programs structure their programs to focus less on winning and more on continuous improvement.

In the cases of local award programs, organizations find that the reduced eligibility requirements, less competition, and more categories and levels of awards are more appealing than participating in a program with only three awards per category, very difficult standards, and national-level competition. State award programs tend to foster greater awareness of productivity and quality, exchange of information, and the building of role models to both strengthen the state's economy and attract business to the state.

QS-9000

In August 1994, the Big Three Automotive Task Force—Ford, Chrysler, and General Motors—released *Quality Systems Requirements QS-9000*, a set of requirements for automotive industry suppliers distributed by the Automotive Industry Action Group (AIAG). Truck manufacturers—Mack Trucks, Freightliner, Navistar International, PACCAR Inc., and Volvo GM—also participated in the creation of QS-9000, which is a collaborative effort of these firms to standardize their individual quality requirements while drawing on the global ISO 9000 standards. Their goal was to develop fundamental quality systems that provide for continuous improvement, emphasizing defect prevention and the reduction of variation and waste in the supply chain.

	Baldrige Award Program	ISO Registration
Focus	Competitiveness; customer value and operational performance	Conformity to ISO 9000-compliant practices specified in the registrant's own quality system
Purpose	Educational; sharing, competitiveness, comparison to world-class criteria	To provide a common basis for assuring buyers that specific practices conform to an internationally recognized standard for quality systems
Quality definition	Customer driven	Conformity of specified operations to documented requirements
Improvement/results	Heavy dependence on results and improvement	Does not assess outcomes or overall results business improvement trends
Role in the marketplace	A form of recognition, but not intended to be a product endorsement or certification	Provides customers with assurances that a registered supplier has and follows a documented quality system
Nature of assessment	Four-stage review process	Evaluation of quality manual and working documents and site audits to ensure conformance to stated practices
Feedback	Diagnostic feedback on approach, deployment, and results	Audit feedback on nonconformances and findings related to practices and documentation
Criteria improvement	Annual revision of criteria	Original 1987, revised 1994; 2000 version under review
Responsibility for information sharing	Winners required to share quality strategies	No obligation to share information
Service quality	Service excellence a principal concern	Standards focused on repetitive processes, without a focus on critical service quality issues, such as customer relationship management and human resource development
Scope of coverage	All organizational functions, operations, and processes throughout all work units	Covers only design/development, production, installation, and servicing; addresses only a small percentage of the areas covered by the Baldrige criteria
Documentation	Not spelled out in criteria	A quality system manual and documented procedures covering all applicable elements of the selected standard
Self-assessment	Primary use of criteria in the area of improvement practices	Standards primarily for "contractual situations" or other external audits

This standardized quality will reduce the cost of doing business with suppliers and enhance the competitive position of both automakers and suppliers. QS-9000 applies to all internal and external suppliers of production and service parts and materials. Ultimately, it is expected that the automakers will require all suppliers to establish, document, and implement quality systems based on these standards.

QS-9000 incorporates the ISO 9001 standard in its entirety, with additional industry requirements geared specifically toward automotive quality improvement programs. With more of a total quality philosophy, QS-9000 goes well beyond ISO 9000 standards by including additional requirements, such as continuous improvement, manufacturing capability, and production part approval processes. Also, whereas the ISO 9001 standard does not prescribe how a supplier must meet the requirements, the QS-9000 standard does prescribe specific actions and forms.

Many of the concepts in the MBNQA criteria are reflected in QS-9000. For example, under management responsibility (the first element in the ISO standards), suppliers are required to document trends in quality, operational performance (productivity, efficiency, effectiveness, and cost of poor quality), and current quality levels for key product and service features and to compare them with those of competitors and/or appropriate benchmarks. Suppliers are also required to have a documented process for determining customer satisfaction, including the frequency of determination and how objectivity and validity are assured. Trends in customer satisfaction and key indicators of customer dissatisfaction must be documented and supported by objective information, compared to competitors or benchmarks, and reviewed by senior management.

In addition, registration to QS-9000 requires demonstrating effectiveness in meeting the intent of the standards rather than simply "doing it as you document it." For example, whereas ISO 9000 requires "suitable maintenance of equipment to ensure continuing process capability" under process control, QS-9000 requires suppliers to identify key process equipment and provide appropriate resources for maintenance and to develop an effective, planned total preventive maintenance system. The system should include a procedure that describes the planned maintenance activities, scheduled maintenance, and predictive maintenance methods. Also, extensive requirements for documenting process monitoring and operator instructions and process capability and performance requirements are built into the standard. Finally, additional requirements pertain specifically to Ford, Chrysler, and GM suppliers. Thus, registration under QS-9000 standards will also achieve ISO 9000 registration, but ISO-certified companies must meet the additional QS-9000 requirements to achieve QS certification.

Additional Readings

Aerospace Basic Quality System Standard. 1997. Warrendale, Pa.: SAE International.

ASQ Chemical and Process Industries Division. 1992. *ANSI/ASQC Q90 ISO 9000 Guidelines: For Use by the Chemical and Process Industries.* Milwaukee: ASQC Quality Press.

AT&T Corporate Quality Office. 1994. *Using ISO 9000 to Improve Business Processes.* July.

Bandyopadhyay, Jayanta K. 1996. *QS-9000 Handbook: A Guide to Registration and Audit.* Delray Beach, Fla.: St. Lucie Press.

Bemoski, K., and B. Stratton. 1995. "How Do People Use the Baldrige Award Criteria?" *Quality Progress,* May.

Benson, R. S., and R. W. Sherman. 1995. "ISO 9000: A Practical, Step-by-Step Approach." *Quality Progress,* October.

Bibby, Thomas. 1995. "ISO 9000, Not a Total Quality Solution, but a Catalyst for Continuous Quality Improvement." *Rubber World,* July, Vol. 14: pp. 15–16.

Bobrowski, P. M., and J. H. Bantham. 1994. "State Quality Initiatives: Mini-Baldrige to Baldrige Plus." *National Productivity Review* (summer): 423–438.

Brown, Mark Graham. 1998. *Baldrige Award Winning Quality: How to Interpret the Baldrige Criteria for Performance Excellence,* 8th ed. Milwaukee: ASQ Quality Press.

Brumm, Eugenia K. 1995. *Managing Records for ISO 9000 Compliance.* Milwaukee: ASQC Quality Press.

Eckstein, Astrid L. H., and Jaydeep Balakrishnan. 1993. "The ISO 9000 Series: Quality Management Systems for the Global Economy." *Production and Inventory Management Journal* (fourth quarter) Vol. 34: pp. 66–71.

Evans, J. R., and W. M. Lindsay. 1996. *The Management and Control of Quality.* 3rd ed. New York: West Publishing.

Feigenbaum, A. V. 1991. *Total Quality Control.* 3rd ed. New York: McGraw-Hill.

Hoyle, David. 1994. *ISO 9000 Quality Systems Handbook,* 2nd ed. Oxford: Butterworth-Heinemann.

Huyink, David Stevenson, and Craig Westover, 1994. *ISO 9000: Motivating the People; Mastering the Process; Achieving Registration.* New York: Irwin Professional Publishing.

Kanter, Rob. 1997. *QS-9000 Answer Book: 101 Questions and Answers about the Automotive Quality System Standard.* New York: John Wiley & Sons.

Kessler, Sheila. 1995. *Total Quality Service: A Simplified Approach to Using the Baldrige Award Criteria.* Milwaukee: ASQC Quality Press.

Lamprecht, James L. 1994. *ISO 9000 and the Service Sector.* Milwaukee: ASQC Quality Press.

Mahoney, F. X., and C. G. Thor. 1994. *The TQM Trilogy.* New York: AMACOM.

Main, Jeremy. 1991. "Is the Baldrige Overblown?" *Fortune,* July 1, pp. 62–65.

The Malcolm Baldrige National Quality Award: 1999 Criteria for Performance Excellence. Gaithersburg, Md., National Institute of Standards and Technology. (Note: Separate criteria are available for the business categories, education category, and health care category.)

Mehta, Praful. 1994. *ISO 9000 Audit Questionnaire and Registration Guidelines.* Milwaukee: ASQC Quality Press.

Nakhai, B., and J. J. Never. 1994. "The Deming, Baldrige, and European Quality Awards." *Quality Progress,* April.

Owen, Dr. Bryn, and Peter Malkovich, 1995. *Understanding the Value of ISO 9000: A Management Guide to Higher Quality, Productivity, and Sales.* Knoxville, Tenn.: SPC Press.

❖❖

Peach, Robert W., ed. 1997. *The ISO 9000 Handbook,* 3rd ed. Chicago: Irwin Professional Publishing.

QS-9000 Series, 3rd ed. Southfield, Mich.: Automotive Industry Action Group. (248) 358-3003.

Rabbitt, John T. and Peter A. Bergh, 1993. *The ISO 9000 BOOK: A Global Competitor's Guide to Compliance and Certification.* White Plains, N.Y.: Quality Resources.

Reimann, Curt W., and Harry S. Hertz. 1993 "The Malcolm Baldrige National Quality Award and ISO Registration." *ASTM Standardization News,* November, pp. 42–53. This paper is a contribution of the U.S. government and is not subject to copyright.

Schlickman, Jay J. 1998. *ISO 9000 Quality Management System Design.* Milwaukee: ASQ Quality Press.

Struebing, L. "9000 Standards". *Quality Progress* (January 1996).

Timbers, Michael J. 1992. "ISO 9000 and Europe's Attempts to Mandate Quality." *The Journal of European Business* March/April: 14-15.

Voehl, F., Johnson P., and D. Aston. 1995. *ISO: An Implementation Guide for Small to Mid-Sized Businesses.* Delray Beach, Fla: St. Lucie Press.

Wilson, Lawrence A. 1996. *Eight-Step Process To Successful ISO 9000 Implementation: A Quality Management System Approach.* Milwaukee: ASQC Quality Press.

☙ Part 1 Endnotes ☙

Chapter 1

1. ASQ TQM Subcommittee.
2. Thomas J. Cartin and Donald J. Jacoby, *A Review of Managing Quality and a Primer for the Certified Quality Manager Exam* (Milwaukee: ASQ Quality Press, 1997), p. 6.
3. Frederick W. Taylor, *The Principles of Scientific Management,* (New York: Harper & Row, 1911).
4. Armand V. Feigenbaum, *Total Quality Control,* 3rd ed. (New York: McGraw-Hill, 1991), p. 6.
5. Kaoru Ishikawa, *What Is Total Quality Control? The Japanese Way,* trans. David J. Lu (Englewood Cliffs, N.J.: Prentice Hall, 1985), p. 90.
6. GOAL/QPC Research Committee, *Total Quality Management Master Plan—an Implementation Strategy* (Methuen, Mass: GOAL/QPC, 1990), pp. 1–4.
7. Joseph M. Juran and Frank M. Gryna, *Quality Planning and Analysis,* 3rd ed. (New York: McGraw-Hill, 1993), p. 12.
8. QPMA definition
9. Glen Gee, Wes Richardson, and Bill Wortman, *The Quality Manager Primer,* 2nd ed. (West Terre Haute: Quality Council of Indiana, 1996), p. II-12.
10. Mary Litsikas, "No One Can Afford to Buy Cheap Any More—an Exclusive Interview with A. Feigenbaum," *Quality,* June 1995, pp. 37–39.
11. Gary L. Parr, "The Customer Is Still the Final Test," *Quality,* March 1995, p. 4.

❖❖

12. Bill Creech, *The Five Pillars of TQM—How to Make Total Quality Management Work for You* (New York: Truman Tally Books/Dutton, 1994), p. 10.

13. Elliot Jacques and Stephen D. Clement, *Executive Leadership—A Practical Guide to Managing Complexity* (Malden, Mass.: Basil Blackwell and Caston Hall and Co.), p. xv.

14. Robert A. Ladner, "Avoiding Fallout from TQM Failure: Measure Twice, Cut Once," *American Business Challenges,* July 1994, pp. 1–6.

15. Robert J. Masters, "Overcoming the Barriers to TQM's Success," *Quality Progress,* May 1996, p. 53.

16. Ibid.

17. Ibid.

18. Ibid., pp. 54–55.

19. Ibid., p. 55.

Chapter 2

1. D. H. Stamatis, *TQM Engineering Handbook* (New York: Marcel Dekker, 1997), p. 84.

Chapter 3

1. H. P. Emerson and D.C. E. Naehring, *Origins of Industrial Engineering* (Norcross, Ga.: Industrial Engineering and Management Press, 1988).

2. Henry Ford, *Today and Tomorrow* (New York: Doubleday Page, 1926).

3. Dianne Galloway, *Mapping Work Processes* (Milwaukee: ASQC Quality Press, 1994), p. 21.

4. Gavriel Salvendy, ed., *Handbook of Industrial Engineering* (John Wiley & Sons, 1982), p. 3.3.2.

5. J. A. Bockerstette and R. L. Shell, *Time Based Manufacturing* (Norcross, Ga.: Industrial Engineering and Management Press and McGraw-Hill, 1993).

Chapter 4

1. W. Edwards Deming, *Out of the Crisis* (Cambridge: Massachusetts Institute of Technology, Center for Advanced Engineering Study, 1986).

2. Thomas J. Cartin and Donald J. Jacoby, *A Review of Managing for Quality and a Primer for the Certified Quality Manager Exam* (Milwaukee: ASQ Quality Press, 1997), pp. 18, 20.

3. Chip Long, *Advanced Supplier Certification* (Seal Beach, Calif.: World Class Consulting Group, 1995), pp. 4–14.

Chapter 5

1. The Marketing Concept is generally credited to Phillip Kotler, author of numerous marketing texts.

2. William H. Davidow and Bro Uttal, *Total Customer Service—the Ultimate Weapon* (New York: Harper and Row, 1989).

3. Karl Albrecht, *At America's Service* (New York: Dow Jones-Irwin, 1988), p. 134.

❖❖❖

4. John Goodman, Scott M. Broetzmann, and Colin Anderson, "Ineffective—That's the Problem with Customer Satisfaction Surveys," *Quality Progress* (May 1992).
5. Carl Sewell and Paul B. Brown, *Customers for Life—How to Turn That One-Time Buyer into a Lifetime Customer* (New York: Doubleday/Currency, 1990), p. xviii.
6. James L. Heskett *et al.*, "Putting the Service-Profit Chain to Work," *Harvard Business Review* (March/April 1994).
7. Hal F. Rosenbluth and Diane McFerrin Peters, *The Customer Comes Second and Other Secrets of Exceptional Service* (New York: William Morrow, 1992).
8. Benson P. Shapiro, V. Kasturi Rangan, and John J. Sviolka, "Staple Yourself to an Order," *Harvard Business Review* (July/August 1992).
9. Michael J. Wing, *Talking with Your Customers—What They Will Tell You about Your Business When You Ask the Right Questions* (Dearborn Financial, 1993).

Chapter 6

1. A. V. Feigenbaum, *Total Quality Control*, 3rd ed. (New York: McGraw-Hill, 1991), pp. 77–78.
2. ANSI/ASQC Q9000-1-1994.
3. J. R. Evans and W. M. Lindsay, *The Management and Control of Quality*, 3rd ed. (New York: West Publishing, 1996).
4. AT&T Corporate Quality Office, *Using ISO 9000 to Improve Business Processes*, July 1994.
5. Thomas Bibby, "ISO 9000, Not a Total Quality Solution, but a Catalyst for Continuous Quality Improvement," *Rubber World* (July 1995).

Part 2

Organizations and Their Functions

Chapter 7

Organizational Assessment

❖ *This chapter should help you*

◆ Become knowledgeable of the different types of assessments, including quality audits

◆ Understand the linkage between assessments and continuous improvement

◆ Understand the generic assessment process

◆ Become familiar with the potential benefits of quality audits and common audit problems

---

Chapter 6 discussed the Malcolm Baldrige National Quality Award criteria and ISO 9000 series standard requirements, two frameworks that organizations often use when seeking recognition or registration. In addition, many organizations use these frameworks to perform self-assessments. This chapter will discuss the use of assessments as a tool for evaluating organizations.

PURPOSES AND TYPES OF ORGANIZATIONAL ASSESSMENTS

Assessments are a management tool used to collect data on organizational performance. They are typically done for the purpose of the following:

◆ diagnosing a problem situation (e.g., low performance in a particular product line or an ongoing conflict between two departments)

◆ identifying opportunities for improvement

◆ measuring progress made in comparison to a previous assessment

Improving organizational performance calls for ensuring that the mission, management systems, operating behaviors, and feedback mechanisms are properly designed and aligned. Organizational assessments might look at culture (e.g., measuring openness to change before moving from a modest employee involvement program to self-managed work teams); measure compliance to regulatory or adopted standards, such as current good manufacturing practices (cGMP) or ISO 9001; or compare the organization to models of excellence such as the Baldrige criteria.

The assessment process consists of (1) understanding the purpose for the study, (2) identifying an appropriate model to guide the assessment, (3) developing or acquiring appropriate data collections tools, (4) collecting the data, and (5) reporting

❖❖❖

on the findings. Data collection methods can include interviews, surveys, observations, and reviews of records, depending on the type of assessment. For example, an assessment of organizational culture is frequently done through a purchased questionnaire, while diagnosing a conflict situation will most likely involve interviews to determine patterns of behavior.

Having a clearly defined conceptual model to guide the assessment is critical to ensuring that there will be structure and consistency in the process and resulting data. Individuals responsible for taking action on the basis of the results should ideally agree on the model to be used. Having the assessment performed by persons believed to be unbiased and objective is also important. Such individuals can also frequently present various models for consideration or help the organization develop a model that defines its current or desired state.

Assessment findings are usually organized into categories that fit the basic model used to guide the study. The findings are viewed for the purpose of identifying patterns or consistency of responses that indicate significant strengths, weaknesses, opportunities, or needs. Because of the myriad of formats the assessment process can take, the analysis and reporting process itself is often quite complex and therefore frequently open to criticism. For example, interviews that yield open-ended responses and observations of artifacts to determine cultural or management philosophy tendencies require interpretation that might be subject to the biases of the researcher. For these reasons, the use of externally validated and numerically scored instruments is often the preferred method. Using a scale of verbal responses from which participants select their answers (e.g., a Likert-type scale using the categories of "Strongly Agree," "Agree," "Neutral," "Disagree," and "Strongly Disagree") is a method frequently used.

Because the assessments for which a quality manager will be the driving force are usually based on a quality standard, such as ISO 9001, the remainder of the chapter will focus on these types of assessments, called a *quality audit.*

QUALITY AUDIT DEFINED

A quality audit is "a systematic and independent examination to determine whether quality activities and related results comply with planned arrangements and whether these arrangements are implemented effectively and are suitable to achieve objectives."[1]

Three principle parties are involved in a quality audit. By function, they are (1) the auditor, or the person(s), who plans and conducts an audit in accordance with an established standard; (2) the client, or the person/organization, who has requested that an audit be conducted; and (3) the auditee, or the organization to be audited.

An audit may be classified as internal or external, depending on the interrelationships that exist among the participants. Internal audits are first-party audits, whereas external audits can be either second- or third-party audits.

A first-party audit is performed within an organization to measure its strengths and weaknesses against its own procedures or methods and/or external standards adopted by the auditee organization (voluntary) or imposed on the auditee organization (mandatory). A first-party audit is an internal audit conducted by auditors who are employed by the organization being audited but who have no vested interest in the audit results of the area being audited.

A second-party audit is an external audit performed on a supplier by a customer or a contracted (consulting) organization on behalf of a customer. A third-party audit is performed on a supplier or regulated entity by an external participant other than a customer. The organization to be audited—or in some cases the client—compensates an independent party to perform an audit.

Quality audits can be performed on a product/service, process, or system. A product quality audit is an in-depth examination of a particular product (or service) to evaluate whether it conforms to product specifications, performance standards, and customer requirements. A product audit should not be confused with inspection, although an auditor might use inspection techniques. Product audits have a broader scope and are a sporadic method of reinspecting or retesting a product to measure the effectiveness of the system in place for product acceptance. Inspection is a regular, constant method of the product approval process and verifies a product's conformance to standards as stipulated by limited product characteristics.[2]

A process quality audit examines a single process or activity—such as marking, stamping, coating, soldering, or welding—to verify that the inputs, actions, and outputs are in accordance with requirements established by procedures, work instructions, or process specifications. A quality system audit is "a documented activity performed to verify, by examination and evaluations of objective evidence, that applicable elements of the quality system are appropriate and have been developed, documented, and effectively implemented in accordance and in conjunction with specified requirements."[3] A system audit examines processes, products, and services as well as all the supporting groups—for example, purchasing, customer service, design engineering, and order entry—that assist in providing an acceptable product or service.[4]

Auditing deals with the last two steps of the quality cycle: the check and act stages of the Plan = Do = Check = Act cycle,[5] which is illustrated in Chapter 33.

PHASES OF THE AUDIT PROCESS

Auditing consists of the following stages: (1) audit preparation, (2) audit performance, and (3) audit reporting, corrective action, follow-up, and closure.

Audit Preparation

The following activities are performed during audit preparation:

- prepare the audit plan
- schedule activities
- define the purpose of the audit
- establish the scope of the audit
- select the audit team
- identify resources needed
- identify authority for the audit

- identify standard(s) to be used
- conduct a technical review
- secure and review quality-related documentation
- develop checklists and other working papers (develop appropriate data collection methods)
- contact auditee

Audit Performance

Audit performance is the actual data collection phase. The following items are accomplished during this audit phase:

- hold the opening meeting
- employ auditing strategies to collect data
- verify documentation
- analyze data and categorize results
- present audit results at closing meeting

Audit Reporting, Corrective Action, Follow-Up, and Closure

Once the audit performance stage has been completed, the audit team must formally report audit results to the client and/or auditee. The appropriate corrective actions, follow up, and closure must be brought to any problem areas noted:

- distribute formal audit report
- request corrective action
- evaluate auditee's response to corrective action requests
- assess the best mode to verify corrective action
- close out audit once corrective action has been verified

A flowchart that shows the sequence of steps performed in quality audits and their interrelationships is shown in Figure 7.1.

BENEFITS OF QUALITY AUDITS

The performance of a quality audit provides management with unbiased facts that can be used to achieve the following:

- inform management of actual or potential risks
- identify input for management decisions (so that quality problems and costs can be prevented or rectified)
- identify areas of opportunity
- assess personnel training and effectiveness and equipment capability
- provide visible management support of the quality program
- verify compliance to regulations[6]

Effective quality audits assess each of the four task elements shown in Figure 7.2.

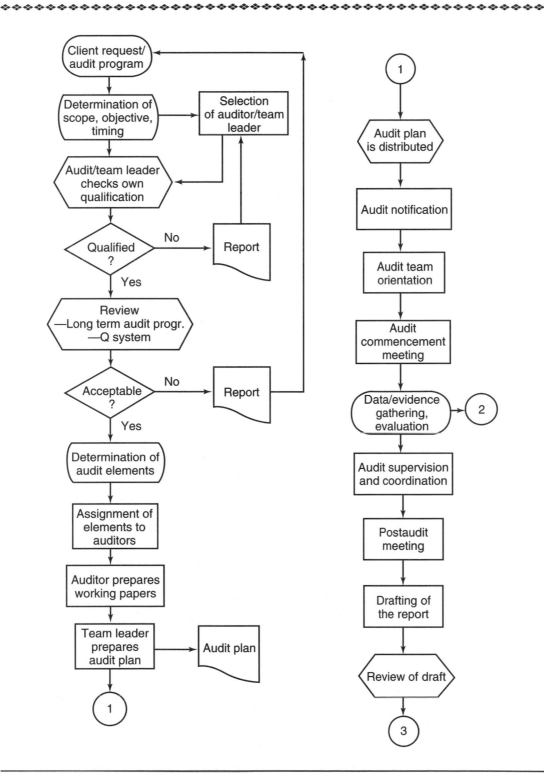

Figure 7.1. Flowchart for quality audit. Source: J.M. Juran and F. Gryna, *Juran's Quality Control Handbook,* 4E (1988), McGraw-Hill. Used with permission.

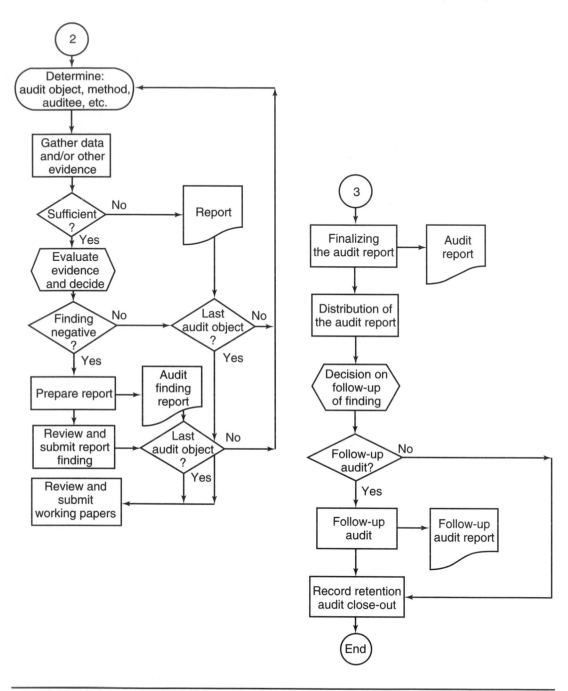

◆ **Figure 7.1.**   Flowchart for quality audit.   *continued*

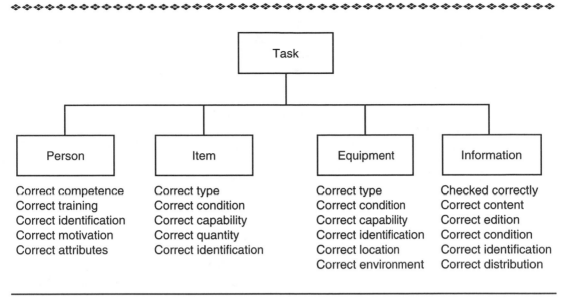

◆ **Figure 7.2.** The four task elements.

COMMON MISTAKES AND BARRIERS TO SUCCESS IN AUDITING

Various problems can hinder the audit process. Some of the more common ones are mentioned here.

Error #1: Equating auditing with inspection.
The quality audit might be used improperly as an alternative to an existing inspection operation or as a crutch in an ineffective inspection or quality program. The quality audit should not be used in verification activities that include disposition (pass/fail) of a product.[7]

Error #2: Fearing the auditing function.
At times management or employees might not recognize that a successful quality system leads to the improvement of operating systems. Fear can arise if the audit function is viewed as an adversarial "gothcha" way for management to monitor what is going on. Additionally, employees might resent the audit process if the results are used inappropriately (i.e., in performance appraisals).

Error #3: Finding fault, not facts.
Quality audits must be fact finding, not fault finding.[8] An auditor measures compliance with and conformance to specified requirements by gathering and analyzing objective evidence, that is, "information which can be proved true, based on facts obtained through observation, measurement, test, or other means."[9]

Error #4: Failing to measure an audit's effectiveness.
It is not enough to simply perform an audit; the effectiveness of the audit should be measured.

Error #5: Not recognizing that quality auditing is a people-oriented activity.
Quality auditing is a people-oriented activity. The auditor needs to be skilled in handling people, as the data by itself often cannot tell the entire story.

Error #6: Not assessing the benefits of the audit compared to the costs involved.
The potential benefits that will result from an audit should outweigh the costs involved. The existence of a measurement system to accurately monitor the cost-benefit relationship is vital.

Error #7: Poorly defining the purpose and scope of an audit.
If the audit's purpose or scope has not been clearly defined, or if the audit team fails to stay within the limits set by them, audit results might be meaningless.

Error #8: Failing to verify corrective action.
The audit cycle is incomplete if the auditing team fails to verify that corrective action has taken place.

🏛 Additional Readings 🏛

American Society for Quality Control Standards Committee for American National Standards Committee Z-1 on Quality Assurance. American Society for Quality Control. 1994. ANSI/ISO/ASQC A8402.

Arter, Dennis R. 1994. *Quality Audits for Improved Performance.* 2nd ed. Milwaukee ASQC Quality Press.

Cummings, Thomas G., and Edgar F. Huse. 1989. *Organization Development and Change.* 4th ed. St. Paul,: West Publishing.

Keeney, Kent, 1995. *The Audit Kit.* Milwaukee: ASQC Quality Press.

___. 1995 *The ISO 9000 Auditor's Companion.* Milwaukee: ASQC Quality Press.

Mills, Charles A. 1989. *The Quality Audit: A Management Evaluation Tool.* New York: McGraw-Hill.

Parsowith, B. Scott. 1995. *Fundamentals of Quality Auditing.* Milwaukee: ASQC Quality Press.

Rice, C. M. 1994. "How to Conduct an Internal Audit and Still Have Friends." *Quality Progress,* June, p. 39.

Robinson, Charles B. 1992. *How to Make the Most of Every Audit: An Etiquette Handbook for Auditing.* Milwaukee: ASQC Quality Press.

Russell, J. P., ed. 1999. *The Quality Audit Handbook.* 2nd ed. Milwaukee: ASQ Quality Press.

Russell, J. P., and Terry Regel. 1996. *After the Quality Audit: Closing the Loop on the Audit Process.* Milwaukee: ASQC Quality Press.

Sayle, Allan J. 1988. *Management Audits: The Assessment of Quality Management Systems.* 2nd ed. Brighton, Mich.: A. Sayle Associates.

Talley, Dorsey J. 1988. *Management Audits for Excellence.* Milwaukee: ASQC Quality Press.

Willborn, Walter. 1993. *Audit Standards: A Comparative Analysis.* 2nd ed. Milwaukee: ASQC Quality Press.

Wilson, P. F., L. D. Dell, and G. F. Anderson, 1993. *Root Cause Analysis: A Tool for Total Quality Management.* Milwaukee: ASQC Quality Press.

Chapter 8

Organizational Structures

❖ *This chapter should help you*

◆ Be familiar with the terms and principles related to organizational structure and design

◆ Understand the benefits of creating an organizational structure

◆ Understand the concepts of vertical and horizontal organizational design as compared to a contingency approach

◆ Be familiar with different organizational design applications

---

We trained very hard, but it seemed that every time we were beginning to form up into teams, we would be reorganized. I was to learn later in life that we tend to meet any new situation by reorganizing. A wonderful method it can be for creating the illusion of progress while producing confusion, inefficiency, and demoralization.

—Gaius Petronius, Roman Author, A.D. 70

DEFINING ORGANIZATIONAL STRUCTURE AND DESIGN

Once an organization's mission, goals, plans, and strategies have been determined, management must develop an effective and efficient structure to accomplish them. The organizational structure is the organization's formal framework or system of communication and authority. An organization's structure can be described by three components: complexity, formalization, and centralization.[1]

Organizational complexity refers to the degree of differentiation that exists in an organization. When division of labor exists in an organization, for example, the hierarchy contains many vertical levels. An organization with geographically dispersed units finds it more difficult (or complex) to coordinate people and their activities. On the other hand, an organization with only six employees in one office location generally has a simple structure.

Organizational formalization is the degree to which an organization relies on rules and procedures to direct employee behavior. Some organizations operate with few standardized guidelines and little formalization, whereas others have countless rules and regulations to instruct employees on appropriate behavior. The more rules and regulations in an organization, the more formalized the organization's structure.

Organizational centralization refers to where the decision-making authority is located. In organizations in which decision making is highly centralized in upper management levels, problems flow up to and are resolved by senior executives. In other organizations decision making is delegated to lower levels of management in a process known as *decentralization.*

When managers develop or change an organization's structure, they are engaged in organizational design. The design process involves decisions about the amount of complexity, formalization, and centralization to be used. These three aspects of organizational structure can be mixed and matched in varying amounts to create various organizational designs.

Managers must design an organizational structure that permits the effective and efficient accomplishment of organizational goals and objectives. Some common reasons for creating an organizational structure are the following:

◆   to divide work to be done into specific jobs and departments

◆   to assign tasks and responsibilities associated with individual jobs

◆   to coordinate diverse organizational tasks

◆   to cluster jobs into units

◆   to establish relationships among individuals, groups, and departments

◆   to establish formal lines of authority

◆   to allocate and deploy organizational resources

To design an appropriate structure, managers must decide how to coordinate work activities and efforts both vertically and horizontally.

BUILDING THE ORGANIZATION'S VERTICAL (HIERARCHICAL) DIMENSION

In organizations, employees typically are categorized as top managers, middle managers, first-line managers, or operative employees. Aspects of an organization's vertical dimension include determining these organizational categories and defining the interaction among the levels by deciding who reports to whom and determining who has the authority to make decisions.

Unity of Command

First presented by Henri Fayol as principle 4 of his 14 principles of management, unity of command refers to the idea that a subordinate normally should be directly responsible to only one superior.[2] Otherwise, a subordinate might be forced to cope with conflicting demands or priorities from several managers. In rare cases in which this principle must be violated, activities or duties taking place under the direction of different supervisors should be clearly separate to avoid conflicts, misunderstandings, or the misuse of resources.

Today, the unity-of-command concept is appropriate when organizations are comparatively simple as well as in most other circumstances. In fact, most organizations adhere strictly to this principle when designing work activities and work relationships. In a few cases, such as when a matrix organization structure (discussed shortly) exists, the inflexibility resulting from the unity- of-command principle could hinder an organization's performance.

Authority and Responsibility

Managers must determine the types and amounts of authority and responsibility that organizational members will have. Authority refers to the rights inherent in a managerial position to give orders and expect them to be followed. Managers acquire specific rights along with their respective positions. When a manager no longer occupies the position, the rights remain with the vacated position, not the manager. Traditionally, authority has been delegated downward to subordinate managers, giving them certain rights while specifying limits within which to operate.

When managers delegate authority, commensurate responsibility must be given as well. That is, when one is given the "right" to do something, one also assumes a corresponding "obligation" to perform. Allocating authority without responsibility can create problems, so people should not be held responsible for things over which they have no authority. Historically, authority could be delegated, but responsibility could not. Rather, the delegator was held responsible for the actions of the people to whom work had been delegated. A seeming contradiction has been avoided through the recognition of two forms of responsibility: operating and ultimate. Today, managers can and do delegate operating responsibility while retaining ultimate responsibility, as managers are responsible for the actions of subordinates to whom operating responsibility has been delegated.

Managers often distinguish between two forms of authority: line and staff. Line authority, the superior–subordinate authority relationship that extends from the top of the organization to its lowest levels (along a chain of command), entitles a manager to direct the work of a subordinate. In Figure 8.1, the chain of command extends from the CEO to the president to the vice president of operations to the director and then to others, as shown by the dashed line to the foreman, and finally to labor. As a link in the chain, a manager with line authority has the right to direct the work of subordinates and to make certain decisions without consulting others. In the chain of command, every manager also is directed by a superior.

As organizations become larger and more complex, line managers might lack the time, expertise, or resources to do their jobs effectively. In response, they create staff authority functions to support, assist, advise, and generally reduce some of their informational burdens. In Figure 8.2 line authority is shown by the solid line from the executive director to the director of operations to the unit 1 and unit 2 managers and from these unit managers to operations. Staff authority is shown by the dotted lines to various positions, such as assistant to the executive director, director of personnel, director of purchasing, and so on.

Historically, managers have been enamored with the concept of authority. They actively assumed that the rights inherent in one's formal organizational position were the sole source of influence and that if an order was given, it would be obeyed. They believed that managers were all powerful. Chester Barnard presented another perspective, the acceptance theory of authority, which proposes that authority comes from the willingness of subordinates to accept it.[3] In other words, if a subordinate

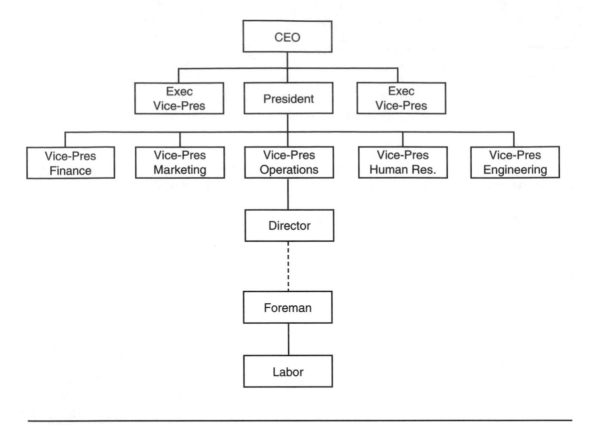

Figure 8.1. Chain of command.

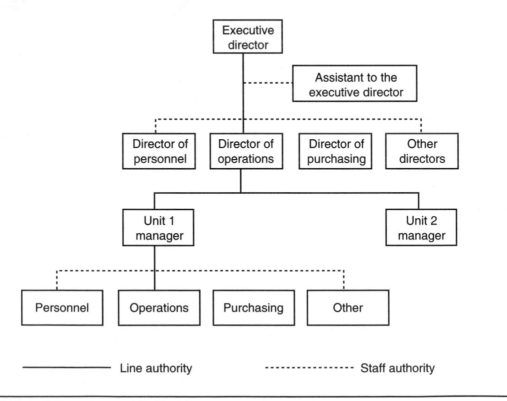

Figure 8.2. Line and staff authority.

does not accept a superior's order, no authority exists. Barnard contends that subordinates will accept orders only if the following conditions are satisfied:

◆   They understand the order.

◆   They feel that the order is consistent with the purpose of the organization.

◆   The order does not conflict with their personal beliefs.

◆   They are able to perform the task as directed.

Managers now recognize that one does not have to be a manager to have influence, nor is influence always correlated to organizational level. Authority is an important concept in organizations, but focusing exclusively on authority produces a narrow, unrealistic view of influential sources in organizations. Today, authority is recognized as one aspect of the larger concept of power.[4] While authority is a legitimate right that is held because of a person's position in an organization, power refers to an individual's capacity to influence decisions. That is, the formal rights that come with an individual's position are just one way in which an individual can affect the decision-making process.

Span of Control

Organizational span of control refers to how many subordinates a manager can effectively and efficiently supervise. Managers must address this aspect of vertical dimension when designing an appropriate organizational structure. Although no consensus exists on an ideal number, many managers favor small spans—typically no more than six—in order to maintain close control.[5] However, the organizational level might be a contingency variable that affects this number. As managers rise in the organizational hierarchy, they deal with a greater variety of complex and ill-structured problems, so top executives should have a smaller span of control than do middle managers, and, likewise, middle managers require a smaller span than do supervisors. Therefore, to a large degree the span of control determines the number of levels and managers in an organization. Other things being equal, the wider or larger the span of control, the more efficient the organizational design.

Contrasting Spans of Control

Today, many organizations have reduced their number of managerial positions through downsizing and restructuring while generally increasing the spans of control for the remaining managers. For example, the span of control for managers at companies such as General Electric and Reynolds Metals has expanded to 10 or 12 subordinates—double the number of 20 years ago.[6] However, even in organizations that have not restructured, the optimum span of control is increasingly being determined by a number of contingency variables. For example, more trained and experienced subordinates need less direct supervision than do others. Therefore, managers who have well-trained and experienced employees can function quite well with a wider span. Other contingency variables include similarity of subordinate tasks, the complexity of those tasks, the physical proximity of subordinates, the degree to which standardized procedures are in place, the sophistication of the organization's management information system, the strength of the organization's culture, and the preferred style of the manager.[7]

❖❖❖

Centralization/Decentralization

As described earlier, a characteristic of an organization's structure is the amount of centralization/decentralization. These terms refer to how much decision-making authority has been delegated to lower management levels. Few organizations could function effectively if all decisions were made by a select group of top managers, nor could they do so if all decisions were delegated to the lowest levels of the organization. Fayol listed centralization as one of his 14 principles of management and noted that the proper amount of centralization or decentralization depended on the situation.[8] As with most of the traditional management principles, the ultimate objective was the optimum and efficient use of the capabilities of the organization's personnel.

Traditionally, organizations were structured as pyramids, with authority and power concentrated at the top. Relatively centralized decision making was popularly practiced. However, as organizational environments became more complex and dynamic, many organizations began to decentralize decision making. Many executives now believe that decisions should be made by those people who have the best information to make those decisions, regardless of their level in the organization. In fact, the trend over the last 35 years, at least among U.S. and Canadian firms, has been decentralization in organizations.[9]

More centralization might be needed under the following conditions:

◆ The environment is more stable.

◆ Lower-level managers are not as capable or experienced at making decisions.

◆ Lower-level managers do not want to have a say in decisions.

◆ Decisions are more significant.

◆ The organization is facing a crisis or the risk of company failure.

◆ Effective implementation of company strategies depends on managers retaining more say over what happens.

More decentralization might be needed under the following conditions:

◆ The environment is complex, uncertain.

◆ Lower-level managers are capable and experienced at making decisions.

◆ Lower-level managers want a voice in decisions.

◆ Decisions are relatively minor.

◆ Corporate culture is more open to allowing managers to have a say in what happens.

◆ The company is geographically dispersed.

◆ Effective implementation of company strategies depends on managers having more involvement and flexibility to make decisions.

Managers should select the amount of centralization/decentralization that best allows them to implement their goals and strategies. What works in one situation might not be best for another, so managers must decide how much decentralization is appropriate for their particular organization or subunit.

The recent shift toward decentralized decision making reflects the importance of managers responding quickly and effectively to environmental changes. Bill Gates, founder and CEO of Microsoft Corporation, is an example of an executive who pushes authority down through the organization. Microsoft employees have the authority to make decisions in their work areas and are held accountable for those decisions.

An aspect of decentralization that has received attention lately is the concept of empowerment. Empowerment refers to the concept of giving employees substantial authority and the ability to make decisions, within guidelines, on their own. Many organizations have empowered individual employees and employee teams to make decisions concerning their particular areas of work. For example, at Gold Coast Yachts, a company in St. Croix, Minn., employees are involved in major business decisions about the design and production of the company's multihull sailboats and power catamarans. Company president Richard Difede says that his employees have the real "power" in the organization because they deal with day-to-day problems and other situations. Therefore, empowering employees involves delegating more authority and operating responsibility to them.

BUILDING THE ORGANIZATION'S HORIZONTAL DIMENSION

In addition to a vertical dimension that focuses on the integration and coordination of work activities between organizational levels, an organization's structure also has a horizontal dimension that examines how work activities are organized at each specific level of the organization. This horizontal dimension of organizational structure involves answering questions such as, How will work activities be divided? or What form of departmentalization will work best?

Division of Labor

Division of labor means that rather than an entire job being performed by one individual, it is broken down into a number of steps, with separate individuals completing each step. In essence, individuals *specialize* in doing part of an activity rather than the entire activity. Assembly-line production, in which each worker repeatedly does a standardized task, is an example of division of labor. Fast-food companies such as Taco Bell, Burger King, and McDonald's use the concept of division of labor to standardize the process of taking a customer's order and filling it quickly and properly.

Because some tasks require highly developed skills while others can be performed by unskilled workers, division of labor makes efficient use of the diverse skills and capabilities of employees. If all workers in an organization were engaged in each step of the production process, every worker would need the skills to perform both the most demanding and the least demanding jobs. The result would be that, except when performing the most highly skilled or highly sophisticated tasks, employees would be working below their skill levels. Because skilled workers are paid more than unskilled workers and their wages tend to reflect their highest level of skills, paying highly skilled workers to do easy tasks would be an inefficient use of resources.

Historically, management has viewed the division of labor as an unending source of increased productivity. At the turn of the 20th century and earlier, this generalization was undoubtedly accurate. Because specialization was not widely practiced, its introduction into a workplace almost always generated higher productivity. However, at a certain point certain human drawbacks (or diseconomies) from division of labor exceed the economic advantages. These human diseconomies include boredom, job stress, low productivity, poor quality, increased absenteeism, and high turnover. By the early 1960s, these drawbacks were so prevalent in some jobs that enlarging rather than narrowing the scope of job activities was necessary to increase production.[10] By giving employees a variety of activities to do, allowing them to do a whole and complete piece of work, and putting them together into teams, managers are able to design more motivating jobs. Each of these ideas, of course, runs counter to the concept of division of labor. Yet, overall the division of labor concept is still alive and well in many organizations. It must be applauded for the cost economies that it brings to certain jobs, but its limitations must be recognized also.

Departmentalization

Each organization has a specific way to classify and group work activities. The process of grouping individuals into separate units or departments to accomplish organizational goals is known as *departmentalization.*

Historically, managers believed that organizational activities should be specialized and grouped into departments. Division of labor creates specialists who need coordination, and this is facilitated when specialists are placed in departments under the direction of a manager. Departments typically are grouped according to (1) the work functions being performed, (2) the product or service being produced, (3) the customer being served, (4) the geographic area or territory covered, or (5) the product–customer flow. The method(s) used should reflect the grouping that would best contribute to the attainment of the organization's objectives as well as the goals of individual units.

Functional. One of the most popular ways to group activities is by functions performed, or functional departmentalization. A manufacturing plant might be organized by separating engineering, accounting, manufacturing, human resources, and purchasing specialists into common departments, as show in Figure 8.3. Functional departmentalization can be used in all types of organizations because only the functions change to reflect the organization's objectives and activities. For example, a hospital might have departments devoted to research, patient care, and accounting.

Product. Figure 8.4 illustrates the product departmentalization used at Bombardier Ltd., a Canadian company. Each major product area in the corporation is placed under the authority of an executive, who is a specialist in and responsible for all aspects of that product line. L.A. Gear, another company that uses product departmentalization, bases its organizational structure on its varied product lines, which include women's and men's footwear and apparel and accessories.

Customer. The particular type of customer that the organization seeks to reach can also be used to group employees. The sales activities shown in Figure 8.5 for an office supply firm, for example, can be broken down into three departments: those serving retail, wholesale, and government customers. Textbook publishers often organize

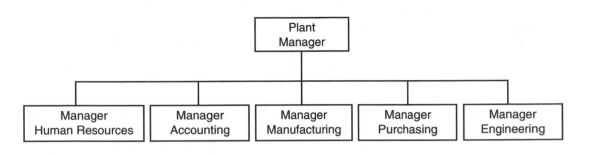

◆ **Figure 8.3.** Functional departmentalization.

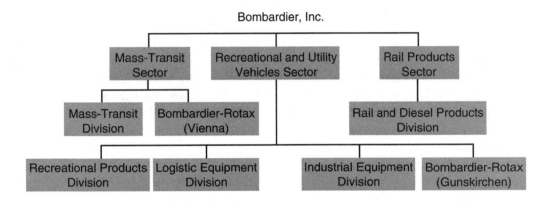

◆ **Figure 8.4.** Product departmentalization.

◆ **Figure 8.5.** Customer departmentalization.

their departments on a customer basis, such as primary-grade-level textbooks, secondary-grade-level textbooks, and college- or university-level textbooks. The assumption underlying customer departmentalization is that customers in each department have a common set of problems and needs that can best be met by having specialists for each.

Geographic. Another way to departmentalize is on the basis of geography or territory—geographic departmentalization. An organization's sales function might have western, southern, midwestern, and eastern regions, as shown in Figure 8.6. A large school district might have six high schools to provide for each of the geographical territories within the district. If an organization's customers are scattered over a large area, geographic departmentalization can be valuable. For example, the organizational structure used by Coca-Cola during the mid-1990s reflects the company's operations in two broad geographic arenas: the North American business sector and the international business sector (which included the Pacific region group, European Community group, northeastern Europe and Africa group, and Latin America).

Process. The final form of departmentalization, process departmentalization, is shown in Figure 8.7, which illustrates the various production departments in an aluminum processing plant. Each department specializes in one specific phase (or process) in the production of aluminum tubing. The metal is cast in huge furnaces and sent to the press department, where it is extruded into aluminum pipe. It is then transferred to the tube mill, where it is stretched into various sizes and shapes of tubing; moved to finishing, where it is cut and cleaned; and finally arrives in the inspect, pack, and ship department. This form of departmentalization focuses on the work processes and can be used for processing customers as well as products. For example, at a state motor vehicle office, the process to get a driver's license involves servicing in several departments. In some states, applicants must go through three steps, each handled by a separate department: (1) validation by the motor vehicles department, (2) processing by the licensing department, and (3) payment collection by the revenues department.

Most large organizations use many or all of the previously mentioned departmental groupings. Recently, two additional areas have been recognized for their effects on departmental grouping decisions. First, organizations have recognized the importance of customer service to success and have responded by emphasizing customer departmentalization. Because customer satisfaction is an important component of total quality management programs, many organizations have renewed their focus on meeting customer needs by adopting organizational structures that support this objective.[11] For example, L.L. Bean has restructured several customer groups based on the type of merchandise the customers generally purchase. Xerox segments its customers according to environment, geography, and the type of decision making employed so that the Xerox unit that best meets a customer's needs is assigned to that customer.

Second, teams often are used today to accomplish organizational objectives. As tasks become more complex and diverse skills are needed to accomplish those tasks, management has increasingly introduced teams and task forces. Rigid departmentalization is being complemented or replaced by a hybrid grouping of individuals who are experts in various specialties and who work together in an organizational arrangement known as a *cross-functional team.*[12] Cross-functional teams are unique in that they bring together experts who might never cross paths in a traditional organization, although their work might be highly interdependent. It is not unusual to find cost accountants teaming up with operations managers, product designers col-

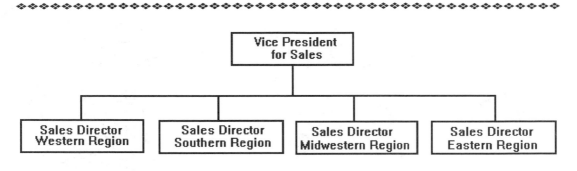

◆ **Figure 8.6.** Geographic departmentalization.

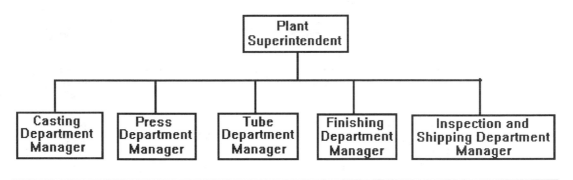

◆ **Figure 8.7.** Process departmentalization.

laborating with purchasing department employees, and marketing professionals working with research engineers.

Such teams cross traditional departmental lines and often are used to form the basis for a matrix organization structure. A matrix organization structure is an organizing approach that assigns specialists from different functional departments to work on one or more projects led by a project manager. This unusual organizational arrangement was developed in the 1960s by the U.S. aerospace industry to cope with the demands of efficiently and effectively managing a number of concurrent projects. Over the last decade the matrix organization form has become an increasingly popular organizing choice. More and more companies are formalizing the development and use of cross-functional teams organization-wide through the implementation of the matrix organization structure. Today, companies such as TRW, Lockheed, and Asea Brown Boveri (ABB) use matrix structures. Even Toyota used a matrix structure to develop its luxury car, the Lexus.

Figure 8.8 shows a matrix organization used in an aerospace firm. The matrix structure creates a dual chain of command that violates the classical principle of unity of command. Functional departmentalization is used to gain the economies that result from specialization, but overlying the functional departments is a set of managers who are responsible for specific products, projects, or programs within the organization. Along the top of the figure are the familiar organizational functions of engineering, accounting, human resources, and so on. Along the vertical dimension,

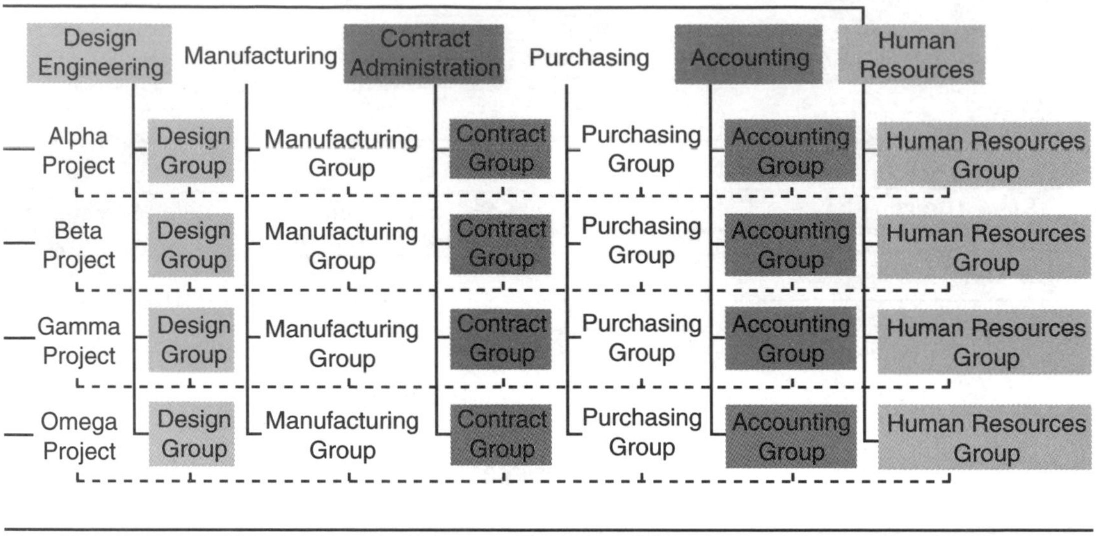

Design Engineering	Manufacturing	Contract Administration	Purchasing	Accounting	Human Resources
__ Alpha Project	Design Group	Manufacturing Group	Contract Group	Purchasing Group	Accounting Group	Human Resources Group
__ Beta Project	Design Group	Manufacturing Group	Contract Group	Purchasing Group	Accounting Group	Human Resources Group
__Gamma Project	Design Group	Manufacturing Group	Contract Group	Purchasing Group	Accounting Group	Human Resources Group
__ Omega Project	Design Group	Manufacturing Group	Contract Group	Purchasing Group	Accounting Group	Human Resources Group

◆ **Figure 8.8.** Matrix organization. Reprinted by permission of Prentice-Hall, Inc., Upper Saddle River, N.J.

however, the various projects that the aerospace firm is currently working on have been listed. Each project is directed by a manager who staffs the project with people from each of the functional departments. The addition of this vertical dimension to the traditional horizontal functional departments weaves together elements of functional and product departmentalization, creating a matrix. Employees in the matrix have two bosses who share authority: a functional departmental manager and a product or project manager. The project managers have authority over the functional members who are part of that manager's project team. Typically, the project manager has authority over project employees relative to the project's goals. However, decisions such as promotions, salary recommendations, and annual reviews remain the functional manager's responsibility. To work effectively, project and functional managers must communicate regularly and coordinate the demands on the common employees.[13]

THE CONTINGENCY APPROACH TO ORGANIZATIONAL DESIGN

In the past, many managers believed the "ideal" structural design to be the mechanistic or bureaucratic organization. Today, managers realize that no single organizational design is ideal for all situations because of the presence of many contingency factors.

Mechanistic and Organic Organizations

Figure 8.9 describes two diverse organizational forms. The mechanistic organization (or bureaucracy) evolved from the early traditional principles of management. Adherence to the unity-of-command principle ensured the existence of a formal hierarchy of authority, with each person controlled and supervised by one superior. Keeping the span of control small at increasingly higher levels in the organization created tall, impersonal structures. As the distance between the top

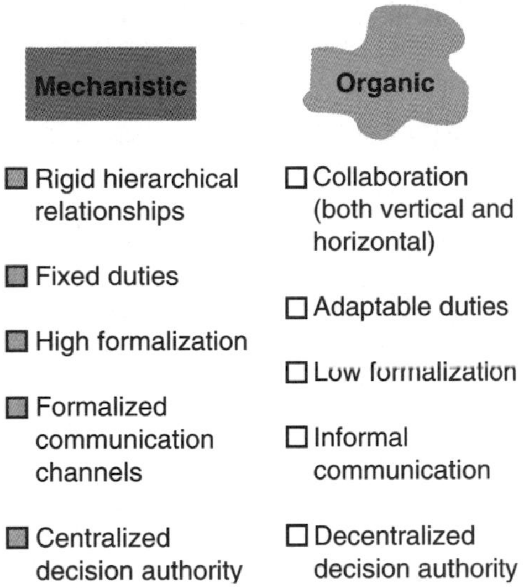

Mechanistic	Organic
■ Rigid hierarchical relationships	☐ Collaboration (both vertical and horizontal)
■ Fixed duties	
■ High formalization	☐ Adaptable duties
	☐ Low formalization
■ Formalized communication channels	☐ Informal communication
■ Centralized decision authority	☐ Decentralized decision authority

◆ **Figure 8.9.** Mechanistic versus organic organizations. Reprinted by permission of Prentice-Hall, Inc., Upper Saddle River, N.J.

and the bottom of the organization expanded, top management increasingly imposed rules and regulations. Because top managers could not control lower-level activities through direct observation and ensure the use of standard practices, they substituted rules and regulations. The historical belief in a high degree of division of labor created jobs that were simple, routine, and standardized. Further specialization through the use of departmentalization increased impersonality and the need for multiple layers of management to coordinate the specialized departments.

Many traditional managers have advocated that all organizations be high in complexity, formalization, and centralization. Organizational structures would be efficiency machines, well oiled by rules, regulations, and routinization. The impact of personalities and human judgments, which impose inefficiencies and inconsistencies, would be minimized. Standardization would lead to stability and predictability, eliminating confusion and ambiguity.

In direct contrast to the mechanistic form of organization is the organic organization (or adhocracy). This organization form is low in complexity and formalization and is decentralized. It is a highly adaptive structure that is as loose and flexible as the mechanistic organization is rigid and stable. Rather than having standardized jobs and regulations, the adhocracy's loose structure allows it to change rapidly as needs require. Organic organizations have division of labor, but the jobs that people do are not standardized. Employees tend to be technically proficient professionals who are trained to handle diverse problems. They need few formal rules and little direct supervision because their training has prepared them to deal with most situations. For example, a computer engineer assigned work does not need procedures on how to do it. Most problems can be solved or resolved independently or after conferring with colleagues. The organic organization is low in centralization so that the professional can respond quickly to problems and because top management cannot be expected to have the expertise to make necessary decisions.

Strategy and Structure

An organization's structure helps management achieve its objectives. Because objectives are derived from the organization's overall strategy, strategy and structure should be closely linked. More specifically, structure follows strategy. If management significantly changes its strategy, it needs to modify the structure to accommodate and support this change. Alfred Chandler studied the strategy–structure relationship of several large U.S. companies and found that organizations usually begin with a single product or line.[14] The simplicity of the strategy requires only a simple or loose structural form to carry it out. Decisions can be centralized in the hands of a single senior manager because complexity and formalization are low. As organizations grow, their strategies become more ambitious and elaborate, and the structure changes to support the chosen strategy.

Size and Structure

Considerable historical evidence suggests that an organization's size significantly affects its structure.[15] For example, large organizations—those typically employing 2000 or more employees—tend to have more specialization, horizontal and vertical differentiation, and rules and regulations than do small organizations. However, the relationship is not linear. Rather, size affects structure at a decreasing rate. That is, the impact of size becomes less important as an organization expands. Essentially, once an organization has around 2000 employees, it is already fairly mechanistic. An additional 500 employees will not have much of an impact. In contrast, adding 500 employees to an organization that has only 300 members is likely to result in a shift toward a more mechanistic structure.

Technology and Structure

Every organization uses some form of technology to convert its inputs into outputs. To reach its objectives, an organization uses equipment, materials, knowledge, and/or experienced individuals and combines them into certain types and patterns of activities. For example, Maytag uses workers on assembly lines to build the washers, dryers, and other home appliances that it manufactures and sells. Kinko's Copies custom produces jobs for individual customers, and Miles, Inc., uses a continuous-flow production line for manufacturing its vitamins. Each of these organizations represents a different type of technology. The common theme in studies of technology is that the processes or methods that transform inputs into outputs differ by their degree of routineness. In general, the more routine the technology, the more standardized the structure can be. Management should expect to structure routine technologies with a mechanistic organization. The more nonroutine the technology, the more organic the structure should be.[16]

Environment and Structure

Environment has been shown to be a major influence on organizational structure.[17] Mechanistic organizations are most effective in stable environments, whereas organic organizations are best matched with dynamic and uncertain environments. The evidence on the environment–structure relationship helps explain why so many managers are restructuring their organizations to be lean, fast, and flexible. Global competition, accelerated product innovation by all competitors, and increased demands from customers for higher-quality and faster deliveries are examples of dynamic environmental forces. Mechanistic organizations tend to be ill- equipped to respond to rapid environmental change. As a result, more managers are redesigning their organizations to make them more organic.

APPLICATIONS OF ORGANIZATIONAL DESIGN

Companies can employ any one of several organizational designs.

Simple Structure

Most organizations start as entrepreneurial ventures with a simple, inelaborate structure consisting of owner(s) and employees. An organization that appears to have almost no structure is probably a simple structure that is low in complexity, has little formalization, and has authority centralized in a single person. The simple structure is a "flat" organization because it usually has only two or three vertical levels, an informal arrangement of employees, and one individual in whom decision-making authority is centralized.

The simple structure is most widely used by small businesses in which the owner and manager are the same person. The strengths of the simple structure are obvious: It is fast, flexible, and inexpensive to maintain, and accountability is clear. One major weakness is that it is effective only in small organizations and becomes increasingly inadequate as an organization grows because its low formalization and high centralization result in information overload at the top. As the organization increases in size, decision making becomes slower and can eventually come to a standstill as the single executive tries to continue making all the decisions. If the structure is not changed and made more elaborate, the firm is likely to lose market momentum and eventually fail. The simple structure's other weakness is that it is risky; everything depends on one person. If anything happens to that person, the organization's information and decision-making center is lost.

Bureaucracy

Many organizations do not, by choice or by design, remain simple structures. As a company increases its sales and production volume, employees generally must be added to cope with the additional duties and requirements of operating at that volume. As the number of employees rises, the organizational structure tends to become more formalized: Rules and regulations are introduced, jobs become specialized, departments are created, levels of management are added, and the organization becomes increasingly bureaucratic.

A bureaucracy is an organizational arrangement based on order, logic, and the legitimate use of authority. When contingency factors—including growth in size—favor a bureaucratic or mechanistic design, one of two options is most likely to be used. One is a functional structure whose primary focus is on achieving the efficiencies of division of labor by grouping like specialists together in functional groupings. The other is the divisional structure, which creates self-contained, autonomous units or divisions. A closer look at each of these variations follows.

Functional Structure. The functional structure expands the concept of functional departmentalization to the entire organization. Under a functional structure, management designs an organization by grouping similar or related occupational specialties. The strength of the functional structure lies in the cost-saving advantages that accrue from specialization. Putting similar specialties together results in economies of scale, minimizes duplication of people and equipment, and makes employees more comfortable because they are with others who "talk the same language." However, the biggest weakness of the functional structure is that the organization can lose sight of its best interests while pursuing functional goals. No one function is totally responsible for end results, so functional specialists often have little understanding of what people in other functions are doing.

Divisional Structure. The divisional or business unit structure is an organizational structure made up of autonomous, self-contained units or divisions. PepsiCo, Daimler-Benz AG, and Johnson & Johnson are examples of organizations that have adopted a divisional structure. Each unit or division in a divisional structure is basically autonomous; a division manager is responsible for performance and has complete strategic and operational decision-making authority over his or her unit. In most divisional structures, a central headquarters provides support services, such as financial and legal, to the various units. Of course, central headquarters also oversees the coordination and control of the various divisions.

The strength of the divisional structure is that it focuses on results. Division executives have full responsibility over what happens to their products or services. The major disadvantage of this approach is the duplication of activities and resources. Because each division has its own functional departments, such as marketing, research and development, and production, the duplication of functions increases the organization's costs and reduces efficiency.

Many contemporary organizations have realized that the traditional hierarchical organizational designs, including functional and divisional structures, are not appropriate for the increasingly dynamic and complex environments they face. In response to marketplace demands for being lean, flexible, and innovative, many managers are finding creative ways to structure and organize work and to make their organizations more responsive to the needs of customers, employees, and other organizational constituents.[18]

Team-Based Structures

In a team-based structure, the entire organization consists of work groups or teams that perform the organization's work.[19] Employee empowerment is crucial because no rigid line of managerial authority flows from top to bottom. Rather, the employee teams are free to design work in the way they think best. The teams are held responsible for all work activity and performance results in their respective areas. Some companies that have made the transition to a team-based structure are discussed in the following paragraph.

Sun Life Assurance of Canada's U.S. office in Wellesley, Massachusetts, has reorganized customer representatives into eight-person teams trained to expedite all customer requests. Customers who call in are switched not from one specialist to another but to a team that takes care of every aspect of the customer's request. At Birkenstock Footprint Sandals, employee teams have been formed in sales, credit, production, warehousing, and other areas, within and across departments. In this company, as in other organizations that have moved to team-based structures, the transition to using teams was a gradual one. At Birkenstock, the team-based structure grew out of the success that a company-formed "eco task force" had with developing suggestions for ways in which the company and its dealers could improve recycling efforts and decrease the amount of energy used in day-to-day operations. The outcomes from the 12-person task force were so popular that Birkenstock managers wanted to further tap into the creativity and enthusiasm of its employees. A team-based structure permits exactly that. Many other for-profit and not-for-profit organizations have successfully implemented a team-based structure.[20]

The Boundaryless Organization

The design of a boundaryless organization (also referred to as a network organization, modular corporation, or a virtual corporation) is not defined by, or limited to, the boundaries imposed by a predefined structure. Many successful organizations operate most effectively in today's environment by remaining flexible and unstructured. The ideal structure for them is not having a rigid, predefined structure. Instead, they want a structure that lets them meet the demands of each situation as it arises.

The boundaryless organization can function efficiently and effectively by breaking down the artificial boundaries created by a fixed structural design. There are the horizontal boundaries imposed by departmentalization, the vertical boundaries that separate employees into organizational levels and hierarchies, and the external boundaries that separate the organization from its all-important suppliers, customers, and other stakeholders. Ideally, by minimizing or eliminating these artificial boundaries, the boundaryless organization streamlines its work activities so that it can respond quickly to the tumultuous and fast-moving marketplace.

Many factors have contributed to the rise of the boundaryless organization. The first factor is the *increasing globalization of markets and competitors.* The need to respond to complex, rapidly changing, and highly competitive global environments has made it imperative for an organization to adapt quickly in order to take advantage of opportunities that arise anywhere in the world. Also, the changing face of global trade has opened new doors for organizations. No longer is a company limited to manufacturing and/or selling in a limited territory. Organizations are moving to a fluid, flexible structure that is, in effect, custom designed as situations arise.

For example, Nike sells billions of dollars of shoes every year and earns a competitive profit even though it outsources its manufacturing to Asian suppliers rather than owning shoe-manufacturing facilities.

The second factor that has contributed to the rise in boundaryless organizations is the *rapidly changing technology* that permits the boundaryless organization to work. Without advanced computing power, software, and telecommunications capabilities, the boundaryless organization could not exist. For example, VeriFone, the world leader in credit card authorization systems, has no corporate headquarters, secretaries, or paper mail. Chief executive officer Hatim Tyabji calls his organizational structure the "blueberry pancake model, very flat, with all blueberries equal."[21] Even without a rigid, defined structure, VeriFone employees have fast information at their fingertips through the company's e-mail network. This type of organizational arrangement would not be possible without the advanced technology that is the backbone of the information network.

Finally, the *need for rapid innovation* has contributed to the evolution and development of the boundaryless organization. Rapidly changing marketplace needs and brief "windows" of opportunity demand that organizations be able to respond quickly and effectively to these situations. A boundaryless organization's flexible and fluid structure might include employee teams, outside contracts with other "specialist" organizations, or sophisticated electronic information networks so that it can respond with the rapid innovation that the global marketplace requires.

🏠 Additional Readings 🏠

Barnard, Chester I. 1968. *The Functions of the Executive.* 30th anniversary ed. Cambridge, Mass.: Harvard University Press.

Bateman, T. S., and S. A. Snell. 1996. *Management Building Competitive Advantage.* Chicago: Richard D. Irwin.

Blau, Peter M., and Richard A. Schoenherr. 1971. *The Structure of Organizations.* New York: Basic Books.

Chandler, Alfred D. 1962. *Strategy and Structure: Chapters in the History of the Industrial Enterprise.* Cambridge: MIT Press.

Child, John. 1984. *Organization: A Guide to Problems and Practices.* London: Kaiser & Row.

Crosby, Philip B. 1990. *Leading: The Art of Becoming an Executive.* New York: McGraw-Hill.

Daft, Richard L. 1994. *Management.* 3rd ed. Fort Worth, Tex.: Dryden Press.

Fayol, Henri. 1949. *General and Industrial Management.* Translated by Constance Storrs. London: Pitman.

___. 1916. *Industrial and General Administration.* Paris: Dunod.

George, Stephen, and Arnold Weimerskerch. 1994. *Total Quality Management.* New York: John Wiley & Sons.

Gerwin, Donald. 1981. "Relationships between Structure and Technology." In *Handbook of Organizational Design*, vol. 2, ed. P. C. Nystrom and W. H. Starbuck. New York: Oxford University Press.

❖❖

Gooding, R. Z., and J. A. Wagner. 1985. "A Meta-Analytic Review of the Relationship between Size and Performance: The Productivity and Efficiency of Organizations and Their Subunits." *Administrative Science Quarterly* (December) Vol. 30: 462–81.

Harrington, H. J., and J. S. Harrington. 1995. *Total Improvement Management: The Next Generation in Performance Improvement.* New York: McGraw-Hill.

Kipnis, David. 1976. *The Powerholders.* Chicago: University of Chicago Press.

McClenahem, John S. 1989. "Managing More People in the '90s." *Industry Week,* 20, March p. 30.

Mintzberg, Henry. 1983. *Power in and around Organizations.* Englewood Cliffs, N.J.: Prentice Hall, 1983.

___. 1983. *Structure in Fives: Designing Effective Organizations.* Englewood Cliffs, N.J.: Prentice Hall.

Moskal, Brian S. 1988. "Supervisors, Begone!" *Industry Week,* (June 20), p. 32.

Patterson, Gregory A. 1988. "Auto Assembly Lines Enter a New Era." *Wall Street Journal,* p. 2.

Peters, Tom. 1994. "Successful Electronic Changeovers Depend on Daring." *Springfield Business Journal,* August 8, p.15.

Pugh, D. S. 1981. "The Aston Program of Research: Retrospect and Prospect." In *Perspectives on Organization Design and Behavior,* ed. A. H. Van de Ven and W. F. Joyce. New York: John Wiley & Sons.

Robbins, S. P. 1990. *Organization Theory: Structure, Design, and Applications.* 3rd ed. Englewood Cliffs, N.J.: Prentice Hall.

___. 1996. *Organizational Behavior.* 7th ed. Englewood Cliffs, N.J.: Prentice Hall.

Robbins, S. P., and M. Coulter. 1996. *Management.* 5th ed. Englewood Cliffs, N.J.: Prentice Hall.

Rousseau, Denise M., and R. A. Cooke. 1984. "Technology and Structure: The Concrete, Abstract, and Activity Systems of Organizations." *Journal of Management* (Fall–Winter): 345–61.

Urwick, Lyndall. 1944. *The Elements of Administration.* New York: Harper & Row.

Van Fleet, David. 1983. "Span of Management Research and Issues." *Academy of Management Journal* (September): 546–52.

Chapter 9

Quality Functions within the Organization

❖ *This chapter should help you*

◆ Understand typical quality functions

◆ Become familiar with common barriers to effective performance of quality functions

---

The quality group in an organization is responsible for ensuring that a product or service is fit for use and meets specified requirements. These requirements can be specified by the purchaser, end user, industry, or society in general.

HISTORY OF THE QUALITY FUNCTION

The "modern" quality group and its functions resulted from the industrial revolution. As industrialization evolved, product manufacturing was broken down into individual tasks, one of which was inspection. Production foremen were very familiar with their products and were able to override inspectors, who reported to the foremen. However, the approach of World War I accelerated new product introductions. Foremen were less familiar with their products and did not know what inspection issues could be safely overridden, and the natural bias to produce and ship began to cause problems. Because of this, the theories of an industrial engineer, Frederick Taylor, were put into practice.

Taylor recommended a hierarchical structure that created an independent inspection organization. This hierarchical structure worked well through the enormous production demands of World War II and through the Cold War. Most companies remain structured in this format; however, it is now realized that every department and every individual needs to produce a quality product. This applies not only to those who actually produce the product or service but also to those who support that production.

FUNCTIONS OF THE QUALITY GROUP

No standard answer exists as to what functions the quality group should perform in any given organization. Product mix, company size, and markets served are influential in determining the role of the quality group. The tasks performed by the quality group include those discussed in the following sections. Not all these functions are performed by separate departments in all companies; when and where these tasks should be divided often is dictated by economics, customers, society, and organizational culture. The following discussion assumes that a company is medium to large in size with both corporate and plant quality organizations. Even in small companies in which these tasks might be performed by one individual, they remain discrete functions.

Quality Assurance

Quality assurance consists of "all the planned and systematic activities implemented with the quality system and demonstrated as needed, to provide adequate confidence that an entity will fulfill requirements for quality."[1] Therefore, the role of quality assurance is to design and implement a system that meets the quality needs of the business. This may include compliance to generic quality system standards (e.g., ISO 9000), specific industry standards, or special customer quality requirements.

Reliability Engineering

The objective of reliability engineering is to determine the probability that a product will perform its intended function for a specified time interval under stated conditions. This individual, department, or group is usually found in industries that build complex mechanical or electronic devices with multiple subcomponents, all of which must function in order for the device to perform as intended. A mission that is obviously critical in nature is keeping the space shuttle flying, but reliability engineering can also include the estimation of the life expectancy of an electric toaster. The performance of this task might involve stress analysis; failure mode, effects, and criticality analysis (FMEA); reliability prediction; supplier selection; reliability testing; and failure reporting and corrective actions.

Quality Engineering

The quality engineering function is involved with the design, production, or servicing of a product. The quality engineer will be involved in advanced quality planning, establishing quality standards, test equipment and gage design or selection, process capability analysis, rejected or held material analysis, and general troubleshooting in any area described as having a "quality problem." Quality engineers ensure that the proper data will be collected and analyzed during all appropriate phases of a product's life. These statistics are used to prevent problems prior to occurrence and to identify and correct problems after they occur.

Supplier Quality

The supplier quality function works with the purchasing department to ensure the quality of purchased parts. This is done by ensuring that the supplier has an effective quality system in place and that the supplier is able to meet specifications for material to be purchased. A partnership relationship might be created to help the supplier meet the standards or to improve—for the benefit of both parties. Problems with purchased materials are reported to the supplier, and both parties should work to prevent them from recurring. The supplier quality department is also responsible for developing and implementing supplier certification programs that will reduce the need for incoming inspection and enable just-in-time shipments.

Quality Control

Quality control is defined as the "operational techniques and activities that are used to fulfill requirements for quality."[2] Quality control is the process of checking to see whether the product conforms and is fit for use and if it is not, responding appropriately.

Inspection

Inspection is the process of monitoring measures of product or service quality. Inspection data can be used for process control purposes and for defect reduction efforts.

Receiving Inspection. In a manufacturing environment, receiving (incoming) inspection is the group that inspects purchased raw materials or components as they are received to ensure that the correct materials have arrived, that they meet specified criteria, and that they are properly identified. Contents might be visually inspected using attribute sampling plans, measurement of variables, or laboratory chemical or physical testing. The materials will be identified as being held until released by receiving inspection. In some regulatory cases they will be in a bonded or quarantined area until released.

In a service organization, receiving inspection is the act of checking the raw materials used to produce the service. In this case it would be the customer's written or verbal order (insurance policy application) or a true raw material for the service (surgical pin). (Note: Most quality functions started with the manufacturing world and are now being translated into the service world. In the receiving inspection of written or verbal orders, most manufacturing firms did little about contract review until required by such standards as ISO 9001-1994.)

In-Process Inspection. In-process inspection is the act of checking materials to a specification or drawing while the product is being produced. It ensures that the product's content and status are properly identified and traceable. Checking specifications might consist of measurement, physical, or chemical testing, and the testing might be destructive or nondestructive. If the material passes the inspection criteria, it is so noted, and the product moves along to the next stage of the process. If it fails inspection, the product will be scrapped or quarantined until disposition can be made. This quarantine can be simple tagging or storage in a bonded area. Immediate corrective action will be taken and then documented to allow long-term evaluation of the effectiveness of the action.

In service industries the interim test might be the review of a credit card application or a travel agent reviewing an itinerary. The concept is still the same: The information or request has been received, and the act of providing the service has started while a review is being performed. In most cases the review is performed by the individual performing the work.

Finished Goods Inspection. Prior to the release of a manufactured product, a final review or test of the product may occur. This can be 100 percent visual, formal sampling of attributes, chemical or physical testing, or a functional test. It can take the form of a batch review in which all records of the production and inspection process are reviewed for anomalies. These tests normally take place when a product is ready for shipping and only packing remains. The product is also checked for identification of content, status, and traceability.

In a service industry finished goods inspection might consist of the final steps before delivery. In a restaurant the chef or waiter might check the presentations of the food (ergo, that the sauce is swirled just right or that the tomatoes are centered on the bun). Another example would be an optometrist polishing a new pair of glasses prior to handing them to the customer.

Metrology

Metrology is the individual or group responsible for the devices used to measure and/or test material or product quality. This function is directly involved with the selection, purchase, and/or redesign of gages, test equipment, measuring devices, and associated jigs and fixtures. Metrology also maintains calibration of the measuring equipment and ensures its maintenance for precision.

Internal Auditing

Internal auditing is responsible for determining whether the quality system is compliant with required standards and whether the system is effective. Internal auditing can be an individual, group, or department but should be independent of the department being audited. It is common practice for an experienced lead auditor to train and lead people from different departments for specific audits. Using personnel from other departments increases employee awareness of the need for and benefits of a quality system and the internal auditing process.

Administration

Administration is a separate entity only in the largest of organizations. Administration is responsible for developing the organization's quality plan and corresponding budget as well as coordinating the activities to achieve the plan and reporting on its status. Changes being introduced are usually of a technological nature, but cultural shifts might be required. Administration will determine the professional qualifications and training requirements for each position in the department. This department's overall mission is to develop and maintain the quality system in order to ensure the quality of the product or service being provided.

Customer Quality

The customer quality group works with customers in almost a mirror image of the supplier quality group. This group should respond to problems presented by customers with a quick and precise action that will prevent recurrence. Successful customer quality groups must work with other internal departments to ensure that problems are effectively addressed and to anticipate and address problems that have not yet occurred.

Consulting and Training

In some companies the quality function is responsible for formal classroom instruction on the tools used for quality improvement. These tools—flowcharting, Pareto analysis, and soon—are covered in Chapter 33. They are often taught in the work environment by quality professionals working as team facilitators to solve existing problems.

COMMON MISCONCEPTIONS IN QUALITY

Several mistakes that commonly occur with the quality functions of a department are as follows:

- forgetting that the quality department is a *service* department
- forgetting that the company is there to make a profit
- feeling that quality's only responsibility is rejecting product
- thinking that it is other people's jobs to improve the process (you can not throw problems over the wall and ignore them)
- feeling as though the customer is out to get you (this means that you do not understand your customer's business)
- waiting on others to provide leadership (lead, or get used to the view)
- feeling like *you* do not need professional training (those who are reading this get it.)

Additional Readings

American Society for Quality Control Standards Committee for American National Standards Committee Z -1 on Quality Assurance. American Society for Quality Control. ANSI\ISO\ASQC A8402.

Juran, Joseph M., and Frank M. Gryna, eds. 1988. *Juran's Quality Control Handbook.* 4th ed. New York: McGraw-Hill.

Chapter 10

Communication within the Organization

❖ *This chapter should help you*

- ◆ Understand the linkage between organizational structure and communication
- ◆ Become familiar with the benefits of open and effective communication
- ◆ Understand the factors that contribute to effective communication as well as those which lead to ineffective communication

---

Because organizations consist of multiple people working toward a common goal, they cannot function without communication—the process of transmitting information. Organizations accomplish their goals by utilizing people in the distribution of work, management and control of work, problem solving and decision making, information processing, information and idea collection, testing and ratifying decisions, coordination and liaison, commitment and involvement, negotiation, and inquiry into the past.[1] Communications is pivotal for accomplishing any of these tasks.

Communications can be written or oral. Examples of written communications media include policy and procedure manuals, performance reports, proposals, memoranda, meeting minutes, newsletters, e-mail, and on-line documents (e.g., company intranets). Examples of oral communications include speeches, meetings (group or one-on-one), informal discussions, and voice mail.

Communication is also either formal or informal. Formal communication is planned and carried out as part of standard operating policies and methods and is typically carried out according to the organizational structure. A letter offering employment, a product test report, the company's annual report, and performance appraisal are examples of formal communication. Informal communication is not mandated or otherwise required but occurs as part of helping individuals function collectively. Examples include a discussion between a test engineer and a production supervisor to clarify a specification or an e-mail message from one employee to another reminding him or her of the need for the two of them to prepare for an upcoming presentation.

The method used for a specific communication should take into account the urgency of the message, the makeup of the audience and how widely dispersed members are, and how the message is likely to be received by the audience. These issues will help in selecting the best communication channel to use (e.g., phone call versus e-mail versus memo or one large meeting versus several smaller meetings) as well as the individual(s) who will deliver the message and how it is organized.

A significant problem in communications is the difference between what the sender says and what the receiver often hears. Because the sender is translating thoughts into words and the receiver is then translating words into thoughts, many opportunities for differences in meaning to occur exist. Misinterpretations can be caused by, for example, background, cultural biases, group norms, and emotional factors.

An increasing problem in communications is information overload. As the pace of change continues to accelerate and choices in types of communications channels likewise expand (e.g., voice mail, newsletters, e-mail, and company intranets), people might find it difficult to sort, understand, and remember large quantities of information.

COMMUNICATION AND ORGANIZATIONAL STRUCTURE

Organizational structure plays an important role in communication. Top-to-bottom vertical communication flows from managers to subordinates. The company's vision and values, strategic objectives and measures, and policies and procedures are typically communicated in this manner. Vertical communication also occurs when a manager assigns tasks to personnel in his or her function.

Rather than utilizing the chain of command for communication, management may find it more efficient to communicate some messages to all employees at monthly meetings. More frequent informal communication helps assure managers that everyone in the system is humming the same tune.[2]

Bottom-to-top vertical communication happens when information flows from subordinates to management. Status updates on assigned tasks, employee suggestion systems, and other types of reports are examples of this form of communication. In addition to vertical communication, information is also transferred horizontally. Information flow among peers or within a team or group is horizontal communication.

Managers and leaders of groups play a key role in effective communication. By exhibiting leadership qualities, they lay the foundations for trust, which will result in open communications.

BENEFITS OF OPEN AND EFFECTIVE COMMUNICATION

Many benefits result from a good internal communications network:

◆ Employees understand company goals and their role in meeting those goals.

◆ Employee involvement increases so the company is better able to meet its goals.

◆ Improved efficiency and effectiveness result when highly motivated employees attempt to accomplish their goals.

◆ Costs are reduced as the organization accomplishes tasks effectively, eliminating the costs and time delays associated with rework or redesign.

◆ Open communication channels make it easier for management to see the real issues and problems.

◆ Employees are receptive to change and offer creative solutions for problems.

Communication is most effective when the following occur:

◆ *Open channels of communications are maintained.* This enables employees to provide the correct information. Trust between the manager and the employee is a key factor in this process.

◆ *Employees are highly motivated.* The organization must ensure that employee morale is high and that people are motivated to give their best.

◆ *An appropriate rewards and recognitions system is in place.* To maintain high motivation, employees must be rewarded and recognized for their accomplishments.

◆ *Communication is timely.* When communication is timely, whether a performance appraisal, a response to employee suggestions, or a quarterly financial update, employees feel that they can trust management and that management will act on the information they provide. This applies to both top-to-bottom and bottom-to-top communications.

◆ *The organization is flat.* Reduction in the number of management layers helps reduce communication distortion.

◆ *Employees are empowered.* When teams or individuals are empowered, their participation and motivation increases, resulting in improved efficiency. Because they are closer to the problems, they are better positioned to make decisions, rather than having to work through several management layers.

◆ *Employee training is provided.* With proper training, people with leadership roles can be effective leaders. Employees can be better team players.

In contrast, communication is ineffective when the following problems occur:

◆ *Communications are not open.* When employees feel that they cannot trust management or that management is not honest, they are not likely to share accurate or complete information.

◆ *Managers lack leadership qualities.* When managers are not effective in their leadership roles, they cannot get tasks accomplished or help resolve issues. This can demoralize employees quickly.

◆ *Communication is not timely.* Timely communication is very essential for sustaining employee morale. For example, if a suggestion system has been in use for a while but management does not respond to the suggestions, employees will no longer contribute. However, when suggestions receive responses, employees feel valued and are motivated to contribute further.[3]

◆ *Many management layers exist.* Information does not flow properly and correctly from top to bottom or vice versa if there are too many management

❖❖❖

layers. In this case, instead of receiving information about the real problems, managers may receive only the information they want to hear.

◆ *Management support and follow-up is lacking.* When companies are ready to start new programs, they need to provide continued support to ensure its success. Teams that have been empowered lose motivation quickly when their decisions are not acted on or are overridden by management.

◆ *Organizations are not prepared for change from status quo.* Successful communications require the organization at all levels to be flexible and open minded. When employees are not ready for such changes, communication is usually not effective.[4]

🏠 Additional Readings 🏠

Coakley, Carolyn Gwynn, and Andrew D. Wolvin, 1991. "Listen to What's Being Said about Listening Training." *Performance & Instruction,* April, pp. 8–10.

Costigan, Robert D. 1995. "Adaptation of Traditional Human Resources Processes for Total Quality Environments." *Quality Management Journal* (spring).

Covey, Stephen R., and Keith A. Gulledge. 1995. "Principle-Centered Leadership and Change." In *The Quality Yearbook, 1995,* ed. James W. Cortada and John A. Woods. New York: McGraw-Hill.

George, Stephen, and Arnold Weimerskirch. 1994. *Total Quality Management— Strategies and Techniques Proven at Today's Most Successful Companies.* New York: John Wiley & Sons.

Handy, Charles. 1993. *Understanding Organizations.* New York: Oxford University Press.

Howe, R., D. Gaeddert, and M. Howe. 1992. *A Failure to Communicate: Quality on Trial.* New York: West Publishing.

Kirrane, Diane E. 1988. *Listening to Learn, Learning to Listen.* Alexandria, Va.: American Society for Training and Development Info-Line.

Raymond, L. 1994. *Reinventing Communication: A Guide to Using Visual Language for Planning, Problem Solving, and Reengineering.* Milwaukee: ASQC Quality Press.

Rice, Elizabeth J. 1998. "Are You Listening?" *Quality Progress,* May, pp. 25–29.

Zaremba, A. J. 1989. *Management in a New Key: Communication in the Modern Organization.* Norcross, Ga.: Institute of Industrial Engineers.

Chapter 11

Change Agents and Their Effects on Organizations

❖ *This chapter should help you*

◆ Understand the roles and principles of change management

◆ Become familiar with the responsibilities of a change agent

◆ Understand the process of managing change, including the relationship between the change agent and the client

◆ Become familiar with common problems encountered in managing change

As an organization operates and evolves, there are not only incremental changes but increasingly major shifts in strategy, technology, and work organization. Change management is a process for ensuring that the people affected by change understand the nature of the change and the reasons for it, with the expectation that the new methods of operating will be internalized without creating undue resistance, conflict, and fear.

TYPES OF CHANGE AGENTS

Change agents are individuals who play a specific role in the planning and implementation of the change management process. They might be members of the organization or outsiders.

Internal Change Agents

An internal change agent is a person within the organization who has been commissioned by management to champion quality improvement efforts. Internal change agents possess an understanding of the organization's culture, infrastructure, and the business and also have a vested interest in seeing change efforts succeed. However, internal change agents can be hindered by political pressures that can prevent them from providing objective feedback when problems arise. They might also lack perspective of the big picture[1] or have a vested interest in preserving certain traditions that keeps them from seeing some opportunities for improvement.

External Change Agents

An external change agent is a person outside the organization who has been hired to facilitate the improvement process. An external change agent has a greater degree of freedom and is better able to objectively assess activities and provide honest feedback to senior management without fear of repercussion. Also, organizational members are less likely to have previous experiences with the change agent that might impact their effectiveness, and they do not have a vested interest in preserving long-held organizational traditions. The danger is, of course, that organizations can become so dependent on an external change agent that the change process is affected when the change agent leaves. Another disadvantage of external change agents is their lack of familiarity with the corporate culture.

External change agents must work diligently to build a relationship with the client organization. This includes becoming familiar with company norms, shared beliefs, and behaviors as well as understanding both formal and informal leadership structures. For most organizations the change agent needs to become acquainted with "influentials," who serve as informal leaders—persons to whom others turn for new ideas.[2] Building a relationship among informal leaders can be beneficial because other members of the organization will check with them for affirmation that it is beneficial or safe to support the change process.

Deming emphasized the role of external change agents in his view of organizational transformation. "A system can not understand itself. The transformation requires a view from outside."[3]

Change Agent Team

To capitalize on the pros of using first- and second-party change agents and to counterbalance the cons, the best practice is to form a change agent team in which an internal change agent and an external change agent work in collaboration.[4]

CHANGE AGENT SKILLS

"The change agent's expertise accordingly consists of knowledge and skill in tapping into the enterprise's interaction processes, in order to discover what members of it do, feel, think, and experience. . . . He or she helps them elaborate appropriate interaction processes, to capture and generate data on themselves and the organization, and to utilize that data . . . . The change agent provides and imparts knowledge and skill in how to work with that data."[5]

As this quote indicates, change agents need a wide range of skills. They need to be systems thinkers who can diagnose problems at the organizational, group, and individual levels. They also need to be familiar with models for diagnosis as well as a multitude of methods for intervening. Following are but a few of the interventions a change agent might be called on to facilitate:

◆ *Human process interventions:* team building, survey feedback, and process consultation

◆ *Technostructural interventions:* sociotechnical systems, job enrichment, and self-managed work teams

◆ *Human resource management interventions:* reward systems, stress management, and career planning

◆ *Strategic interventions:* open-systems planning and culture change[6]

Change agents also need to have a high level of self-confidence and good communication skills. Depending on the change they are facilitating, they might be called on to work with the following:

◆ senior executives on strategic change issues or leadership development processes

◆ product or department managers for resolving conflict or implementing changes in mission

◆ teams for developing new work system design

◆ individuals for coaching and development

A change agent should be a team player skilled in the arts of negotiating, conflict resolution, problem solving, and project management. They must be able to communicate effectively with senior management and should possess the qualities of patience, persistence, and a sense of humor. Familiarity with the specific business environment, the organization, and its people is important.

For implementing improvement efforts, a change agent should be familiar with quality management theories and concepts and be experienced in the use of quality improvement tools.[7] As part of working with groups at various levels of the organization, they might be called on to facilitate the use of the seven quality control tools, the seven management tools, or other specific improvement tools (e.g., reengineering and lean manufacturing). The effective integration of the skills of working with people with the skills of working with improvement techniques provide the more successful results.[8]

Force-field analysis, a method for looking at the driving forces for change in comparison to the restraining forces that resist change, is frequently used in change management. As seen in Figure 11.1, change will occur when the force of resistance is less than that driving the change. Unfortunately, management usually wants to add more driving force when time and energy are better spent reducing the restraining forces. For example, fear of loss of jobs or lack of congruences between the stated desired behaviors and what is actually rewarded by the organization are restraining forces that only management can address. Force-field analysis is useful for providing an understanding of the status quo and a starting point for action.[9]

DUTIES OF THE CHANGE AGENT

A change agent is responsible for assisting the client (usually the management team) in the planning and execution of a change effort. In doing so they work to support the group responsible for initiating and implementing the change. This group might be the executive council for a strategic change, such as total quality management, or a subset of the executive group plus a vertical slice of the organization for implementing

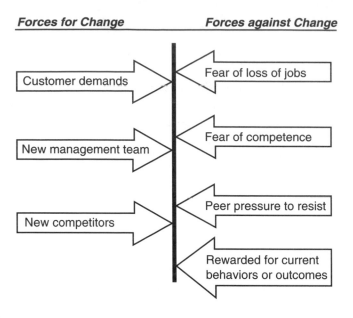

Forces for Change | **Forces against Change**

Customer demands → Fear of loss of jobs

New management team → Fear of competence

New competitors → Peer pressure to resist

Rewarded for current behaviors or outcomes

◆ **Figure 11.1.** Force-field analysis.

a sociotechnical work redesign. Although the group will oversee the process, a senior executive is often named as sponsor of the initiative, and the change agent will work closely with this sponsor on a day-to-day basis in monitoring the change process.

The change agent must ensure that the client has a clear understanding of both the current and the desired situation (where we are now and where we want to go). Once this gap is clearly identified, a plan for achieving the future vision can be developed. The change process must take human behavior as well as technical performance issues into account.

Responsibilities of the change agent might include providing progress reports to the sponsor; challenging the sponsor if commitment falters; developing and managing the internal support network that provides training, coaching, and feedback; and managing specific projects.[10] The change agent also balances the varying needs or desires of the sponsor, the guiding team, and the workforce. The change agent must be careful not to demonstrate inappropriate behaviors, such as taking credit for progress, performing activities that the sponsor or line managers should be doing, micromanaging progress (cattle prodding others to take action), or taking on the role of informant.

A change agent is most useful or necessary during the initial stages of instituting a transformation by providing models, insights, and objectivity for the process. As other managers in the organization gain experience in planning and executing change, the change agent's role should be reduced or phased out.

CHARACTERISTICS OF THE CHANGE AGENT–CLIENT RELATIONSHIP

The following characteristics should be present in the relationship between the change agent and the client.

◆ *Reciprocity:* Give-and-take is required by both parties in the transfer of information. Reciprocity increases mutual understanding of the status quo and makes diagnosis more accurate. If the client is already committed to a particular solution and has enlisted a change agent to help prove a point or affirm a predetermined position, no reciprocity exists.

◆ *Openness:* Both the change agent and the change management team should be willing to freely express new inputs and give authentic feedback.

◆ *Realistic expectations:* The change agent is not a miracle worker and must work with the change management team to set realistic expectations and not oversell themselves on what can be achieved.

◆ *Expectations of reward:* The change agent must be viewed as a value-added resource in helping to improve how work is done. Pilot programs sometimes serve the purpose of demonstrating a change agent's worth before a long-term contractual agreement is made.

◆ *Structure:* Roles, working procedures, and mutual goals and expectations should be defined.

◆ *Equal power:* A balance of power should be regulated by the sponsor between the external change agent and the change management team. When the power of the two parties is balanced, power itself no longer plays the significant role in bringing about change. Where there is an imbalance, the appearance of change might be brought about through compliance of the weaker partner without any buy-in for lasting effectiveness.[11]

GUIDELINES FOR IMPLEMENTING CHANGE

The following eight steps are a guideline for implementing the change process:

1. *Establish a sense of urgency:* examine market and competitive threats and opportunities

2. *Form a guiding coalition:* assemble a core group to lead the change effort

3. *Create a vision:* create a vision to direct the change effort and develop strategies for achieving it

4. *Communicate the vision:* find useful mechanisms for communicating the new vision and strategies

5. *Empower others to act on the vision:* identify and remove obstacles to change

6. *Establish short-term goals:* plan for visible improvements and recognition of accomplishments of people who make them happen

7. *Consolidate results to drive continuous improvement:* piggyback on achievements to stimulate continuous improvement

8. *Institutionalize new approaches:* establish linkages between new behaviors and improvement in performance results[12]

PROBLEMS IN CHANGE MANAGEMENT

The following problems are common in change management:

Error #1: Failing to establishing a sense of urgency.
Management often underestimates how hard it can be to drive people out of their comfort zones. When less than 75 percent of company management is convinced that business as usual is totally unacceptable, serious problems are likely to interfere with the change process.[13]

Error #2: Failing to create a powerful guiding coalition.
Significant renewal programs often start with just one or two people. In cases of successful change management, the leadership coalition expands over time. "Efforts that don't have a powerful enough guiding coalition can make apparent progress for a while. But, sooner or later, the opposition gathers itself together and stops the change."[14]

Error #3: Lacking a vision.
Without a sensible vision, a transformation effort can easily dissolve into a list of confusing and incompatible projects that can take the organization in the wrong direction or nowhere at all. Failed transformations often have plenty of plans, directives, and programs but no vision.[15]

Error #4: Undercommunicating the vision.
Change is not likely to happen unless there is widespread willingness among the workforce to participate. Communication is vital in motivating those who must make the necessary sacrifices for changing how work is done. Without credible communication, the hearts and minds of the troops are never captured.[16]

Error #5: Failing to manage resisting forces.
Inaction on the part of management in dealing with resisting forces, including non-supporters, can threaten the credibility of the change effort as a whole.[17]

Error #6: Failing to plan for short-term successes.
Real transformation takes time, and a renewal effort risks losing momentum without short-term goals to meet and celebrate. Most people will not go on the long march unless they see compelling evidence within 12 to 14 months that the journey is producing expected results. Without short-term wins, too many people give up or actively join the ranks of those who have been resisting change.[18]

Error #7: Celebrating victory prematurely.
Initiators of change can be overanxious to report progress and have a conflict of interest in making sure that the "right" results are achieved on time. This can actually incite resistors to join the bandwagon in the hopes of making the initiators think that they are finished and can then go away.[19]

❖❖

Error #8: Failing to make permanent change.

Change happens when it becomes "the way we do things around here." Until new behaviors are rooted in social norms and shared values, they are subject to degradation as soon as the pressure for change is removed. This is a common occurrence when a relationship of dependency evolves between the external change agent and the client organization so that when the change agent is phased out, so is the pressure for sustaining improvement activities.[20]

Error #9: Lack of involvement or participation by process owners.

When process owners are not given the opportunity to become involved and participate in planning and implementing changes, the change management effort is compromised because of a probable lack of buy-in by those affected by the change and by a lack of synergy in being able to formulate the best possible solution for improving the way work is done.

Error #10: Lack of planning in assessing the impact of change and the time to make it happen.

Many change management teams are guilty of not posing the question as to what threats a change will pose to the existing organization. Discovery of what habits, whose status, and what beliefs might be threatened by a change is critical in understanding the reasons that it might be rejected.[21]

The most general lesson to be learned from companies that have endeavored to initiate improvement programs is that the change process is a progressive one that happens through a series of steps that, in total, usually require a considerable length of time. Taking shortcuts only creates the illusion of speed and never produces the desired results.[22]

PERVASIVE CHANGE

One early model for viewing change was proposed by Kurt Lewin, who stated that three steps must occur:

◆ *Unfreezing:* getting people to recognize the need for change and being willing to try

◆ *Moving:* actually trying the behaviors, processes, attitudes, or other desired changes

◆ *Refreezing:* the change has been implemented and is now the norm[23]

Although this model can still be a useful frame of reference for thinking about change, the pace of change in some industries is now so rapid that there appears to be no time to refreeze before a need for a new unfreezing arrives. This pace of change might indicate that all managers—in fact, all employees—need to become knowledgeable of change management and be their own agents of change.

🏠 Additional Readings 🏠

Brassard, Michael. 1989. *Memory Jogger Plus.* Methuen, Mass.: GOAL/QPC.

Caravatta, Michael. 1997. *Let's Work Smarter, Not Harder: How to Engage Your Entire Organization in the Execution of Change.* Milwaukee: ASQ Quality Press.

Cummings, Thomas G. and Edgar F. Huse. 1989. *Organizational Development and Change*. 4th ed. St. Paul, West Publishing.

Deming, W. Edwards. 1996. *The New Economics.* 2nd ed. Cambridge: MIT. Center for Advanced Engineering Study.

Havelock, Ronald G. 1982. *The Change Agent's Guide to Innovation in Education.* 6th ed. Englewood Cliffs, N.J.: Educational Technology Publications.

Hutton, David W. 1994. *The Change Agents' Handbook: A Survival Guide for Quality Improvement Champions.* Milwaukee: ASQC Quality Press.

Juran, Joseph M., and Frank M. Gryna, eds. 1988. *Juran's Quality Control Handbook.* 4th ed. New York: McGraw-Hill.

Kanter, R. M. 1983. *The Change Masters.* New York: Simon & Schuster.

Kotter, John P. 1996. *Leading Change.* Boston: Harvard Business School Press.

___. 1995. "Leading Change: Why Transformation Efforts Fail." *Harvard Business Review* (March–April): 59–67.

The Malcolm Baldrige National Quality Award Criteria: 1999 Criteria for Performance Excellence. Gaithersburg, Md., National Institute of Standards and Technology.

McLennan, Roy. *Managing Organizational Change.* Englewood Cliffs, N.J.: Prentice Hall, 1989.

Okes, Duke W. 1991. "Quality Improvement and Organization Development." The Quality Management Forum, ASQ Management Division, winter.

Stevens, N. 1996. "The Challenge of Change." *Manufacturing Systems,* April, 84–86.

Chapter 12

Management Styles

❖ *This chapter should help you*

- ◆ Recognize some well-known motivational theories
- ◆ Become familiar with various types of management styles
- ◆ Understand the problems encountered with autocratic and participative systems

---

MOTIVATIONAL THEORIES

A manager is "one who handles, controls, or directs." Throughout history the people who handle, direct, or control the efforts of others have been called by many names, including chief, shaman, and monarch. Leadership, on the other hand, is "the process through which a person tries to get organizational members to do something that the person desires."[1] Modern management theory holds that a manager should be a leader rather than a handler, controller, or director.

John Kotter defines the tasks of management as planning and budgeting, organizing and staffing, and controlling and problem solving. He defines leadership as establishing direction, aligning people, and motivating and inspiring.[2] For the purposes of this chapter, the role of a manager is that of an individual responsible for all these activities.

Motivating others to work at their best is a constant challenge for managers, who must attempt to understand the many factors that motivate individuals. For example, some people are motivated when their work is rewarding and satisfying, whereas others are motivated by incentives associated with successful task accomplishment. Still others are motivated by encouragement or by the importance of their work.

In fact, each individual might be motivated by different things at different times, making the human side of the job of management quite complex. Following are a few of the basic theories of management that have been developed since the early 1900s.

Scientific Management

In 1911 Frederick Taylor introduced one of the first contributions to the scientific theory of management. The aim of scientific management was to find the one best way to perform a task, which would result in increased productivity. Taylor emphasized the efficiency, not the satisfaction, of workers. He did this by breaking a job down into small-task components that could be studied to find the more efficient way of doing it.

Scientific management ideas were expanded when Henry Gantt added the concept of providing an incentive system to workers and supervisors on the basis of their output, whereas Frank and Lillian Gilbreth began to study how work design affected worker fatigue.

Classical Organizational Theory

As organizations became larger and more complex, the study of management enlarged to look at the management of not only individual tasks but also the larger enterprise. Henri Fayol was an early pioneer in this regard, developing his own Fourteen Principles of Management, including issues such as Unity of Command (discussed in Chapter 8) and subordination of individual interest to the common good.

Max Weber added the idea of bureaucracy as being the ideal organizational structure. He felt that a clear definition of work responsibilities and lines of authority would provide predictable and more efficient output. Mary Parker Follett added the factor of relationships, both within the organization and between the organization and its environment, to consideration for management.

The Behavioral View

In the 1930s researchers performed a series of studies at the Hawthorne Plant of Western Electric Company to determine the best level of lighting, length of workday, and length of rest periods to maximize worker productivity. As the lighting in the plant was increased, production levels rose. Surprisingly, production levels also rose as light levels decreased. Researchers eventually determined that the increase in productivity was correlated not to lighting levels but to the fact that the workers had been chosen for the study. This change in behavior due to being singled out for attention, now commonly called the *Hawthorne effect*, clearly shows the importance of human factors in motivating employees.

In 1954 Abraham Maslow conceptualized a hierarchy of worker needs. Shown in Figure 12. 1, this pyramid assumes that human needs progress from the most basic-or physiological-needs to what Maslow terms *self-actualization*. In terms of work, the lower stages must be satisfied before an employee can perform at the highest level. Maslow also proposed that a satisfied need is no longer a motivator.

In contrast to Maslow, who believed that individuals are born with a particular set of needs, Douglas McClelland believed that needs were acquired through an individual's interaction with his or her environment. McClelland described three manifest needs: the need for achievement, the need for affiliation, and the need for power over others.

Douglas McGregor formulated the Theory X and Theory Y models in 1960 to explain two leadership styles. Theory X managers take a negative view of human nature and assume that most workers do not like work and will try to avoid it. Theory Y managers take a positive view of human nature, believing that employees want to work, will seek responsibility, and can offer creative solutions to organizational problems.

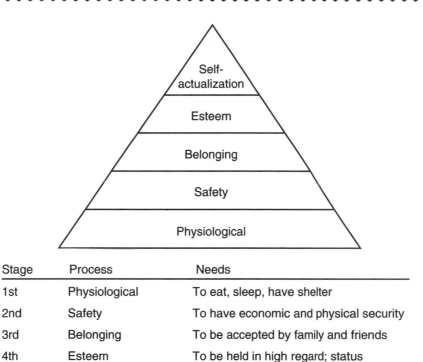

Stage	Process	Needs
1st	Physiological	To eat, sleep, have shelter
2nd	Safety	To have economic and physical security
3rd	Belonging	To be accepted by family and friends
4th	Esteem	To be held in high regard; status
5th	Self-actualization	To achieve one's best

◆ **Figure 12.1.**   Maslow's hierarchy of needs.

In 1971 Frederick Herzberg identified factors at work considered to be hygenic in nature. These include wages, working conditions, challenging work, growth and learning, group identity, and participation in work planning. The factors were identified as being hygienic because they create dissatisfaction if they are not adequate but do not necessarily create satisfaction if they are present.

MANAGEMENT STYLES

Because each manager is a unique composite of his or her beliefs, values, priorities, and the organization in which he or she works, many different styles of management exist. Some of the more universally recognized styles are discussed here.

Autocratic Management

Autocratic managers are concerned with developing an efficient workplace and have little concern for people. They typically make decisions without input from their subordinates. This style relies on the positional power created by the management role.

Participative Management

Participative managers are primarily concerned with people but might attempt to balance this concern with the business concerns of the organization. Participative managers allow and encourage others to be active in the decision-making process.

❖❖

Continuous improvement teams evolved largely because of the idea that employees should be allowed to participate in the decision-making processes that affect their work.

Theory Z, a term coined by William Ouchi, refers to a Japanese style of management that is characterized by long-term employment, slow promotions, considerable job rotation, consensus style decision making, and concern for the employee as a whole. Theory Z organizations have consistent cultures in which relationships are egalitarian and based on trust. Organizational goals are obvious and are integrated into individual's belief systems, so self-direction is dominant.

Another approach to participative management is "management by wandering (walking) around" (MBWA). This technique encourages managers, especially high-level managers, to periodically walk around and talk to subordinates. They are encouraged to listen naively and to look for improvement opportunities. This technique forces managers to stay in touch with the people who actually perform the work—those who experience problems firsthand.

Charismatic Leadership

Charismatic managers or leaders are able to articulate a view that subordinates accept and thereby become a model for others to follow. Business leaders who fit this category include Lee Iaccoca of Chrysler and Bob Galvin of Motorola. Many political leaders, (ergo, Winston Churchill and Franklin D. Roosevelt) exhibited the characteristics of charismatic leaders. The less positive side of the same management style was exhibited by Adolf Hitler and Charles Manson.

Transactional and Transformational Leadership

B. M. Bass has introduced a distinction between transactional and transformational leadership.[3] Transactional leadership refers to the exchanges that take place between supervisor and subordinate on a daily basis. The transaction is based on the implied rewards (positive or negative) associated with achieving a desired performance. Transformational leadership, on the other hand, implies reshaping entire strategies of an organization. This concept might overlap with charismatic leadership but is aimed at elevating the goals of subordinates and enhancing their self-confidence to achieve those goals. Bob Galvin accomplished this transformational leadership at Motorola with the Six Sigma program, which positioned Motorola to become a high-quality, reliable competitor in its market.

Management by Fact

A key contribution of quality management to business philosophy is that decisions should be based on data. Reinforced by the Baldrige Award's category of "Information and Analysis," the QS-9000 requirements of "Analysis and Use of Company Level Data" and "Customer Satisfaction," and the use of the seven quality tools for process improvement, performance measures and information have become recognized for their utility in making business decisions.

Coaching

As competing organizations attain the same levels of technology, a key differentiation in organizational performance is their ability to develop and effectively empower employees. Providing guidance and constructive feedback to employees to help them better apply their natural talents and to move beyond previous limitations has become a style of management. In this role, managers ask questions that will help others reach a conclusion rather than the manager making the decision for them.

Contingency Approach

Although employee participation or other management philosophies have the potential to positively affect performance, substantial obstacles exist for managers who try to use a formula or single theory to try to improve performance. For example, Locke and Schweiger,[4] in their research into the subject of whether participation enhances productivity, did not find clear support for this premise. One reason, of course, might be the difficulty in fully implementing a participative management system. However, other management styles might be more productive in certain environments and conditions. For example, in some cases the costs of employee participation (ergo, training and support) might be more than the cost reductions and intangible benefits that can be achieved because of the particular process technology being applied. In some situations an autocratic management style might achieve superior performance over a participative style, such as when decisions must be made rapidly with information only available to the manager. For example, it is difficult to imagine that the captain of a sinking ship would have better results if he or she approached the crew with a participative style.

Additional Readings

Bass, B. M. 1988. "Policy Implications of Transformational Leadership." In *Research in Organizational Change and Development.* Edited by R. W. Woodman and W. A. Pasmore. Greenwich, Conn.: JAI Press.

Blake, R., and J. Mouton. 1978. *The New Managerial Grid.* Houston: Gulf Publishing.

Burns, J. M. 1978. *Leadership.* New York: Harper & Row.

Herzberg, F., B. Mausman, and B. Snuderman. 1959. *The Motivation to Work.* 2nd ed. New York: John Wiley & Sons.

Kotter, John P. 1996. *Leading Change.* Boston: Harvard Business School Press.

Locke, E. A., and D. M. Schweiger. 1979. "Participation in Decision Making: One More Look." In *Research in Organizational Behavior,* Vol. 1. Ed. B. Staw and L. L. Cummings. Greenwich, Conn.: JAI Press.

Maslow, Abraham H. 1943. "A Theory of Human Motivation." *Psychological Review,* 50: 370–96.

McClelland, David C. 1962. "Business Drive and National Achievement." *Harvard Business Review* (July-August) Vol. 40, No. 4: 99–112.

McGregor, Douglas. 1960. *The Human Side of Enterprise.* New York: McGraw-Hill.

Stoner, James, Edward Freeman, and Daniel Gilbert Jr. 1995. *Management.* 6th ed. Englewood Cliffs, N.J.: Prentice Hall.

Taylor, Frederick W. 1911. *The Principles of Scientific Management.* New York: Harper & Bros.

Vecchio, Robert P. 1995. *Organizational Behavior.* (Jackson Center, Ohio:) Dryden Press.

❖❖

Chapter 13

Business Functions

❖❖

❖ *This chapter should help you*

- ◆ Distinguish between internal and external business functions
- ◆ Understand the purpose and scope of external business functions
- ◆ Understand the purpose and scope of internal business functions

---

A business organization is a system—a group of interrelated processes designed to accomplish a mission. Many of these processes call for specialized skills or functions. At the same time, the organization is not a stand-alone entity—it is part of a larger system that includes other organizations, society, and the earth. An organization must ensure that its role in the larger system is carried out appropriately. This requires (1) an awareness of outside issues that affect the organization and (2) knowledge of how to manage the process of interfacing with those external functions.

Business functions can be classified as external or internal. External business functions are those that deal with the outside world, such as safety, legal, regulatory, product liability, and environmental standards legislated by authorities at the local, state, federal, and/or international levels. Other external business functions that must be managed include technological and process-oriented activities that might be driven by the competitive or industry environment within which a company operates.

Internal business functions are those that operate within the boundaries of the organization and include human resources, engineering, sales and marketing, finance, research and development, and purchasing. Collectively, these types of business functions affect the ability of the organization to meet and adapt to changes in customer and market requirements.

The distinction between external and internal functions exists in traditional, for-profit businesses as well as in nonprofit, educational, or government organizations. Regardless of whether the organization is departmentalized according to function, product, customer, geography, or process or according to a matrix form, both internal and external business functions will exist.

The size and priority of a firm's various functions will also depend on the particular product or service being provided. For example, a firm that deals with dangerous chemicals or drugs will have larger legal, environmental, and safety functions.

Companies in fast-changing fields, such as the semiconductor industry, will have a larger research-and-development function. In a labor-intensive business, human resources and training might be classified as separate functions; in a capital-intensive business, these functions might be combined, with training being a subset of the human resource function.

This chapter provides an overview of some vital external and internal business functions. The list should not be considered exhaustive, as businesses can be structured in many ways, and new ways of organizing for work are continually being attempted. In addition, new societal problems (e.g., discrimination) and needs (e.g., child-care issues) are more frequently being passed on to business to address.

EXTERNAL FUNCTIONS

A company often has very little control over external requirements placed on it. Laws and regulations, industry or product standards, emerging technology, and product safety concerns (as determined by society) often develop in response to factors outside the day-to-day scope of the organization's operations. In these circumstances an authority inside the organization must be able to interpret the criteria for compliance and determine what the organization needs to do to achieve compliance.

Safety

Organizations must pay attention to workplace safety issues that might affect employees as well as product safety regulations and concerns. The federal Occupational Safety and Health Administration (OSHA), through state agencies, monitors workplace safety. OSHA sets and enforces regulatory guidelines on issues, such as required eye and ear protection, the operation of moving equipment (e.g., forklifts), and fire protection. The Food and Drug Administration (FDA) is charged with protecting customers by controlling public access to new products (e.g., drugs). The FDA also provides operational guidelines in the form of current good manufacturing practices (cGMP) for the organizations and processes that produce these products. Other U.S. agencies charged with protecting public health include the U.S. Department of Agriculture (USDA), Centers for Disease Control (CDC), and the Bureau of Alcohol, Tobacco, and Firearms (BATF). For products such as toys, medical devices, and machinery, the European Union (EU) has issued similar directives that define requirements for products to be sold within their borders.

Legal and Regulatory

Most of the regulations enforced by the previously mentioned organizations are actually issued as federal laws listed in the Code of Federal Regulations. Therefore, compliance is mandatory, not voluntary. Unannounced audits or inspections can be performed by the agencies, which have the ability to leverage fines or mandate closing of the facility if violations are found. Therefore, organizations need to embed such requirements in day-to-day operational procedures, including self-monitoring (e.g., safety audits). Record keeping is an important part of demonstrating compliance to regulations, although the quality department often is not responsible for the maintenance of such records.

Voluntary Compliance

Not all external standards to which an organization might be required to work are legal documents. Standards developed and maintained by organizations such as the American Society for Testing and Materials (ASTM), Underwriters Laboratories (UL), and the International Organization for Standardization (ISO) are often required as part of a contractual agreement with customers, with loss of contract being the primary implication of noncompliance.

Product Liability

Compliance to regulatory requirements or other generally accepted standards is intended to reduce the likelihood of injury to the user of the product or service. However, this compliance does not guarantee that failure will not happen; in fact, many other errors could occur that might result in damage. A new product might fail when used outside the parameters for which the designer tested it, or an undetected error during the production cycle might produce a product that is less safe than was specified by design. Regardless of the cause of the failure, companies might find it necessary to defend their products and business practices and typically retain legal counsel (frequently outsourced) to help in legal interpretation and to organize the company's defense.

Environment

In the United States, the Environmental Protection Agency (EPA) is responsible for overseeing regulations meant to protect the land, air, and water. Businesses need to assess what impact their processes might have on the environment and implement controls to meet standards that have been set. The ISO 14000 standards series provides a voluntary framework for structuring the environmental management process.

Technology Process

In today's rapidly changing world, a new technological development (which often occurs outside one's own industry) can have a dramatic impact on competitiveness. Organizations must have a means for monitoring such developments, assessing the potential for use in their industry, and effectively acquiring and implementing those practices deemed to provide competitive advantage.

INTERNAL FUNCTIONS

Internal functions are those activities that create and operate the processes that enable the organization to accomplish its mission. In a manufacturing organization, these functions typically include information technology, finance, human resources, sales and marketing, customer service, materials, engineering, research and development, quality, maintenance, and production. In a hospital these internal functions might include billing, reception, acute care, nursing, psychiatry, maternity, housekeeping, pharmacy, dietetics and food service, laundry, management engineering, mechanical engineering, instrumentation engineering, and so on. Similar lists of internal functions can easily be visualized for educational and government institutions.

The following list examines internal business functions found in a manufacturing setting.

Information Technology

Information is a core enabler for business, and the information technology group is responsible for providing technology that will allow the organization to effectively acquire, process, and store the information. Information technology strategy should also be driven by business strategy rather than just adopting the latest technology.

Mainframe computers, workstations (e.g., for computer-aided design or other high-speed graphics applications), and personal computers must be appropriately connected both internally and externally (e.g., receiving orders through electronic data interchange). Software to support other business functions (e.g., finance, purchasing, sales, and production control) must be effectively integrated. Corporate intranets are increasingly being used to provide employees access to company information, and electronic commerce via the Internet is radically changing relationships between businesses and their customers.

Because of the pace of change in information technology, most of these functions are frequently outsourced in all but larger organizations. This requires an effective process for managing the subcontractor.

Finance

The finance function is responsible for planning, controlling, and reporting the flow of dollars into and out of the business. It oversees the acquisition of funds through stock and bond offerings as well as shorter-term loans. The finance function provides a structure used by the business for budgeting and accounting for operating receipts and expenditures and ensures that any excess funds are invested until needed. This group reports on the organization's financial status both internally (e.g., for monthly operating reviews) and externally (e.g., to the Securities amd Exchange Commission [SEC] and to shareholders) in the form of cash flow statements and balance sheets.

Human Resources

The human resource function is responsible for recruiting, training, and sometimes "dehiring" the personnel needed for operation of the business. It also oversees compensation systems, development of people for future needs (e.g., career and succession planning), and resolution of problem people issues in accordance with company policies. The human resource function also is usually responsible for ensuring that company policies do not violate laws, such as the American with Disabilities Act (ADA) and discrimination laws regulated by the Employee Equal Opportunity

Commission (EEOC). In unionized companies the function also coordinates, or is involved with, negotiating labor contracts.

Marketing

The marketing function has the responsibility for seeing that potential customers are aware of who the company is and what it does as well as to help translate customer needs into potential opportunities for the company. It develops communication channels (e.g., advertising and timely news releases) to keep the company visible.

Sales and Customer Service

The sales function works closely with potential customers to match their specific needs to current product offerings, resulting in a customer order. Customer service supports sales to ensure that order requirements are clearly and accurately defined and are communicated to the scheduling function. The sales function also monitors orders to ensure that they are fulfilled as contracted.

Materials

The materials function is often broken into two different departments: purchasing and production control. The purchasing process is responsible for identifying suppliers who can deliver needed materials (for production as well as maintenance/repair/operations/MRO) on time and at an appropriate price. The supplier management process also includes placing orders and monitoring supplier performance (helping to improve them, or replacing them if necessary improvements are not made).

The production control process starts where purchasing leaves off, that is, when purchased materials are received. Production control schedules production of each order, manages inventories (received materials, in-process, and finished goods), and arranges for transportation of finished products to the customer.

Engineering

Engineering can take many forms, depending on the particular industry, product line, or company philosophy. However, the types of engineering functions that must be accomplished include the following:

◆ *Product engineering:* converting the concepts from marketing or the research and development functions into viable products and specifications

◆ *Process engineering:* development, acquisition, and installation of equipment (e.g., machinery, tooling, gaging) that can consistently produce the company's products

◆ *Industrial engineering:* optimizing equipment layout and material work flow, consideration of ergonomics in process design, and setting and monitoring productivity standards

◆ *Facilities engineering:* maintaining the building, land, central services (HVAC and water), and machinery

❖❖

Research and Development

Research and development is the process of exploring new developments and new ideas in order to identify potential new products or processes that can fulfill previously untapped opportunities and/or replace those that are in the later stages of the product life cycle.

Production

The production function is the key element of any manufacturing operation. In fact, many plants have no responsibility but production, as all other functions are performed off-site in various office complexes. The production function manages the flow of material and its conversion from a raw state to a finished state. All resources—energy, supplies, equipment, and human labor — combine to make this conversion.

Quality

Because the quality function is the major focus of this book, the details of the function are covered in other chapters (17, 18, and 21). The key role of the quality function is to support the other functions of the business. The quality department might support external functions by helping to interpret externally imposed requirements and by defining the processes necessary for maintaining requirements. The quality function also supports internal functions by providing special skills necessary for day-to-day operations (e.g., supporting human resources in developing a quality-related training curriculum for new employees) as well as assisting other functions in their continuous improvement efforts. Quality managers need to understand the purpose and basic processes managed by all other business functions, especially those processes that can affect quality and customer satisfaction.

🏚 Additional Readings 🏚

Levinson, William A. 1994. *The Way of Strategy.* Milwaukee: ASQC Quality Press.
Weber, Richard T., and Ross H. Johnson. 1993. *Buying and Supplying Quality.*
   Milwaukee: ASQC Quality Press.

🗒 Part 2 Endnotes 🗒

Chapter 7

1. ANSI/ISO/ASQC A8402-1994, p. 8.
2. J. P. Russell, ed., *The Quality Audit Handbook* (Milwaukee: ASQ Quality Press, 1997), p. 9.
3. ASQ Certification Department.
4. Russell, p. 11.
5. Dennis R. Arter, *Quality Audits for Improved Performance*, 2nd ed. (Milwaukee: ASQ Quality Press, 1997), p. 4.
6. Russell, pp. 15–16.
7. Charles A. Mills, *The Quality Audit: A Management Evaluation Tool* (New York: McGraw-Hill, 1989), p. 5.

8. Allan J. Sayle, *Management Audits: The Assessment of Quality Management Systems,* 2nd ed. (Brighton, Mich.: A. Sayle Associates, 1988), pp. 1–6.
9. ANSI/ISO/ASQC A8402-1994, p. 5.

Chapter 8

1. S. P. Robbins and M. Coulter, *Management,* 5th ed. (Upper Saddle River, N.J.: Prentice-Hall, Inc., 1996).
2. Henri Fayol, *Industrial and General Administration* (Paris: Dunod, 1916).
3. Chester I. Barnard, *The Functions of the Executive,* 30th anniversary edition (Cambridge, Mass.: Harvard University Press, 1968), pp. 165–66.
4. David Kipnis, *The Powerholders* (Chicago: University of Chicago Press, 1976).
5. Lyndall Urwick, *The Elements of Administration* (New York: Harper & Row, 1944), pp. 52–53.
6. John S. McClenahem, "Managing More People in the '90s," *Industry Week,* March 20, 1989, p. 30.
7. David Van Fleet, "Span of Management Research and Issues," *Academy of Management Journal* (September 1983) Vol. 26: 546–52.
8. Henri Fayol, *Industrial and General Administration* (Paris: Dunod, 1916), pp. 19–42.
9. Richard L. Daft, *Management,* 3rd ed. (Fort Worth, Tex.: Dryden Press, 1994), p. 298.
10. Brian S. Moskal, "Supervisors, Begone!" *Industry Week,* June 20, 1988, p. 32; Gregory A. Patterson, "Auto Assembly Lines Enter a New Era," *Wall Street Journal,* 1988, p. 2.
11. Stephen George and Arnold Weimerskerch, Total Quality Management (New York: John Wiley & Sons, 1994).
12. Robbins.
13. Ibid.
14. Alfred D. Chandler, *Strategy and Structure: Chapters in the History of the Industrial Enterprise* (Cambridge: MIT Press, 1962).
15. Peter M. Blau and Richard A. Schoenherr, *The Structure of Organizations* (New York: Basic Books, 1971); D. S. Pugh, "The Aston Program of Research: Retrospect and Prospect," in *Perspectives on Organization Design and Behavior,* ed. A. H. Van de Ven and W. F. Joyce, (New York: John Wiley & Sons, 1981); R. Z. Gooding and J. A. Wagner, "A Meta-Analytic Review of the Relationship between Size and Performance: The Productivity and Efficiency of Organizations and Their Subunits," *Administrative Science Quarterly* (December 1985).
16. Donald Gerwin, "Relationships between Structure and Technology," in *Handbook of Organizational Design,* vol. 2, ed. P. C. Nystrom and W. H. Starbuck, (New York: Oxford University Press, 1981); Denise M. Rousseau and R. A. Cooke, "Technology and Structure: The Concrete, Abstract, and Activity Systems of Organizations," *Journal of Management* (Fall–Winter 1984) Vol. 10.
17. Robbins.
18. Ibid.
19. Ibid.

20. Ibid.
21. Tom Peters, "Successful Electronic Changeovers Depend on Daring," *Springfield Business Journal* August 8, 1994, p. 15.

Chapter 9

1. ANSI/ISO/ASQC A8402-1994.
2. Ibid.

Chapter 10

1. Charles Handy, *Understanding Organizations* (New York: Oxford University Press, 1993).
2. Stephen George and Arnold Weimerskirch, *Total Quality Management—Strategies and Techniques Proven at Today's Most Successful Companies* (New York: John Wiley & Sons, 1994), chapter 8.
3. Ibid.
4. Stephen R. Covey and Keith A. Gulledge, "Principle-Centered Leadership and Change," in *The Quality Yearbook, 1995,* ed. James W. Cortada and John A. Woods, (New York: McGraw-Hill, 1995).

Chapter 11

1. Ronald G. Havelock, *The Change Agent's Guide to Innovation in Education,* 6th ed. (Englewood Cliffs, N.J.: Educational Technology Publications, 1982), p. 51.
2. Ibid., p. 44.
3. W. Edwards Deming, *The New Economics,* 2nd ed. (Cambridge: MIT Center for Advanced Engineering Study, 1996).
4. Havelock, p. 53.
5. Roy McLennan, *Managing Organizational Change* (Englewood Cliffs, N.J.: Prentice Hall, 1989), p. xix.
6. Thomas G. Cummings and Edgar F. Huse, *Organizational Development and Change,* 4th ed. (St. Paul,: West Publishing, 1989), pp. vi–vii.
7. David W. Hutton, *The Change Agents' Handbook: A Survival Guide for Quality Improvement Champions* (Milwaukee: ASQC Quality Press, 1994), pp. 10–13.
8. Duke W. Okes, *Quality Improvement and Organization Development,* The Quality Management Forum, ASQ Management Division, winter 1991, p. 4.
9. Michael Brassard, *Memory Jogger Plus* (Metheun, Mass.: GOAL/QPC, 1989), p. 299.
10. Hutton, pp. 6–8.
11. Havelock, pp. 55–58.
12. John P. Kotter, *Leading Change* (Boston: Harvard Business School Press, 1996), p. 61.
13. Ibid., p. 60.
14. Ibid., pp. 62–63.
15. Ibid., p. 63.
16. Ibid., pp. 63–64.
17. Ibid., pp. 64–65.

18. Ibid., p. 65.
19. Ibid., p. 66.
20. Ibid., p. 67.
21. Joseph M. Juran and Frank M. Gryna, *Juran's Quality Control Handbook,* 4th ed. (New York: McGraw-Hill, 1988), p. 22.66.
22. Kotter, p. 59.
23. Cummings, p. 47.

Chapter 12

1. Robert P. Vecchio, *Organizational Behavior* (Fort Worth, Tex.: Dryden Press, 1995), p. 332.
2. John Kotter, p. 61.
3. B. M. Bass, "Policy Implications of Transformational Leadership," in *Research in Organizational Change and Development,* ed. R. W. Woodman and W. A. Pasmore, (Greenwich, Conn.: JAI Press, 1988).
4. E. A. Locke and D. M. Schweiger, "Participation in Decision Making: One More Look," in *Research in Organizational Behavior,* vol. 1, ed. B. Staw and L. L. Cummings, (Greenwich, Conn.: JAI Press, 1979).

Part 3
Quality Needs and Overall Strategic Plans

Chapter 14

Linkage between Quality Function Needs and Overall Strategic Plan

❖ *This chapter should help you*

- ◆ Understand the rationale for strategic planning
- ◆ Appreciate that the strategic planning process is dynamic
- ◆ Realize that, when fully implemented, all plans and actions within an organization form a structure of interdependent linkages, top to bottom
- ◆ Appreciate why quality function plans and actions must support the overall strategic plan and organizational goals and objectives

---

The origin of the term strategic plan has been traced to Ansoff's *Corporate Strategy*, published in 1965. For the following two decades, Ansoff continued to write about this concept of planning and managing with a strategic intent. By the mid-1990s, Henry Mintzberg had contributed a vast amount of writings on strategic planning. A critical issue in strategic planning is the subject of quality.

The quality function is the group within the organization responsible for the implementation of the quality plan in the conduct of *quality-related* activities. Quality function needs, then, are the quality-related resources and support systems (e.g., people who possess knowledge and skills, money, and equipment) required to help the organization achieve its overall strategic plan.

DEFINING STRATEGIC PLAN AND THE QUALITY FUNCTION

Strategy is "the approach to using resources within the constraints of a competitive environment in order to achieve a set of goals." Mintzberg further describes strategy as a plan or a course of action into the future; as a pattern providing consistency over time; as a position or the determination of certain products in certain markets; and as an organization's perspective or way of doing things.[1]

Strategic planning is the continuous process of making present entrepreneurial decisions systematically and with the greatest knowledge of their futurity, organizing systematically the efforts needed to carry out these decisions; and measuring the results of these decisions against the expectations through organized, systematic feedback.[2] Planning is a continuous process because the competitive environment is

❖❖❖

dynamic. Effective, continuous planning guides an organization toward achievement of goals and prepares it for changes in internal and external factors that can affect its future.[3]

The criteria for the Malcolm Baldrige National Quality Award (MBNQA) and the requirements for ISO 9000 certification are useful guidelines for evaluating a company's strategic planning process. An organization can use this information to perform a self-assessment that evaluates how it sets strategic directions and how it develops the critical strategies and action plans to support these directions. Action plans, sometimes called *operational plans,* are specific plans or projects necessary to meet the shorter-term objectives of the strategic plan. At this level, the action planning and implementation process is essentially the same as project management. "In simplest terms, action plans are set to accomplish those things the company must do well for its strategy to succeed."[4] The self-assessment can also examine how strategic plans are deployed and how performance is tracked.

The MBNQA criteria describe strategic planning as the process that addresses strategic and business planning and deployment of plans, with strong customer and operational performance requirements. The award's strategic planning category emphasizes that customer-driven quality and operational performance excellence are key strategic business issues integral to company planning.

DEVELOPING A STRATEGIC PLAN

Strategic plans communicate the company's priorities throughout the organization. A strategic plan provides a roadmap of how to get to a specific target and directs everyone in the organization to work to reach that same target. Strategic planning is not the job of a few select managers. Involving people from all levels of the organization in the planning process helps the organization focus on customer needs, remain flexible and responsive, retain employees, and avoid management burnout.

The development of an overall strategic plan, also called a *company-wide strategic plan,* is affected by various internal and external forces. Internal forces are things within the organization that have an effect on the strategic plan, such as corporate culture, finances, worker skills, and other resources. External forces are things outside the organization that have an effect on the strategic plan, such as changes in technology, customers' requirements, regulatory agencies' rules, and competitors' actions or products. In addition, various functions within the company have their own strategic plans that are closely aligned and integrated with the overall strategic plan. Examples of these strategies are service strategies, marketing strategies, quality strategies, operational strategies, and so on.

An ongoing strategic planning process is needed to assist in the development of a strategic plan. This is not a one-time process, as part of the planning process is to determine whether previous strategic plans have been met. If the plans have not been met, the organization needs to determine why. Answers might range from a flawed planning process that needs improvement, to unrealistic objectives, to organizational weaknesses.[5]

Strategic planning is not forecasting or extrapolating the present and does not deal with future decisions; rather; it is concerned with the futurity of present decisions. Although it does not attempt to minimize or eliminate risk, strategic planning can help an organization choose among risk-taking alternatives.

Controversy has arisen over the viability of strategic planning. Longer-range planning does seem somewhat less useful for organizations that face extremely rapid change, such as a volatile marketplace, exploding technological advances, or the production of products with short-term appeal (ergo toy action figures and computers).

Define Mission and Guiding Principles

To effectively develop a strategic plan with all its ancillary objectives, strategies, and action plans, the organization must first state its mission and guiding principles. These statements are used to create a vision for the organization.

The mission defines the purpose of the organization. "Mission defines the core purpose of being in terms of the accomplishments needed that will result in realization of the vision."[6] The following are examples of mission statements:

The mission of Levi Strauss & Co. is to sustain profitable and responsible commercial success by marketing jeans and selected apparel under the Levi's brand name. We must balance goals of superior profitability and return on investment, leadership market positions, and superior products and service. We will conduct our business ethically and demonstrate leadership in satisfying our responsibilities to our communities and to society. Our work environment will be safe and productive and characterized by fair treatment, teamwork, open communications, personal accountability and opportunities for growth and development.[7]

Our mission is to continuously provide unprecedented customer satisfaction.

We administer Prudential Assurance life business. Our purpose is to delight our customers by delivering a quality service, in a cost-effective manner, through the contribution of everyone.[8]

We are Bread Loaf, a family of building professionals dedicated to and empowered by the strength of our people. We seek challenges to create innovative solutions which make statements demonstrating our commitment to excellence. As we grow into the 21st century, we shall continually focus upon employee wellness, community responsibility and a sensitive balance between personal and professional fulfillment.[9]

To deliver a high-quality pizza, hot, within 30 minutes, at a fair price.[10]

The terms *goals* and *objectives* are often used interchangeably. However, goals are more global, loftier concepts embedded in the mission statement, whereas objectives are more specific, measurable, and time-bound outputs of the planning process.

Finally, guiding principles specify how business is to be conducted. Guiding principles, or values, help establish and define the corporate culture and form the basis for decision making. Examples of guiding principles are customer focused, innovative, ethical, and risk taking. Guiding principles are the fundamental beliefs that guide actions while bridging the gap between the organization's mission and vision.

Creating a Vision

Once the organization has clearly formulated its mission statement and guiding principles, it can create a vision statement to express what it would like to accomplish or where it would like to be in the future. A vision statement should be brief, it should inspire and challenge, it should describe an ideal condition, it should appeal to all stakeholders, and it should provide direction for the future state of the organization. The following are examples of vision statements:

To become a $125 billion company by the year 2000.

Wal-Mart, 1990

To knock off RJR as the number one tobacco company in the world.

Philip Morris, 1950s

To become number one or two in every market we serve and revolutionize this company to have the strengths of a big company combined with the leanness and agility of a small company.

General Electric Company, 1980s

The vision, or desired future state of the organization, is born from its mission and values. To articulate a vision, an organization should scan the future and define its role in it. Once the vision becomes clear, the organization can work toward achieving it by developing the strategic plan.

Although the terms are often used interchangeably, mission statements and vision statements are distinctly different. "A mission is for today's goals and the vision is for tomorrow's goals."[11] Vince Lombardi, Super Bowl–winning coach of the Green Bay Packers, is credited with saying, "The best coaches know what the end result looks like, whether it's an offensive play, a defensive play, a defensive coverage, or just some area of the organization. If you don't know what the end result is supposed to look like, you can't get there. All teams basically do the same thing. We all have drafts, we all have training camps, we all have practices. But the bad coaches don't know what they want. The good coaches do."[12]

Likewise, all companies basically do the same thing. They all sell products and services to customers, and they all utilize the same resources (e.g., people, equipment, and money). Successful companies know where they are headed and have plans to get there.

LEVELS OF STRATEGIC PLANNING

Once an organization has defined its mission, guiding principles, and vision, it can begin the strategic planning process. Numerous strategic planning models have been developed to assist in the planning process.

In *The Rise and Fall of Strategic Planning*, Mintzberg includes several models of strategic planning, one of which is shown in Figure 14.1. Planning is typically divided into three levels: strategic, tactical, and operational.

The strategic plan is what the organization wants to achieve in the future. Strategic plans forecast ahead three to five years. Determining the firm's future quality position and deciding what broad strategy will be required to achieve that position is the basis of strategic planning.

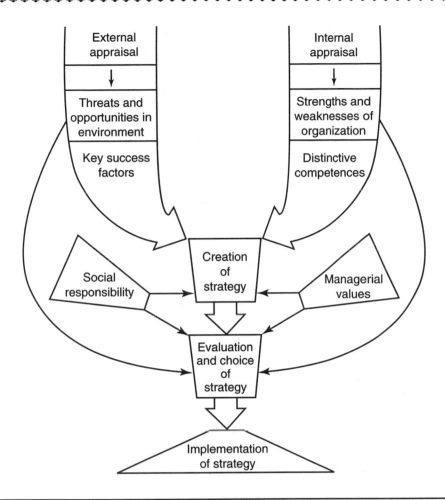

◆ **Figure 14.1.**   Mintzberg planning model. Reprinted with permission of The Free Press, a Division of Simon and Schuster, Inc., from *The Rise and Fall of Strategic Planning: Reconceiving Roles for Planning, Plans, Planners,* by Henry Mintzberg. Copyright © 1994 by Henry Mintzberg.

Tactical plans identify how the organization will implement the strategic plan. Tactical plans are those that occupy most of the attention of quality engineers, especially when a new product is being planned. The quality engineer works with suppliers, testers, designers, and market and financial analysts to specify what tasks need to be completed to ensure that a product meets its goals.

Operational plans, or action plans, are the day-to-day action-oriented plans concerned with the details of who performs what tasks and within what time frame. Operational plans include scheduling inspections, tests, calibrations, process capability studies, training courses, and other essential day-to-day activities.

Another way to view these levels of planning is that strategic planning is composed of two phases. The first phase is formulation, in which strategies and objectives are formulated or defined. The second phase, implementation, encompasses the tactical and operational plans.

STRATEGIC PLANNING PROCESS

Involvement of people during the strategic planning process also changes as the process is deployed throughout the organization. Typically, the organization's leadership drives the strategic planning with input from all functional areas. Next, functional areas formulate their own objectives and strategies (tactical plans) to support the strategic plan in achieving its vision. Further into the process, individuals become involved in developing action plans, budgets, and measures to monitor performance against the plans. The strategic planning process continues with budget information being funneled back up the organization to develop the functional budgets, division budgets, and overall corporate budget.

Measurements complete the process by providing information back to the various levels. Individuals receive information on how well they are meeting their operational/action plans, functions and divisions receive information on how performance relates to their tactical plans, and the organization gets valuable feedback on how well it is achieving its vision. Measurements close the loop by providing the information needed to make course adjustments over time, thus ensuring that the strategic plan is met.

TOOLS USEFUL IN STRATEGIC PLANNING

Several tools are available to assist in developing a strategic plan.

SWOT Analysis

Probably the most common set of concepts underlying many strategic plans is generated using a SWOT analysis (also referred to as the Design School Model or the Harvard Policy Model). SWOT is an acronym for "strengths, weakness, opportunities, and threats." A SWOT analysis is a systematic assessment of an organization's internal and external environment and identifies attributes that affect its ability to achieve its vision and to improve and protect its competitive position.

Scenario Planning

Scenario planning is another tool used for strategic planning. "Scenario planning is a disciplined method for imagining possible futures that companies have applied to a great range of issues."[13] By identifying basic trends and uncertainties, a series of scenarios can be constructed that will help compensate for the usual errors in decision making: overconfidence and tunnel vision. In its simplest form, scenario planning uses three macro (or all-embracing) scenarios: good future, bad future, and wild card. Once scenarios are visualized, alternate strategic (contingency plans) can be developed.

Hoshin Planning

Hoshin planning is a Japanese-based, closed-loop strategic planning process that includes the implementation of what is planned as well as the review of what is done.[14] "The Japanese words *hoshin kanri* can be generally interpreted as direction (setting) management for the entity. The words *nichijo kanri* can be interpreted as daily (fundamental) management for the entity."[15] In the United States, *hoshin kanri* translates to "direction" and "control" and is usually shortened to *hoshin planning*.

Hoshin planning employs intensive visioning and top-level goal setting. From these, the objectives for achieving the goals are established. Through as many iterations of downward deployment and upward feedback ("catchball") as are necessary throughout the organization, objectives are honed and action plans developed for the implementation of the plans. Every action plan is linked upward (and laterally) with the objectives and goals it supports. At the action plan level, which usually consists of identified projects, the process closely resembles project management, that is, a work breakdown of steps, responsibilities, resources, timelines, tracking, measuring, reporting, and corrective action.

The hoshin planning process should not be confused with management by objectives, which it superficially resembles. Hoshin planning is a tightly knit planning and implementation system that can involve every member of the organization. Hoshin planning is a vehicle for communicating, through every organizational level, the direction of the organization and for controlling the outcomes. Every person in the organization knows where his or her efforts and ideas fit in the overall scheme. Documented evidence exists at every stage in the process to enable all planners to learn from the process, improve the process, and achieve the planned goals of the organization. Hoshin planning engenders and reinforces team-based problem solving and decision making. It literally forces management to "walk the talk" and to integrate the implementation of strategic plans with daily operations. It surfaces resource conflicts and forces trade-off analysis and resolution. Hoshin planning is a fact-based system for stimulating and managing the growth and development of the organization and its people.

Hoshin planning uses a number of tools, including the following:

◆ environmental trend charts
◆ SWOT analysis
◆ macro process flowcharts
◆ affinity diagram
◆ weighted interrelationship diagram
◆ radar chart
◆ relationship matrix
◆ prioritization (priorities) matrix
◆ tree diagram
◆ contingency planning tree
◆ activity network diagram
◆ catchball matrix
◆ supportive review matrix[16]

Hoshin planning is not an easy journey. It requires solid top management support and personal involvement. For organizations that are not accustomed to soliciting feedback from below or that have never done formal planning before it involves a significant cultural change, an effectively functioning hoshin planning process might take two to three years, or even longer, to work out the smooth flow of information and to build realism into the planning.

Quality Function Deployment

Quality function deployment (QFD) is an organized, cross-functional technique that uses structured thoughtware (known as the House of Quality) to translate and deploy important customer requirements (the voice of the customer) throughout a design cycle. As a strategic planning tool, QFD delivers prioritized actions that support the strategic intent. Because of its emphasis on customer requirements, QFD is discussed in Chapter 24.

Management and Planning Tools

The seven management and planning tools (activity network diagram, affinity diagram, weighted interrelationship diagram, matrix diagram, priorities matrix, process decision program chart, and tree diagram) assist in the development of strategic plans by turning the qualitative data that are gathered into useable information to plan strategies. These tools are discussed in Chapter 33.

Benchmarking

Benchmarking is the process of identifying best practices from noncompeting/other organizations that will lead to superiority. Once identified, best practices can be incorporated into the organization's vision. For an in-depth discussion of benchmarking, see Chapter 31.

BARRIERS TO SUCCESSFUL STRATEGIC PLANNING

Undefined and ambiguous terms can be one of the biggest roadblocks to the strategic planning process. Terms can be easily misunderstood because they are often used interchangeably. The term *goal* is often substituted for *objective*. Likewise, *action plan* and *program* are sometimes used interchangeably. Organizations must clearly define the terms they will be using in their strategic planning process and communicate them clearly to ensure that they are understood by all people involved in the planning process. When priorities and strategies are unclear, people do not know what to aim for or what to do. Company vision alone, in most cases, is not specific enough to allow people to know the company's priorities.

Strategic planning sometimes fails because reward and recognition systems do not support the planning process or promote a sense of urgency. People are motivated to act quickly when they receive rewards and recognition, but in most organizations people are not rewarded this for sense of urgency.

At times, individual departments might have their own set of plans, goals, and strategies that might or might not fit in with those of other departments. When fragmented responsibilities and functional systems do not support the planning process, the organization cannot work together toward a common goal.

Additionally, when management does not "walk the talk" of strategic planning, people become confused by the mixed signals they receive. Excessive procedures, paperwork, and meetings choke out a sense of urgency by miring employees in mundane tasks.

These problems are supported by the list of the 10 most important pitfalls of planning as compiled by Steiner[17]:

1. Top management's assumption that it can delegate the planning function to a planner.

2. Top management becomes so engrossed in current problems that it spends insufficient time on long-range planning, and the process becomes discredited among other managers and staff.

3. Failure to develop company goals suitable as a basis for formulating long-range plans.

4. Failure to assume the necessary involvement in the planning process of major line personnel.

5. Failure to use plans as standards for measuring managerial performance.

6. Failure to create a climate in the company which is congenial and not resistant to planning.

7. Assuming that corporate comprehensive planning is something separate from the entire management process.

8. Injecting so much formality into the system that it lacks flexibility, looseness, and simplicity, and restrains creativity.

9. Failure of top management to review with departmental and divisional heads the long-range plans, which they have developed.

10. Top management's consistently rejecting the formal planning mechanism by making intuitive decisions which conflict with the formal plans."[17]

🏛 Additional Readings 🏛

Ansoff, H. I. 1965. *Corporate Strategy.* New York: McGraw-Hill.

Anthony, William P. 1985. *Practical Strategic Planning: A Guide and Manual for Line Managers.* Westport, Conn.: Quorum Books.

Calhoun, Kenneth. 1992. "Strategic Quality Planning: An Integrated Systems Approach." *The Quality Management Forum* (newsletter of the Quality Management Division of ASQ), summer, pp. 4–5, 12.

Cartin, Thomas J., and Donald J. Jacoby. 1997. *A Review of Managing Quality and a Primer for the Certified Quality Manager Exam.* Milwaukee: ASQ Quality Press.

Colleti, Joe. 1995. *A Field Guide to Focused Planning: Hoshin Kanri—American Style.* East Granby, Conn.: The Woodledge Group.

Collins, James C., and Jerry I. Porras. 1996. "Building Your Company's Vision." *Harvard Business Review* (September–October), pp. 65–77.

Courtney, Hugh, Jane Kirkland, and Patrick Viguerie. 1997. "Strategy under Uncertainty." *Harvard Business Review* (November–December), pp. 67–79.

❖❖

Cowley, Michael, and Ellen Domb. 1997. *Beyond Strategic Vision: Effective Corporate Action with Hoshin Planning.* Boston: Butterworth-Heinemann.

Dew, John R. 1998. "Developing a Quality-Centered Strategic Plan." *Quality Digest,* May, pp. 48–52.

Drucker, Peter. 1995. "The Information Executives Truly Need." *Harvard Business Review* (January–February), p. 54.

GOAL/QPC Research Committee. 1990. *Hoshin Planning: A Planning System for Implementing Total Quality Management.* Methuen, Mass.: GOAL/QPC.

Godfrey, A. Blanton. 1996. "Integrating Quality and Strategic Planning." *Quality Digest,* March, p. 1.

Graves, Suzanne, and John Moran. 1995. "Developing an Organization's Strategic Intent and Operational Plan." *The Quality Management Forum* (newsletter of the Quality Management Division of ASQ), spring, pp. 1–4.

Harris, M. C. 1998. *Value Leadership: Winning Competitive Advantage in the Information Age.* Milwaukee: ASQ Quality Press.

Kenyon, David A. 1997. "Strategic Planning with the Hoshin Process." *Quality Digest,* May, pp. 55–63.

King, Robert. 1989. *Hoshin Planning: The Developmental Approach.* Methuen, Mass.: GOAL/QPC.

Kuhn, Jerry A., and Tena Carson Figgins. 1994. "You Need a Strategic Plan to Win." *Journal of Quality and Participation* (July/August) Vol. 17: pp. 44–48.

Lammers, Teri. 1992. "The Effective and Indispensable Mission Statement." *INC.* August, pp. 75–77.

Latham, John R. 1995. "Visioning: The Concept, Trilogy, and Process." *Quality Progress,* July, p. 89.

Lee, Chris. 1993. "The Vision Thing." *Training,* February, p. 29.

Lipton, Mark. 1996. "Demystifying the Development of an Organizational Vision." *Sloan Management Review* (summer), pp. 83–92.

Lyman, Dilworth, Robert F. Buesinger, and John P. Keating. 1994. "QFD in Strategic Planning." *Quality Digest,* May, pp. 45–52.

Madden, J., and D. Anderson. 1985. *Hey, Wait a Minute, I Wrote a Book.* New York: Ballantine.

The Malcolm Baldrige National Quality Award, 1999 Criteria for Performance Excellence. Gaithersburg, Md., National Institute of Standards and Technology.

Mazur, Glen Howard, Hisashi Takasu, and Michiteru Ono.1998. *Policy Management: Quality Approach to the Strategic Planning.* Torrance, Calif.: Integrated Quality Dynamics.

Mears, Peter, and Frank Voehl. 1995. *The Guide to Implementing Quality Systems.* Delray Beach, Fla.: St. Lucie Press.

Miller, Lawrence M. 1994.*Whole System Architecture—Beyond Reengineering: Designing the High Performance Organization.* Atlanta: The Miller Consulting Group.

Mintzberg, Henry. 1994. "The Fall and Rise of Strategic Planning." *Harvard Business Review* (January–February) Vol. 72: pp. 107–14.

___. 1994. *The Rise and Fall of Strategic Planning.* New York: The Free Press.

___. 1990. "Strategy Formation: Schools of Thought." In *Perspectives on Strategic Management, ed.* J. Frederickson. Boston: Ballinger.

1987. "Put Your Mission Statement to Work." *Customers!* (May) Vol. 8: p. 38.

Schoemaker, P. 1995. "Scenario Planning: A Tool for Strategic Thinking." *Sloan Management Review* (winter): 41–56.

Steiner, George A. 1979. *Strategic Planning: What Every Manager Must Know.* New York: The Free Press.

Torrence, Samuel, and William Montgomery. 1997. "Heavy Duty Hoshin Deployment: Real World Applications for Accelerating Strategic Business Breakthrough." *Journal of Innovative Management* (spring) Vol. 17: p. 109.

Chapter 15

Linkage between Overall Strategic Plan and Quality Plan

❖ *This chapter should help you*

- ◆ Understand the concept of a value chain
- ◆ Appreciate that quality must be integrated with the highest level of planning
- ◆ Identify the reasons that quality plans fall short

Strategic planning drives change that is needed to help an organization meet its vision. The overall strategic plan does just that: It communicates a direction for the entire organization. In turn, each functional area develops a tactical plan. In the quality function, this plan is called a *quality plan*. The quality policy, procedures, and documentation are used for the implementation of the quality system. The quality plan is an integral part of this process.

The quality plan is the "document setting out the specific quality practices, resources, and sequence of activities relevant to a particular product, project, or contract."[1] The quality plan documents how the requirements for quality will be met and should be consistent with the requirements of the quality system and the strategic plan.

LINKAGES BETWEEN VALUE CHAIN ACTIVITIES

Quality planning is an important subset of the overall strategic plan. The linkage between the quality plan and the overall strategic plan can be a powerful source of competitive advantage. Linkages exist when the performance of one activity affects the cost or effectiveness of other activities. Trade-offs are often created when one activity is optimized at the expense of another. A company must resolve such trade-offs in accordance with its strategy to achieve a competitive advantage.

The linkage activities bind the independent activities throughout the value chain. A company's value chain identifies the primary activities that create value for customers and the related support activities. Value chains are a tool for thinking strategically about the relationship among activities performed inside and outside the firm. The value chain is not a collection of independent activities but rather a system of interdependent activities. These activities are the building blocks of competitive advantage. Linkages are relationships between the way one value activity is performed and the cost of performance of another. Competitive advantage frequently derives from linkages among activities, just as it does from the individual activities themselves.

QUALITY AND STRATEGIC PLANNING

Strategic planning focuses on the opportunities that lie in the future and subsequent decision making that defines an organization's goals and objectives, policies, and plans. An important element of strategic quality planning is differentiation on the basis of quality.

Quality must be involved at the highest level of planning: the strategic level. Top management must decide whether the organization desires to excel at quality or whether it will offer just enough quality to avoid being cited for poor quality. If the decision is to excel, then strategic planning is used to identify what specific quality attributes will be emphasized and what additional resources will be required.

A major application of the quality planning concept is *strategic quality planning,* or *company-wide quality management* (CWQM), which is an extension or subset of the company's strategic plan. Strategic planning consists of a sequence of activities similar to the following:

◆ establish broad business goals

◆ determine the deeds needed to meet the goals

◆ organize: assign clear responsibilities for those deeds

◆ provide the resources needed to meet those responsibilities

◆ provide the needed training

◆ establish the means to evaluate actual performance against goals

◆ establish a process for periodic review of performance against goals

◆ establish a reward system that relates rewards to performance[2]

Linking the quality plan to the overall strategic plan allows the quality function to contribute to the company's mission and vision.

WHY QUALITY PLANS FAIL

Quality plans fall short in their ability to be assimilated within an organization's overall strategic plan for many reasons.

Communication Problems

Because terms such as *mission, objective, strategy,* and *goal* are frequently misunderstood, the organization must define these and other terms and use them consistently to convey the intended meaning. To be meaningful, an organization's mission statements and vision statements must be discrete, measurable, and finite.

Likewise, the organization's quality plan needs to be effectively communicated and monitored. All employees should understand the relevance of quality to their jobs. Employees actively involved in the strategic planning process have a clearer understanding and demonstrate a higher level of commitment to it.

❖❖❖

Problem Tolerance or Inaction

Strategic planning should not tolerate major unresolved issues. Emerging issues pertaining to quality should be addressed immediately because quality cannot result if corrective action is inadequate or untimely. Problems can sometimes be avoided when emerging issues are examined from a strategic viewpoint.

Talking about quality is not enough. Unless it is encouraged and provided for, unless it is the focus of organized project teams or simultaneous engineering teams (which should include statisticians, engineers, manufacturing people, accountants, and others), there is little chance that improvement will take place.

☗ Additional Readings ☗

Calingo, Luis Ma. R. 1995. *Business Strategy and Total Quality Management: Stages on the Way to Total Integration.* ASQC 49th Annual Quality Proceedings, pp. 847–55.

Covey, Stephen R. 1990. *Principle-Centered Leadership.* New York: Simon & Schuster.

Edelen, Richard. 1997. "Implementing a Total Quality Program." *The Fabricator,* February, pp. 34–36.

Frohman, Mark A. 1996. "Unleash Urgency and Action." *Industry Week,* November 4, pp. 13–16.

Gardner, James R., Robert Rachlin, and H. W. Allen Sweeny. 1986. *Handbook of Strategic Planning.* New York: John Wiley & Sons.

Garvin, David A. 1987. "Competing on the Eight Dimensions of Quality." *Harvard Business Review* (November–December) Vol. 65, No. 6: pp. 103–9.

Hayden, Catherinc. 1986. *The Handbook of Strategic Expertise.* New York: The Free Press.

Juran, Joseph M. 1992. *Juran on Quality by Design: The New Steps for Designing Quality into Goods and Services.* New York: The Free Press.

___., eds. 1988. *Juran's Quality Control Handbook.* 4th ed. New York: McGraw-Hill.

Juran, Joseph M., and Frank M. Gryna. 1993. *Quality Planning and Analysis.* 3rd ed. New York: McGraw-IIill.

Nanus, Bart. 1996. *Leading the Way to Organization Renewal.* Portland, Ore.: Productivity Press.

Porter, Michael E. 1985. *Competitive Advantage: Creating and Sustaining Superior Performance.* New York: The Free Press.

Pyzdek, Thomas, and Roger W. Berger, eds. 1992. *Quality Engineering Handbook.* Milwaukee: ASQC Quality Press.

Saraph, Jayant V., and Richard J. Sebastian. 1993. "Developing a Quality Culture." *Quality Progress,* September, pp. 73–78.

Sheridan, Bruce M. 1996. *Achieving a Truly Integrated Strategic Plan.* ASQC 50th Annual Quality Proceedings, pp. 61–67.

St. Lawrence, Dennis, and Bob Stinnett. 1994. "Powerful Planning with Simple Techniques." *Quality Progress,* July, pp. 57–64.

Strickland, Thompson. 1996. *Strategic Management: Concepts and Cases.* Chicago: Richard D. Irwin.

Chapter 16

Theory of Variation

❖ *This chapter should help you*

  ◆ Realize that variation exists in everything

  ◆ Differentiate common causes of variation from special causes of variation

  ◆ Understand that common causes are typically those that require management's action

---

Variation is inherent; it exists in all things. No two entities in the world have the same measurable characteristics. The variation might be small and unnoticeable without the aid of precise and discriminative measuring instruments, or it might be quite large and easily noticeable. Two entities might appear to have the same measurement because of the limitations of the measuring device.

FACTORS AFFECTING VARIATION

Everything is the result of some process, so the chance for some variation in output is built into every process. Because material inputs are the outputs of some prior process, they are subject to variation, and that variation is transferred to the outputs. Variation will exist even in identical processes using identical resources. Even though a task is defined and performed in the same manner repeatedly, different operators performing the same task and the same operator performing the same task repeatedly introduce variation. Precision and resolution of the measuring devices and techniques used to collect data also introduce variation into the output data.

Variation can result from changes in various factors, normally classified as follows:

◆ people (worker) influences

◆ machinery influences

◆ environmental factors

◆ material influences

◆ measurement influences

◆ method influences

The resulting total variation present in any product is a result of the variations from these six main sources. A cause-and-effect (fishbone) diagram can be used to illustrate this point very effectively.

❖❖

Because the ramifications of variation in quality are enormous for managers, knowing a process's capabilities prior to production provides for better utilization of resources. Operating costs are reduced when inspection, rework, safety stock storage, and troubleshooting are eliminated. Proper management requires a deep appreciation of the existence of variation as well as an understanding of its causes and how they can be corrected.

TYPES OF VARIATION

Walter Shewhart, the father of modern quality control, was concerned with the low-cost reduction of variation. Shewhart distinguished two kinds of processes: (1) a stable process with predictable (controlled) variation and (2) an unstable process with unpredictable (uncontrolled) variation. If the limits of process variation are well within the band of customer tolerance (specification), then the process is stable. The product can be made and shipped with reasonable assurance that the customer will be satisfied. If the limits of process variation just match the band of customer tolerance, then the process should be monitored closely and adjusted when necessary to maximize the amount of satisfactory output. If the limits of process variation extend beyond the band of customer tolerance, output should be inspected to determine whether it meets customer requirements.

When the amount of variation to be expected can be predicted with confidence, the process is said to be in a state of statistical control. Although a singular output value cannot be predicted exactly, it can be anticipated to fall within certain limits. Similarly, the long-term average value can be predicted.

In an unstable process every batch of product is a source of excitement! It is impossible to predict how much, if any, of the product will fall within the band of customer tolerance. The costs necessary to produce satisfactory product are unknown because the organization is forced to carry large quantities of safety stock and bids for new work must include a (big) safety factor. Crisis and firefighting are the order of the day. Unless competitors are in the same situation, the organization's days are probably numbered.

Shewhart developed simple statistical and graphical tools to inform operators and managers about their processes and to detect promptly when a stable process becomes unstable and vice versa. These tools, called control charts, come in various forms to accommodate whether measures are attributes or variables, whether samples are of constant size or not, and so on.

Building on Shewhart's notions, Deming recognized two different sources of variation: special causes and common causes. He also distinguished between the duties of those who work in the process and the managers who work on the process.

Common Causes

Variation that is always present or inherent in a process is called *common cause variation*. It occurs when one or more of the previously mentioned factors fluctuate within the normal or expected manner and can be improved only by changing that factor(s). Common causes of variation occur continually and result in controlled variation. They ensue, for example, from the choice of supplier, quality of inputs, worker hiring and training practices, equipment selection, machinery maintenance or lack of maintenance, and working conditions. If the process variation is excessive, then the process must be changed.

Eradicating these stable and predictable causes of variation is the responsibility of the managers of the process, as managers must change the process—the workers cannot. Common causes are beyond the control of workers, as was demonstrated by Deming's famous red bead experiment (described in the glossary). Volunteers were told to produce only white beads from a bowl containing a mixture of white and red beads. Haranguing the workers had no outcome on the output. No matter what the workers did, they got red beads—sometimes more, sometimes less, but always some because the red beads were in the system. Deming estimated that common causes account for 80 percent to 95 percent of workforce variation. This is not the fault of the workers, who normally do their best even in less-than-ideal circumstances. Rather, this is the responsibility of the managers, who work on, not in, the process.

Special Causes

When one or more of the variations from the identified factors is abnormal or unexpected, the resultant variation is known as *special cause variation*. This unexpected level of variation that is observed for a stable process is due to special causes that are not inherent in the process. Special causes of variation are usually local in time and space, for example, specific to a change in a particular machine or a difference in shift, operator, or weather condition. They appear in a detectable pattern and cause uncontrolled variation. Special causes of variation often result in sudden and extreme departures from the usual but can occur in the form of gradual shifts (or drifts) in a characteristic of a process. When a control chart shows a lack of control, skilled investigation should reveal what special causes affect the output. The workers in the process often have the detailed knowledge necessary to guide this investigation.

ACHIEVING BREAKTHROUGH IMPROVEMENT

Building on Shewhart's notions to develop a systematic method for improvement, Juran distinguished between sporadic and chronic problems for quality improvement projects (QIPS). Starting from a state of chaos, a QIP should first seek to control variation by eliminating sporadic problems. When a state of controlled variation is reached, the QIP should then break through to higher levels of quality by eliminating chronic problems, thereby reducing the controlled variation. The notions of "control" and "breakthrough" are critical to Juran's thinking.

The following scenario demonstrates this concept:

A dart player throws darts at two different targets. The darts on the first target are all fairly close to the bull's-eye, but the darts are scattered all over the target. It is difficult for the player to determine whether changing his stance (or any other variable) will result in an improved score. The darts thrown at the second target are well off target from the bull's-eye, but the location of the darts is clustered and therefore predictable. When the player determines what variable is causing the darts to miss the bull's-eye, immediate and obvious improvement should result.

❖❖❖

This is the impetus behind Juran's work: to achieve repeatable and predictable results. Until that happens, it will be almost impossible to determine whether a quality improvement effort has had any effect. Once a process is in control, breakthroughs are possible because they are detectable.

The following points are essential to an understanding of variation:

◆ Everything is the result or outcome of some process.

◆ Variation always exists, although it is sometimes too small to notice.

◆ Variation can be controlled if its causes are known. The causes should be determined through the practical experience of workers in the process as well as by the expertise of managers.

◆ Variation can result from special or common causes. Corrective action cannot be taken unless the variation has been assigned to the proper type of cause. For example, in Deming's bead experiment the workers who deliver the red beads should not be blamed; the problem is the fault of the system that contains the red beads.

◆ Practical tools exist to detect variation and to distinguish controlled from uncontrolled variation. These proven tools should be used because relying on judgment or intuition is not an accurate method of making these distinctions.

Finally, an organization must focus its attempts at reducing variation. Variation does not need to be eliminated from all aspects of production; rather, the organization should focus on reducing variation in those areas most critical to meeting customers' requirements.

🏠 Additional Readings 🏠

Deming, W. Edwards. 1994. *The New Economics*. 2nd ed. Cambridge: Massachusetts Institute of Technology.

___. 1986. *Out of the Crisis*. Cambridge: Massachusetts Institute of Technology, Center for Advanced Engineering Study.

Feigenbaum, Armand V. 1991. *Total Quality Control*. 3rd rev. ed. New York: McGraw-Hill.

Joiner, B. L., and M. A. Gaudard. 1990. "Variation Management and W. Edwards Deming." *Quality Progress*, December, p. 77.

Chapter 17

Quality Function Mission

❖ *This chapter should help you*

◆ Understand the concept of "little-Q" and "big-Q"

◆ Comprehend how the quality function mission and the role of the quality manager differ, depending on a "little-Q" or "big-Q" focus

---

ELEMENTS OF QUALITY FUNCTION MISSION STATEMENTS

For most quality functions, the quality function mission will include some common elements. These are to ensure the following:

◆ customer focus and quality are part of the organization's mission

◆ all suppliers understand fundamental principles of quality

◆ all employees understand fundamental principles of quality and how to apply them

◆ all employees master the quality tools needed to carry out their mission within the organization

The quality function mission is derived from, yet feeds into, the organization's mission. This is a particular instance of a much more general situation. It is a mistake to have everything driven top-down and an equal mistake to have everything driven bottom-up. Corporate collaboration is essential in quality planning as well as in other areas.

The quality function mission has changed since the introduction of total quality management (TQM; Feigenbaum's term), or company-wide quality control (Ishikawa's term). Juran introduced a distinction in 1992 that captures part of the change in the mission of the quality function. He called the usually narrow focus on quality "little-Q." An example of little-Q quality is catching a bad batch of product before it goes too far. Another example is a team of workers and their manager improving some process to break through to higher levels of quality. This type of quality is important but is limited in scope and impact. This was the customary (in fact, the only), kind of quality before TQM. Juran calls the new focus on quality "big-Q." An example of big-Q quality is having cross-functional teams throughout the organization working to prevent problems.

❖❖❖

Likewise, the quality function mission can be divided into two parts, one old (little-Q quality) and one new (big-Q quality). In organizations that have not yet adopted TQM, little-Q quality, the specific departmental mission, is the only part articulated.

These traditional functions might include one or more of the following:

◆ conducting quality control and assurance

◆ performing reliability and quality engineering

◆ handling procurement, incoming inspection, and supplier management

◆ auditing of procedures, products, and incoming materials

◆ laboratory testing and measuring

◆ reporting and administration

Big-Q quality emphasizes the coordination of various activities conducted in other functions and groups so that all plans contribute to the achievement of the organization's goals for quality. These new functions may include one or more of the following:

◆ establishing quality costing, or cost of poor quality

◆ implementing a quality information system

◆ planning quality goals, objectives, and plans

◆ establishing process operation quality requirements

◆ leading and facilitating teams

◆ working with research and development (R&D) and new product design and development

◆ managing supplier and subcontractor relations

Certain functions could be classified either way, depending on the organization. These include improving accuracy and reducing variation in laboratory results, calibrating instruments and gages, establishing sampling procedures, and conducting feedback processes for the improvement of internal operations.

DEVELOPING A QUALITY FUNCTION MISSION

A quality function mission can be developed in several successive steps:

1. Identify one particular service or product provided by the quality function.

2. Determine the customer(s) of that service or product.

3. Discuss with the customer(s), whether they need this service or product? What attributes are valuable? Which are not valuable? (Consider such attributes as speed, accuracy, schedule, packaging, or formatting.)

4. Quantify the gap between current practice and customer needs. If the service or product is not needed, eliminate it.

5. Define a schedule for improvement of that particular service or product on the basis of resources, and relative priorities.

The quality function mission statement should be clear and complete so that strategies with quantitative objectives and definite plans can be developed. The quality function mission statement must be linked to the organization's mission statement. For example, if the organization's mission statement emphasizes timeliness, then the quality function mission statement should emphasize that characteristic rather than, say, cost.

RESPONSIBILITIES AND GOALS OF THE QUALITY MANAGER

A quality manager might be responsible for the following:

- reporting to management on the level of quality achieved
- identifying for management those areas requiring quality breakthroughs
- working with other managers (both line and staff) to formulate quality policies and procedures
- working with other managers to establish quality goals for new and existing products
- working with finance to identify the true costs of quality and the opportunities for savings
- directing laboratories to check conformance of materials and processes to standards and requirements
- developing and delivering training programs that teach the appropriate use of quality tools at work
- participating in feedback loops to build on successes and to learn from failures
- participating in reviews of product or service design to ensure that quality requirements are identified
- participating in reviews of production to ensure that quality requirements are being met

The goals of the quality manager must support the organization's mission. A successful quality manager (or manager of any other function) balances the needs to maintain the best possible efforts, to operate at the least possible costs, and to satisfy strategic goals and business plans.

For organizations with a functional hierarchy that contains a distinct quality function, the following assumptions normally hold true:

- The organization has formulated a mission statement.
- The mission of the quality function is derived from the organization's mission.
- Because the organization's mission is unique, so is the mission of the quality function.
- The combined missions of all functions are designed to achieve the organization's overall mission.

The quality function should exhibit the following characteristics.

Customer Focused

The quality function should be customer focused, using results-oriented measures for success. Best-in-class firms orient their approach to quality around meeting customers' requirements rather than focusing on competitors' actions. What is right for a competitor might not be right for another company, because of different strengths, visions, and so on.

Employees at firms that emphasize quality can trace a chain of thought from "Our customer values X" down through the layers of organization to "My department must do Y, on schedule, at low cost, and so on. " Komatsu, a maker of heavy construction equipment, is famed for its banner system. A banner hangs at the factory door, proclaiming to all, and reminding employees of, the factory's goals. Similar banners hang over major sections, translating the factory aims into subgoals. Smaller banners hang over departments and even over workstations, providing each worker with a "short list" of what matters and how it is measured.

Known Quality Orientation

It serves no purpose to be oriented toward quality if that orientation is unknown to customers. The best firms are proud to, and prone to, present their particular view on quality at every opportunity. They ensure that everyone knows how to register a complaint or compliment, and they actively solicit feedback and then act on it.

The automobile manufacturer Saturn is noted for its orientation toward quality. Line workers call recent customers and ask, "I installed the seats in your car. Do they work right for you?" Designers call and ask, "We designed the ventilation controls. How did you like them?"

Autonomous and Independent

The quality function needs autonomy and independence to do its job. Best-in-class companies elevate the quality function to the highest levels of management structure. The title "Director of Quality" is often seen at leading organizations. This ensures that quality is viewed as having an essential place in all corporate discussions rather than being considered a useless appendage.

Motorola and Hewlett-Packard, among others, route promotions for managers through the quality function. A candidate for high office must have a track record of doing, not just talking about, quality.

COMMON PROBLEMS AND BENEFITS ASSOCIATED WITH THE QUALITY FUNCTION MISSION

The mission of the quality function cannot be developed in isolation from the mission of the organization. This problem occurs commonly in staff organizations. The mission of the quality function is not to produce quality in the organization's products and services and establish quality goals. The finance and quality functions can be compared in this regard. The finance function does not make the money, and it does not set the financial goals; rather, it provides honest, trustworthy records of what is really happening so that others can make informed decisions. It also supplies various tools to enable others to meet their goals. Similarly, the quality function provides quality measures and supplies the tools needed to meet quality goals.

Quality is an investment, not an expense. An investment is an outgo (expenditure) now that is expected to produce a stream of income later so as to recover the initial outlay and to provide a surplus. Quality does cost money, but carefully spent money can be recovered. The problem with making this distinction is that usually the accounting is done department by department, function by function, so that outlays and income are separated both in time and in space.

Organizations that focus on quality enjoy many benefits. In a study commissioned by Congress, winners of the Baldrige Award as a group outperformed Standard and Poor's index of 500 leading companies in the stock market (see Chapter 6). In addition, data from Profit Impact of Market Strategy (PIMS) show that organizations that focus on quality and achieve it have higher returns on resources. They frequently are major players in their markets, and their products command a premium price.

Greater revenues and lower costs are potent inducements to consider quality. Companies that focus on what most customers need instead of what their rivals are doing enjoy higher growth rates. Finally, Crosby claims that quality is free. This is not to say that no costs are associated with achieving quality but rather that resources prudently allocated to quality have a positive yield that is greater than almost any other investment option the firm could explore.

Additional Readings

Crosby, Philip B. 1979. *Quality is Free: The Art of Making Quality Certain.* New York: McGraw-Hill.

___. 1984. Quality without Tears: The Art of Hassle-Free Management. New York: New American Library.

Feigenbaum, Armand V. 1991. *Total Quality Control.* 3rd ed. New York: McGraw-Hill.

Ishikawa, Kaoru. 1989. *Guide to Quality Control.* White Plains, N.Y.: Quality Resources.

Juran, Joseph M. 1988. *Juran on Planning for Quality.* New York: The Free Press.

___. 1992. *Juran on Quality for Design.* New York: The Free Press.

Juran, Joseph M., and Frank M. Gryna, eds. 1988. *Juran's Quality Control Handbook.* 4th ed. New York: McGraw-Hill.

Kim, W. Chan, and Renee Mauborgne. 1997. "Value Innovation: The Strategic Logic of High Growth." *Harvard Business Review* (January–February), Vol. 75, pp. 102–15.

Chapter 18

Priority of Quality Function within the Organization

❖ *This chapter should help you*

◆ Understand the evolution of the quality function

◆ Understand some of the false assumptions and lessons learned when working toward excellence

---

In the British parliamentary system, the prime minister is termed "first among equals," and this expression might be used to describe the status of quality in an organization. Well-being comes from acting as a harmonious, integrated whole, not from any one function within the organization seeking preeminence. For most firms, cost, schedule, and product performance features are the primary areas of concern. Safety and reliability are important considerations as well for other firms.

If a firm strives for quality and X (whatever X might be), then it is likely to achieve both quality and X. Firms that have won the Deming Prize or the Baldrige Award report that the drive for quality is an enabler, as the struggle for quality often leads to the achievement of other business goals. However, if a firm has X for its primary goal and considers quality as an optional, secondary goal, then it is likely to achieve neither X nor quality over the long term.

HISTORY OF QUALITY FUNCTION

In early agricultural situations, quality resulted largely from screening, culling inferior product, and grading the acceptable product. Careful selection of seed and breeding stock, attention to site, and good husbandry lowered the incidence of poor product but did not eliminate the need to cull and grade. Farmers did their best, but their output was the result of natural processes, mostly beyond their control. The "make it, then sort it" approach to quality is still prevalent. Craft workers had somewhat more control over their inputs and their processes. Potters, for example, recognized that their outputs varied, depending on the type of clay, glaze, and the firing method used. Inherent (undetectable or uncontrollable) variations in materials and methods still limited their ability to make a uniformly high-quality product. Their best work was excellent, but consistency varied.

In most preindustrial era settings, sales, design, manufacturing, finance, and quality were integrated: One worker performed all these functions, perhaps with the help of an apprentice or family members. This tradition persisted until the development of the factory system, in which supervisors were placed over workers. All employees were concerned with production, but only the supervisor judged quality. A distinction between making product and checking it had been introduced. Factories developed into highly organized enterprises, with a great deal of specialization of labor. Quality was still tested in, and the testers and inspectors became a separate, specialized group. Usually, this group was part of manufacturing, close to the point of use and familiar with the needs of other workers. It was believed that these workers, most of whom had little formal education, had to specialize to master a task.

These assumptions are still made by many: we can only make so much; it will come out in various grades, and better product is rare, so high quality is opposed to high productivity. If quality and productivity are opposed, then it is a conflict of interest for quality control workers and production workers to report to the same managers. To get independent judgment, the quality organizations became autonomous, reporting to their own managers rather than to managers of manufacturing. This was also institutionalized in government contracts.

The foundations of modern quality control were developed by Walter Shewhart, who published *The Economic Control of Quality of Manufactured Goods* in 1931 based on his years of experience at Western Electric. This book advocated techniques better than "make a lot and sort out the good ones." The concepts of measuring and controlling the process, reducing the variation in the system, and distinguishing between special causes and common causes contributed to a new approach to achieving quality.

During World War II (1940–1945), the military needed large quantities of highly uniform product. A three-second fuse needed to take exactly that long; the consequences of variation were unsatisfactory. The propellant charges for artillery shells had to be uniform to control trajectory. Tanks, airplanes, and other equipment had to have closely matched parts to function reliably. Deming and others trained thousands of personnel in the American war industries in the practice of statistical process control (SPC).

The American Society for Quality Control (ASQC), now called the American Society for Quality (ASQ), was formed in 1946. Its mission statement is: "The American Society for Quality advances individual and organizational performance excellence worldwide by providing opportunities for learning, quality improvement, and knowledge exchange."

For the most part, some engineers (not operators or statisticians) applied quality principles and technologies (especially SPC) and came to be called quality engineers. Because it was recognized that many of the problems experienced in production and service were due to design practices and decisions, a specialized group, reliability engineers, emerged. The experiences of the best-performing organizations made it clear that high levels of quality demanded careful planning, analysis, communication between functions, and close cooperation among all departments.

The modern, enlightened understanding recognizes that increased quality and productivity go hand in hand, so the need for independence and autonomy of the quality function is lessened. The enterprise should become more integrated with the adoption of this new view. Each worker is responsible for work quality and must have the necessary tools and powers to perform work correctly. The production cycle is returning to the earlier situation when each worker was master in the shop, dealing with customers, making the product, and checking its quality. Management of the total process or subprocess requires many skills that are increasingly being found in today's highly educated and extremely capable workers.

STRUCTURE OF THE QUALITY FUNCTION

Quality and manufacturing are often organized in parallel, whether by product or by process. Factors to consider in devising a good structure include size and complexity of the operation, the nature of the customers or markets served, the variety and quantity of products involved, and the variety of processes used. If Firm A employs several dozen people to produce one or two products from one site to be distributed locally while Firm B employs 10,000 people on four continents to make and support dozens of product lines, clearly their quality functions will be very different from a staffing and organizational standpoint.

Decentralization

If various parts of the firm are very different, then it might be beneficial to have training groups (or groups for other activities) located in each plant. In such decentralized structures, the intent is to have what is needed where it is needed. Even when common approaches are used and adopted by the firm, "best practices" should be adapted to the local plant environment.

Centralization

The larger the firm, the easier it is to justify the costs of specialized groups gathered in one central place to serve other groups. Some common examples are laboratories, calibration facilities, auditors, and trainers. It is often more cost effective to divide the expense of a central "shared" service among many users than to divide the facility.

The notion of critical mass says that a certain threshold in size and amount of activity is required for some facilities to work well. For example, if equipment used in the quality function requires calibrating only a few times per year, then it makes little sense to own all the necessary equipment and to have an under utilized expert in calibration. It might be better to make arrangements to share equipment and personnel with an outside supplier or to share the facility with manufacturing. In such circumstances, the quality function might be distributed throughout many other existing organizations.

❖❖

❖ TABLE 18.1.   Staff and Line Functions

	Staff Functions	Line Functions
Location	At headquarters	In the field
Characteristic activities	Plan, analyze, advise, and recommend	Implement and execute (action)
Typical duties	Coordinate resources	Command forces
Direction of goals	Internal operations	External threats
Scope	Widespread theaters of operation	Local situations
Time frame	Medium to long term	Short term
Focus	Strategies	Tactics

Staff and Line Functions

The distinction between staff functions and line functions first arose in the military's command-and-control hierarchy. When other enterprises became as large as military units, they adopted the structures and the organizations of the military.

The differences between military staff officers and line officers are many; these job definitions have been adopted in many large companies. Table 18.1 shows a few of these differences. In most modern organizations, financial matters, legal affairs, human relations, quality, and so on are usually considered staff functions. Selling, designing, producing, distributing, and soon are often categorized as line functions. However, other allocations are possible.

Most managers are concerned with activities listed in both columns in Table 18.1. They might command, but they also must coordinate their functions with others. They are usually involved in both making and executing plans. When TQM has been successfully implemented, the distinctions between staff and line activities can become blurred as empowered teams become responsible for both plans and action as management layers decrease.

DUTIES AND PRIORITIES OF THE QUALITY FUNCTION

Regardless of structure, the quality function must perform the following duties:

- ❖ plan activities to achieve corporate objectives
- ❖ delegate authority and assign responsibility
- ❖ monitor execution of those activities
- ❖ report on performance
- ❖ learn from past successes and failures

◆   maintain lines of communication (both up and down)

◆   serve as an example of "how to do it"

These duties can be classified as performing one of the following functions:

Quality control (QC): Operational techniques and individual activities that focus on controlling or regulating processes and materials to fulfill requirements for quality. The focus is on preventing defective products or services from being passed on.

Quality assurance (QA): Planned and systematic activities necessary to provide adequate confidence that the product or service will meet the given requirements.

Quality systems (QS): Defined organizational structure, responsibilities, procedures, processes, and resources for implementing and coordinating the QA and QC activities.

Metrology: Ensuring that the measurements are meaningful. Calibration of equipment should be traceable to the National Institute of Standards and Technology (NIST).

Another way of grouping activities is by the kind of quality costs. Prevention costs include such areas as training, planning, calibrating, and qualifying suppliers. Appraisal costs include auditing, inspecting, testing, and checking (when done to provide information about the status of a process or product) and performing process capability studies. Failure costs (both internal and external) result from activities such as recalling, sorting (when done to sort good from bad), reinspecting, reworking, repairing, retesting, and handling customer complaints. These types of quality costs are explained in more detail in Chapter 34.

To perform these functions, subsidiary organizations of the quality function might include the following:

◆   a *laboratory* analyzing work product (intermediate or final)

◆   a *calibration facility* ensuring that gages and test equipment are provably accurate and precise

◆   *inspectors* working with manufacturing to check incoming materials, intermediate work products, and final goods

◆   *auditors* checking that work, storage, labeling, and other procedures are followed and are effective

◆   *reliability engineers* working with design and production, determining the probability of performing adequately for a specified length of time under stated conditions and lowering total cost of ownership of the product

◆   *liaison engineers* working with certifiers (including the International Standards Organization), regulators (such as the Food and Drug Administration), and other oversight bodies ensuring that external requirements are both known and complied with

◆   *problem-solving teams* working where needed to apply expertise, such as the tools of quality control and root cause analyis

❖❖

◆ *quality trainers* transferring knowledge of the tools of quality control, quality management, and root cause analysis as well as other techniques to employees at all levels

◆ *supplier quality engineers* ensuring that purchased parts and materials are acceptable in grade, timeliness, and other characteristics

◆ *quality engineers* planning and working with sales, design, and other functions to ensure quality in products under development

◆ *cross-functional teams* ensuring that all parts of the firm work together to achieve the organization's vision; might work on internal assessments as well as including the Baldrige Award or various state-sponsored awards

The priority of the quality function is not measured by the size of the quality department (budget, head count, floor space, or location in the organization chart) but can be estimated from a number of factors:

◆ the emphasis placed on quality objectives relative to goals (examine practices and actions, not written policies and procedures). (e.g., "When in doubt, ship it out, because we need to meet quota—the customer may be able to use it after all" demonstrates that quality is a very low priority)

◆ the total costs of quality and the allocation to the various parts of the total (prevention, appraisal, and failure)

◆ the resources allocated and the time spent on quality by management at all level, but especially the higher levels

◆ the active involvement in quality efforts by senior leadership

WHAT THE QUALITY FUNCTION IS NOT

When the quality department is viewed as the owner of quality, the rest of the firm abdicates its role and responsibility. It can improperly be perceived as the product prevention squad, a protective screen, or as just one more (unimportant) goal.

Product Prevention Squad

The quality function is sometimes viewed as the product prevention squad—the people who say, "You can't do/ship/use that!" This occurs when quality is oriented toward *defect detection*, a negative approach of eliminating the bad so that only the good remains. The quality function is much more effective when it works toward *defect prevention*. This approach focuses on process improvement, finding good processes (internal or external to the organization), and adapting them for local use.

Protective Screen

The quality function is not a screen or barrier to protect the customer from problems and defects. Several advertisements emphasize that the customer can be confident of satisfaction "because we have x number of inspectors and testers checking the product." Actually, this statement is an admission that an organization does not have dependable processes for making a good product. Inspecting and sorting is an expensive, ineffective way to find the good product to deliver. An effective quality function works toward reducing defects and minimizing process variation so that screening and inspection is not required because the incidence of defects is so low that it is too expensive to search for them.

One More Goal

Quality is sometimes mistakenly viewed as just one more goal among many. This mistake occurs when managers and workers approach quality as another task on top of all the other tasks; or, perhaps the more truthful image is quality viewed as coming *after* all other tasks. In such cases, quality needs to be reframed as the way in which all tasks are accomplished rather than as another separate and distinct task. Quality is doing one's job effectively.

Quality is an extremely important function in an organization, but it is not the only important function. The quality function needs to practice humility in dealing with other functions within the organization. Quality might be first, but quality is not alone in bringing about success for the firm. Quality is not exempt from blunders, mistakes, poor judgment, or human error. There are good and bad ways to work for quality. Thus, the quality function should be scrutinized just as any other function is evaluated and subsequently improved.

🎋 Additional Readings 🎋

Dobyns, Lloyd, and Clare Crawford-Mason. 1991. *Quality or Else: The Revolution in World Business*. Boston: Houghton Mifflin.

Freeman, Michael G. 1996. "Don't Throw Scientific Management Out with the Bathwater." *Quality Progress*, April, pp. 61–64.

Gershon, Mark. 1996. "A Look at the Past to Predict the Present." *Quality Progress*, July, pp. 29–34.

Hiam, Alexander. 1992. *Closing the Quality Gap: Lessons from America's Leading Companies*. Englewood Cliffs, N.J.: Prentice Hall.

Juran, Joseph M., ed. 1995. *A History of Managing for Quality: The Evolution, Trends, and Future Directions of Managing for Quality*. Milwaukee: ASQC Quality Press.

Lawton, Robin L. 1993. *Creating a Customer-Centered Culture Leadership in Quality, Innovations and Speed*. Milwaukee: ASQC Quality Press.

Runmler, Geary A., and Alan P. Brache. 1995. *Improving Performance: How to Measure the White Space on the Organization Chart*. San Francisco: Jossey-Bass.

Shewhart, Walter. 1931. *The Economic Control of Quality of Manufactured Goods*. New York: D. Van Nostrand Company, Inc.

Shiba, Shoji, Alan Graham, and David Walden. 1993. *A New American TQM: Four Practical Revolutions in Management*. Cambridg, Mass.: Productivity Press.

Swatton, Brad. 1996. "Not the Best Years of Their Lives." *Quality Progress*, May, pp. 24–30.

Tenner, Arthur R., and Irving J. DeToro. 1992. *Total Quality Management: Three Steps to Continuous Improvement*. Reading, Mass.: Addison-Wesley.

Chapter 19

Metrics and Goals That Drive Organizational Performance

❖ *This chapter should help you*

◆ Understand the importance of metrics in organizational performance

◆ Appreciate metrics alignment to company goals

◆ Realize the need to use balanced proactive metrics

Most of us have some experience folding and flying paper airplanes, hoping that they would fly straight and true to their targets. Once launched, those planes went where they went. Many of us also have seen enthusiasts flying model planes controlled by radio or wires. When the wind blows them off course, the operator adjusts the rudder and ailerons, and the craft is soon back on course. When a downdraft occurs, the operator adjusts the power and the elevators, and the plane is back at the desired altitude.

This difference in operation is known as *open loop* versus *closed loop*. The difference is the use of feedback to continually monitor the discrepancy between goals and reality and making changes to reduce the gap. In closed-loop processes and operations, the output affects the inputs to keep the output close to the target. This feedback loop must have sensitivity to the goal and should be tied directly to key controlling inputs. It must be monitored continuously so that the need for adjustments—sometimes major, sometimes minor—is recognized.

The better the design and construction of the paper plane and the more experienced the operator, the more likely the plane will fly close to its desired target. This is true of all open-loop operations. Good planning, anticipation of the potential causes of disruption, "tightening" the process so that it is not easily deflected from the target—all these are useful practices that are effective in the hands of skilled managers. However, closed-loop processes are more likely to succeed in reaching their goals because they can better handle disruption from unforeseen causes.

Every process should have two outputs: (1) valuable product with which to satisfy the customer and (2) information with which to manage, control, and improve the process. The closed-loop process has many advantages over the open-loop operation. Unfortunately, many processes are open loop, and managers resort to intuition, emotions, and other ineffectual methods in an attempt to eliminate common causes of variation. Management by fact—that is, using closed-loop processes and trend data to monitor continuous improvement—is the preferred approach.

DIFFERENCES IN PLANNING AND MEASUREMENT

The differences between open-loop and closed-loop operations show up early in the planning stages. Typically, in open-loop operations the planning focuses on how to detect or measure problems in the inputs and how to plan for contingencies. "What if the Barlow shipment is late?" "How late is too late?" or "What if the weather is too cold?" and "How cold is too cold?" In contrast, in closed-loop operations the planning focuses on how to measure the outputs and how to determine the control points where adjustments can be made.

Consider an example from the metal fabrication industry. One shop measures tool wear regularly and replaces worn cutters promptly. This is a typical open-loop operation. Another shop uses statistical process control (SPC) to monitor the diameter of the output pieces and adjusts the tool position as needed. This is typical of many closed-loop operations.

What happens if something other than tool wear causes the pieces to come out undersized? The open-loop operation probably will not detect that problem until the customer complains and then will not know what caused the problem. The closed-loop operation will detect the problem and take corrective action before the customer experiences defects.

Metrics and Organizational Alignment

It has been said that "whatever gets measured, gets done." This is true in many applications and organizations. Unfortunately, the organization that has too many measures dilutes its ability to achieve breakthrough results in any of them. When metrics are considered an integrated element of organizational strategy, they are a powerful means of policy deployment throughout the firm.

An annual closed-loop assessment process, such as the one shown in Table 19.1, can be based on the Baldrige Award criteria, state-sponsored award criteria, or independent criteria. In any case, the overall organizational goal should be to assess progress toward excellence and initiate a new plan to close the gap. Relatively few (4 to 10) of these strategic metrics can focus an organization's efforts and achieve breakthrough performance. More tactical measures might be important to individual departments or sites that support the strategic plan, but metric collection should be limited to the actual process drivers because too many metrics can lead to ineffectiveness. A metric should lead to an action to attain the goal (i.e., they should be attainable).

A popular technique is to use the "balanced scorecard approach" introduced by Kaplan and Norton in their groundbreaking articles in the *Harvard Business Review*.[1] This approach defines metrics in four areas: customers, people (employees), shareholders, and process. Six common process metrics are cost, time, quality, agility (ability to adapt), capacity, and variability. Sometimes these areas overlap and can even conflict. In this case, they must be linked in a business process so as not to suboptimize operations by making effective performance trade-offs.

◆ TABLE 19.1. Annual Closed-Loop Assessment	
Annual Closed-Loop Assessment	**Use of Metrics**
1. Define "business excellence" for your business	Establish strategic measures of success
2. Assess your progress	Compare your progress to world-class competitors and to strategic objectives; identify gaps
3. Identify improvement opportunities	Set annual priorities and improvement goals
4. Deploy action plan	Align key metrics and deploy to all levels of the organization

A balanced approach considers metrics in all four areas and recognizes that all four are important to the firm's success. Leading indicators tend to be predictive of future performance, whereas lagging indicators (which are easier to collect) might report on past successes or failures. Taking action to affect leading indicators is the secret to managing and understanding a process.

An example might be an auto trip from Dallas to Houston with a result metric—a 3:00 P.M. arrival time. The process metric would be departure time and average speed. If the departure time is 11:00 A.M. for this 240-mile trip and an average speed is 65 miles per hour, then there is a high probability that the 3:00 P.M. arrival time will be achieved.

Goals are cascaded from one level of an organization to the next. Any large undertaking will be represented by a vast number of goals, which generate action items, which generate more detailed, more specific action items, until the level of individual teams and contributors is reached, as shown in the following example:

The CEO says that the goal of the firm is to increase customer delight. One manager says that there is some evidence that customers would be delighted with a product that never breaks down unexpectedly and agrees to take action on it, with other managers taking other action items to support the goal of customer delight. Some time later, at a second meeting, the division manager says, "We have a goal—to make sure our product never breaks down unexpectedly!" One of the attendees says that she believes changes in material might make a difference and agrees to take action. Other attendees take other action items to support the goal of a product that never breaks down unexpectedly. Some time later, there is a third meeting, and the department manager says . . .

Good questions to ask are "Why am I doing this?" and "How do I contribute to company goals?" If you do not know where you are heading, then it does not matter what direction you take. How will you know whether things are progressing? How will you know whether you are succeeding? This is where metrics can tell you whether you are progressing toward your goal.

Consider another example: An organization has decided to pursue a larger market share and needs more output. An analysis shows that the bottleneck is being caused by a shortage of people. A likely action item is "hire more people." The question is, "How do you verify action toward the goal?"

Some plausible measurements are the following:

◆ *Number of open personnel requisitions remaining.* If this stays high or levels off, then corrective action should be taken.

◆ *Number of hours of labor worked each week.* It is possible that people were hired but were unable to report for work or were placed in training classes; if this amount does not increase, then adjustments should be made.

◆ *Amount of product produced each week.* This was the output goal; if the goal is not being reached, then adjustments should be made.

"Measures and indicators refer to the numerical information that quantifies (measures) input, output, and performance dimensions of processes, products, services, and the overall company. Measures and indicators might be simple (derived from one measurement) or composite."[2] Some measurements verify that the action item is being done, and other measurements verify that the goal is being reached. Usually, both types of measurements are required.

Frequency of Measurements (Periodicity)

It costs money to take measurements. There is the time involved in doing it, possibly equipment and space, training in how to measure, and so on; it can be a diversion of resources from the main task of producing useful output. Taking measurements should be not a burden but part of the process.

When determining the appropriate intervals at which to measure, one factor to consider is how fast input conditions can change. In Galway, Ireland, the temperature and relative humidity vary slowly within fairly narrow limits. In Tijuana, Mexico, these can change greatly and rapidly. An SPC procedure that was perfectly satisfactory in one place might be unsatisfactory in another. (This assumes that you know the factors that affect your process.)

Six factors influence how frequently measurements should be taken:

1. *Purpose:* Does the metric indicate a trend or control output?
2. *Cost:* How much time/money is spent measuring?
3. *Rate of change:* What is the maximum time between measurements?
4. *Degree of control:* Can an unfavorable change be corrected? How soon?
5. *Consequences:* What is the risk?
6. *Baseline:* Is there existing data on how the metric performs over time?

Process maps for closed-loop operations should indicate the monitor points (where measurements are taken in a process) and the processing of those measurements. To truly understand a process, all individuals involved should create a baseline "as is" process map, including all current steps and the current performance measures. Too many times a false assumption is made that "we understand the process."

Ultimately, all lower-level goals must be aligned with the major goals of the balanced scorecard approach:

Why measure? To take action to ensure success of reaching your goals.

What to measure? Key actionable process elements that will help you monitor the process.

Where to measure? As close as possible to the variation.

When to measure? As often as necessary, but no more often.

How to measure? As unobtrusively as possible.

Measurements and indicators can be gathered at all points in the supply chain: external customers, internal operations, and suppliers.

BENEFITS OF MEASURING

When you can measure what you are speaking about and express it in numbers, you know something about it; but when you cannot measure it, when you can't express it in numbers, your knowledge is of a meager and unsatisfactory kind.

Lord Kelvin

Achieving Goals

"If you don't know where you are supposed to be going, you aren't likely to get there." A Roman proverb says that when you do not know what harbor you want to get to, then no wind is the right wind. Ignorance of purpose is a demoralizer for any organization. In contrast, clarity of purpose is a motivator for organizations. If everyone knows what is at stake and what is to be achieved, and if everyone can follow progress toward that goal, then each person can make a contribution.

Detecting Problems

An effective measurement system can provide the ability to detect and correct problems before they become overwhelming. A good system for measuring progress, or lack thereof, can enable operators and managers to determine whether things are proceeding according to plan and provides a clear goal and constant feedback on progress toward that goal.

Understanding the Process

Measuring helps process owners learn which factors make a difference and which do not. Many people, in the course of process improvement efforts, find themselves asking, "Now that we have changed something, did it make a difference?" Without an effective way of measuring, there will be no clear answer. Instead of understanding and knowledge about the process, there will be only opinion and conjecture. Management by fact, not emotion, is desired.

❖❖❖

BEST PRACTICES

The following techniques are considered best practices in the area of measurement.

Benchmarking

Benchmarking is the process of comparing your progress to other best-in-class organizations. Best-in-class firms use benchmarking as a key activity in setting goals as well as in determining how to meet them. Benchmarking ensures managers that chosen goals are competitive and attainable. Benchmarks are the measures of a best-in-class process.

Customer-Focused Goals

Goals should focus on customer satisfaction. The best companies use customer and marketplace goal including market share, customer retention, customer satisfaction, and delight. Of course, all these goals are interrelated, not independent. Delighted customers form an unpaid sales force, increasing market share. Increasing the retention of customers, instead of "churning," increases market share.

Business Goals

Business goals should specify a balanced approach, process quality, customer satisfaction, productivity, and financial performance. Best-in-class firms do not wait to measure results; they check on the leading process measurements to continually improve and reduce defects and variability.

Policy Deployment

Best-in-class firms set strategic goals, determine a few strategic metrics, and then cascade these goals throughout the company to ensure alignment as well as attainment of breakthrough performance.

COMMON MISTAKES

The use of metrics is not easy and can result in many mistakes.

Goals Too Easy or Too Hard

Goals can be set too low or too high. This often shows that management is out of touch with organizational realities. One of the solutions is benchmarking, which helps set challenging but possible stretch goals. Another solution is anything that improves communication up and down the various levels; some form of catchball can be instituted by which goals are negotiated at each level.

Goals Only for the Top

A failure to percolate goals down through an organization can be caused by upper management being out of touch with lower levels of the organization. Each level must know its goals and must develop action plans to achieve them. Hoshin planning (discussed in Chapter 14) can be used to ensure that all levels of an organization have known goals.

Wrong Frequency of Measurement

Having the wrong frequency for changing the way in which the numbers are defined, collected, or analyzed can cause problems. Both never and too often are killers. No rules regarding the frequency of measurement fit all circumstances. Those employees closest to and most knowledgeable of the process usually have a feel for the rate at which things change—the natural rhythm or pulse of the system. These process owners can probably estimate a good frequency for measuring. However, it is preferable to start by measuring more often rather than less often and cutting back the frequency when this can be justified. If the process has unexpected transients, or hiccups, it is important not to miss them.

Too Many Metrics

Too many metrics can dilute the focus and energy of the firm and create confusion on priorities. Normally, a handful of metrics is sufficient to manage the business on a strategic level.

Pretty Metrics

Metrics should be local, friendly, and dirty. They should be used by many people to manage the daily business. Having a pretty chart on the wall is not the goal; rather, having ones that are understood and frequently used is the goal.

Metrics Not Clearly Defined

Metrics should be clearly and concisely defined to eliminate assumptions that could invalidate the data. These definitions should be published and strict configuration control exercised to ensure accurate data.

🛕 Additional Readings 🛕

Camp, Robert C. 1995. *Business Process Benchmarking: Finding and Implementing Best Practices*. Milwaukee: ASQC Quality Press.

Harbour, Jerry L. 1997. *The Basics of Performance Measurement*. New York: Quality Resources.

Harrington, H. James. 1987. *The Improvement Process: How America's Leading Companies Improve Quality*. New York: McGraw-Hill.

Hronec, Steven M. 1993. *Vital Signs: Using Time, and Cost Performance Measurements to Chart Your Company's Future*. New York: AMACOM.

Kaplan, Robert S., and David Norton. "The Balanced Scorecard." *Harvard Busines Review 74*, 1996.

Lynch, Richard L., and Kelvin F. Cross. 1994. *Measure Up! Yardsticks for Continuo Improvement*. Cambridge, Mass.: Blackwell Publishers.

Maskell, Brian H. 1991. *Performance Measurement for World Class Manufacturing.* Portland, Ore.: Productivity Press.

Rust, Roland T., et al. 1994. *Return on Quality: Measuring the Financial Impact of Your Company's Quest for Quality.* Chicago: Probus Publishing.

Tenner, Arthur, and Irving J. DeToro. 1992. *Total Quality Management: Three Steps to Continuous Improvement.* Reading, Mass.: Addison-Wesley.

Chapter 20

Formulation of Quality Principles and Policies

❖ *This chapter should help you*

◆ Differentiate between principles, policies, and procedures

◆ Understand that principles, policies, and procedures promote uniformity of conduct and approach

Without a goal, what will be achieved? Without direction, how can the goal be achieved? These same principles apply to business. For quality to be part of the strategic business plan, the quality goal must be formulated and documented.

In a one-person organization, all the personnel are familiar with all the organization's knowledge, goals, policies, and procedures. As organizations grow in size and complexity, personnel are added, each of whom makes significant decisions. To unify the decision process, principles and policies need to be defined and communicated.

DEFINING PRINCIPLES, POLICIES, AND PROCEDURES

Business principles are comprehensive fundamental beliefs or values that are intended to guide behavior. They tend to be grounded in the history of the organization and to be descriptions of what has mattered or explanations of what has made the firm distinctive. Some examples of business principles follow:

We believe that it is better for the firm and easier too, to retain customers than to replace them.

We value each customer, and we grow as they grow.

We believe in honesty and mutual respect with our customers. This forms the basis for our shared prosperity.

Applied more specifically to the quality function, quality management principles are "comprehensive rules or beliefs for leading and operating an organization, aimed at continually improving performance over the long term by focusing on customers while addressing the needs of all stakeholders." The quality management principles are the basis for all levels of objectives and demonstrate the depth of the organization's commitment to quality.

Examples of specific quality principles follow:

Problems have special causes and common causes.

Management must take responsibility for common causes.

It is better to prevent defects from getting in than to sort them out.

Well-formulated principles should be "timeless," not dependent on temporary circumstances. Certain principles can foster particular strategies and goals. However, goals with numerical targets usually depend on outside influences, not on the organization's principles.

Eight supporting principles nested within the quality management principle are shown in Table 20.1. Quality principles are the foundation on which a quality policy is built. Policies differ from guiding principles. Organizational policies (directives, procedures, guidelines, and rules) are a more specific and directive version of values. Usually, the most important are communicated to the workforce through employee handbooks, to suppliers through supplier guidelines, and to customers through product or service guides and warranty and disclosure information. The trend of value-focused organizations is toward simplicity in the communication of values and policies.

A policy is a high-level overall plan embracing the general goals and acceptable procedures of a group. It is a definite course or method of action selected from among alternatives and in light of given conditions to guide and determine present and future decisions. Policies state how goals will be achieved and are intended to guide decisions. They are future oriented, sometimes for the indefinite future and sometimes conditioned by the presence or absence of some constraining factor. For example, a financial policy might be this: "For as long as interest rates remain high, it will be our policy to avoid debt." As visions, strategies, and goals are unique to each organization, policies are also (in general) unique to an organization.

A quality policy is a formalized document whose purpose is to communicate the overall intentions and directions of the organization as they relate to quality. Feigenbaum states that a quality policy "is the broad strategic pattern to guide and govern all management decisions in the product-quality areas, including safety, reliability, and other necessary quality characteristics." A quality policy indicates the principles to be followed or what is to be done but does not stipulate how.

The first task of senior management in embarking on a campaign for total quality management and ISO 9000 is drafting the company's quality policy. Because every company is unique in its history, management, and state of development, its quality policy should be developed to fit its current situation. The quality policy should summarize the organization's view on the definition of quality, the importance of quality, quality competitiveness, customer relations, internal customers, workforce involvement, quality improvement, planning and organization, and additional subject matter as required.

Establishing a quality policy is the "first step in creating a comprehensive quality plan that will allow a company to compete in world markets that are demanding quality and service." Quality policy statements of clarity and brevity help people in

◆ TABLE 20.1. Principles of Quality Management	
Principle 1: Customer-focused organization	Organizations depend on their customers and therefore should understand current and future customer needs, meet customer requirements, and strive to exceed customer expectations.
Principle 2: Leadership	Leaders establish unity of purpose and direction of organization. They should create and maintain the internal environment in which people can become fully involved in achieving the organization's objectives.
Principle 3: Involvement of people	People at all levels are the essence of an organization, and their full involvement enables their abilities to be used for the organization's benefit.
Principle 4: Process approach	A desired result is achieved more efficiently when related resources and activities are managed as a process.
Principle 5: System approach to management	Identifying, understanding, and managing a system of interrelated processes for a given objective improves the organization's effectiveness and efficiency.
Principle 6: Continual improvement	Continual improvement should be a permanent objective of the organization.
Principle 7: Factual approach to decision making	Effective decisions and actions are based on the analysis of data and information.
Principle 8: Mutually beneficial supplier relationships	An organization and its suppliers are independent, and a mutually beneficial relationship enhances the ability to create value.

the organization develop a common understanding about the aims of the organization in dealing with management processes and work activities that affect all aspects of quality performance.

Procedures are statements of current practice—of how to do things at the detailed level. These evolve naturally as the organization finds better ways to work toward its goals or to act on its principles.

Clearly, there are tight connections between the terms principles, policies, and procedures. This can lead to long discussions about "which comes first?" Some organizations resolve the matter by binding two or all three of the statements into one document and calling it the Policies and Procedures Manual.

The following statements are examples of a quality principle and policies with reference to procedures:

[*Principle*] We believe in striving for customer satisfaction at all times.

[*Policy*] Therefore, all small billing discrepancies will be routinely settled in favor of the customer. Procedure P-123 describes how to determine whether a discrepancy is small.

[*Policy*] An exception will be allowed if a pattern of abuse can be established. Procedure P-456 describes how to establish a pattern of abuse.

DOCUMENTATION OF PRINCIPLES, POLICIES, AND PROCEDURES

The quality policy should be documented and consistent with other organizational policies. Management should take all necessary measures to ensure that the quality policy is understood, implemented, and reviewed at all levels.

Documentation of the organization's quality policy and objectives commonly occurs in the quality manual. This is where the organization's commitment to quality is presented and where the organization's objectives for quality are outlined. This section of the quality manual should also describe how the quality policy is made known to and understood by all employees and how it is implemented and maintained at all levels. Specific quality policy statements might also be included under the system element concerned.

Juran notes five benefits resulting from the documentation of written policies:

◆ All parties involved with the company are provided a written guide to managerial action, lending a stability to the organization.

◆ The organization is forced to consider quality problems and their ramifications.

◆ The organization is legitimized and can communicate authoritatively.

◆ Management is conducted by communicated policy rather than firefighting or crisis.

◆ Practice is audited to policy.[1]

As determined by Baldrige Award criteria, an organization's approach to quality must be documented and functional throughout the organization. Companies that have been Baldrige Award winners demonstrate this type of culture.

The following list of companies are examples of organizations whose quality policies have translated into phenomenal quality improvements throughout their businesses:

◆ General Motors Corporation, Cadillac Motor Car Company, Detroit, Michigan

◆ International Business Machines, Rochester, Minnesota

◆ Motorola Inc., Schaumburg, Illinois

◆ Westinghouse Electric Corporation, Commercial Nuclear Fuel Division, Pittsburgh, Pennsylvania

◆ Xerox Corporation, Business Products and Systems, Fairport, New York

The following improvements have occurred at these companies as a result of articulating a clear vision for their future: lower employee turnover, safety and health rates better than the industry average, increased number of quality improvement suggestions, attendance rates above the industry average, overall employee job satisfaction improvements, increased customer satisfaction, and improved quality measures.

FORMULATING PRINCIPLES, POLICIES, AND PROCEDURES

In general, staff functions formulate policies concerning those matters in their realm of concern, and then prescribe the procedures that they feel are necessary to ensure that the policy will be executed. The process of formulating an effective quality policy should be based on inputs from many stakeholders: line organizations, such as design, manufacturing, and distribution; staff functions, such as budget/finance, human resources, and legal; customers; regulators; shareholders; communities in which business is conducted; and senior management and corporate planners.

Ideally, quality policies should be derived from corporate policies and principles and should be consistent with quality principles. Therefore, it would be premature to develop quality policies before senior management has formulated the corporate principles, stated corporate strategies and goals, and developed corporate policies.

The development of procedures should take place with the parties who will carry out the procedures. The quality function usually contributes expertise in methods that work in general; the line organizations have experience in what is practical and possible, given current conditions. Procedures usually change more quickly than do policies and principles. They must be kept current and accessible so that everyone knows which procedures to use. The transition from one procedure to another must be managed with care.

The following questions should be settled before formulating quality goals:

◆ What market segments does the firm deal with (high end, mass markets, specialized niches, and so on)?

◆ What does the firm sell (commodities, total packages, and so on)?

◆ Is the firm striving for leadership, for industry average, or for adequacy?

◆ How does the firm position itself (low cost, premium supplier, and so on)?

Every organization has a policy for quality, but until it is documented, it is unknown. In the absence of a written policy, each employee will do whatever seems best in his or her own eyes, whatever seems "natural," whatever comes to mind. The word for that is chaos. It is not enough to pull and to pull hard; rather the organization has to pull together.

Until the quality goals of the organization are written down, presented, discussed, clarified, rephrased, and made available to all, achieving those goals will depend more on luck than on anything else. The major disadvantage of written policies is the great amount of work required to develop them. In addition, extensive input from high-level management is required to determine and/or approve the policy. When high-level management neglects to establish policy, policy will be established at low levels. Another concern expressed by managers is that written policies can restrict or limit the ability of employees to adapt to changing situations.

Everyone has a procedure for doing X, in fact, probably several procedures, depending on whim and circumstance. There is great value in documenting the variety, examining the costs and benefits of each, and determining when to use each method. Training is enhanced, continuity is established, and the organization is better off knowing how things are done. Once a method is "out in the open," it can be studied, measured, and improved. As long as there is some mystery or uncertainty about how to do things right, things will often be done poorly and inconsistently. Principles, policies, and procedures set forth criteria against which to judge a particular course of action or a particular implementation. Employees, suppliers, and customers do not have to fear arbitrary or erratic decisions. In an organization that works in a consistent, understandable way toward known goals, "you know where you stand" is commonly heard.

Likewise, the formulation of principles, policies, and procedures can promote uniformity of conduct and of approach. A common image is that of a construction crew erecting a building from blueprints. The electrical crew can string wires while the plumbing crew routes pipes—they know that they will not get in one another's way.

Principles, policies, and procedures establish and support a culture that can bind employees into an effective whole. A common comparison, or metaphor, is that of a choir singing from the same sheet of music. The altos know when to sing their parts, the basses know when to sing theirs, and together they harmonize. This image presumes that there is a sheet of music, which can be provided by well-written principles, policies, and procedures.

BEST PRACTICES/WORST MISTAKES

In the formulation of quality principles, policies, and procedures, several concepts are important to success:

◆ *Focusing on customers, not rivals.* This has been characteristic of high-growth companies and distinguishes them from their less successful competitors.

◆ *Establishing cross-functional teams.* This results in policies and procedures that are complete and consistent throughout the organization and serve the corporate strategies and goals. There is a constant temptation to consider only the local situation, but best in class firms know that it might be necessary, for example, to institute procedures that increase manufacturing costs in order to lower total costs and thereby to benefit the customer.

◆ *Establishing cross-level teams.* Cross-level teams can be formed to ensure that principles are communicated throughout the organization. Best-in-class firms confirm that all employees know what the firm considers important and that employees fully understand their roles in achieving the organization's goals.

The following list indicates common mistakes made in the formulation of principles, policies, and procedures:

◆ Quality policies are vague and do not provide guides for conduct.

◆ Attempting to force one quality policy upon multiple markets or divisions when the culture does not permit or fit.

◆ Mistakenly believing that company policies are "holy ground" and cannot be adapted.

◆ Publishing a quality policy when reasonable doubt exists that the policy will be followed. Cynicism occurs when deed and policy differ.

◆ Not gaining cooperation early enough with marketing, product development, and the manufacturing functions when developing the policy.

In addition, organizations can fail to establish a reasonable time frame for implementation. This can occur when goals are not challenging enough or when goals are impossible. The balance can be delicate, and may need continual adjustment and review. Failure to review progress and to reset goals on a timely basis may be another form of this mistake.

🏛 Additional Readings 🏛

Cartin, Thomas J., and Donald J. Jacoby. 1997. *A Review of Managing Quality and a Primer for the Certified Quality Manager Exam.* Milwaukee: ASQ Quality Press.

Harris, Michael C. 1998. *Value Leadership, Winning Competitive.* Milwaukee: ASQ Quality Press.

Whimey, John O. "Strategic Renewal for Business Units." *Harvard Business Review* 74 (Sept–Oct 1996): 84–98.

Chapter 21

Resource Requirements to Manage the Quality Function

❖ *This chapter should help you*

- ◆ List the five key resources required for managing the quality function
- ◆ Understand why these resources are important for the quality function
- ◆ Initiate budgeting for the quality function using a four-step process

---

QUALITY FUNCTIONS RESOURCES

Each function in an organization requires certain resources in order to be managed effectively. Many of these (e.g., money) are common across functions; others (e.g., a particular skill set) are unique. However, even common needs must be specified and justified differently for different functions, depending on the particular manner in which they are used by that function. Traditionally, any discussion of the resource requirements of an organization has been completely aligned with the resource requirements of its key functions (e.g., manufacturing, design, or sales). Functions such as quality use unique resources and often use similar resources in different ways. This is why a separate discussion is required for the resource requirements of this function.

The key distinguishing feature of the quality function is that it is an *enabling* function. It does not directly produce goods or services. However, when managed well, it enables increasingly effective and efficient creation and delivery of goods and services by the organization. Because this function is a catalyst, it follows that the resources used by it can yield disproportionate benefits. This in turn requires that these resources meet the dual requirements of quality and timeliness (e.g., the right resources provided in time).

Many of the resources required for the quality function are tangible and familiar from other contexts, such as manufacturing and sales. Some of them are somewhat less tangible. This does not mean that they are any less important for the effective management of this function; rather, it means simply that they often are overlooked when this function is being deployed. Such neglect always leads to poor or unsustainable quality in the organization.

People

The quality function needs people who can ensure that everything is done right the first time. The function requires the right people in the right numbers. Because quality is an enabling function, staff members need to possess certain unique attributes. Table 21.1 summarizes the four key attributes needed, explains the importance of each attribute, and lists how each attribute manifests itself. Even when these key attributes are recognized, an organization might still struggle to create a profile to use to screen prospective internal or external candidates for quality function positions. A useful tip is to find an existing successful quality professional in your organization (or another organization if you are responsible for starting this function in your organization), build an actual profile, and then remove specifics and generalize attributes using Table 21.1.

The nature of the organization's work and the maturity of existing quality systems determines the right number of people to staff the quality function. However, many practicing quality professionals figure that 2 percent of the organizational staff is the required staff strength for the quality function. This rule of thumb should be qualified by adding that this is the requirement of full-time equivalents, not actual numbers hired for the quality function. These requirements can be met by a variety of means, including the following:

◆ *Full-time hires.* This is the most common mode of staffing but suffers from the problem of inflexibility and the attendant danger of creating an unresponsive bureaucracy in the quality function.

◆ *Part-time hires (i.e., individuals working for part of the day or week).* This increases flexibility while decreasing payroll costs for the organization. However, management might need to closely oversee part-time employees to ensure continuity in job performance and motivate individuals who might not feel as committed to the organization's success as is desirable.

◆ *Outsourcing (e.g., through consultants).* This works especially well for areas such as quality training, problem-solving facilitation, and specific calibration and data analysis activities.

◆ *Rotation of existing line staff through the quality function on short-term assignments with a small core group of quality professionals.* This requires a great deal of management in order to ensure continuity but has the advantage of building quality awareness and skills through a wider cross section of the organization.

The manager of the quality function needs to determine the number and configuration of people needed. This can be done effectively by keeping the attribute list in mind, remembering the rule of thumb on numbers, and considering the options available for meeting those numbers.

Hardware

The second key resource needed by quality professionals to discharge their function effectively is hardware. This is an especially vital resource when the function involves

❖ TABLE 21.1.   Key Attributes of Quality Function Personnel

Attribute	Importance	Visible Evidence
1 Technical literacy	The quality professional needs to talk the language of the organization. In an organization supplying automotive parts, it helps to be an automotive or mechanical engineer or to have worked closely with similar organizations in the past.	Appropriate educational qualifications. Past experience in a similar industry. Past experience in a role where there was a lot of interaction with this industry (i.e., a supplier industry, a customer industry, an industry association, a technical institute, training establishment or a design/standardization body). Demonstrated evidence of quickly picking up the language of the organization (i.e., successful tenure in a variety of different industries).
2 Quality literacy	The quality professional should know what she need to do (i.e. design and deployment of quality systems, tools, training and measurement).	Formal quality qualification (which would ensure familiarity with concepts, evolution, standards, tools, measurement, statistical analysis, and deployment mechanisms). Successful past experiences in similar roles in either industry or consulting.
3 Facilitation skills	This function works through others in the organization by helping them solve problems and uncover better ways of working. This requires minimizing prescription and maximizing facilitation of individuals and groups in identifying and solving their problems using the right tools.	Demonstrated evidence of working effectively with teams. (People who are used to working by themselves are uncomfortable with this role). Formal facilitation training. Better-than-average communication skills.

Continued

◆❖◆

◆ TABLE 21.1. *Continued*		
Attribute	**Importance**	**Visible Evidence**
4 Positive attitude	Since the quality professional does not create quality herself she needs to be persistent in her efforts at working through others who may even resist or delay these initiatives. She also needs to be positive about the outcome of her initiatives because there is inevitably a gestation period for quality initiatives to yield bottom-line improvements. Finally, she needs to keep other people in the organization confident about the usefulness of quality tools, many of whom may be unfamiliar to first-time users who may even doubt their validity as they struggle to establish competence at using them.	High levels of energy. Past experience of overcoming organizational challenges at paid or volunteer work through persistence. Demonstrated evidence of helping teams learn and use unfamiliar tools successfully.

verifying measurements, ensuring the use of calibrated measurement devices, sampling and analyzing process data, verifying compliance to claimed specifications, and training personnel in quality concepts and techniques. Hardware in this sense does not refer to office furniture or personal computers used to support the normal office functions of word processing and electronic mail. Rather, depending on the business, specific items needed by the quality function could include the following:

- ◆ measurement devices, such as gages
- ◆ calibration systems of a higher degree of accuracy and stability compared to their counterparts used in the normal line functions
- ◆ data logging and analysis systems, especially in process industries
- ◆ laboratory equipment for destructive and nondestructive testing
- ◆ special facilities for simulating extreme environmental conditions
- ◆ training aids

Software

Quality professionals also need the right software to support their work. The software needed depends on the nature of the organization's business and the specific scope of the quality function. Software can be divided into three types:

◆ *Analysis software.* This includes packaged software for statistical analysis, flowcharting, and modeling. This type of software is routinely used during the day-to-day activities comprising the quality function.

◆ *Documentation software.* This software includes various packages that provide template-based support for creating quality management system documentation, audit plans and checklists, and organization self-assessment capabilities.

◆ *Training software.* This includes multimedia instructional software to train people on specific problem-solving tools or benchmarking as well as packaged software that can be used to create awareness of quality standards, such as ISO 9000 or QS-9000. Training software is not confined to computer software alone but also includes books, videotapes, and journals that would go into the organizational library for supporting the quality function.

Certain other enablers (e.g., corporate memberships in professional bodies and support organizations, perhaps a benchmarking clearinghouse) do not qualify as software. However, they are worth mentioning here because they usually are manifested in the form of regular bulletins, journals, and CD-ROMs as well as access to members-only sites on the Internet.

Money

A resource required to secure the resources already mentioned is money. Inadequate provisioning for this resource can cripple the effectiveness of the quality function because of the gestation period required for the quality initiative to show results. During this gestation period, money continues to flow out without any measurable improvement in the organization. However, unseen to casual observers, the quality initiatives usually continue to gather critical mass, and after a certain time, depending on the size of the organization, management commitment, and prior maturity, visible results begin to flow in terms of reduced rejects, faster deliveries, and better customer satisfaction. It is important that the quality function continues to access this resource during the period of gestation, which has been recognized by each quality "guru" in his own way. For example, Philip Crosby talks of the right sequence for improving quality in an organization. According to him, this consists of the following:

◆ *Determination.* This is the realization, across the organization and especially at the top levels of management, that things need to change for the better. Often this comes about after a calculation of the cost of quality or even a widely administered diagnostic questionnaire.

◆ *Education.* This includes organization-wide training in quality concepts, tools, and measures.

◆ *Implementation.* This is the phase in which quality systems are developed or refined, individual or group problem-solving and quality improvement projects take root, and measurable benefits start flowing.

In this sequence, money will continue to flow out in all three stages and will flow back as benefits only after commencement of the third stage. Short-term return-on-

❖❖❖

investment (ROI) calculation can cripple funding requirements for the quality function in the crucial early phases. Over a longer time span, money spent on quality pays for itself.

The availability of money in organizations is mediated by the budgeting process. This means that the quality manager should be proficient in developing, defending, and executing budgets. Each organization usually has a well-defined process for developing budgets. Many even have detailed templates that, coupled with a suitable groupware package, allow smooth development and seamless integration of the budgets prepared by different functions. However, a generic approach to the budgeting process is worth describing for someone who might be doing it for the first time. This consists of the usual disaggregation–aggregation cycle, which consists of four steps:

1. List the broad actions forming the mission of the quality function. These could include, but are not limited to, the following:

   ◆ accreditation of the organizational quality management system to a global standard

   ◆ identifying and executing benchmarking and process improvement projects

   ◆ equipping selected levels within the organization with specific tools and skills and

   ◆ preparing the organization for a corporate excellence award requiring self-assessment

2. Detail each item in the mission statement into specific constituent activities and further detail these into subactivities and sub-subactivities if necessary until the required resources and associated funding requirements can be confidently estimated in terms of both value and time frame.

3. Estimate resource requirements for each subactivity or sub-subactivity as the case may be. Use past data available from previous budgeting exercises, similar activities performed in other functions, industry norms as experienced in other companies or reported in literature, and information provided by suppliers of the required products and services. If the organization has a strong activity-based costing system, the estimation exercise becomes somewhat easier to perform.

4. Group the money requirements using common classifications occurring in the different activities. For example, travel would appear as an item of expenditure in several activities. Also arrange the money requirements by time intervals to generate the cash requirement plan, which helps the finance function in scheduling funds as required. Preserve detailed worksheets of the activity breakdown for tracking progress and for improving estimations in the next budgeting or review cycle.

The importance of clear and detailed budgeting cannot be overestimated because the quality function is often required to explain and defend its money requirements at several forums within the organization. The effort spent on developing a mission statement, a detailed work breakdown structure, and accurate estimation usually pays for itself in the form of quick internal approvals, a reliable aid for tracking progress, and, most important, enhanced confidence in actual execution of planned activities. However, effective management of the quality function requires one more enabler: organizational structure.

Structure

Some would argue that structure cannot be classified as a resource. However, it is such a crucial enabler and is often provided by management through the same process of internal dialogue required for other resources that a brief discussion is essential.

The quality function should have a clear place on the organizational chart, preferably with a direct, independent reporting relationship to the chief executive. This is not to say that the function cannot work effectively if structured in any other way; however, such success would be rare. This is because the quality function affects the entire enterprise and often challenges the suboptimizing behavior exhibited by other organizational functions. Also, the gestation period associated with several quality initiatives mandates this type of structure to avoid the perception of quality as a burden on the budgets of other functions.

Apart from finding its own place in the organization, the quality function should be structurally supported by other functions for the best results. One way of doing this, championed most strongly by Crosby, is through the quality organization that overlays the functional organization. In this scheme, each function within the organization, such as finance, marketing, and production, holds a clear and measurable responsibility for one quality measure, such as measurement, company-wide education, or corrective action. The quality function then becomes an enabler to help deploy this element successfully. The advantage of this approach is that quality becomes everyone's responsibility, and the perception of quality-related work as something that needs to be done over and above one's regular work is greatly diluted. Another successful although somewhat less direct approach is to use a structure, such as an organizational quality council consisting of senior heads of all key functions, to debate, evaluate, and support quality initiatives. What is important is that the quality function is supported by appropriate organizational structures that go beyond mere goodwill in order to be truly effective.

SUMMARY

The discussion of the five key enablers for the effective discharge of the quality function and the four-step process for budgeting that mediates the release of the most closely controlled resource has sidestepped a discussion of how the utilization of these resources is best measured. Although the key enterprise-level indicators of corporate success (ROI, market share, and customer and employee satisfaction) are positively affected by quality initiatives, most organizations supplement these long-term measures by using a set of shorter-term measures, such as quality costs (see Chapter 34). It is sufficient to note here that the organization continually incurs costs of preventing poor quality, appraising quality, and correcting internal and external failures of its products and services. These costs decline with effective management of the quality function, and this saving is a direct measure of the utilization of resources.

❖❖

🏛 Additional Readings 🏛

Crosby, Philip B. 1979. *Quality Is Free.* New York: New American Library.

___. 1984. *Quality without Tears.* New York: McGraw-Hill.

Deming, W. Edwards. 1986. *Out of the Crisis.* Cambridge: Massachusetts Institute of Technology, Center for Advanced Engineering Study.

Garvin, David A. 1988. *Managing Quality: The Strategic and Competitive Edge.* New York: The Free Press.

Hunt, V. Daniel. 1992. *Managing for Quality: Integrating Quality and Business Strategy.* Chicago: Business One Irwin.

Rao, Askok, et al. 1996. *Total Quality Management: A Cross-Functional Perspective.* New York: John Wiley & Sons.

📑 Part 3 Endnotes 📑

Chapter 14

1. Henry Mintzberg, *The Rise and Fall of Strategic Planning* (New York: The Free Press, 1994).
2. Peter Drucker, "The Information Executives Truly Need," *Harvard Business Review* (January–February 1995) Vol. 73: 125.
3. Thomas J. Cartin and Donald J. Jacoby, *A Review of Managing for Quality and a Primer for the Certified Quality Manager Exam* (Milwaukee: ASQ Quality Press, 1997), p. 79.
4. 1998 Baldrige Criteria, p. 3.
5. Cartin and Jacoby, p. 81.
6. Peter Mears and Frank Voehl, *The Guide to Implementing Quality Systems* (Delray Beach, Fla.: St. Lucie Press, 1995), p. 32.
7. Chris Lee, "The Vision Thing," *Training,* February 1993, 29.
8. Jay Cook, "Teams Need a Vision to Work," *Journal of Quality and Participation* (December 1994) Vol. 12: 59.
9. Teri Lammers, "The Effective and Indispensable Mission Statement," *INC.,* August 1992, pp. 75–77.
10. "Put Your Mission Statement to Work," *Customers!,* May 1987.
11. John R. Latham, "Visioning: The Concept, Trilogy, and Process," *Quality Progress,* July 1995, Vol. 7: p. 89.
12. J. Madden and D. Anderson, *Hey, Wait a Minute, I Wrote a Book* (New York: Ballantine, 1985).
13. P. Schoemaker, "Scenario Planning: A Tool for Strategic Thinking," *Sloan Management Review* (winter 1995) Vol. 37: p. 82.
14. Michael Cowley and Ellen Domb, *Beyond Strategic Vision: Effective Corporate Action with Hoshin Planning* (Boston: Butterworth-Heinemann, 1997), p. 2.

15. David A. Kenyon, "Strategic Planning with the Hoshin Process," *Quality Digest,* May 1997, p. 55.
16. Samuel Torrence and William Montgomery, "Heavy Duty Hoshin Deployment: Real World Applications for Accelerating Strategic Business Breakthrough," *Journal of Innovative Management,* (spring 1997) Vol. 15: 31.
17. Steiner, 1979, p. 294.

Chapter 15

1. ANSI/ASQC Q9004-1-1994.
2. Joseph M. Juran and Frank M. Gryna, eds., *Juran's Quality Control Handbook,* 4th ed. (New York: McGraw-Hill, 1988), p. 6.24.

Chapter 19

1. Robert S. Kaplan and David Norton, "The Balanced Scorecard," *Harvard Business Review,* 1996. (Nov.–Dec.) Vol. 74: p. 86.
2. 1998 Baldrige Criteria, p. 3.

Chapter 20

1. Joseph M. Juran and Frank M. Gryna, eds., *Juran's Quality Control Handbook,* 4th ed. (New York: McGraw-Hill, 1988), p. 5.3.

Part 4

Customer Satisfaction and Focus

Chapter 22

Types of Customers

❖ *This chapter should help you*

◆ Define the term *customer* and identify and describe types of customers in a business process

DEFINING THE CUSTOMER

Virtually all quality management techniques begin with and focus on the customer. The first step in Juran's road map for quality planning, shown in Figure 22.1, is the identification of customers. Correctly identifying customers is essential to quality planning because all activities are based on the fulfillment of customers' needs or requirements. Today, most quality professionals consider the *customer* to be any individual or group that receives and must be satisfied with the work product or output of a process. In other words, the customer is the individual or group whose requirements a process is intended to fulfill. However, this is a fairly narrow definition of the term. Juran and Gryna broadly describe a customer as "anyone who is impacted by the product or process."[1] Clearly, this definition includes more than just those who receive and must be satisfied with the output of a process.

The quality professional should realize that a process and its output touch many people both within and beyond organizational boundaries. These include suppliers, employees, management, government bodies, the community, and so on. Whether or not an organization's definition of customer encompasses all these groups, it is important to recognize that all of them might have requirements to be satisfied.

CUSTOMER TYPES

The first five types of customers discussed in the following sections are identified by Harrington in *Business Process Improvement*.[2] Others have identified and described other categories of customers; three of these customer types are mentioned here. Customers can belong to more than one of these categories.

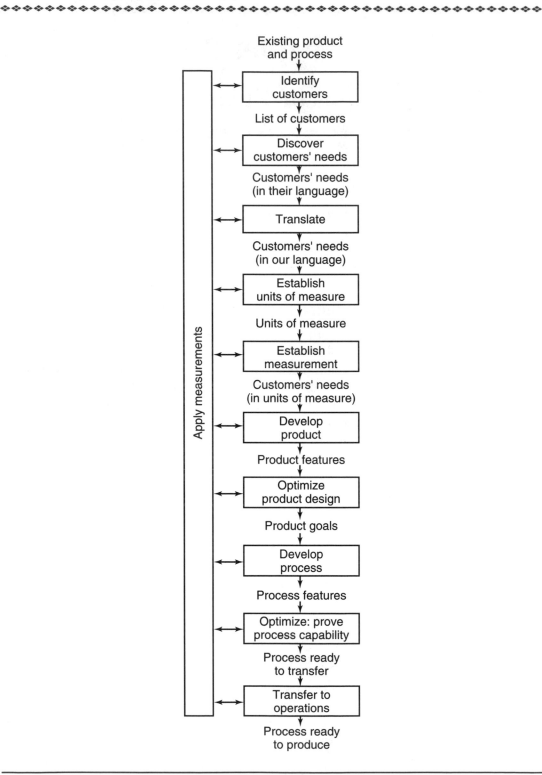

◆ Figure 22.1. Quality planning road map. Source: J.M. Juran and F. Gryna, *Juran's Quality Control Handbook*, 4E (1988), McGraw–Hill. Used with permission.

Primary Customer

The primary customer is the individual or group who directly receives the output of a process. For a bank loan officer, the primary customer is the individual or organization that is requesting a loan. For a test laboratory, it is the individual or department who needs the requested test results in order to make a decision. The primary customer is a major source of product and process requirements.

Secondary Customer

Secondary customers are those individuals or groups from outside of the process boundaries who also receive process output but who are not the reason for the process' existence. For example, a business process that produces invoices for an organization's primary customer might also send copies of those invoices to an internal department for sales reporting. In this case, the internal department is a secondary customer.

Indirect Customer

Like secondary customers, indirect customers are within the organizational boundaries. They do not receive process output directly but are affected if the process output is incorrect or late. The output passes through other steps before leaving the organization. For example, the logistics function within a manufacturing company is not the final user of the production process output, but logistics cannot ensure that shipments will be made on time if the product is late coming from production.

External Customer

External customers are located outside the organizational boundaries and receive the end product or service but might not be the actual user. For example, Baldrige Award winner Zytec makes power suppliers for computers, copiers, and other business machines. Zytec's external customers are companies such as IBM and Kodak. However, these customers are not the final users of the power supply.

Consumer/End User

Consumers, also called end users, are the final users of a product or service. This term describes where a product or service is finally used or consumed. Sometimes the external customer and the end user are the same, but more often products and/or services are delivered to a distributor, representative, or retailer that sells them to the consumer. Figure 22.2 shows five consumer types in an order entry process. Early in the process shown in Figure 22.2, a secondary output (a report generated to balance work loads between manufacturing plants) goes to corporate headquarters, the secondary customer. Final output (a parts order form) goes to purchasing, the primary customer. Manufacturing is an indirect customer that receives the parts to manufacture a television set. Manufacturing's output goes to a distributor of television sets, an external customer. The last customer is the end user who purchases and uses the television set.

❖❖

1. Purchasing (primary)
2. Corporate headquarters (secondary)
3. Manufacturing (indirect)
4. Distributor (external)
5. End user

❖ **Figure 22.2.**   Order entry customer profile. Source: H. James Harrington, *Business Process Improvement* (1991), McGraw–Hill. Used with permission.

Intermediary

An intermediary performs tasks in the steps between production and transfer of a product to the end user, such as transporting vehicles from the manufacturer to the dealer.[3] These tasks are transparent to the consumer or end user.

False Customer

A false customer is an individual or group within a process that performs activities that do not add value to the product or service. Obviously, an objective of process improvement projects is to identify and eliminate as many false customers as possible. Examples of false customers include an inspector who monitors 100 percent of process output because of poor up-front quality planning, a manager who reviews all memos written by all of his or her employees before they can be distributed, and a process or business function that cannot identify its customer.

"If a function or process does not seem to have a real customer, then that function should be reevaluated. The function may be unnecessary, or it may simply be part of a larger process."[4] When a function does not add value, it should be eliminated unless mandated.

Internal Customer

The term *internal customer* has come into popular use to generally refer to individuals or groups within a process who are inside the organizational boundaries. It is used to refer to the idea that everyone who works in a process has a customer and that their objective is to identify and meet their internal customer's requirements. This concept has value in process management; however, some companies have discovered that the term often lessens the focus on the external customer and consumer. To avoid confusion and ensure a customer focus, one company refers to these individuals or groups as "process partners." A company that chooses to use the internal customer label must be sure that all employees recognize that the company's ultimate responsibility is to the external customer, as it is the purpose of the process and the company to serve them.

IMPORTANCE OF IDENTIFYING CUSTOMER TYPES

Identifying and defining customer types is an important part of process management and improvement. Defining a process through documentation and process mapping requires that process owners and improvement teams identify every customer type and source of process and product requirements. Measuring process effectiveness also requires customer input.

Generally, customer satisfaction research is performed among the end users of an organization's products or services. These decision makers might be the same or different people and are usually categorized as primary customers or consumers. However, when an organization performs market research, it should look beyond its current customers. Surveying lost customers, prospective customers, and competitors' customers can also provide useful insights as to what satisfies customers and provide information as to what new or improved products, services, or processes might fulfill a customer's requirements and ultimately result in customer satisfaction. Methods used to gather customer satisfaction data are discussed in Chapter 28.

🏛 Additional Readings 🏛

Deming, W. Edwards. 1986. *Out of the Crisis.* Cambridge: Massachusetts Institute of Technology, Center for Advanced Engineering Study.

Harrington, H. James. 1991. *Business Process Improvement.* New York: McGraw-Hill.

Hradesky, John L. 1995. *Total Quality Management Handbook.* New York: McGraw-Hill.

___, eds. 1988. *Juran's Quality Control Handbook.* 4th ed. New York: McGraw-Hill.

Juran, Joseph M. and Frank M. Gryna. 1993. *Quality Planning and Analysis: From Product Development through Use.* 3rd ed. New York: McGraw-Hill.

Pyzdek, Thomas J. 1996. *The Complete Guide to the CQM.* Tucson, Ariz.: Quality Publishing.

Chapter 23

Elements of Customer-Driven Organizations

❖ *This chapter should help you*

◆ Identify the factors that contribute to customer value

◆ Describe the benefits of a customer-driven organization

◆ List the characteristics common to the strategies of service leaders

◆ Identify barriers to becoming a customer-driven organization

---

Chapter 22 defined several types of customers and described their relationship with one another. This chapter focuses on the most important customer type, the one the organization was created to serve: the primary customer. This customer establishes most product requirements, makes purchasing decisions, and judges product or service quality. The primary customer is almost always an external customer and is frequently the consumer, or end user, of the organization's product or service. As used throughout this chapter, the word *customer* is synonymous with *consumer* or *end user*.

DEFINING CUSTOMER FOCUS

Organizations that recognize the importance of customers and focus on their wants and needs are commonly referred to as being "customer focused" or "customer driven." In business literature, the terms *customer driven* and *market driven* are often used interchangeably. In best-in-class organizations, virtually every activity is undertaken with customers' interests in mind. It is important to note that undertaking "virtually every activity with customers' interests in mind" does not imply that an organization should do so at a financial loss. After all, organizations that are not profitable ultimately cease to do business.

Many of today's sophisticated customers define their requirements in terms of value, a collection of factors that drive their buying decisions. Fredericks and Salter have identified five factors that make up the "customer value package": price, product quality, innovation, service quality, and company image relative to the competition.[1] These factors combine to drive business results, as shown in Figure 23.1. Customer-driven organizations that address the elements of the customer value

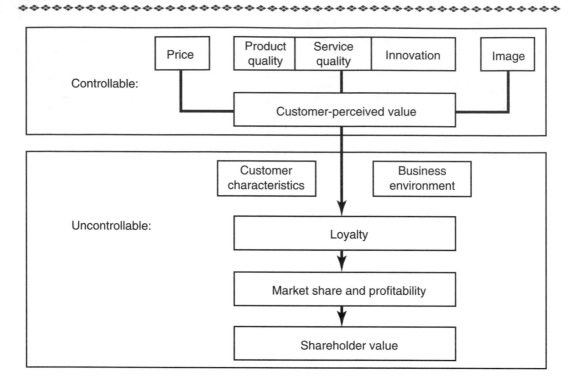

◆ **Figure 23.1.** The customer value package. Reprinted from *Management Review,* May 1995. Copyright © 1995 American Management Association International. Reprinted by permission of American Management Association International, New York, NY. All rights reserved. http://www.amanet.org.

package enjoy significant competitive advantages. Companies such as Amica Insurance, USAA, Nordstrom, L.L. Bean, Lexus, and Ritz-Carlton—all known for their outstanding customer service—enjoy the benefits afforded by greater customer loyalty (discussed in Chapter 30).

CREATING A SERVICE-ORIENTED FRAMEWORK

Figure 23.2 presents a framework for customer service that can be used to develop the key elements of a customer-driven organization. As discussed in the following sections, the framework consists of nurturing service leadership, building a service quality information system, creating a service strategy, and implementing the service strategy.

Nurturing Service Leadership

To achieve a customer service culture, an organization requires senior management's commitment, leadership, and support. In *On Great Service,* Berry identifies the following characteristics of service leaders:

◆ *Service vision:* Service leaders view excellent service as the driving force of the business.

◆ *Belief in others:* Service leaders believe in the fundamental capacity of people to achieve and view their own role as setting a standard of excellence, providing

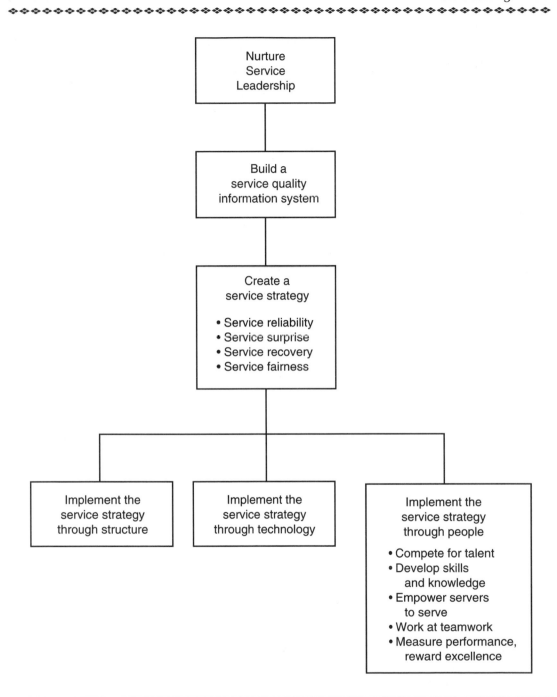

◆ **Figure 23.2.**   Framework for customer service. Reprinted with permission of The Free Press, a Division of Simon and Schuster, Inc. from *On Great Service: A Framework for Action* by Leonard Berry. Copyright © 1995 by Leonard Berry.

the tools needed for success, and encouraging leadership behavior throughout the organization.

◆ *Love of the business:* Service leaders would rather be running the business than doing anything else. They have deep feelings about operating the business well.

◆ *Integrity:* Service leaders do the right thing—even when inconvenient or expensive. They place a premium on being fair, consistent, and truthful with customers, employees, suppliers, and other stakeholders, thereby earning the opportunity to lead.[2]

Successful leaders communicate and reinforce the values by which their organizations function. Albrecht has identified six basic values, or abiding principles, that have emerged as hallmarks in fostering customer-focused, quality-committed cultures. The following values are imparted by strong service leaders:

◆ *Spirit of service:* a general attitude and set of beliefs, shared by all levels of the organization, that serving others is an important thing to do

◆ *Shared fate:* a group loyalty and cooperation that is inseparably intertwined with individual, coworker, and corporate success

◆ *Codetermination:* a searching together for solutions to organizational problems by leaders and employees alike, viewing change management as a matter of cooperatively inducing change

◆ *Mutuality:* recognizing that throughout the entire supply chain, everyone has a customer

◆ *Empowerment:* providing employees the tools (training, education, and information) that they need to make decisions and take actions that will improve their work and add value for the customer

◆ *Creative dissatisfaction:* an attitude of not being satisfied with the status quo and encouragement to think outside the box, which reflects the idea that there is a better way to do something[3]

Building a Service Quality Information System

Customer information is another cornerstone of the committed customer-driven organization. These organizations create "service quality information systems" that use *"multiple research approaches to systematically capture and disseminate service quality information to support decision making."*[4]

A service quality information system must do the following:

◆ encourage and enable management to incorporate "the voice of the customer" (discussed in Chapter 24) into decision making

◆ reveal customers' service priorities

◆ identify service improvement priorities and guide resource allocation decisions

◆ allow the tracking of company and competitor service performance over time

◆ disclose the impact of service quality initiatives and investments

◆ offer performance-based data to reward excellent service and correct poor service[5]

Creating a Service Strategy

Successful service strategies have several key characteristics: the role of quality service is central; they offer customers genuine value, giving customers more for the costs they incur; and they foster genuine achievement in the organization.[6]

To identify a specific service strategy, ask the following questions:

What attributes of service are—and will continue to be—most important to our target markets?

On which important service attributes is the competition weakest?

What are the existing and potential service capabilities of our company?[7]

The answers to these questions can be used to perform an *opportunity analysis*. The results of the analysis will provide the foundation for a service strategy that will meet customer expectations, exploit competitor weaknesses, and fit the organization's potential. They will also provide the basis for service standards and performance measurements that reflect customers' expectations in terms that all employees can understand.

Implementing the Service Strategy

After the service strategy has been developed and accepted by senior management, the next step is implementation. Three elements to be considered in implementing the strategy are structure (or organization), technology, and people.

Structure. Traditional organizational structures, such as the hierarchical structure based on functional units or departments, frequently do not support the customer-focused company and make it difficult to achieve world-class customer service. Senior management often measures departments in these organizations in ways that do not reflect the desired behavior. For example, the sales department might be asked to focus on customer satisfaction, which requires spending sufficient time with each customer to address their specific needs. However, the department might actually be measured and rewarded on the basis of the number of calls handled per day.

The first step in implementing a service strategy is establishing common, customer-focused measurements that encourage everyone to keep customers' interests in mind. The next step is to use a process management approach that ensures that business processes are designed, measured, and improved on the basis of the needs of primary customers.

Some organizations have successfully used a figurative "inverted pyramid"[8] structure to communicate the idea of customor focus. In this structure, the customer is shown to be on top of the organizatmon. The next level includes the people who work with or support the customer. Senior management's place at the bottom of the pyramid demonstrates that it is senior management's responsibility to provide resources and support to those who support the primary customer.

Having the right organizational structure facilitates the following elements of an effective service strategy:

◆ cultural leadership for continuous service improvement

◆ guidance and coordination of service improvement initiatives

◆ technical expertise and resources to support service improvement

◆ solutions or recommendations concerning specific service quality issues

◆ service delivery that meets or exceeds customers' expectations day in and day out

◆ excellent recovery when the original service fails customers[9]

Technology. The rapid development and availability of sophisticated technology continues to provide an array of new tools and techniques at an ever-expanding rate. Many customers use tools such as the Internet to gain immediate access to product catalogs, on-order and account status, and customer service information. Conversely, on-line databases contain and make available detailed customer information for sales and customer service representatives who might use this information for product development, complaint tracking, and financial analysis.

These applications and many others can be a part of a service strategy in a customer-focused organization. However, technology is not a panacea and should be implemented with forethought and planning. In using technology to improve service, Berry suggests six basic guidelines:

1. *Take a holistic approach.* Technology investments are strategic. Management needs not only a technology strategy to facilitate the service strategy, but also a behavior-changing strategy to implement the technology.

2. *Automate efficient systems.* Superimposing new technology on inefficient, outmoded systems will almost always lead to disappointing results.

3. *Solve a genuine problem.* Why should the customer undergo the effort of learning to use new technology, plus risk the possibility of poor results, without the promise of tangible benefits?

4. *Offer more—not less—control.* Technology should be the servant, not the master. It should give its users more control in accomplishing what they want to accomplish, not less.

5. *Optimize basic technologies.* Executives aspiring to use technology to improve service quality need to make sure that low-tech materials, methods, and machines work and that they are well integrated with newer, more advanced technologies.

6. *Combine high tech with high touch.* Firms need to "act small." Rather than referring to size, this refers to an organization's willingness and ability to personalize and customize service and to deliver it promptly and with a minimum of bureaucratic fumbling.[10]

Through People. For an organization to successfully provide service quality, it must have the human resources available for the task. People, not companies, provide service.

To meet the goals of the service strategy through people, a company must (1) compete for and get the best talent available, (2) develop service skills and knowledge in the workforce, (3) empower the servers to serve, (4) work at teamwork, and (5) measure performance and reward excellence.[11]

BARRIERS TO BECOMING A CUSTOMER-DRIVEN ORGANIZATION

The primary barrier to becoming a successful customer-driven organization is the absence of commitment by senior management. It is impossible for an organization to make the changes necessary to achieve customer focus and implement a service strategy without senior managements commitment, leadership, and support described at the beginning of this chapter,

Organizations without senior management commitment to customer focus will display symptoms such as the following:

◆ Products are designed without a clear understanding of customer requirements, especially in the areas of reliability and serviceability.

◆ Customer-oriented measurements are absent.

◆ The organization's various functions do not work together to support customer focus.

◆ Technology is used to reduce costs at the expense of customer service.

◆ The organization's infrastructure does not support resolution of customer service issues.

◆ Customer complaints are resolved with quick fixes rather than long-term process improvements.

◆ Customer contact is impersonal.

Today, some quality managers still find themselves in organizations that are not and have not made a commitment to become customer driven. However, when organizational leaders recognize the benefits and competitive advantage of being customer driven, they frequently look to their quality managers and professionals for help in overcoming the barriers. Many quality managers have made a significant contribution to their organizations in this way.

Even if a company-wide commitment to being customer driven does not exist, the quality manager can still be a role model for being customer driven. He or she could begin by meeting with internal and external customers to get feedback on how the quality department is currently meeting customers' needs. The department would then establish customer-oriented measurements and a process for gathering ongoing customer feedback on how well requirements are being met. These topics are discussed in Chapters 24 and 28.

❖❖

🏠 Additional Readings 🏠

Albrecht, Karl. 1998. *At America's Service.* Homewood, Ill.: Dow Jones/Irwin.

———. 1995. *Delivering Customer Value.* Portland, Ore.: Productivity Press.

Berry, Leonard L. 1995. *On Great Service.* New York: The Free Press.

Edosomwan, Johnson A. 1993. *Customer and Market-Driven Quality Management.* Milwaukee: ASQC Quality Press.

Fredericks, Joan O., and James M. Salter II. 1995. "Beyond Customer Satisfaction." *Management Review,* May, pp. 29–32.

Kotler, Philip. 1991. *Marketing Management: Analysis, Planning, Implementation, and Control.* Englewood Cliffs, N.J.: Prentice Hall.

Chapter 24

Customer Expectations, Priorities, Needs, and "Voice"

❖ *This chapter should help you*

- ◆ List and describe the elements of a customer satisfaction strategy
- ◆ Understand what is meant by listening to the voice of the customer
- ◆ Describe the Kano model and give an example of each element
- ◆ Understand and describe the structure of quality function deployment

---

DETERMINING CUSTOMER SATISFACTION LEVELS

Many leading companies, including IBM and Xerox, have measured and tracked customer satisfaction levels for decades. Results can be used to identify problems and opportunities, measure the performance of managers and executives, and reveal relative competitive performance. These leading companies have also integrated findings (e.g., obtained through customer surveys) into their corporate strategies, new product development, manufacturing quality, product and service delivery, and competitive positioning. They make marketing decisions on the basis of statistical analysis that shows what factors are most important in their customers' buying decisions.

Customer satisfaction measurement has also become an integral part of the quality management process as companies use customer satisfaction survey results to drive improvement initiatives. Customer satisfaction levels are impossible to assess unless customers' expectations, priorities, and needs have been determined. This is known as listening to the voice of the customer. A system for utilizing customer feedback is shown in Figure 24.1. Leading-edge customer satisfaction systems include several key elements. First, they have formal processes for collecting and analyzing customer data and for communicating results to the appropriate business functions for action. Data can be used for company or market segment analysis to develop marketing strategies or used at the account level to gain an understanding of that customer's opinion of the company. To be useful, data must be stored appropriately and made available to those who need it.

Every organization benefits from a better understanding of customer requirements. Feedback on how well an organization is meeting those requirements is gathered by using some combination of the methods (e.g., surveys and focus groups)

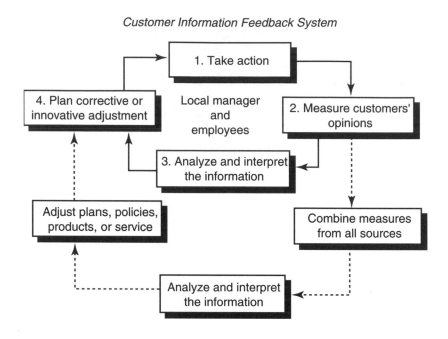

◆ Figure 24.1. System for utilizing customer feedback. Source: *Cornell Hotel and Restaurant Administration Quarterly,* Arthur J. Daltas, "Protecting Service Markets with Consumer Feedback," May 1977. Used with permission.

listed and described in Chapter 28. Most companies use several formal methods for collecting customer satisfaction data. By using several sources, they are better able to validate results and increase their credibility within the organization. Because each method of gathering customer feedback has its benefits, disadvantages, and specific applications, most companies choose a combination of methods to get a complete picture. Once information has been gathered, sophisticated techniques can be used to analyze the information.

ANALYZING CUSTOMER SATISFACTION DATA

Several methods are used to analyze customer satisfaction data. Two commonly used methods, the Kano model and quality function deployment, are described here.

The Kano Model

The Kano model, shown in Figure 24.2, was developed by Naritaki Kano to show the relationship between three types of product characteristics, or "qualities." These include qualities that "must be" present, those that are "one-dimensional," and those that are "delighters."

The presence or absence of must-be characteristics is shown by the curved line in the lower-right quadrant. When a must-be characteristic is not present or is not present in sufficient quantity, dissatisfaction exists. As the characteristic becomes more available or of a higher quality, customer satisfaction increases, but only to a neutral state. In other words, the factor can only satisfy, not delight, the customer.

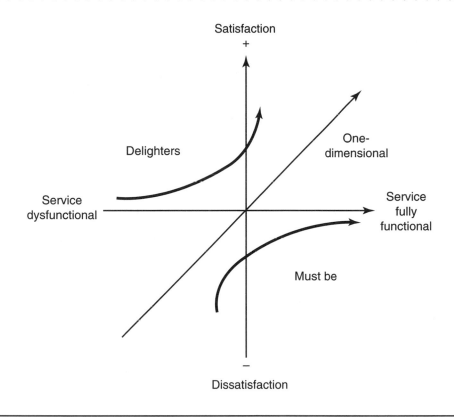

Satisfaction
+

Delighters

One-
dimensional

Service
dysfunctional

Service
fully
functional

Must be

–

Dissatisfaction

◆ **Figure 24.2.**   The Kano model.

One-dimensional factors drive satisfaction in direct relationship to their presence, and thus they are represented by a straight line. For example, as the interest rate on a savings account rises, so does satisfaction.

The curved line in the upper left to center area represents delighters. If absent, these factors have no impact on satisfaction. However, when present, these features delight the customer. An example would be automobile cup holders. When first introduced, cup holders were delighters. This example also demonstrates an important point about delighters. As they become more available, they tend to move from the upper-left side of the model to the lower left. Today, an automobile without cup holders would not be well received in the market. Cup holders have become a must-be feature.

Quality Function Deployment

Quality function deployment (QFD) is a technique that is used to translate a customer's requirements into internal processes by graphically showing the linkages between the two. The data obtained from customer listening surveys and customer focus groups can be used as the starting point for the customer requirements, or "what needs to be done," part of the matrix. The "how things are done" part of the matrix comes from the processes, systems, or other technical descriptions that are

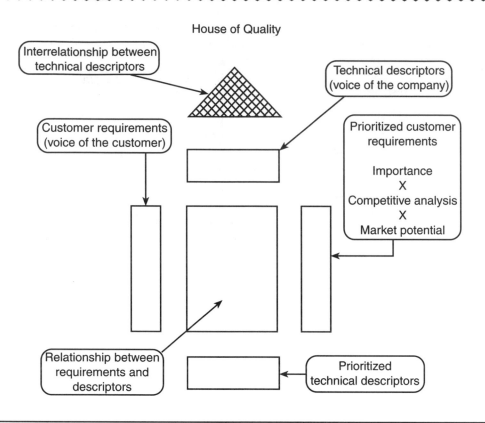

❖ **Figure 24.3.** QFD process matrix. Source: James Bossert, *Quality Function Deployment,* Copyright © 1991 ASQC Quality Press. Used with permission.

used within the company to meet customer needs. Where the rows and columns of this matrix meet, relationship codes can be inserted. Usually, these codes are classified as (1) strongly related, (2) moderately related, (3) weakly related, or (4) by default, which means that no relationship exists between the customer requirements and the company descriptors.

The QFD process matrix, shown in Figure 24.3 graphically depicts the relationship between the voice of the customer and the voice of the company. If desired, the customer requirements can be prioritized by importance, competitive analysis, and market potential by adding an additional matrix to the right-hand side of the QFD matrix. The company descriptors can also be prioritized by importance, target values, and competitive evaluation by adding another matrix to the bottom of the QFD matrix. The "house of quality" is completed by adding a "roof," which is a matrix to correlate the interrelationship between company descriptors. Usually, the same codes are used in both the roof and the body of the matrix to show the strength of relationships. The completed QFD matrix indicates which activities for problem solving or continuous improvement should be given the highest priority. This graphical representation helps management and personnel involved in an improvement effort understand how an improvement will affect customer satisfaction and helps prevent deviations from that objective. Although the QFD process was developed to prioritize design processes, it can be used very effectively for other process-related systems.

Customer listening techniques that use objective and valid statistical methods will provide information for the QFD analysis with a minimum possibility of invalid conclusions. Quality function deployment has been used to develop products that delight the customer by providing features that were beyond their stated requirements. In many cases, the customer did not know that these options were possible, so they were not on his or her list of needs or priorities. By comparing the customer's requirements to product and service features the company typically focuses on and identifying and prioritizing the agreements and gaps, innovative new offerings are more likely to become apparent. These can provide a greater probability of moving the company into the delighting-quality level. Including an analysis of where the competition is in the process can also identify opportunities for significant improvement.

Additional Readings

Akao, Y., ed. 1990. *Quality Function Deployment: Integrating Customer Requirements into Product Design.* Cambridge, Mass.: Productivity Press.

Bossert, James L. 1991. *Quality Function Deployment—Practitioner's Approach.* Milwaukee: ASQC Quality Press.

Hayes, Bob E. 1997. *Measuring Customer Satisfaction: Survey Design, Use, and Statistical Analysis Methods.* 2nd ed. Milwaukee: ASQ Quality Press.

Hinton, Tom, and Wini Schaeffer. 1994. *Customer-Focused Quality: What to Do on Monday Morning.* Milwaukee: ASQC Quality Press.

King, B. 1987. *Better Designs in Half the Time: Implementing QFD in America.* Menthuen, Mass.: Goal/QPC.

McRobb, R. M. 1982. "Customer-Perceived Quality Levels." *In ASQC Quality Congress Transactions.* Milwaukee: ASQC Quality Press, pp. 428–32.

Sheridan, B. M. 1993. *Policy Deployment: The TQM Approach to Long-Range Planning.* Milwaukee: ASQC Quality Press.

Stamatis, D. H. 1997. *TQM Engineering Handbook.* New York: Marcel Dekker.

Chapter 25

Customer Relationship Management and Commitment

❖ *This chapter should help you*

◆ Understand the key principles of relationship management, including when the practice makes the most sense

◆ Learn the major benefits of practicing customer relationship management

---

MANAGING CUSTOMER RELATIONSHIPS

Customer relationships, in their most advanced form, become customer–supplier partnerships or alliances (see Chapter 27). Although partnerships or alliances are not always the ultimate objective of a customer relationship, an effective relationship exists when a customer has a strong preference for a particular supplier. This might be based on any of a number of factors, such as performance history or experience, responsiveness, flexibility, trust, and other aspects that lead to value for the customer. The practice of customer relationship management is most appropriate with those customers who can most affect a company's future (see Chapter 26).

Customer relationship management, a relatively new way of thinking about marketing and doing business, is one of the major advancements in business disciplines in the 1990s. Maintaining satisfactory relationships with customers requires the commitment of both management and the entire workforce. Also referred to as *relationship marketing* or *one-to-one marketing*, customer relationship management is a concept profoundly influenced by Regis McKenna, Don Peppers, and Martha Rogers.[1]

McKenna offers the following perspective on the topic: "Differentiation, from the customer's viewpoint, is not something that is product or service related as much as it is related to the way you do business. In the age of information, it is no longer possible to manufacture an image. The distinction between perception and reality is getting finer. Further, in a world where customers have so many choices they can be fickle. This means modern marketing is a battle for customer loyalty. Positioning must involve more than simple awareness of a hierarchy of brands and company names. It demands a special relationship with the customer and infrastructure of the marketplace."[2]

In what is certain to become a landmark reference, Peppers, Rogers, and Dorf define the concept of customer relationship management as "being willing and able to change your behavior toward an individual customer based on what the customer tells you and what else you know about the customer."[3] This chapter emphasizes a number of ideas from these authors regarding the benefits, implementation practices, and barriers related to this evolving discipline.

Customer-focus teams improve the ability of an organization to execute the strategies of customer relationship management. Often these teams provide a point of focus for customers that cuts across different functions. Typical team composition includes an account manager, customer service representative, field engineer/tech support, and plant advocates. The purpose of the customer-focus team is to provide a near-seamless interface in the customer relationship. Further, it ensures that all the key stakeholders in the supplying organization are in alignment in strategy and actions on behalf of the customer.[4]

Complaint handling is one aspect of managing relationships with customers. Empirical data from *Consumer Complaint Handling in America—an Update Study* shows the importance of effective complaint handling systems. The data show the importance of making it easy and convenient for customers to complain when they experience problems and for complaint handling to be effective and efficient as well. For example, for a product costing over $100, the research results show that 9.5 percent of noncomplainants experiencing problems would repurchase. Repurchase intent increases to 19 percent for complainants whose issues are unresolved and jumps to 54.3 percent when complaints were resolved satisfactorily.[5] Additional research by the U.S. Office of Consumer Affairs/Technical Assistance Research Programs (TARP) shows that the speed of complaint resolution also affects repurchase intent, which is significantly higher when resolution is achieved quickly. John Goodman and TARP have helped shed light on how effective complaint handling affects customer loyalty as manifested in repeat purchases.

The discipline of customer relationship management forces an organization to reevaluate its methods of measuring the satisfaction of the targets of its initiatives. Satisfaction surveys conducted only with purchasing customers can be too limited in these enhanced business relationships. The nature of the customer–supplier interface will be dramatically expanded from the traditional seller/purchaser relationship to include cross-functional teams from both organizations. As a result, surveys will increasingly need to examine the needs of a cross section of stakeholders from the customer's organization. In addition, organizations will be increasingly likely to implement internal satisfaction measurement systems, using in-person surveys as a vehicle to improve communications and customer satisfaction and to strengthen relationships with core customers.[6]

Entering into the discipline of customer relationship management has profound implications and is not something that happens by accident. Rather, it is a conscious and even strategic act that requires the commitment not only of leadership but also of the entire organization. An organization must consider how quickly and extensively to embark in the area of customer relationship management. Some organizations enter into this practice on a very limited scale (e.g., by starting with one key customer) and expand as they are able. Others take a more radical approach by positioning themselves for enterprise-wide programs. Peppers, Rogers, and Dorf suggest starting with a small initiative and evaluating initial gains before deciding how heavily to invest in the practice. These authors offer a readiness assessment tool, called the One-to-One Gap Tool, to evaluate processes, technology, knowledge strategy, partnerships, customer relationships, employee management, and competitive strategy. The tool is used to conduct an internal assessment and compare it with a similar assessment from a representative group of customers. These results will bring to attention the gaps that have the most impact on a company's migration to a culture of one-to-one marketing (their term for customer relationship management).

FRAMEWORK FOR IMPLEMENTING CUSTOMER RELATIONSHIP MANAGEMENT

Peppers, Rogers, and Dorf suggest the following framework for success in implementing one-to-one marketing.[7] The four key steps of their framework are listed here.

Identify Candidates

This step includes recognizing which customers are candidates for a one-on-one marketing program as well as having current information on customer needs/requirements and the systems in place to document, retrieve, and analyze customer information.

Differentiate between Customers

This step entails several activities, including identifying the organization's key customers, that is, high-volume customers or those a high level of impact on the firm's current or future profitability. Customers who are unprofitable because of the amount of rework required, low profit margins, or other factors should be deemphasized. Orders from important customers who have had problems in the past should be closely guarded ("babysat"), possibly by adding a quality assurance professional to the relationship team. Customers whose orders have dropped by 50 percent or more in the past year should be contacted so that the reasons for the decline can be ascertained. Once customers have been classified as listed here or into similar categories, they can be ranked by priority into A, B, and C groupings, with activities being emphasized for A customers and deemphasized for C customers.

Interact with Key Customers

This step involves initiating more extensive dialogue with key customers. Examples include personalized written communications, multilevel officer-to-officer contact between organizations, and offering lost key customers a reason to return. Internal service levels should be evaluated and compared to those of competitors. If a voice response unit (VRU) is used for customer service, recordings must be friendly and helpful and should ensure that customers can move through the system in a quick and direct manner. The transaction paper trail through the organization can be studied to determine ways to reduce cycle times and responsiveness to customers. Improved complaint handling practices, combined with the use of technology, should ensure that customers find it easy and desirable to continue to do business with you.

Customize the System

To determine customers' unique requirements, the organization can ask its top 10 customers what improvements should be made and then act on the suggestions. Customers should be asked to specify the best ways to communicate under different settings and the desired frequency for sales calls and technical briefings. Customized customer relation systems supported by management add value for customers but still offer standardization in delivery (e.g., specialty catalogs based on lifestyle or sales force organized by industry).

CUSTOMER RELATIONSHIP MANAGEMENT: MAKING THE TRANSITION

The future success of companies such as Amazon.com, Dell, and American Express will continue to build on the direct customer interaction that has been a hallmark since their inception. Customer relationship management is strategically compatible for these businesses, given their existing emphasis on customer relationships.

3M, Hewlett-Packard, and Wells Fargo are established companies that have benefited from creating stronger, more interactive customer relationships. The transition from their old cultures toward one of true customer relationship management has been deliberate, as an organization cannot commit to customer relationship management while continuing to run business the same as always. It is difficult for a company to overcome many obstacles at once, so transition strategies often must be implemented piece by piece, business unit by business unit. However, the potential rewards for establishing an effective customer relationship management program are highly worthwhile and often provide numerous and significant competitive advantages.

Section 3.2 of the 1999 Baldrige Award criteria outlines several areas that can be used to assess how well an organization builds relationships to retain current business and develop new opportunities. The criteria questions include the following:

1. How do you determine key access mechanisms to facilitate the ability of customers to conduct business, seek assistance and information, and make complaints?

2. How do you determine key customer contact requirements and deploy these requirements to all employees involved in the response chain?

3. What is your complaint management process? How do you ensure that complaints are resolved effectively and promptly and that all complaints received are aggregated and analyzed for use in overall organizational improvement?

4. How do you build relationships with customers for repeat business and/or positive referral?

5. How do you keep your approaches to customer access and relationships current with business needs and directions?

Organizations might find it helpful to perform a self-assessment against the Baldrige criteria to see where efforts to create effective customer relationships should focus. Organizations that are successful in adopting the innovative practice of customer relationship management are most likely to achieve performance breakthroughs with their customers.

BENEFITS OF EFFECTIVE CUSTOMER RELATIONSHIP MANAGEMENT

Some of the many benefits to adopting and implementing effective customer relationship management practices are summarized here.

Creation of Learning Relationships

An organization should establish learning relationships with each customer, starting with those who are considered most valuable.[9] In a learning relationship, the customer and supplier become intertwined over time. The supplier learns to meet and exceed a customer's expectations far better than a competitor could hope to. A competitor would have many lessons to learn before the customer would enjoy the same levels of service and convenience that an established supplier provides.

Increased Cross-Selling

An organization practicing effective customer relationship management should expect gains in increased product-line purchases (more products per customers) as well as higher unit margins. The opportunity for up-selling (i.e., getting customers to purchase more expensive or higher-value products and services) might also be present.

Reduced Customer Attrition

A major benefit of customer relationship management is increased customer loyalty. Measuring retention levels with both one-to-one marketing customers and traditional customers can provide the economic evidence needed to accelerate the organization's transition to a culture that supports customer relationship management.

Higher Customer Satisfaction Levels

Implementing and monitoring customer satisfaction measures for both traditional and one-to-one marketing customers will help justify future one-to-one marketing efforts. Traditional measures (e.g., overall satisfaction) as well as more insightful metrics for willingness to recommend, performance versus competing suppliers, and other indicators of loyalty should be included.

Reduced Transaction Costs and Faster Cycle Times

Increased convenience for the customer is a key goal of customer relationship management. Over time, customers need to specify less and less information for the supplier to meet their requirements. The result is that the transaction becomes more efficient, costs less, and takes less time.

❖❖

COMMON MISTAKES AND BARRIERS TO SUCCESS IN CUSTOMER RELATIONSHIP MANAGEMENT

The following mistakes or barriers can hinder attempts at effective customer relationship management.

All Customers Seen as Equal

Some companies feel honor-bound to deliver the same standards of service to every customer. Unfortunately, this has the unintended consequence of diluting effectiveness for the most important, or key, customers. When a key customer experiences a service failure, that customer might choose to switch to a competitor's products or services. The financial impact of losing a key customer can be substantial and often justifies the creation of discriminating standards based on the customer's value. The creation of a key account selling system is one way to avoid this limiting mind-set.

Information Technology Systems Insufficient

Full relationship deployment presumes the ability to manage a wide range of information about customers. This information likely will include past sales transactions, volume, profitability, customer satisfaction results, profiles of product and service requirements, complaint/inquiry histories, and so on. The efficient management of this type of information is fostered by effective information technology (IT) systems, a capability that many organizations lack. To successfully gather, use, and store this information, a company might need to invest in a data mart or data warehouse.

Lack of Cross-Functional Alignment

An organization will find it easier to manage customer relationships if it is proficient in using adhoc cross-functional teams and if it is accustomed to looking at service processes from the customer's vantage point.

"Ownership" of a Customer

If multiple business units and functions have contact with a customer's organization, where does the ultimate decision-making ability and accountability lie? All stakeholders should be in alignment and working together to create customer satisfaction.

Excessive Customization

An obvious concern exists when organizations attempt to become all things to all people. Organizations should limit themselves within the strategic advantages of their core competencies and deliver products and services in ways that benefit key customers in particular. Failure to focus on key customers will lead an organization to spend too much time pursuing business that is likely to be ultimately classified as low volume, unprofitable, or nonpurchaser.

🏮 Additional Readings 🏮

Israel, Jeff T. 1997. "Feedback to Improve Core Customer Relationships: A Framework to Implement Face-to-Face Surveys." *ASQC 52nd Annual Quality Congress Transactions.*

The Malcolm Baldrige National Quality Award: 1999 Criteria for Performance Excellence. Gaithersburg, Md.: National Institute of Standards and Technology.

McKenna, Regis. 1991. *Relationship Marketing: Successful Strategies for the Age of the Customer.* New York: Addison-Wesley.

Peppers, Don, Martha Rogers, and Bob Dorf. 1999. "Is Your Company Ready for One-to-One Marketing?" *Harvard Business Review* (January–February).

Pine, B. Joseph II, Don Peppers, Martha Rogers, and Bob Dorf. 1995. "Do You Want to Keep Your Customers Forever?" *Harvard Business Review* (March–April).

U.S. Office of Consumer Affairs/Technical Assistance Research Programs. 1986. *Consumer Complaint Handling in America: An Update Study, Part II.* Washington, D.C.: U.S. Department of Consumer Affairs, March 31.

Chapter 26

Customer Identification and Segmentation

❖ *This chapter should help you*

- ◆ Understand how key customers are identified
- ◆ Understand how the concept of market segmentation is used to help organizations realize more efficient returns on their resources
- ◆ Become familiar with common segmentation concepts and patterns
- ◆ Understand how companies choose a segmentation strategy

One key legacy of the industrial age was the trend of mass production. Henry Ford has often been credited with saying the following about the people waiting to buy his company's Model T's: "They can have any color car they want, so long as it's black." In reality, not every customer would have chosen to purchase a black car, but this was the only choice, given Ford's initial concept of mass production. For many decades the idea of mass production was associated with the concept of mass markets.

Market segmentation has its roots in the "marketing concept," generally attributed to Philip Kotler. The basic premise of the marketing concept is that a company should determine what consumers need and want, and then try to satisfy those wants and needs, provided that (1) doing so is consistent with the company's strategy and (2) the expected rate of return meets company objectives."[1] By encouraging organizations to structure products and services around customer needs and wants rather than being driven strictly by technological capability, this idea has helped organizations move from a product-driven approach toward a market- or customer-driven emphasis.

In *The Third Wave*, Alvin and Heidi Toffler offer clues on trends relating to mass production, mass markets, and the changing workplace. They coined the term *demassification* to describe these changes, including a trend where organizations' homogenous customer groups begin to splinter into many groups with unique needs and expectations.[2] In his keynote address at the 50th Annual Quality Congress in 1996, Alvin Toffler used the term *mass customization* to further characterize this trend, suggesting that nearly every customer has unique requirements that product and service providers need to address on a customer-by-customer basis.

❖❖

The implication of such a trend is staggering for most organizations, especially in view of their current practices to serve their customers. Organizations that surpass competitors in serving key market segments should find themselves in a commanding position in the marketplace. The challenge to an organization is to clearly know its customers and their unique requirements and expectations.

"The biggest single barrier to the development of an effective corporate strategy is the strongly held belief that a company has to appeal to the entire market."[3] Organizations can often realize more efficient returns on their marketing resources when they narrow the scope of their focus. This chapter discusses some of the ways to identify and segment particular customers or markets.

Identifying Customers

The identification of customers is straightforward for some organizations and very difficult in others. When the supplier and customer have a direct relationship, identifying customers and their requirements is a relatively simple task. For example, new car dealers have detailed information on the purchasers of new cars and frequently provide postpurchase service and support for some time after a sale. However, when the supplier and end user never come into direct contact, it is much more difficult for the product or service provider to identify the customer and his or her unique needs. For example, manufacturers of consumer products distributed through various retail outlets rarely have detailed information about their end users unless these customers return warranty registration cards or respond to special offers. In either case, the product or service provider might understand the requirements of the key customer segment(s) served, but knowing the actual identity of the customer (as in the case of the automobile dealership) enables the provider to collect information and make special offers to that customer.

An organization must be able to meet or exceed the needs of key customers or customer groups. If product features and service delivery processes are designed to satisfy needs and expectations of one homogeneous group, some customer groups will be satisfied; however, many other groups might experience failed expectations. An organization that fails to explore the ways in which customer needs or wants vary across market segments misses an opportunity to maximize customer satisfaction in segments vital to the organization's well-being. Scarce service delivery resources might be allocated in a manner that maximizes satisfaction among the key business segments once the needs and expectations of core customer groups are determined.

Core/Key Customers

Core, or key, customers typically are those customers most vital to the organization's economic success. These can be high-volume customers, customers from selected industries, customers with the greatest impact on the organization's profitability, or customers deemed most likely to have significant impact on the firm's future viability.

A company can identify its core customers by doing a detailed analysis of their performance financially as well as by putting together a possible scenario for the future to decide whether they really are key customers. As discussed in Chapter 27, core customers are often willing and eager to enter into partnerships or other forms of strategic alliances with a business so that both companies can grow and be more profitable.

Non-Core Customers

Non-core customers might or might not have unique requirements from those of core customers. Whether an organization chooses to serve these customers should be contingent on an evaluation of the cost of service versus the economic benefit. Cost of service can vary, depending on whether the same service delivery process (resources) is used for both core and non-core customer segments, and on whether the non-core segment requires or justifies its own service delivery system.

Potential Customers

Potential customers are not currently on the customer list but could use the product or service offered. A strategy to reach this group needs to be developed and implemented as the business grows.

SEGMENTING CUSTOMERS

The term *market segments* refers to the concept that there are groups of potential customers sharing particular wants or needs (rather than simply one large gelatinous market) and that these groups are objectively identifiable.[4] In contrast to customer service segmentation, which focuses on what customers expect, market segmentation focuses on what various people and organizations need.[5]

Segmentation Variables

Many variables or differentiating factors can be considered in creating customer or market segments. Examples follow for some commonly used variables.

Purchase Volume. With volume segmentation, some organizations split their customer base into two or more groupings on the basis of volume. High-volume customers are often thought of as core customers and might account for only 20 percent of the customer base but as much as 80 percent of the total business volume.

Profitability. Profitability segmentation can yield different results than volume segmentation. The key distinction is that the criteria would be based on customer profit contribution rather than on sales revenue.

Industry. One common basis of segmentation in business-to-business markets is the North American Industrial Classification System (NAICS), formerly known as the Standard Industrial Classification (SIC). Organizations often discover that customers from different industries have unique requirements that determine the value they receive from products and services. For example, customers in the energy utility business might differ from customers in high-technology manufacturing in terms of their requirements for telecommunications services. The implication might lead a telecommunications organization to offer different products or services to each or at least to market an identical product differently to address different requirements.

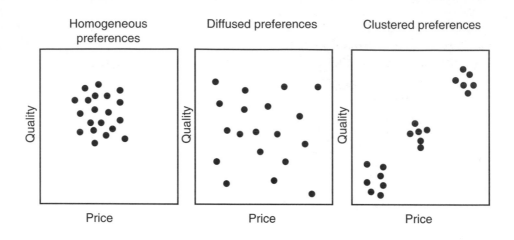

◆ **Figure 26.1.** Segmentation concepts. Source: Quality Publishing. Used with permission.

Geographic. Often customers and markets are segmented geographically, but usually this is a method of allocating resources (e.g., sales and field support) to a region rather than being driven by unique customer requirements.

Demographic. Examples of demographic-based segments could include groupings based on any combination of factors, such as age, income, marital status, education, and gender. Sometimes demographic characteristics are combined. For example, family life cycle usually combines head-of-household age, marital status, and a factor indicating both the presence and the ages of children living at home to determine a resulting segment. Some of the unique resulting segments include single adult head of household, young marrieds (no children), households with young children, households with teenagers, empty nest (working age but children have left home), and golden years (retired). Marketers have long used these kinds of segments to identify and characterize key target markets. Certain products (e.g., diapers and educational software) appeal to or are best suited for one life cycle segment or another.

Psychographic. Psychographic segmentation leads to groupings based on values, attitudes, and beliefs. Insurance marketers might want to target consumers with a balanced, healthy lifestyle as manifested by attitudes. For example, a key target segment might include individuals who believe that smoking is unhealthy and that a good diet, a regular exercise regimen, and getting plenty of rest are all important.

Segmentation Concepts

Marketers must study characteristics of customers within a selected group (cluster) by using specific or multiple variables.[6] Target market segments can be formed on the basis of the following key segmentation concepts, shown in Figure 26.2.

No Segmentation. In Figure 26.2a the customers are completely undifferentiated; that is, all customers are perceived as having the same expectations. Uniform quality is the goal, and mass marketing is used.

A. No market segmentation

B. Complete market segmentation

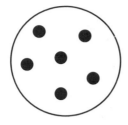

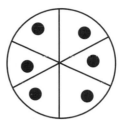

C. Segmented by income classes 1, 2, and 3

D. Segmented by age classes A and B

E. Segmented by income-age class

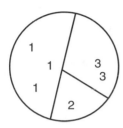

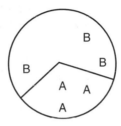

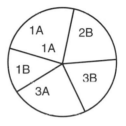

◆ **Figure 26.2.**   Preference segment patterns. Source: Quality Publishing. Used with permission.

Complete Market Segmentation. Each customer in Figure 26.2b has a unique set of requirements. The quality requirements are set by each customer's individual demands, and customized marketing is used.

Segmentation by a Single Criterion. Figure 26.2d shows segmentation based on a single differentiating factor (age in this example). Each distinct class requires a different marketing approach, and quality requirements differ for each class.

Segmentation by Multiple Criteria. Two differentiating factors (income and age) are used in Figure 26.2e. Customers are classified according to both factors. Marketing strategy and quality requirements can vary for each class identified.

Patterns of Segmentation

Customers are often segmented by demographic (e.g., age and income) or psychographic (lifestyle and attitudes) criteria, but segmentation by product attributes is especially helpful to quality managers.[7] Customers' likes and dislikes indicate their preferences. Three broad preference patterns are shown in Figure 26.1.

Homogeneous Preferences. Customers with homogeneous preferences have roughly the same preferences. In Figure 26.1a the two product attributes (quality and price) graphed do not appear to cause a natural segmentation. Competing brands are likely to be similar and located near the center.

Diffused Preferences. In Figure 26.1b no natural segments exist, but customer preferences vary greatly. Competitors would be expected to offer dissimilar products in response to customer preferences.

Clustered Preferences. Natural market segmentation occurs in Figure 26.1c. Distinct preference clusters exist, and competing products are expected to be dissimilar between clusters and similar within clusters.

Market segmentation must be based on sound statistical techniques that ensure that samples taken are representative of the market as a whole as well as of the individual segment being studied. This aids in the identification of key segments of potential customers. Cluster analysis is a multivariate technique that creates groupings on the basis of minimizing variation within groups and maximizing variation between groups, according to a list of variables or criteria. Factor analysis is sometimes used to map the perceptual space of customer needs and wants for a market for a particular good or service. Used together, the resulting perceptual maps identify both the location of segments and the market perceptions of competitors in meeting key needs and wants. For example, creation of multiple fragrances of cleaning products was based on research that identified market segments with the requirements of something other than lemon or pine fragrances for cleaning products. As none of the existing brands were positioned to meet these requirements, fragrances such as "Sea Breeze," "Spring Rain," and "Mountain Fresh" were created and marketed specifically to meet those needs.

CHOOSING A SEGMENTATION STRATEGY

Identifying customers and providing benefits targeted to meet or exceed their unique requirements is a prescription for extraordinary levels of customer satisfaction, loyalty, and profitability. The principal reasoning behind this axiom is that a market includes individuals and organizations from all circumstances. If all individuals and organizations had the same needs and expectations, it would be easy to standardize product features and service delivery processes to maximize the value that each desired.

However, in reality a market is far more complex. Many subsets of customer needs and requirements (segments) exist. An organization attempting to appeal to the needs of all in the market might actually fail to deliver the value expected by any of its segments. The key is to identify the segment(s) that should be the primary focus of the organization. High rates of segment penetration are likely when product features and service processes are in alignment with customer requirements.

Best practices in customer identification and segmentation include the following:

◆ Create and maintain a customer information system to provide information on customer identity, potential segmentation criteria, and, if possible, information on customer needs and requirements. If a comprehensive customer database is not feasible, market research can be used to characterize customer segments.

◆ Use SWOT analysis as a preliminary indication of competitive position. Segmentation strategies that offer the most leverage for building on current strengths and minimizing current weaknesses should be explored.

◆ Use customer and market surveys to evaluate customer and market perceptions of the organization and compare these perceptions to those held toward others in the business. This information can be used to identify current position (in the minds of both customers and noncustomers) relative to current and potential market opportunities.

◆ Choose a segmentation strategy that fits strategic intent in the context of opportunity. Segmentation can be integrated into marketing planning, strategic planning, and quality and service process improvement plans.

An organization's marketing strategy must take into consideration whether the organization is interested most in pursuing more customers or in targeting the right customers. Effectively targeting a market requires a clear understanding of the current customer strata and how each contributes to revenue and profit. Anthony suggests a focused approach for developing "the right customers":

◆ Precisely direct marketing efforts (focus to avoid undisciplined expansion).

◆ Tailor marketing plans/campaigns (and service delivery processes) to meet the needs of core customer segments. This translates into properly allocating marketing resources across segments, as underfunding efforts directed at core segments could result in lost opportunities.

◆ Use appropriate marketing performance indicators to monitor and guide the relative success of segmentation initiatives. Move away from indicators such as number of customers and gross sales in favor of cost of sales, cost of retention (a cost-of-quality component), potential for expansion, and customer profit contribution.[8]

BARRIERS TO EFFECTIVE CUSTOMER IDENTIFICATION AND SEGMENTATION

Many factors can contribute to lack of effectiveness in customer identification and segmentation.

Failure to Identify Customers

Some organizations sell through wholesalers and retailers and have no idea of the identity of their customers. These organizations can build customer databases through product registrations and warranty work but generally must rely on market research to characterize customers and the market at large. Similarly, they must rely on research to identify their competitive position and opportunities within the market. Other organizations know who their customers are and have the capability to identify their market position and opportunities but lack the systems and infrastructure needed to capture and use the information.

The "We Know Our Customers" Myth

Many organizations believe that they know who their customers are and what they want. Unfortunately, the evidence might be anecdotal and unsupported by hard data. Effective segmentation requires metrics to classify customers into groups as well as to evaluate their value to the organization (e.g., sales revenue and profit contribution).

Failure to Align Operations with Marketing Strategies

Segmentation generally comes from the marketing side of the organization. Stakeholders in quality and operations planning need to integrate the thinking and systems of the organization to align service delivery processes and quality with the customer requirements dictated by the segmentation strategy.

Failure to Distinguish Need for Separate Service Delivery Processes

When an organization adopts a segmentation strategy, it is tempting to optimize the service delivery system to maximize customer satisfaction for the core customers or the strategically most significant segment. In some cases, a separate service delivery process might be desired to serve non-core segments. This can entail whole-systems duplication in infrastructure (e.g., call centers and distribution facilities) and staff functions, such as sales, technical support, and installation and repair personnel.

In the 1990s, businesses have operated under a tendency toward consolidation of customer service and call center functions. Intuitively, this is a contradiction of what might be required for effective deployment of segmentation strategies. By disaggregating these functions at the segment level, an organization can excel in the expertise and knowledge required to provide world-class value in a particular segment.

🏛 Additional Readings 🏛

Anthony, Michael. 1998. "More Customers or Right Customers: Your Choice." *Marketing News*, August 31, p. 13.

Daetz, Doug, Bill Barnard, and Rick Norman. 1995. *Customer Integration—the Quality Function Deployment Leader's Guide for Decision Making.* New York: John Wiley & Sons.

Davidow, William H., and Bro Uttal. 1989. *Total Customer Service: The Ultimate Weapon.* New York: Harper & Row.

Lawton, Robin L. 1993. *Creating a Customer-Centered Culture: Leadership in Quality, Innovation, and Speed.* Milwaukee: ASQC Quality Press.

Levitt, Theodore. 1983. *The Marketing Imagination.* New exp. ed. New York: The Free Press.

Pyzdek, Thomas J. 1996. *The Complete Guide to the CQM.* Tucson, Ariz.: Quality Publishing.

Reis, Al. 1996. *Focus.* New York: HarperCollins.

Toffler, Alvin, and Heidi Toffler. 1996. *Powershift.* New York: Bantam.

Chapter 27

Partnerships and Alliances between Customers and Suppliers

❖ *This chapter should help you*

◆ Understand the characteristics of customer–supplier strategic relationships

◆ Recognize how both parties can benefit from strategic relationships

TREND TOWARD CUSTOMER–SUPPLIER RELATIONSHIP INFORMATION

By nature, customer–supplier relationships are often less than win-win and are sometimes even adversarial in nature. A customer typically wants the highest quality, the shortest cycle times, and the lowest possible price and often views suppliers as interchangeable commodity providers. Conversely, suppliers are motivated to sell goods and services at a price that provides an acceptable profit but are also motivated to build customer loyalty and create a close-knit relationship to secure future business.

As discussed in Chapter 4, supplier management has evolved to emphasize the importance of both parties working together so that each can benefit. Increasingly, organizations have discovered the benefits of forming strategic relationships both within and outside their organization. Strategic relationships are known by many terms: coalition, joint venture, strategic alliance, partnership, and so on. An alliance implies that two parties are working together for a common purpose. The notion of partnerships goes even further, implying a shared fate, mutual benefits, and equal relationship. Strategic relationships involve cooperative undertaking among companies and can involve technology, licenses, or supply/marketing agreements.

Strategic relationships between customers and suppliers involving all business issues, not just quality, are clearly the wave of the future. Teamwork actions include training a supplier's staff in quality techniques, including suppliers in a design review meeting to gain ideas on how supplier parts can best be used and sharing confidential sales projections with suppliers to assist in supplier production scheduling. Such partnerships often lead to new approaches that benefit both the purchaser and suppliers.[1]

Some common situations that might lead an organization to develop a customer–supplier partnership include the following:

◆ On the basis of a review of core competencies, an organization might recognize that a supplier's capabilities exceed internal capabilities. In such cases, a better return on assets might be attained by outsourcing the production of key components or services to this supplier.

◆ Cost-cutting pressures resulting from substantial price competition in the market might force an organization to search for ways to lower costs, both internally and externally, so that profit margins can be maintained.

◆ Combining resources can increase capabilities so that they exceed those realized by customers and suppliers engaged in more traditional customer–supplier relationships. Strategic relationships are a viable option when an organization desires to attain technological breakthroughs, enter new markets, and/or develop new products or services.

Organizations might strive to build two different kinds of partnerships: internal or external. Internal customer–supplier partnering is briefly discussed in the following section. This chapter's primary focus is on external customer–supplier partnering.

INTERNAL CUSTOMER–SUPPLIER RELATIONSHIPS

Internal partnerships, those created within an organization, can result in improved effectiveness whether based on cross-functional processes, labor-management relations, or other internal organization stakeholders. Areas for internal partnering often can be identified by flowcharting production and service processes and studying the relationships that exist between functions. Although most functional departments understand their part of the process quite well, they might lack a systems perspective of how their particular function relates to the activities performed by other functional departments. This failure to integrate the various functions affecting a process affects effectiveness and is likely to result in dissatisfied internal and external customers.

A customer–supplier agreement that resembles those used between organizations and their external suppliers can be created to clear up any confusion of the integration of functions between departments. The customer–supplier agreement clearly states the customer's and supplier's expectations so that customer satisfaction can be achieved. "Establish departmental teams to identify their internal customers, what their requirements are, and how to measure satisfaction and come to agreement with the internal customers. In the event the internal customers are not satisfied, a recovery plan should be developed. The status of a department's internal customer satisfaction agreement should be reviewed monthly."[2]

PARTNERSHIPS WITH KEY SUPPLIERS

The importance of creating and maintaining partnering relationships with key suppliers is reflected in the 1999 Baldrige Award criteria for supplier and partnering processes (Section 6.3). Organizations are asked to describe how they manage key suppliers as well as the interactions and processes related to partnering. The following response areas from the criteria provide guidelines for organizations looking for ways to effectively manage partnership relations:

◆ What key products/services do you purchase from suppliers and/or partners?

◆ How do you incorporate performance requirements into supplier and/or partner process management? What key performance requirements must your suppliers and/or partners meet to fulfill your overall requirements?

◆ How do you ensure that your performance requirements are met? How do you provide timely and actionable feedback to suppliers and/or partners? Include the key performance measures and/or indicators and any targets you use for supplier and/or partner assessment.

◆ How do you minimize overall costs associated with inspections, tests, and process and/or performance audits?

◆ How do you provide business assistance and/or incentives to suppliers and/or partners to help them improve their overall performance and to improve their abilities to contribute to your current and longer-term performance?

◆ How do you improve your supplier and/or partnering processes, including your role as supportive customer/partner, to keep current with your business needs and directions? How are improvements shared throughout your organization, as appropriate?

In a 1996 survey of customers,[3] a silicon wafer manufacturer asked its customers various questions on the nature of customer-supplier partnerships. The questions addressed the nature of supplier partnerships, expected benefits from partnerships, and the characteristics exhibited by key suppliers.

What is a supplier partnership? In defining the nature of customer–supplier partnerships, nearly half the customers interviewed spoke of shared risks and rewards. Two-fifths (40 percent) described the nature of the relationship as embodying a mutual give-and-take (analogies ranging from marriage to virtual mergers). One-third articulated good communications that emphasize honesty and openness. One-fifth talked of the idea of extending the factory to the supplier.

What benefits do you expect (as the customer) from a supplier partnership relationship? Nearly half (48 percent) the customers surveyed indicated that the expected benefits from a partnership-type relationship would be realized through higher quality (supplier and product); guaranteed supply; and/or attaining desired customer–supplier synergies. About 30 percent expected improved communications and/or improved costs or pricing to be important benefits.

What are the characteristics of your best suppliers? The leading characteristics that customers listed to describe their best suppliers included providing high product quality (52 percent), responsive and flexible service (48 percent), and good communications (29 percent). Nearly one-fifth each (19 percent) described their best suppliers as those who would either go the extra mile or hold a "can-do" attitude, would honor their commitments, and/or would provide problem-solving support.

As shown by these answers, especially important characteristics of successful partnerships and alliances include mutual benefit, trust building, open and complete communication, and interdependence of parties.

Mutual Benefit

Both parties in a strategic relationship must profit from the relationship. Unless the product is satisfactory and the level of service provided is acceptable, no customer will desire to continue a relationship.[4] Problems should be approached collaboratively; both parties should strive to make money while reducing cycle time. The spirit of a win-win mutual benefit is pervasive and encourages both parties to seek creative solutions.[5]

Trust Building

Both parties should be in the relationship for the "long haul" so that the relationship is not jeopardized by momentary problems or opportunistic behavior. "Even when the relationship is expected to be a short-term one, the element of trust is still essential to the relationship."[6] Suppliers and customers must feel free to exchange ideas without fearing that proprietary information will be divulged to competitors.

Open and Complete Communication

All responsibilities and expectations of the relationship must be clearly and frequently communicated. The most indispensable element of a customer–supplier relationship is dialogue and feedback.[7] "Immediate feedback from the client company's market directly to the supplier allows the parties to make quick global estimates and promptly introduce the required changes or improvements. It makes available information and ideas that are very useful to both parties."[8]

Interdependence of Parties

Effective partnerships foster mutual assistance, joint planning, and other forms of close collaboration.[9] "As the organization becomes more permeable, insiders flow out and outsiders flow in with ease. Suppliers, strategic partners, customers and experts . . . become involved in open managerial meetings relating to planning, product design, capital budgeting, personnel systems and operations. Lead users join product planning and design teams. Customer representatives work directly with in-house personnel . . . the 'organization chart' becomes a series of overlapping circles representing cross-disciplinary projects, alliances, and stakeholding relationships, many of which cut across national borders."[10]

BENEFITS RESULTING FROM CUSTOMER– SUPPLIER RELATIONSHIPS

Both customers and suppliers experience many benefits from a partnership or alliance relationship. As companies focus on becoming the "best-in-class" in serving their customers' needs, they seek partners who have capabilities they lack. Companies can respond to customers' desires with excellence and increase the value customers derive from their products and services when they partner with customers, make alliances with competing firms, or outsource entire functions and departments.[11]

Other recognized benefits of partnerships and alliances between customers and suppliers include the increased effectiveness that results from faster time-to-market for new products, the development of a joint technology base with shared core competencies, stable demand forecasting, improved quality, and improved communication through electronic information exchange.

The demands that world-class customers place on their suppliers result in improvements for both organizations. The below examples show how companies gained cost and time savings, or increased quality of product or service by forming alliances. Additionally, world-class customers encourage their suppliers to become world class also.

Cost/Time Savings

World-class customers lower their administrative costs and cut lead times through effective and timely communications with suppliers. Successful customer–supplier partnerships and alliances often involve leading-edge electronic data interchange (EDI). On the basis of expanded EDI and just-in-time (JIT) systems, Ford Motor Company has literally opened a portion of its database to Dana Corporation employees, who use this knowledge of Ford's actual parts usage requirements to replenish parts as they are needed. The system functions at higher levels of efficiency, and both companies enjoy the resulting cost savings.[12] In other cases, supplier management costs, such as those associated with incoming inspection, can be significantly reduced or eliminated when scrap or rework caused by supplier quality problems declines.

Better Products and Services

World-class customers improve their technology and process knowledge when they draw on specialized expertise that naturally resides within highly focused suppliers. Nike, the powerhouse shoe company, manufactures nothing. The company is world class at design and marketing but totally outsources shoe production to others more capable.[13]

Outsourcing refers to the practice of hiring an outside supplier to perform a function that could be (and perhaps has been) done within the company. The following are commonly cited reasons for outsourcing:

◆ to improve the company's focus by allowing it to concentrate on essential activities

◆ to gain access to world-class capabilities

◆ to accelerate the benefits of reengineering

◆ to share, and thus reduce, risks

◆ to free noncapital resources or to make capital funds available

◆ to reduce operating costs

◆ to secure resources not available internally

◆ to increase production capacity

◆ to eliminate a function that is difficult to manage[14]

Supplier Improvement

Suppliers benefit from the pressure that world-class customers bring to bear to improve quality.[15] Bose Corporation prospers in the Japanese-dominated world of consumer electronics by inviting suppliers to station individuals full time in Bose's corporate headquarters.[16] This gives both parties opportunities to cooperatively coordinate the relationship and suggest creative solutions to problems.

BARRIERS TO SUCCESSFUL PARTNERSHIPS

Today, many customer companies are more progressive, but it is still common for the customer to dictate requirements and the terms and conditions of the relationship to the supplier. The phrase "supplier partnership" is heard frequently, but many organizations fail to achieve true equality or balance in the relationship. Many customer-–supplier "partnerships" are superficial and one-sided. In many cases, one partner (usually the supplier) goes out of its way to provide extraordinary service for a valued customer. Seldom do customers go out of their way to help a supplier. In these cases, the concept of mutual benefit is not being met.[17]

Not all customers or suppliers desire to quickly enter into a partnership or alliance relationship. There is a "courtship" period in establishing a customer–supplier relationship, much as there is between people who eventually get married. It is during this time that a determination is made as to the viability of entering into a more formal relationship.

It is worthwhile to overcome these barriers because a successful partnership not only can be economically rewarding but also can endure more mistakes and produce greater rewards than partners could expect if no such relationship existed.[18]

🏯 Additional Readings 🏯

ANSI/ISO/ASQC A8402-1994 Quality Management and Quality Assurance—Vocabulary

Bell, Chip R. 1994. *Customers as Partners*. San Francisco: Berrett-Koehler Publishers.

Broecker, Edward J. 1989. "Build a Better Supplier-Customer Relationship." *Quality Progress,* September, pp. 67–68.

Conway, W. 1994. "Partnering for Quality Improvement." *Quality,* April, p. 16.

Drew, J. H., and T. R. Fussell. 1996. "Becoming Partners with Internal Customers." *Quality Progress,* October, p. 51.

Erickson, K., and A. Kanagal. 1992. "Partnering for Total Quality." *Quality,* September, p. 17.

Hayden, Catherine. 1986. *The Handbook of Strategic Expertise*. New York: The Free Press.

Hradesky, John L. 1995. *Total Quality Management Handbook*. New York: McGraw-Hill.

Imparato, Nicholas, and Onen Harari. 1994. *Jumping the Curve.* San Francisco: Jossey-Bass.

Israel, Jeff T. 1997. "Feedback to Improve Core Customer Relationships: A Framework to Implement Face-to-Face Surveys." In *ASQC 52nd Annual Quality Congress Transactions.*

Juran, Joseph M., and Frank M. Gryna. 1993. *Quality Planning and Analysis,* 3rd ed. New York: McGraw-Hill.

Merli, Giorgio. 1991. *Co-Makership.* Cambridge, Mass.: Productivity Press.

Moody, Patricia E. 1993. *Breakthrough Partnering.* Essex Junction, Vt.: Oliver Wight Publications.

Peppers, Don, Martha Rogers, and Bob Dorf. 1999. "Is Your Company Ready for One-to-One Marketing?" *Harvard Business Review* (January–February), Vol 77: p. 68.

Poirier, Charles C., and Stephen E. Reiter. 1996. *Supply Chain Optimization.* San Francisco: Berrett-Koehler Publishers.

Williams, Gordon, and Leigh Reed. 1994. "Enhancing Customer–Supplier Relationships" *Quality.* April, p. 20.

Whitely, Richard, and Diane Hessan. 1996. *Customer Centered Growth.* Reading, Mass.: Addison-Wesley.

Chapter 28

Communication Techniques

❖ *This chapter should help you*

- ◆ Understand techniques used to solicit customer feedback
- ◆ Become familiar with survey methods
- ◆ Become familiar with methods of directing communications to customers
- ◆ Understand how improved communications enable strategic planning and deployment of improvement initiatives

Organizations rely on various methods to gather, assess, and act on information to serve customers and drive marketing activities. In the past, product development was typically dictated by a product-driven approach (i.e., if you build a better mousetrap, the world will beat a path to your door). Since the 1970s, successful organizations have increasingly adopted a market- or customer-driven approach. Such an approach explores the needs and wants of the marketplace and customers to determine the features and benefits to be designed into products and service delivery processes.

The shift toward a market focus has been aided by the development and refinement of a variety of techniques used to gather data from customers and markets. *Inc.* magazine published the results of an Ernst & Young survey that asked businesses what sources they used to collect information on customer needs and expectations. The adapted results are presented in Figure 28.1. Survey results indicate that a majority of surveyed firms rely on reactive feedback methods (complaint monitoring, 800 numbers, and warranty systems) to bring the voice of the customer into their organization. Less commonly used are proactive feedback methods, such as written surveys, telephoning, and visiting customers. However, proactive methods, such as customer surveys, are increasing in prominence since the advent of the Baldrige Award in 1987. Competitive and financial performance pressures have encouraged many organizations to strive to improve performance and increase customer satisfaction.

Several experts offer outstanding guidance in the area of assessing customer satisfaction. Don Dillman, an expert in survey methodology and implementation, suggests many time-tested ways to increase survey response rates and successfully implement surveys in *Mail and Telephone Surveys: The Total Design Method.*

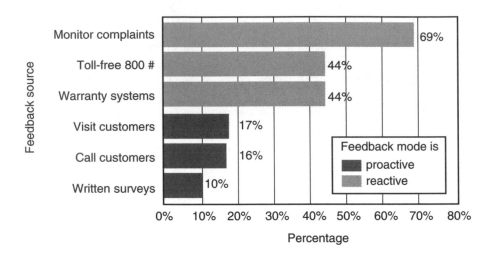

◆ **Figure 28.1.** Sources used to collect information on customer needs and expectations. Reprinted with permission of *Inc.* magazine, Goldhirsh Group, Inc., 38 Commercial Wharf, Boston, MA 02110 (http://www.inc.com). *Ernst and Young Survey of the Institute of American Entrepreneurs* (adapted figure), Inc. Staff, January 1993. Reproduced by permission of the publisher via Copyright Clearance Center, Inc.

Bob Hayes's *Measuring Customer Satisfaction: Development and Use of Questionnaires* provides an excellent discussion on determining customer requirements prior to implementing customer surveys. Likewise, John Goodman has made significant contributions in the areas of complaint handling, call center management, and estimating the market damage due to problems experienced by customers.

Terry Vavra successfully merges marketing and quality principles in *Improving Your Measurement of Customer Satisfaction: A Guide to Creating, Conducting, Analyzing, and Reporting Customer Satisfaction Measurement Programs*. According to Vavra, "Customer satisfaction measurement has its roots in the Total Quality Management movement, but was also explored early on from a social-psychological perspective by marketing theorists. While the TQM school focused on the more pragmatic application of satisfaction information to design and manufacture, the marketers explored the psychology of satisfaction—how it was formed and the nature of its impact on future purchase behavior."[1]

INFORMATION GATHERING

Businesses collect customer and/or market data using many tools and from many corners of the organization. The organization's systems for gathering data as well as for analyzing and disseminating this information are key to an effective communications system.

A framework for gathering, analyzing, and disseminating data (the voice-of-the-customer system) is presented in Figure 28.2. The framework illustrates the relationship of the critical activities associated with an effective communications system. The model shows how different data streams can be merged to address important marketing and customer satisfaction issues. Customer records could include infor-

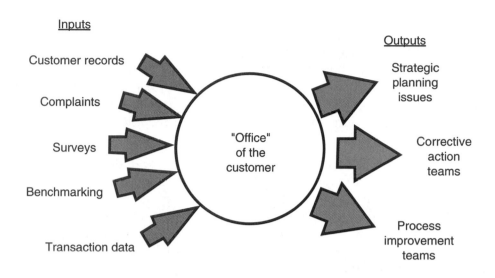

Figure 28.2. Voice-of-the-customer communications model. Source: Jeff Israel, *Satisfaction Strategies,* © 1993. Used with permission.

mation gathered from product warranty registration information. Complaints, if logged and tracked, can be integrated with other sources of customer feedback. Customer and market surveys are proactive and provide opportunities to assess performance and project results to key segments, all customers, or entire markets. Benchmarking information can lead to rapid innovation of best practices that enhance customer value. Transaction data can provide the basis for determining frequent and high-volume purchasers.

When integrated, this information is extremely valuable to the organization's stakeholders. Unfortunately, individual departments often own this information and do not commonly share it with others who could benefit. Regarded separately, the data streams might suggest one course of action but if considered collectively might suggest another course altogether. Organizations need to integrate and process data and then disseminate the resulting information in a manner that facilitates the maximum positive impact on the organization.

The "office of the customer" represents the employees or systems entrusted to process feedback inputs by converting raw data into valuable information with strategic, corrective action, and process improvement implications. This information is then disseminated to the stakeholder groups accountable for strategy, corrective action, and process improvement.

Competitive pressures are driving today's organizations to significantly improve three vital components of their communication systems: customer databases, customer satisfaction/market perception systems (surveys), and complaint handling systems.

COMMUNICATIONS TECHNIQUES/TOOLS

This section explains some of the key concepts and tools employed in the area of communications techniques.

❖❖❖

Survey Research Applications

Some of the most common applications of customer and market surveys include customer needs identification, baseline satisfaction surveys, customer satisfaction tracking, market perception surveys, lost customer surveys, product/service concept development and testing, and segmentation surveys. For any of these surveys to be statistically valid, distinctions must be made between the following terms.

Population versus Sample. A population refers to the universe of targeted respondents. An example might be all U.S. households. A sample refers to the subset of the population chosen to represent all targeted respondents. In our example, the sample frame might be drawn from the most recent census or generated using random digit dialing within working phone exchanges in the United States. In either case, a random sample of sufficient size ensures that survey results from the sample can be accurately projected to the population. The response rate indicates the percent of the sample that responds to the survey.

Validity. Validity is one of the most important concepts in survey research. In general, it is the ability of survey questions to accurately determine respondent attitudes, behaviors, or beliefs. Question wording is crucial, as it is important that the intended meaning be conveyed to the respondent. Wording should be clear so that all respondents perceive the intent of the question in the same way.

Reliability. Reliability refers to a survey's repeatability. With good sampling techniques and consistent application of the research method, the results of two independent random samples of a conducted survey would be expected to be statistically comparable. Typically, reliability is expressed with terms such as *sample error* or *precision.* For example, "Survey results will not vary by more than 5% given a 95% level of confidence." Survey reliability is a direct function of sample size. With large populations, a sample size of 400 is usually sufficient to attain the desired precision.

Bias. Many potential sources of bias, usually introduced unwittingly, can severely influence survey responses. Bias can result from poor question wording, choice of inappropriate scales, or even the order or positioning of questions within a survey. Bias from interviewer effects can be introduced in many ways, including interviewer–respondent dynamics related to gender, age, or ethnicity. Interviewer paraphrasing of questions, asking leading questions, tone, rate of speech, volume, and demeanor can have biasing impacts. Other potential sources of bias can result from the interviewer knowing the respondent, identifying the sponsorship of the survey, and survey nonresponse. Potential sources of bias should be minimized if possible, but sometimes there are trade-offs. For example, for a customer satisfaction survey the identification of the sponsoring company can tend to positively skew results, but sponsorship generally minimizes nonresponse bias by helping to secure higher response rates.

Quantitative versus Qualitative Research. Quantitative research provides empirical data from which statistical inferences can be drawn and projected to the population at large. Typically, rating scale questions and multiple-choice questions are thought of as quantitative. The sample for quantitative research must be random and large enough to draw statistical inferences.

Qualitative research is highly useful in identifying key themes related to the research issues and in capturing affect (likes, dislikes, and preferences). However, qualitative research does not allow for statistical inferences that can be projected back to the population.

Survey Tools/Methods

The following methods of surveying are frequently used.

Written/Mail Surveys. The most common survey method is the written customer satisfaction or mail survey. Many companies periodically mail out company-wide surveys, tabulate the results, and provide the feedback to all areas of the organization. Some companies survey their customers annually; others send out questionnaires monthly to a random sample of customers.

Mail surveys take longer to implement than phone surveys and some in-person interviews but are the least obtrusive of all survey techniques because respondents can complete the survey at a time of their own choosing. Mail surveys are less expensive than personal interviews and are usually less expensive than telephone surveys.

Maximizing the response rate of a mail survey is a key concern. Prior notification, a well-written cover letter, and a follow-up survey mailing to nonrespondents in the sample are some of the most effective tactics to boost response rates. With customer satisfaction surveys, response rates between 30 percent and 50 percent are attainable.

This approach has a low cost per response, and the results lend themselves to statistical analysis. Mail surveys can include both quantitative and qualitative questions, but the quality of open-ended qualitative data is not as good as that of telephone and in-person surveys because there is no interviewer to probe or clarify incomplete or vague responses.

To be effective, written surveys must be relatively short, with no more than a page or two of questions. This limits the number of questions dedicated to specific areas of the business and minimizes the recipient's desire to throw away the survey. The responses of written surveys are not random, as the least and most satisfied customers tend to respond more frequently than those who do not have strong feelings. To overcome this problem, leading companies are using telephone surveys to contact a random sampling of their customers to measure and correct the bias in their written survey results.

Telephone Surveys. Many companies use telephone surveys to supplement or even replace written surveys. Phone surveys are very effective for collecting information about the company as a whole or about functional areas such as sales and services. Interviewers call customer decision makers and influencers directly to identify their requirements and find out how well the company is meeting those requirements. The survey can be conducted and the findings made available more quickly.

Phone surveys are less subject to the biases inherent in written surveys. Because response rates tend to be much higher than those for written surveys, phone survey results more accurately reflect the attitudes of the customer set. Sample sizes can be much smaller, and the company knows for sure who answered the survey questions.

Phone surveys also offer more flexibility than do written surveys because an experienced interviewer can deviate from a prepared call guide to pursue specific areas of customer interest. The quality of open-ended comment data is good, given adequate interviewer training and supervision. Care must be taken with phone surveys that all interviewers conduct surveys in a consistent manner to minimize potentially biasing interviewer effects. It is more difficult to ask respondents to evaluate complex concepts by phone than it is by mail or in-person because visual props are not available.

Because there is a practical time limit for telephone calls, maximum survey length is generally longer than that for mail surveys but shorter than that for in-person interviews. Phone surveys have a higher cost per response than well-executed written surveys but are less expensive than in-person interviews. Also, telephone calls are interruptive by nature, and there is an increasing resistance to them, especially by consumers. Widespread adoption of voice mail and answering machines has necessitated that numerous attempts be made to attain reasonable survey response rates. Finally, in some consumer markets, customers might have unlisted telephone numbers or no phone service. However, even with these disadvantages, the telephone survey continues to grow in popularity and is an excellent source of input for the quality improvement process in sales.

In-Person Interviews (One-on-Ones). The in-person, or face-to-face, interview is one of the most powerful information gathering techniques available. It can be used to identify the issues that are most important to customers so that these issues can then be addressed in written or telephone surveys. The in-person interview is also an effective stand-alone method for gathering qualitative information. A skilled interviewer can quickly elicit information critical to improving the sales process. He or she can pursue the areas of greatest importance, probe for details, and discuss new ideas and approaches. The in-person interview is an excellent tool for getting input from both external and internal customers.

The cost of conducting a large number of in-person interviews virtually precludes the use of this technique to gather statistically significant data. This is especially true if the company has a large number of customers or if customers are widely dispersed, as scheduling logistics and geography tend to magnify costs and time requirements. The technique also requires the use of skilled, unbiased interviewers. This usually means using people from outside the company.

However, in-person interviews have other advantages. If a sufficient number of surveys are conducted, quantitative results can be projected to the population. In addition, these types of surveys allow for the longest interviews with minimal respondent fatigue. Unlike with focus groups, the attitudes expressed are truly owned by the respondent and not in any way influenced by group consensus or dominant participants.

Focus Groups. Focus groups are qualitative group discussions, usually with 8 to 10 participants generally recruited to meet segmentation criteria, such as level of product use, age, income, and gender. A discussion guide that outlines questions is prepared in advance. The questions are asked and facilitated by a focus group moderator. Depending on the research design, between 2 and 10 groups will be conducted with different segments in different geographic areas. Focus groups can identify important recurring themes with regard to product or service likes and dislikes, important service factors (customer requirements), and performance improvement opportunities.

The focus group has many of the benefits and uses of the in-person interview and the added benefit of a group's synergy at a lower cost per response. Focus groups are often used as a first step in developing written or phone surveys but are also used by themselves to get customer feedback on sales and marketing programs. Focus groups of internal customers can provide input to improve business, manufacturing, development, administrative, and even sales processes.

External customer focus groups are usually conducted in specialized facilities. This means that the participants have to spend time away from their work locations. All focus groups require a skilled facilitator to ensure that the sessions stay on track and are not unduly influenced by a few participants.

Customer Councils. Many companies have established customer councils that meet periodically to discuss common issues and concerns. These councils are an excellent way to develop supplier partnerships. Council meetings provide a forum for in-depth discussions of the company's sales process and for identifying ways in which sales can add value to the company's products and services.

Because council members usually come from the company's largest and best customers, their input might not represent the attitudes of all customers. Therefore, customer councils should not be a company's only source of customer input.

Joint Planning Meetings. One of the most effective ways to identify customer requirements and gather feedback is by conducting joint planning meetings. Several leading companies, including AT&T, Calgon, General Electric, and Texas Instruments, have developed this approach independently. Although joint planning meetings are called by many names and the process might vary slightly, common characteristics exist.

Joint planning meetings begin with a meeting between representatives of a key customer and the sales and service team for that account. The meeting objective is to determine how the company can better meet the customer's requirements and expectations locally. A skilled facilitator leads the participants through a planning process to create a prioritized list of improvement activities. At follow-up meetings, the customer provides feedback on how well the improvements work, and the participants work together to identify more items on which to focus. The company consolidates input from all the joint planning sessions to identify common issues that can be addressed on a company-wide basis.

This approach will not work for every company because this method is most useful when salespeople or teams support one or a few large customers. Also, the objective of these planning meetings is improvement; customers must never perceive that the intent is to sell additional business. However, users of the technique do report that it often results in the identification of additional business opportunities.

❖❖❖

Panels. Typically, a panel is a group of customers recruited by an organization to provide adhoc feedback on performance or product development ideas. Panel composition can vary, depending on strategic intent. Frequently, panels include customers who are strategic business partners, and accustomed to communicating openly and familiar with the sponsoring organization's business practices and technical capabilities. In high-technology industries, panel members might fit the "power user" description because they understand current state-of-the-art applications and therefore have a better understanding of the potential for new applications and benefits proposed during the product design phase. Like focus groups, data gathered from panels are not projectable to the population of customers.

Comment Cards/Suggestion Boxes. Comment cards and suggestion boxes are often used on premise (e.g., at fast-food restaurants, hotels, and doctor offices) to gather customer feedback. They are almost always very brief and provide the benefit of fostering communications with customers from whom the organization most needs to hear. They give dissatisfied customers an opportunity to vent and the establishment an opportunity to make amends (often building loyalty). Customers who receive astonishing service often find themselves compelled to tell management about their wonderful experiences. The main problem with this survey method is that it is often ignored by a majority of customers, resulting in substantial bias due to nonresponse. Many customers will not "volunteer" their time to answer a questionnaire unless they receive something in the mail, are contacted by phone, or are approached in person as they are leaving the establishment. Therefore, results might be useful in identifying sources of problems or causes that drive customer delight but would be woefully inadequate in describing an "average" customer's experience.

Observation (Murmurs). Murmurs, a technique with origins in Japan, is used to gather information on customer behavior. In the late 1980s, Honda dispatched a team of engineers to the parking lots of Disney World to discover customers' requirements for their car trunks. The engineers reportedly watched people drive into the theme parks and unload their trunks. On departure, the engineers observed how people packed and loaded their gear into the trunks. As a result, many new design ideas were integrated into future Honda trunks to add benefits and make them easier for customers to use.

Mystery Shoppers. Mystery shoppers can be very useful to monitor the effectiveness of policy deployment, training, and new product/program launches. Shoppers (either internal employees or third party) pretend to be customers with certain needs and get a bird's-eye view of the service process in action (not just the way it is supposed to work). Shoppers can be trained to minimize personal biases and focus performance ratings on the basis of carefully defined (objective) service levels. However, high shopper scores do not imply that the organization's performance is aligned with customers' needs and expectations.

Other. A variety of other sources of valuable information exists about current and potential customers. Some of the potentially richest sources of information include product/warranty registration cards, call center data (800 phone numbers), complaint systems, customer databases, and data generated from sales forces (customer visits).

Each of these sources has useful applications in terms of identifying strategic planning, process improvement, and corrective action opportunities. Today's organizations increasingly have information about their customers—problems experienced, needs and wants, and other competitive intelligence—from many sources. It is important that each data stream be considered in the context of the value it might hold for various stakeholders throughout the organization.

MISTAKES MADE IN DETERMINING CUSTOMER SATISFACTION

The most common mistake companies make in determining customer satisfaction is assuming that they know how satisfied the customer is and what the customer wants. This is based on the existence of a long-term relationship or on the absence of complaints.

Another mistake is designing surveys using questions that the company wants the customer to answer. Proper survey design requires that the customers be asked what is most important to them and what they want to have included on the survey. As a quality vice president from a Baldrige Award winner once said, "We tended to include survey questions to which we already knew the answers." A similar mistake is developing the survey questions in such a way as to lead the customer to answer the way the company wants. Survey question design is almost an art form.

Another common mistake is to survey samples of customers that are neither random nor representative. This results in responses that are not statistically valid. This can also happen when customers are surveyed by mail and the responses from the 30 percent of customers who sent back the form are analyzed. The problem is that customers at the extremes of satisfaction or dissatisfaction tend to respond to surveys more frequently than those who are neutral.

Poor question definition and invalid statistical samples can cause the company to focus its improvement efforts in the wrong area or on areas that are not important to the customer. This wastes resources without achieving improved customer satisfaction or competitive position.

BENEFITS OF EFFECTIVE COMMUNICATION TECHNIQUES

Some of the key benefits of the effective deployment of communication techniques include the following:

- increased responsiveness to important performance issues
- better anticipation of customers' future requirements
- management by fact (data-driven corrective action/process improvement)
- improved customer satisfaction, retention, and advocacy (positive word of mouth)
- pinpoint-perceived performance and market position in terms of competition

Communication techniques are used to discover customers' needs and requirements because knowing customers' needs and requirements is far superior to speculation. Most organizations face significant pressures from competitors for customers. Further, customers' requirements and expectations are constantly changing. When organizations fully understand what customers expect, priorities can be established in service improvement initiatives as well as in product development. Superior performance in meeting customer and market needs leads to sustainable competitive advantages. These advantages are due to higher levels of customer loyalty and positive market perceptions among potential customers.

Communication techniques are also a means for gathering performance information. Effective information and feedback systems capture and collect performance measurement data that are critical to the objective evaluation of customer satisfaction and perceptions held by the market-at-large of the value and quality offered by the organization.

Knowing both what is important to customers (and/or market) and how well the organization performs according to those requirements enables strategic planning and deployment of improvement initiatives. For existing customers, this information should drive retention strategies and corrective action processes. From a market development point of view, it clarifies perceived market strengths and weaknesses in terms of the competition, providing useful insights on competitive positioning and opportunities to increase market penetration.

Highly successful customer-focused/market-driven organizations integrate a variety of communication tools, methods, and systems. An approach for best practice includes the following:

- define customer requirements
- regularly measure performance and customer satisfaction
- systematically review survey and other customer information
- create strategies, corrective action, and process improvement plans on the basis of the information

Companies noted for their customer information systems include L.L. Bean, Nordstrom, and Federal Express.

BARRIERS TO EFFECTIVE COMMUNICATION

The following problems are common mistakes in the areas of communication as it relates to customer satisfaction and focus.

Failure to Be Proactive

Relying too heavily on reactive data (such as complaint data) is a common mistake. The problem is that complaint data (and other reactive techniques) are usually not projectable to the population. For example, complaints might help identify key problems that need to be addressed, but they fail to quantify the true frequency at which a problem occurs. Typically 25 to 50 times more customers experience a problem than those who bother with, or succeed in, registering a complaint with management.[2]

Customer Does Not Know/Cannot Articulate Requirements

The customer is not always able to clearly articulate requirements and expectations. Andy Grove, the chairman of Intel, once stated that if Intel had relied exclusively on customers' stated needs and expectations (forsaking vision, technology, and instincts), the company would have gone into the memory business rather than create a breakthrough generation of microprocessors (he was referring to the 386 chip).[3]

Failure to Use the Customer's Language

Often the constructs evaluated in surveys are generated internally. It is common for these constructs to be worded differently than they would be if they were generated by external customers. The likely result is that ratings do not represent the intended construct, and survey validity is compromised.

Poor Research Design

Often survey objectives (problem statements) are not well thought out. It is very important to consider how the information will be used and what decisions will be made on the basis of the results. Every question to be included should meet the "need to know" rather than the "nice to know" test. Scrutinizing every question by asking "Why are we asking this?" helps prevent the inclusion of questions of limited value.

Ineffective Use of Results

Another frequent barrier is that good information is not always acted on by the organization. It is fairly common for an organization to conduct surveys but fail to integrate the results into the strategic planning, continuous improvement, and corrective action processes. A failure to disseminate the right information to the right person(s) in the organization (i.e., process owners or champions) is the most common reason for this type of breakdown. Other common reasons for ineffective survey use include a failure by leadership to set expectations for action as well as a lack of discipline to apply a rigorous Plan-Do-Check-Act (PDCA) cycle to the survey process.

DIRECTING COMMUNICATIONS TO CUSTOMERS

The previous sections of this chapter have dealt with the many ways in which organizations listen to the customer—the often neglected part of a two-way communication process. However, organizations also use communication directed at customers to acquaint them with products, services, channels, and the value that they provide.

Two broad approaches are used to direct communications to the customer. The organization can give unsolicited information or make information available on demand. Advertisements, direct mail, telemarketing, and fliers are examples of unsolicited information. Help-desk phone lines and Web sites are two examples of providing information on demand. These two approaches are related because advertisements can whet the desire for more information, which can then be obtained from a Web site.

Any good handbook on communications will provide guidelines for composing communication messages that grab the attention of the customer and can be easily understood and retained. However, companies are increasingly outsourcing this

❖❖

activity and restricting their own role to providing the bare facts that they want to communicate to the service provider who specializes in designing messages for specific channels. The proliferation of potential channels, or options, for communicating with customers—due largely to technological developments—has strengthened this trend. Such channels include the following:

◆ private print media, such as letters and fliers

◆ public print media, such as journals and newspapers

◆ electronic media, such as fax, e-mail, and multimedia presentations (distributed by e-mail attachments or on computer media such as CD-ROMs)

◆ voice channels, including telemarketing options and toll-free help lines

◆ Web-based communications, including information available on Web sites, moderated discussion lists, and information disseminated to Web users using "push" technology

Using a judicious mix of channels that provide both unsolicited and demanded information in the form of mutually reinforcing messages is the key to successful communication with customers.

🏠 Additional Readings 🏠

Complaint Handling in America: An Update Study: Part I, 1985; Part II, 1986. Washington, D.C.: U.S. Office of Consumer Affairs and TARP.

Dillman, Don A. 1978. *Mail and Telephone Surveys: The Total Design Method.* New York: John Wiley & Sons.

Hayes, Bob. 1992. *Measuring Customer Satisfaction: Development and Use of Questionnaires.* Milwaukee: ASQC Quality Press.

"Measuring and Quantifying the Market Impact of Customer Problems." ASQC course presented by John Goodman, Technical Assistance Research, February 1991.

Vavra, Terry G. 1997. *Improving Your Measurement of Customer Satisfaction: A Guide to Creating, Conducting, Analyzing, and Reporting Customer Satisfaction Measurement Programs.* Milwaukee: ASQ Quality Press.

Chapter 29

Multiple Customer Management
and Conflict Resolution

❖ *This chapter should help you*

- ◆ Understand what multiple customer management means
- ◆ Recognize systems needed to deal with multiple customer issues
- ◆ Recognize potential sources of conflict between customers and suppliers
- ◆ Understand how to resolve conflicts between customers and suppliers

MANAGING MULTIPLE CUSTOMERS

Most businesses have more than one customer, each with their own needs/expectations for the product or service being purchased. To meet the needs/expectations of its customers, an organization must first understand its own business. This begins with knowing what it costs to produce the product or provide the service being offered and building these costs into the price of the product or service.

Next, the organization needs to determine the needs/expectations of specific customers. This can be done by studying the industry, such as by forming focus groups in which industry representatives express their needs. An organization should be aware that customers purchasing the same product might have very different needs. For example, the supplier of a line of cleaning products might have customers from both the food industry and the metalworking industry, and these customers will obviously have different requirements, even though certain products might perform well in either application. The metalworking industry might need a product to remove dirt, but the food industry has the additional requirement of wanting to create a nearly sterile environment to protect customers from contaminants.

In addition to different product requirements, customers might have varying delivery requirements. Some customers might need truckloads of quantities but are flexible with delivery lead times, whereas others might want small volumes of material delivered just in time. A supplier must weigh these types of logistical problems and consider the additional costs that could be incurred in either case.

Other customers might require the same product but at different stages of completion. For example, one customer might prefer to purchase material that is less finished, lower in purity, and so on because these materials meet their needs at the best value. When selling partially finished product, suppliers might find it necessary to modify their pricing structure to prevent others from buying and finishing the product and becoming strong competitors.

Suppliers need to evaluate each potential sales opportunity to make an informed decision as to whether it is worthwhile business to pursue. Once management has decided on which areas to focus, customers can be ranked so that research-and-development efforts can anticipate the needs of key customers. Generally, key customers are those that generate the most profits or have a high potential for generating profits. The value of a customer should be projected over the long term because business with a customer can lead to other business with that customer or to a referral to a new customer.

A strong system of strategic planning and a good understanding of statistics as well as management and accounting practices is necessary to manage multiple suppliers. Such practices/mechanisms can allow the company to balance/optimize business processes to suit both their customers' and their own needs.

RESOLVING CONFLICT

Many times, conflicts arise between suppliers and customers, and having multiple customers who compete with one another can present special challenges for a supplier. For example, conflicts can result when delivery schedules overlap or when material or other resources are in short supply.

When conflicts arise, high priority should be given to communicating with the customer in a calm manner and conducting root cause investigations and implementing corrective action. Results of corrective action should be fed back to the customer, and response action should not be discontinued until both parties are satisfied that the conflict has been resolved. Customer service representatives should be trained to deal with the irate customers and also need to be given the authority to solve or resolve customer problems immediately. Passing problems along does not help resolve customers' problems: The faster the problem can be dealt with, the happier the customer will be.

Establishing a relationship based on trust is critical to avoiding or resolving conflict with a customer. A customer must know that confidential or proprietary information is safeguarded from competitors. A supplier should have procedures for protecting proprietary information, such as by limiting access to drawings and specifications and restricting competitors' access to a customer's product. An organization without these provisions faces legal liability from patent or copyright infringement or violations of a contract (usually the purchase order) with the customer.

However, other than safeguarding proprietary or protected information, there is an economic aspect to managing customer conflict. If the systems and resources required to resolve conflict with a demanding customer exceed the economic benefit of meeting the customer's needs and resolving the conflict, it might be more expedient to take no steps to resolve the conflict and let that customer go to a competitor. However, when making such a decision, the intangible impact should be considered. A supplier needs to consider how the loss of that customer will affect business. Unhappy customers talk to many more people than do satisfied ones, and this needs to be considered when dealing with customers. In some industries, ceasing to do business with a customer might not have adverse effects, but in a small retail company, which is heavily dependent on word of mouth for its reputation and future business, this solution could be disastrous.

Resolving conflict with a customer helps establish trust and promotes a long-term relationship. This is a competitive advantage in industries in which customers are reducing supply bases to deal with fewer suppliers. A supplier should develop a relationship with its customers and clearly understand their needs. When conflicts arise, the supplier should try to understand the customer's point of view and negotiate a resolution.

The biggest mistake a supplier can make is believing that the customer is unreasonable and not reacting to resolve the conflict or making a halfhearted attempt at conflict resolution. Many times, this lack of action is rooted in the supplier's focus on optimizing the internal processes even if these processes do not serve the customer well. Conflict resolution is seldom possible in an environment in which the supplier tells the customer, "That's the way we do it, take it or leave it." Unfortunately, this is a common occurrence.

The most important criteria for both multiple customer management and resolving conflict is excellent human relations. Employees need to be trained in good human relations and use these skills when dealing with customers and among themselves. Good human relations can turn an irate customer into a good repeat customer that will bring friends along. The intangible benefits are huge and must be considered in all customer relations.

🏮 Additional Readings 🏮

Carnegie, Dale, 1964. *How to Win Friends and Influence People.* New York: Simon & Schuster.

Goldratt, Eliyahu M., and Jeff Cox, 1992. *The Goal.* 2nd rev. ed. Great Barrington, Mass.: North River Press.

Lapin, Lawrence L., 1982. *Statistics for Modern Business Decisions.* 3rd ed. New York: Harcourt Brace Jovanovich.

Maddux, Robert B., 1988. *Successful Negotiation.* Menlo Park, Calif.: Crisp Publications.

Schaaf, Dick, 1995. *Keeping the Edge.* New York: Penguin.

Steiner, George A., 1979. *Strategic Planning: What Every Manager Must Know.* New York: The Free Press.

Chapter 30

Customer Retention and Loyalty

❖ *This chapter should help you*

◆ Understand the importance of customer satisfaction to a firm's well-being

◆ Learn about the ways in which companies retain customers

◆ Become familiar with the steps in a recovery program for handling customer complaints

---

Deming defines the customer as the most important part of the production line: This concept should be expanded to include the complete value chain. Senior management must take an active role in knowing customers' needs and concerns. Listening to customers' complaints and taking action demonstrates commitment to customers and their needs. Because it costs five to six times more to get a new customer than it does to keep a current customer, customers should never be taken for granted.

Communicating with customers is the most widely used method in learning customers' needs. Most published quality policies declare the intention to meet customers' needs. This intention can be stated as, for example, "to provide customer satisfaction" or "to meet customer perceptions of good quality."

An effective system for integrating the quality-development, quality-maintenance, and quality-improvement efforts of the various groups in an organization should enable marketing, engineering, production, and service at the most economical levels, allowing for full customer satisfaction.

Feigenbaum recognized the importance of customer satisfaction in his definition of total quality control. Ciampa defines *total quality* as total dedication to the customer and states that a company with a total quality mind-set is totally dedicated to the customer's satisfaction in every way possible.[1]

BENEFITS ARISING FROM CUSTOMER SATISFACTION

One of the key measures of business success is customer satisfaction and retention. The number-one benefit of total dedication to the customer—customer satisfaction—is that it ensures an organization's future success.

Customers are assets. Creating customers for life provides an organization's livelihood. By making systems customer friendly, an organization lays the foundation for survival and growth. Encouraging and welcoming complaints provides valuable feedback. Complaints should be considered in a positive rather than a negative light. Building success on a good customer complaint system will strengthen revenues and profits. Customers whose complaints and needs are properly handled will be delighted; not only will they return, but will they tell others how well they were treated.

Seven steps to a successful customer service system are listed here:

Step 1: Total management commitment

Step 2: Get to know your customer

Step 3: Develop standards of service quality performance

Step 4: Hire, train, and compensate good staff

Step 5: Reward service accomplishments

Step 6: Stay close to your customers

Step 7: Work toward continuous improvement

An organization that follows these seven steps will give customers more than they expected. Customers must be kept through a proactive retention program. The three basic components of a value chain retention program are to treat suppliers right, to treat employees right, and to treat customers right. Finally, never take customers, whether internal or external, for granted.

Other methods used to retain customers include frequent-buyer programs, frequent referral programs, thank-you cards, newsletters and personal letters, telephone recalls, customer reward and recognition programs, customer special events, and strategic alliances or partnerships.

RETAINING CUSTOMERS

Although it is true that satisfied customers rarely take their business elsewhere, companies also take specific steps to lock in customers. This is because customer satisfaction is notoriously difficult to measure and manage and because competitors often offer attractive choices to entice even satisfied customers. Also, with the passage of time and greater experience in using a company's products or services, the customer gradually revises his or her expectations. This means that the customer's satisfaction with the same level of product or service quality cannot be taken for granted.

Companies protect their customer base by the following:

- *Rewarding usage.* This can take the form of discount coupons provided inside a product pack for buying additional quantities of the same product.
- *Rewarding loyalty.* Airlines' frequent-flyer programs are an example of this phenomenon.
- *Providing unpaid services.* Some companies offer free lessons on how to use their products.
- *Establishing personal relationships.* Publicly honoring loyal customers during company events, greeting them on their birthdays and anniversaries, and giving them preferential treatment (e.g., upgrading economy-class fliers to business class when space is available) are examples of ways in which companies build personal relationships with customers.

Retaining customers costs money but is still much less expensive than garnering new customers. Companies protect their customer base by building an organization-wide focus on retention. They must first design appropriate metrics, such as percentage revenue from repeat purchases or percentage of memberships into their third year of renewal. Then data must be collected and managers appraised on how well they meet their targets for retention.

RESOLVING CUSTOMER COMPLAINTS

All organizations occasionally encounter an unhappy customer. Making the effort to successfully resolve customer complaints shows the customer that you care and can be used as a continuous improvement tool. Listed here is a five-step recovery program:

1. *Apologize.* First and foremost, say that you are sorry for the inconvenience the customer has experienced and be sincere. Also, personally accept responsibility for the problem and its resolution.

2. *Urgent restatement.* Restate the problem as the customer described it to you to make certain that you understand exactly what the customer means. Then tell or show the customer that you will do everything possible to solve the problem and resolve the complaint immediately.

3. *Empathy.* Make certain that you communicate clearly to your customers so that they understand that you know how they feel.

4. *Restitution.* Not only tell your customers that you will take immediate action to resolve their complaints (e.g., refunding their money), but tell and show them that you will make it up to them in some special way. You might need to provide them with a free gift or a discount on their next purchase.

5. *Follow up.* Check to see whether your customers are now satisfied. This area is where most programs fail.

The commitment and loyalty of the internal customer is an important element of total customer satisfaction. A leader must be able to gain true commitment from the workforce in developing, implementing, and maintaining a total customer satisfaction program. Peter Senge defines three stages of commitment:

◆ *Compliance:* follows the letter of the law, vision, and mission

◆ *Enrolled:* free choice to follow the vision or mission

◆ *Commitment:* wants the vision or mission to come alive; a committed team will do whatever is necessary to satisfy the customer.[2]

COMMON MISTAKES LEADING TO LOST CUSTOMERS

Common mistakes leading to poor service and ultimately to lost customers are a failure to listen, apathetic employees, negative attitudes, poor complaint handling, and a lack of understanding of customers' needs.

Many organizations view complaints or customer dissatisfaction as negative feedback. When organizations ignore customer complaints, they lose a second

❖❖

opportunity to delight the customer, a second opportunity to retain the customer's business, and a second opportunity to develop stronger customer loyalty.

When organizations listen to customers with open minds and more flexible viewpoints, they can experience complaints as gifts. Complaints should be viewed as a powerful information feedback tool. A complaint is a customer's statement about expectations that have not been met. Your customer is giving you a second chance to delight him, keep his business, and develop stronger customer ties: retention and loyalty.

Finally, a common error is introducing dimensions of quality that are unimportant to the customer. Know what is important to the customer: Ask, then listen.

🏠 Additional Readings 🏠

American National Standards—Quality Management and Quality Assurance—Vocabulary. ASQC, 1994.

Albrecht, Karl. 1995. *Delivering Customer Value: It's Everyone's Job.* Portland, Oreg.: Productivity Press.

Barlow, Janelle, and Claus Moller. 1996. *A Complaint Is a Gift: Using Customer Feedback as a Strategic Tool.* San Francisco: Berrett-Koehler Publishers.

Bergstrom, R. Y. 1996. "Voices of the Customer and Supplier." *Automotive Production,* March, pp. 53–55.

Berkowitz, Ralph, 1994. *Moving to the Next Generation of Quality.* Franklin, Tenn.: Resource Systems Management.

Broydrick, S. C. 1996. *The Seven Universal Laws of Customer Value.* Burr Ridge, Ill.: Irwin Professional.

Cannie, J. K., and D. Caplin. 1991. *Keeping Customers for Life.* New York: American Management Association.

Ciampa, Dan. 1991. *Total Quality: A User's Guide for Implementation.* New York: Addison-Wesley.

Deming, W. Edwards. 1986. *Out of the Crisis.* Cambridge: Massachusetts Institute of Technology, Center for Advanced Engineering Study.

Feigenbaum, A. V. 1991. *Total Quality Control,* 3rd ed., rev. New York: McGraw-Hill.

Garvin, David A. 1987. "Competing on the Eight Dimensions of Quality." *Harvard Business Review,* (November–December) Vol. 65: 103–9.

Gerson, Richard F. 1992. *Beyond Customer Service: Keeping Customers for Life.* Menlo Park, Calif.: Crisp Publications.

Griffin, J. 1995. *Customer Loyalty.* New York: Lexington Books.

Harrington, H. James, and James S. Harrington. 1995. *Total Improvement Management: The Next Generation in Performance Improvement.* New York: McGraw-Hill.

Hopkins, E. J. 1995. "Strategies for Defusing Customer Defections." *Quality Digest,* December, pp. 26–29.

Juran, Joseph M. 1998. *Juran on Planning for Quality.* New York: The Free Press.

❖❖❖

___. 1992. *Juran on Quality by Design: The Nine Steps for Planning Quality into Goods and Services.* New York: The Free Press.

Lowenstein, Michael, W. 1995. *Customer Retention: An Integrated Process for Keeping Your Best Customers.* Milwaukee: ASQC Quality Press.

Naumann, Earl. 1995. *Creating Customer Value: The Path to Sustainable Competitive Advantage.* Milwaukee: ASQC Quality Press.

Reichheld, F. F. 1996. *The Loyalty Effect: The Hidden Force behind Growth, Profits, and Lasting Value.* New York: McGraw-Hill.

Scheuing, Eberhard E. 1995. *Creating Customers for Life.* Portland, Ore.: Productivity Press.

Scott, Dru. 1991. *Customer Satisfaction: The Other Half of Your Job.* Menlo Park, Calif.: Crisp Publications.

Senge, Peter. 1990. *The Fifth Discipline.* New York: Doubleday.

Stewart, T. A. 1995. "After All You've Done for Your Customers, Why Are They Still NOT HAPPY?" *Fortune*, December 11, p. 11.

Stratton, Brad. 1996. "Connecting with Customers and Other Sage Advice." *Quality Progress*, February, pp. 58–61.

Willingham, Ron. 1992. *Hey, I'm the Customer.* New York: Prentice Hall.

Zemke, R., and K. Anderson. 1991. *Delivering Knock-Your-Socks-Off Service.* New York: AMACOM.

🗒 Part 4 Endnotes 🗒

Part 4

Chapter 22

1. Joseph M. Juran and Frank M. Gryna, eds., *Juran's Quality Control Handbook,* 4th ed. (New York: McGraw-Hill, 1988), p. 64.
2. H. James Harrington, *Business Process Improvement* (New York: McGraw-Hill, 1991), pp. 72–73.
3. Thomas J. Pyzdek, *The Complete Guide to the CQM* (Tucson, Ariz.: Quality Publishing, 1996), p. 278.
4. John L. Hradesky, *Total Quality Management Handbook* (New York: McGraw-Hill, 1995), p. 29.

Chapter 23

1. Joan O. Fredericks and James M. Salter II, "Beyond Satisfaction," *Management Review,* May 1995, p. 29.
2. Leonard L. Berry, *On Great Service* (New York: The Free Press, 1995), pp. 8–16.
3. Karl Albrecht, *Delivering Customer Value* (Portland, Ore.: Productivity Press, 1995), pp. 36–39.
4. Leonard L. Berry, *On Great Service* (New York: The Free Press, 1995), p. 33.
5. *Ibid., p. 34.*

6. *Ibid., pp. 65–68.*

7. *Ibid., pp. 68, 69.*

8. *Karl Albrecht, At America's Service* (Homewood, Ill.: Dow Jones/Irwin, 1988).

9. Berry, p. 111.

10. Ibid., p. 147ff.

11. Ibid., p. 166ff.

Chapter 24

1. Don Peppers, Martha Rogers, and Bob Dorf, "Is Your Company Ready for One-to-One Marketing?" *Harvard Business Review* (January–February 1999), p. 3.

2. Regis McKenna, *Relationship Marketing: Successful Strategies for the Age of the Customer.* (New York: Addison-Wesley, 1991), Vol. 77: p. 44.

3. Peppers et al., p. 3.

4. Jeff T. Israel, "Feedback to Improve Core Customer Relationships: A Framework to Implement Face-to-Face Surveys," *ASQC 52nd Annual Quality Congress Transactions,* May 6, 1997, p. 420.

5. U.S. Office of Consumer Affairs/Technical Assistance Research Programs, *Consumer Complaint Handling in America: An Update Study, Part II,* (Washington, D.C.: U. S. Office of Consumer Affairs, March 31, 1986), pp. 42–43.

6. Israel, p. 425.

7. Peppers et al., pp. 4–7.

8. Ibid., pp. 4, 8.

9. B. Joseph Pine, Don Peppers, and Martha Rogers, "Do You Want to Keep Your Customers Forever?" *Harvard Business Review* (March–April 1995), Vol. 73: p. 26.

Chapter 26

1. Theodore Levitt, *The Marketing Imagination,* new exp. ed. (New York: The Free Press, 1983), pp 216–17.

2. Alvin Toffler and Heidi Toffler, *Powershift* (New York: Bantam, 1990).

3. Al Ries, *Focus* (New York: HarperCollins, 1996), p 128.

4. Levitt, p. 217.

5. William H. Davidow and Bro Uttal, *Total Customer Service: The Ultimate Weapon* (New York: Harper & Row, 1989), p. 55.

6. Thomas J. Pyzdek, *The Complete Guide to the CQM* (Tucson, Ariz.: Quality Publishing, 1996), p. 299.

7. Pyzdek, pp. 301–2.

8. Michael Anthony, "More Customers or Right Customers: Your Choice," *Marketing News,* August 31, 1998, p. 13.

Chapter 27

1. Joseph M. Juran and Frank M. Gryna, *Quality Planning and Analysis,* 3rd ed. (New York: McGraw-Hill, 1993), p. 321.

2. John L. Hradesky, *Total Quality Management* (New York: McGraw-Hill, 1995), p. 35.

3. Jeff T. Israel, "Feedback to Improve Core Customer Relationships: A Framework to Implement Face-to-Face Surveys," In *ASQC 52nd Annual Quality Congress Transactions,* May 6, 1997, pp. 423, 424.

4. Don Peppers, Martha Rogers, and Bob Dorf, "Is Your Company Ready for One-to-One Marketing?" *Harvard Business Review* (January–February 1999), Vol. 77: p. 16.

5. Nicholas Imparato and Onen Harari, *Jumping the Curve* (San Francisco: Jossey-Bass, 1994), p. 227.

6. Chip R. Bell, *Customers as Partners* (San Francisco: Berrett-Koehler Publishers, 1994), p. 5.

7. Peppers et al., p. 16.

8. Giorgio Merli, *Co-Makership* (Cambridge, Mass.: Productivity Press, 1991), p. 63.

9. Edward J. Broecker, "Build a Better Supplier-Customer Relationship," *Quality Progress,* September 1989, p. 67.

10. Imparato and Harari, pp. 190, 191.

11. Richard Whitely and Diane Hessan, *Customer Centered Growth* (Reading, Mass.: Addison-Wesley, 1996), pp. 36, 37.

12. Charles C. Poirier and Stephen E. Reiter, *Supply Chain Optimization* (San Francisco: Berrett-Koehler Publishers, 1996), pp. 88, 89.

13. Whitely and Hessan, p. 34.

14. Ibid.

15. Patricia E. Moody, *Breakthrough Partnering* (Essex Junction, Vt.: Oliver Wright Publications, 1993), pp. 206–9.

16. Whitely and Hessan, pp. 38, 39.

17. Poirier and Reiter, p. 84.

18. Bell, p. 7.

Chapter 28

1. Terry G Vavra, *Improving Your Measurement of Customer Satisfaction* (Milwaukee: ASQ Quality Press, 1997), pp. 16–17.

2. "Measuring and Quantifying the Market Impact of Customer Problems," ASQC course presented by John Goodman, Technical Assistance Research, February 1991

3. Paraphrased quotations from Andy Grove of Intel, during Quality Forum X, October 25, 1994.

Chapter 30

1. Dan Ciampa, *Total Quality: A User's Guide for Implementation* (New York: Addison-Wesley, 1991).

2. Peter Senge, *The Fifth Discipline* (New York: Doubleday, 1990).

Part 5
Project Management

Chapter 31 Planning
Chapter 32 Implementation

◆◆

Chapter 31

Planning

◆◆

❖ *This chapter should help you*

- ◆ Understand basic project planning concepts and stages
- ◆ Distinguish between short- and long-term quality plans and objectives
- ◆ Become familiar with the use of feedback loops to monitor project success, including the establishment of performance measures
- ◆ Recognize and use familiar project planning tools
- ◆ Understand that risk is inherent in business activities but can be minimized through careful planning
- ◆ Understand the use of benchmarking in project planning
- ◆ Understand the relationship of budgeting and project planning
- ◆ Realize the importance of benefit-cost analysis in project selection and monitoring

INTEGRATED QUALITY INITIATIVES

The strategic planning process and ongoing organizational performance reviews can identify many different opportunities for improvement. However, because of resource constraints, a limited number of potential changes can be addressed at any particular point in time. Project management is an excellent tool to use to ensure effective resource allocation when an organization is pursuing improvements with multiple goals.

Projects are tasks performed by people, constrained by limited resources, and described as processes or subprocesses. They are planned, executed, and controlled within definite time limits.[1] Examples of improvement projects include developing a new or modifying an existing product or service, implementing a new business procedure or process, or changing an organization's structure or support systems (e.g., human resources or information technology).

As in any project, two phases exist in an integrated quality initiative: planning (design) and implementation. Planning is the more critical phase because it directly influences the actions taken in the implementation phase. The project planning phase is discussed here. Project implementation is the topic of Chapter 32.

A well-defined project plan leads to timely and satisfactory project completion and helps optimize project costs. Most projects are cross-functional, which means

261

❖❖

that they require resources and/or direction from more than one functional unit within the organization. For example, in a manufacturing environment, changing a component's outer case from aluminum to plastic would affect purchasing, production, shipping, sales, and possibly other functions. Because various organizational initiatives can compete for many of the same resources, project leaders should take the needs of all organizational segments into account.

In the project design phase, the following steps are central to project planning:

Developing a Mission Statement

The mission statement provides guidance to the project team as to the ultimate goal to be accomplished. Often included in a written charter used to sanction a new project team, the mission statement should define how the project is linked to the organization's strategic plan. It should be specific enough to help the project team understand the scope of the project and identify the major stakeholders. The mission statement might include a target project completion date and specify the objectives to be accomplished during the project. The mission statement is usually developed by the manager or group sponsoring the project but can be created by the project team and reviewed by the sponsor(s) for concurrence.

Identifying Stakeholders' Requirements

Once the mission is defined, stakeholders—individuals or groups with a vital interest in the project—should be identified so that their needs can be evaluated. Stakeholders are those who will be directly or indirectly affected by the project and its outcomes. A process map can be used as an aid to ensure that all stakeholders are identified. In addition to helping to identify important areas from which team members should be selected, a process map provides the project team with an understanding of the current process.

Cleland defines two types of stakeholders: primary (those with a direct obligation to the team, such as a maintenance manager who must provide a skilled craftsperson to serve on a process improvement team that is working to reduce machine downtime) and secondary (those without direct involvement but who can influence project results, such as the purchasing department which might be required to process orders for some new components for the machine).[2]

All stakeholders have their own interests, priorities, and concerns regarding a project's outcome as well as the processes used to achieve it. Any stakeholder groups not represented on the project team should have an opportunity to provide input. Such information is important for identifying processes to be used, boundaries (e.g., of authority) to be observed, and performance measures to be tracked. The formation of a cross-functional team that consists of key stakeholders and that takes other stakeholders' needs into account helps ensure a project's success.

Selecting the Project Team

Once all stakeholders have been clearly identified, a project team is selected. The team should consist of representatives from as many stakeholder groups as is feasible. It is especially important that those responsible for implementing any project recommendations are represented on the project team. Team membership should also take into account any particular technical skills that might be required. When the need for a member with specialized skills will vary over the life of the project, a decision might be made to involve that member on an as-needed basis.

When an opportunity exists to be selective in project team membership, the level of sincere project interest shown by potential team members should be considered. Some organizations take into account the personal styles of potential members (as identified through a personality profile, such as the Myers-Briggs analysis) to ensure team diversity. When a team consists of individuals who are not familiar with one another (e.g., because they come from different geographical areas of the organization), a team building process might be used to get the group focused on the mission. The team building process might include spending some initial meeting time simply getting familiar with the background of each team member and what their personal hobbies are. This can be partially done through open discussion but is aided through structure questionnaires that provide a "profile" of the individual answering the questions. Gaining an understanding of the different values and priorities that each member brings to the project team can help the team become more productive than what might naturally develop.

How team members are selected can vary widely. Team members can be selected by the project sponsors (e.g., a management group) or can be representatives appointed by the various stakeholder groups affected. At times, a project team leader is appointed and given the authority to select or solicit other project team members. The approach used for selecting members for a particular project might depend on the scope and importance of the project, the likelihood of success or the potential impact of failure, the culture and values of the organization, and the dominant style of management.

Designating Quality Checkpoints

Because there is usually a relatively long period between project initiation and completion, it is important to identify interim points at which progress will be evaluated. Reviews are usually done at the end of each project phase or at milestones—points at which something significant should have been completed. However, a very complex project might need to be scrutinized more closely. In such case, a work breakdown structure (WBS) might be used to define activities in detail by specifying a task, indicating who is responsible for its performance, and describing when it should occur. This information might then be used for progress reviews at regular time intervals, such as monthly. Regardless of the method, both the project team and management should know when and how the reviews will occur as well who is involved and what information is to be communicated.

Providing Documentation

Documentation of a project often begins with a charter, which might specify the following:

- the project mission and goals
- project personnel (team members, team leader, sponsor, and facilitator, if used)

◆ project boundaries, timing, and objectives

◆ process to be used and major phases or milestones

◆ project checkpoints

Two additional project documents are a project time plan (e.g., in the form of a Gantt chart) and project communications (meeting minutes or project-tracking reports distributed to the team, management sponsors, and other stakeholders).

SHORT- AND LONG-TERM QUALITY PLANS AND OBJECTIVES

Short-term quality plans and objectives are generally regarded as those that can be completed within one year. Short-term quality objectives are *tactical* in that they help achieve a given near-term objective. In contrast, long-term quality plans are those that will take longer than a year to implement. Long-term quality objectives are *strategic* in that they help achieve a long-term overall position.

As with any project, short-term quality plans should have measurable goals with stated milestone dates. A short-term quality plan usually results in immediate cost savings; these can take the form of reduced labor or materials, fewer customer rejections, or customer retention.

Types of short-term projects include the following:

◆ improving output by 25 percent on production line 1

◆ reducing defects from 5 percent to 1 percent on production line 2

◆ reducing the cost of poor quality by 10 percent in the calendar year

Short-term plans and objectives usually require fewer resources (these can include the size and composition of a team or reporting methods and procedures) than do long-term projects and might require a smaller team. However, these differences do not reduce the need for formally stating the mission, identifying stakeholders, mapping processes, developing measurements, and setting milestones. The project team's failure to keep minutes of brief meetings concerning short-term plans can lead to the completion of a project with no history. This makes midcourse corrections difficult and costly and does not permit follow-up assessment or use of information by future teams.

Long-term quality plans are not quick fixes or adjustments to the current system, as they usually result in a fundamental change in the quality system. Events that constitute a quality system change include working to a new standard or introducing statistical process control (SPC) to the plant. Long-term quality plans also can result in a breakthrough in a product line or change in the organization's culture.

Long-term plans require more forethought regarding objectives, team selection, and allocation of other resources. Finally, one common caveat with long-term plans is the belief that plenty of time exists for the project to be completed. Regardless of the amount of time allotted for project completion, time should be used effectively and not wasted.

FEEDBACK LOOPS

Feedback loops are those measurements or metrics that reflect the effectiveness of actions taken so that progress can be verified (the "check" stage in the Plan-Do-

Check-Act cycle). Developed and set in place early in the planning stage, feedback loops are designed to monitor the project. Deviations from the plan must be detected and reported so that midcourse corrections can be made. Once the plan has been implemented, feedback loops are used for corrective action and as the basis for any adjustments to the project plan. They are also useful for identifying learning opportunities for the current or future team.

Feedback loops provide the information needed to ascertain whether a project is "in control" and permit the project team to react in a timely manner when the need for change is observed. The information provided also assists in rational decision making if the need for any subsequent changes in the project becomes apparent. Feedback loops are needed to offset communication barriers, which can include physical distances, priority conflicts within the company, language difficulties (foreign, technical, and perception), shift differences, interpretation of drawings and requirements, and rumors concerning the project status.

Feedback loops are most effective when a routine of communications has been created. A report due on Friday should be distributed on Friday because information is useful only if it flows in a timely and reliable manner. However, complex communication requirements often lead to a drop in communication as people stop filling out useless reports. When problems are created by a lack of communication, failure of the project or replacement of the project team are two possible outcomes.

Project feedback can be provided through formal written reports or by informal reports, such as correspondence, presentations, meetings, and conversations. All these reporting methods can be appropriate; however, the project team must be careful to leave a document trail that shows the project's status at key junctures. A worst-case scenario would be allowing management to think that the project is proceeding as planned when problems exist. Failing to inform management of the project's true status or forcing people to make uninformed decisions can lead to failure of the project or dismissal of the project team.

Status Reports

Information-generating points in a feedback loop include status reports, in which all responsible parties formally report where they are in relation to the posted time lines. Status reports are formal in the sense that they are complete and for the record. Written presentations, multimedia shows, and verbal reports made while standing around a clipboard at a construction site are examples of status reports. Status reports should include information on the project's progress, resource utilization, and problems encountered (e.g., availability of resources, technical issues, and organizational resistance).

The project plan should define the frequency or timing of reports (e.g., daily, weekly, or monthly). It should define the purpose of each type of communication required and its format (e.g., in writing, or in person). The plan should require that project team request help when necessary and should specify how to obtain that help. In most cases, this will be a formal, written method rather than a verbal request.

The simplest, most common feedback loop in the project planning stage is the updating of plans and timetables. Written reports generated by the project manager and team on a predefined basis provide a fair and accurate picture of where the project is in relation to the official time line. These status reports allow resources to be redirected in a timely fashion to achieve the desired ends.

Management or budget reviews are other forms of status reports and are almost always formal in presentation. A management review is done by management personnel on the basis of presentations by members of the project team. A budget review can be a formal meeting or a standalone written report of the project's standing in relation to the forecast budget.

Customer Audits

Customer audits, typically done by organizations that are purchasing the results of a project, are common in extremely large projects that take years and millions of work hours and dollars. In this case, the customer might perform a detailed physical audit to assess the project's status. The audit will consist of a review of current progress, methods, and results of the project that can be used to determine how these align with the original mission, contract, timing plan, and expected resource utilization. The audit process is not unlike a quality audit (covered in Chapter 7).

PERFORMANCE MEASURES

Performance measures provide quantitative data in a format that easily demonstrates trends. They are usually numerical rather than narrative, ensuring that the data are clear and easy to interpret. Performance measures to be tracked should be specified early in a project (along with the mission, stakeholder requirements, and project plan) as a way of clarifying priorities and limitations.

Timeliness

By definition, a project is usually something that needs to be done within a particular time frame. Therefore, time lines are a critical planning and tracking mechanism for projects. Timing to be tracked includes overall progress (i.e., percentage complete), the status of major phases or milestones, and completion of specific WBS activities. It is important to track both late and early variances because they affect the probability of timely success, costs, and the status of other projects vying for the same resources. Reports on the status of a project's timing can take the form of Gantt charts, process decision program charts, or PERT charts. Each is discussed here.

Gantt Charts. Gantt charts list specific tasks and their timing relative to the overall project plan. Showing relationships between the tasks also allows the identification of the critical path. The Gantt chart can be updated as the project progresses to show planned versus actual status of activities. Gantt charts can also include milestones, which show an event that does not produce time or resources. Figure 31.1 shows a Gantt chart.

Process Decision Program Charts. Process decision program charts are used to develop contingency plans when the project is not progressing according to schedule. Normally, these are used on complex projects in which delays could be very

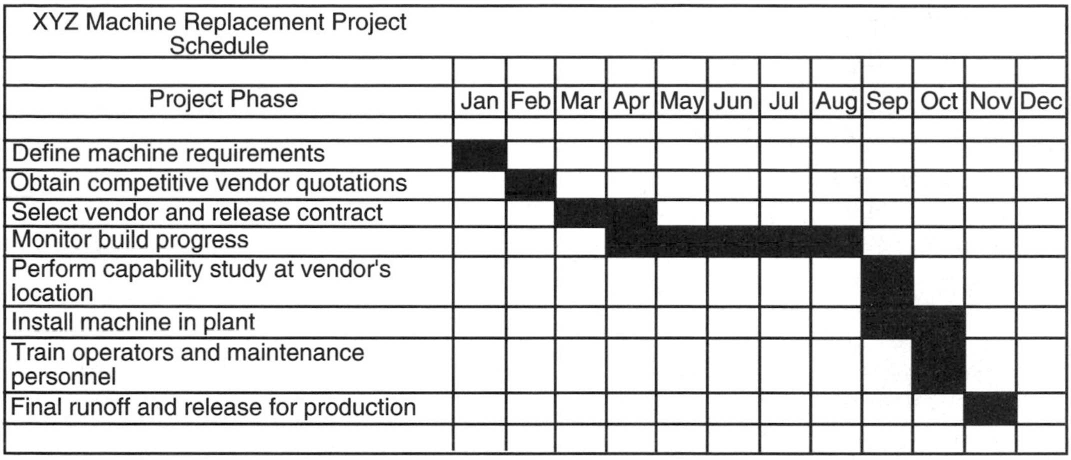

XYZ Machine Replacement Project Schedule													
Project Phase	Jan	Feb	Mar	Apr	May	Jun	Jul	Aug	Sep	Oct	Nov	Dec
Define machine requirements	■											
Obtain competitive vendor quotations		■										
Select vendor and release contract			■									
Monitor build progress				■	■	■	■	■				
Perform capability study at vendor's location									■			
Install machine in plant										■		
Train operators and maintenance personnel										■		
Final runoff and release for production											■	

◆ **Figure 31.1.** Gantt chart.

costly. The cost of delays could be in construction overtime or in missing a product's scheduled introduction date, such as prior to Christmas or in the computer market where a product's shelf life often can be measured in months. A process decision program chart is shown in Chapter 33.

PERT Charts. A PERT chart is a project network diagram that graphically demonstrates the interrelationships between project elements. It shows the order in which items are to be performed, with "branches" (lines) representing activities and a "node" (box) representing an event. The event is usually the completion of all activities leading to that node. Arrowheads are used to show the direction of the activity flow. The node that shows final completion is called the "sink of the network." Activity branches represented by solid lines have precedence over those represented by dashed lines.

PERT charts often include additional time information, showing the earliest and the latest date that each event could be started and completed without affecting the critical path and therefore the project completion date. The term *slack time* denotes the difference between the earliest and the latest time for an event. Events that lie on the project's critical path will have zero slack time.

Resources

The project plan should specify what resources (e.g., facilities, human, equipment, information, and financial) are required as well as when they will be needed. Using resources owned or controlled by the organization can make the project easier to manage, but the need for special equipment or skills or high variation in resource utilization patterns often means that external resources will also be necessary.

How resources are to be acquired, including special needs that might not have been predicted in advance, should be determined as part of the project plan (e.g., who

❖❖

has the authority to make such decisions?) and communicated to personnel responsible for allocating resources. Some questions to ask are the following:

◆ *What resources will be furnished, and by whom?* For example, if one resource is a work area within existing space, have arrangements been made and affected departments informed that they must provide such space? If the resources are people, what qualifications must they have?

◆ *When must these resources be available?* A piece of equipment might need to be available immediately or only during a particular phase of the project. Scheduled holidays and vacations might conflict with the project schedule.

◆ *How will the resource be delivered?* This factor can affect both cost and timing (e.g., consider the difference between ship-bound freight and airfreight).

◆ *How much will it cost, and when will payment be made?* The detailed costs and timing must be known to plan for cash flow.

◆ *Who will pay?* This must be known for each direct stakeholder to budget and make decisions about the project's timing.

Methodology and Tools

Most companies prefer to use a standardized project management methodology unless a new one is absolutely necessary (e.g., because of the makeup of a particular project or contractual requirements). However, a project might involve specific changes in methodology, such as a different project reporting process or the introduction of computerized project management tools. A project team must avoid becoming so involved in learning the new methodology that it loses sight of the project's goals.

Computerization is a definite trend in project management as the cost and complexity of software has becomes reduced. Although a manual system has its own strengths (low cost and a hands-on feeling), a computer provides the ability to do what-if scenarios (e.g., how will the project timing and cost be affected by adding additional resources?) and making it easier to create more complex Gantt and PERT charts. Computerization also permits the integration of multiple projects utilizing some of the same resources, making it easy to assess how a necessary change in one project will affect other projects.

RELEVANT STAKEHOLDERS

Stakeholders are those people who have a vested interest in a project. These include the following:

◆ departments that will be changed as a result of the project

◆ departments that must provide support for the project

◆ direct customers of the project, including end users

◆ indirect customers, such as regulatory agencies that provide guidelines or rules

◆ stockholders or others who will be affected financially by the project

Once stakeholders are identified (see previous discussion), the project team should outline a strategy for working with each stakeholder group. This might entail the direct involvement of a stakeholder representative in the project, asking for input on an as-needed basis, or simply communicating project status. Stakeholders should be notified of the impending project through their own chain of command to ensure that they understand that the project is properly authorized and has management's support. Concerns expressed by stakeholders at this point should be weighed; the nature and legitimacy of their concerns might suggest who is likely to support or obstruct the project.

Aspects of change management were discussed in Chapter 11. As noted there, reasons for resistance to an improvement project or any type of change are usually quite logical and can include the following:

◆ people like how things currently work

◆ the desire for change is often perceived as indicating that the organization is not currently a good one

◆ the organization has a poor history of effective change

◆ the reasons and method for change are poorly communicated

◆ the people, method, or timing of the project are considered inappropriate

◆ the new process is perceived as changing power relationships

◆ the change will increase workloads

The project team should maintain contact with both stakeholders and project sponsor(s) throughout the project. If people who are not part of the team try to delay or obstruct the project, management has the responsibility and authority to address the problem.

RISK ASSESSMENT

All projects that consume organizational assets involve risk. The outcome of the project might not achieve a level of quality acceptable to stakeholders, might not be accomplished on time, or might require more financial capital than was allocated. Therefore, risk assessment, is an important component of project planning.

Wideman identifies four major steps involved in risk management:

◆ risk identification

◆ assessment and quantification

◆ response development

◆ documentation and control[3]

Potential risks can be identified through brainstorming (discussed in Chapter 33) by the project team, input from stakeholders, a methodical review of the project plan, or reviews of other projects. Quantifying risks involves looking at the probability of a particular event's occurrence and its resulting impact by using a tool such as failure mode and effects analysis (discussed in Chapter 37). For those risks having both a high probability of occurrence and a high level of negative consequences, a strategy should

❖❖

be developed for offsetting (e.g., through the purchase of insurance) or remediating (e.g., through the development of a contingency plan) the event. Documentation of the risk management plan provides a guide for responding to events that occur.

Project managers should be careful to take into account the risk orientation of the particular organization and stakeholders for which the project is being undertaken and not allow their own perspective to overly influence subsequent decisions.

BENCHMARKING

Benchmarking, "the process of identifying, understanding, and adapting outstanding practices and processes from organizations anywhere in the world to help your organization improve its performance," is a popular method that organizations use to improve their products and processes.[4] As a project management tool, benchmarking can help a project team determine early in the planning phase what levels of performance other organizations have achieved and how the results have been accomplished. The steps to take in benchmarking are as follows:

1. identify the activity to benchmark
2. determine how to measure the activity
3. identify a benchmarking partner
4. collect data on how the partner is successful
5. analyze the data
6. set goals and develop an action plan
7. monitor plan implementation

Benchmarking involves identifying potential sources of best practices. However, it first requires gaining a complete understanding of one's own process because it is impossible to do an accurate comparison to others without such an understanding. This requires understanding the boundaries of the process to be studied, the steps involved (as identified through a process map), and the resulting current performance level of the process.

A source of comparison can be identified by examining trade publications that list companies deemed best in their industries, perusing best-practices databases available from major consulting firms, or talking with award-winning companies or others from whom it is expected that significant learning can occur. The Internet is likely to become a widely used resource for benchmarking, although the reliability of information found should be confirmed.

If process results or outcomes are all that are to be benchmarked, then available performance figures might be sufficient and no further analysis necessary. However, if how the process achieves those results is to be benchmarked, then a visit to the comparison organization can be arranged. Once performance data has been analyzed, the project team can determine how the partner is achieving that performance and then set goals and an action plan to achieve similar success.

However, process benchmarking can become so large that it becomes a project within its own right. Before using it as a key decision-making tool, an organization should determine whether benchmarking is the best use of its resources. A benchmarking effort might initially be limited to discovering whether anyone has overcome the same or similar restraints. If so, the project team can decide whether benchmarking is required to replicate the success. If process benchmarking is to be done, then this information should be included in the overall project plan with sponsorship from management as with other aspects of the project.

If done correctly, benchmarking offers many benefits. It allows the project team to look beyond its own company and even its industry. Looking beyond normal, everyday boundaries allows new ideas to filter into the organization. In addition, a successful relationship with a partner can create a mutually beneficial sales tool for both companies. Significant research-and-development resources can be saved when mistakes are avoided. Finally, benchmarking can allow a company to gain ground on the competition in a very short time.

Pitfalls to avoid in benchmarking include the following:

- having the wrong people on the team
- the inability to successfully break a process into its components
- taking on too large a process
- lack of long-term management commitment
- focusing only on metrics rather than on processes
- failing to integrate the benchmarking criteria with broader goals
- trying to copy a process from one organization into another without considering differences in culture, skill level, and other processes that might be related

Finally, competitive or comparative analysis should not be mistaken for benchmarking. Such analyses have a purpose mainly of assessing one's own strengths and weaknesses as compared to the competition.

BUDGETING

A project budget is a management tool that sets financial expectations for project implementation. It is a plan that details the magnitude and timing of projected financial resource inflows and outflows over the project's duration.

"In the end, top management is primarily concerned with how much a new quality project will return, how soon returns will occur, and what risks must be taken by the business."[5] Profitable projects can lead to the organization's growth, whereas losing projects can lead to the company's demise. A budgeted quality project is expected to be (1) on time—that is, it should meet the proposed schedule; (2) on budget, or meeting proposed costs; and (3) within specifications. This means that the expected performance should be met and good human relations maintained.

"Each quality project budget must be reasonable, attainable, and based on estimates of tasks to be accomplished"[6] within management-defined guidelines. Usually, the following steps are followed for each project: define the activities, identify resource requirements, estimate costs to complete the activities, and communicate the requirements to top management for funding.

Some typical budget revenue estimating factors include the following:

◆ increased sales
◆ improved process capability
◆ increased profits
◆ increased equipment uptime
◆ reduced defects
◆ reduced spare parts inventories
◆ reduced scrap
◆ reduced customer cancellations
◆ lowered warranty claims
◆ less returned product

Some quantifiable budget cost estimate factors include the following:

◆ money
◆ energy
◆ personnel costs
◆ subcontracted work
◆ overhead allocations
◆ materials, both consumables and project direct
◆ equipment costs: purchase, rentals, leases
◆ fees: permits, licenses, applications, and so on
◆ consulting charges reserve or contingency for unanticipated events

In general, a project budget should do the following:

◆ be the mechanism for planning, authorizing, allocating, and controlling resources
◆ be the timely allocation of scarce resources to the various endeavors of an organization
◆ be precisely the pattern of constraints that embodies organizational policy
◆ be a standard for comparison
◆ be a baseline from which to measure the difference between the actual and planned uses of resources
◆ tie resource usage to organizational achievement that facilitates management's evaluation of project cost/effectiveness
◆ prioritize work
◆ communicate the importance of activities
◆ reinforce and remunerate performance
◆ ensure that all organizational areas are going in the same direction

The astute project manager must be wary of several possible pitfalls. A project might take too long and/or start too early. Top management might want more done using fewer resources, including people.[7]

Budgeting effectiveness often is affected first by the fact that corporate goals, strategies, and plans are sometimes vague or unknown. Second, competition for finite resources can be fierce. Third, the future can be uncertain and unknown. Fourth, internal politics and game playing are inherent in the budgeting process. Finally, external requirements can change rapidly.[8]

> Project revenues and costs are described by four project budget factors: original budget, forecast amount, actual amount during implementation, and variance amount. The original budget is the approved written plan of the total costs and cash inflows, expressed in dollar amounts per time period, for the project as funded by top management. The forecast amount is the predicted revenues and costs, adjusting the budget costs/revenue magnitudes to reflect the reality that becomes apparent only during actual implementation. The actual amount is the actual revenues and costs that have occurred, and for which the amounts are known instead of estimated. The difference between the original budget and actual revenues and costs is known as the variance amount. Usually, any variance exceeding 10% needs an explanation and possibly an analysis.
>
> During the project implementation, the actual cash amounts are documented and the information is provided to the project manager so that the appropriate adjustments and decisions can be made during the project to control costs. Any number of types of variances may be calculated for the project. These may include cost variances for materials, labor, overtime, schedule delays, unplanned activities, etc., by activity or department. The importance of using variances is to highlight those items which are significantly different from originally budgeted so that corrective action can be taken.[9]

BENEFIT-COST ANALYSIS

As businesses respond to changes in markets, technology, and strategic emphasis, they allocate or reallocate financial resources for many purposes. The careful selection and successful implementation of business projects plays a large role in organizational change. Project managers can spend large amounts of funds over a number of years to acquire assets needed by the business. An organization's future economic success and long-term survival is dependent on the benefits of projects outweighing the associated costs.

Top management must approve and fund most projects that will require significant financial resources. Therefore, before a proposed project is initiated, a benefit-cost analysis of its projected revenues, costs, and net cash flows will be performed to determine the project's financial feasibility. This analysis is based on estimates of the project's benefits and costs and the timing thereof, and the results are one key factor in deciding which projects will be funded. On project completion, accounting data are analyzed to verify the project's financial impact on the organization. In other words, management must confirm whether the project added to or detracted from the company's financial well-being.

In the past, based on middle management's proposals to upper management, proposed quality improvement projects were often unconditionally accepted. According to required guidelines, top management authorized them and allocated resources for project implementation. Each quality project was assumed to be critical to organizational success, and most dealt with obvious problems, such as a high rate of customer returns or complaints or high levels of internal scrap or rework. In today's competitive global environment, resource allocation is complicated by the facts that business needs and opportunities are greater and that improvements are often more difficult to achieve, as the easier improvements have already been done. Therefore, top management requires that project benefits and costs be evaluated so that projects can be correlated to revenues, costs, customer satisfaction, market share, and other criteria. These factors are analyzed to maximize business returns and to limit risks, costs, and exposures. Therefore, quality improvement projects are considered to be business investments—as are all cash or capital investments—in which benefits must exceed costs. Quality managers are additionally challenged in that many of these benefits and costs are not easily quantifiable, as is normally expected by top management executives, accountants, and financial committee members.

Characteristics of Benefit-Cost Analysis

Benefit-cost analysis attempts to evaluate the benefits and costs associated with a project or initiative. Two types of benefits can be evaluated: direct or indirect. Direct benefits are measured easily and include issues such as increased production, higher quality, increased sales, reduced delivery costs, higher reliability, decreased deficiencies, and lower warranty costs. Indirect benefits are more difficult to measure and include such items as improved quality of work life, increased internal customer satisfaction, and better-trained employees. Similarly, two types of costs can be evaluated. Direct costs include equipment, labor, training, machinery, and salaries. Indirect costs include downtime, opportunity costs, pollution, and displaced workers.

Generally, a benefit-cost analysis is conducted on the basis of direct costs and direct benefits, or to (1) assist in the performance of a what-if analysis; (2) compare the benefits, costs, and risks of competing projects; (3) allocate resources among multiple projects; and (4) justify expenditures for equipment, products, or people. Benefit-cost analysis justifies quality decisions and the allocation of scarce corporate resources. Because many indirect benefits and costs cannot be quantified, some worthy quality projects or initiatives might fail to obtain the necessary funding.

Project benefit-cost decision making can be used to evaluate nearly any proposed investment by determining whether and by how much accrued benefits surpass costs for the project in question. Some project examples include purchasing a new machine, adding a new process line, and justifying the outsourcing of parts instead of making them in-house.

Linking Profitability and Quality

Quality managers are expected to help their companies profit from quality investments, so no project should receive automatic approval and resource allocation. To be competitive, companies must find ways to increase profitability while providing customers with high levels of satisfaction. The challenge, then, is to find the link between critical business performance measurements, such as profitability, and quality investments, such as improvement projects, programs, and initiatives. Although some quality benefits and costs are difficult to measure or are unknowable, the quality manager still must help determine and measure quality's effect on company finances. One way to do this is by measuring the cost of quality (discussed in Chapter 34).

Excellence in quality alone is not sufficient for differentiating and positioning a company. An increasing number of companies provide cost-competitive, high-quality products and services in a courteous and timely manner. With so many companies providing top quality, aggressive cost-reduction strategies have become as important as quality for many companies and often are included in overall company strategic plans.

Understanding the relationship between quality and profitability requires knowledge of the following:

◆ how customer quality requirements affect customer satisfaction

◆ how quality initiatives need to be linked to satisfying customer requirements and expectations

◆ the relationship between quality investments and gross profits

◆ how to ensure that quality improvement projects focus on providing the greatest returns

◆ how to track the various elements of the cost of quality

◆ how customer returns and customer satisfaction affect revenues

◆ how to quantify customer satisfaction

A study conducted in 1974 showed a direct relationship between market share and product quality.[10] This is obvious from the fact that once earnings surpass fixed costs, profitability is in direct correlation to the number of units sold (which equates to market share).

Screening Project Proposals

Projects approved and funded by top management affect a firm's growth and development as well as its ability to remain competitive and to survive. Success depends on a constant flow of new investment ideas that are activated through these projects. Accordingly, well-managed firms go to great lengths to develop a good process for submitting project proposals.

Project screening procedures must be established so that those projects with the most merit are approved. Screening quality capital expenditure proposals can be a very complex exercise. Benefits can be gained from a careful analysis, but such an investigation does have its own associated costs. Projects should be selected not only on the basis of their prospective financial payback but also on the basis of their fit to overall business needs (e.g., new product development, improvements in support systems, and improvement of the order fulfillment process).

Ranking Projects with Capital Budgeting Decision Rules (Benefit-Cost Analysis Rules)

A number of different methods are used to rank projects and to decide whether they should be accepted for inclusion in the organization's cash/capital budget. Each project can be accepted or rejected or can be delayed because of limited availability of capital or other resources. Three ranking methods are mainly used for financial analysis: payback, net present value (NPV), and internal rate of return (IRR).

Payback Period. The payback period, defined as the number of years a firm expects it will take to recover its original investment from net cash flows, was the first formal method developed to evaluate capital budgeting projects. The easiest way to calculate the payback period is to accumulate the project's net cash flows and see when they sum to zero.

The payback method was originally used because of its simplicity and ease, which was an important consideration in precomputer days. Even today, some sophisticated firms still use the payback method to evaluate small capital expenditure decisions. Also, the payback method is useful because it provides a measure of project liquidity, or the speed with which cash invested in the project will be returned. Firms that are short of cash must necessarily place a higher value on projects with a higher degree of liquidity. Finally, the payback period is often considered to be an indicator of the relative risk of projects because managers can generally forecast near-term events better than more distant ones. When other factors are constant, projects with relatively rapid returns are generally less risky than longer-term projects.

Net Present Value (NPV). As flaws in the payback method were recognized, managers began to search for methods that would improve the accuracy of quality cash/capital project evaluations. This effort led to the development of discounted cash flow (DCF) techniques, which take into account the time value of money. One such DCF method is the NPV method, which consists of the following steps. First, find the present value of each cash flow, discounted at an appropriate percentage rate, which is determined by the cost of capital to the firm and the projected risk of the flow; the higher the risk, the higher the discount rate required. Next, determine the project's NPV by adding the discounted net cash flows. If the NPV is positive, the project should be accepted; if negative, it should be rejected. If two projects are mutually exclusive, the one with the higher positive NPV should be chosen.

Internal Rate of Return. The internal rate of return (IRR) is defined as the discount rate that makes the NPV equal to zero.[11] If the IRR is greater than the minimum required by the company (e.g., cost of capital or alternative investment options), then the project is likely to be accepted.

Evaluating Capital Budgeting Decision Rules

In practice, all three of the capital budgeting rules described previously are used. However, these methods can lead to different accept/reject decisions. Obviously, the best method is the one that selects the set of quality cash/capital projects that will maximize a company's value.

Three properties must be exhibited by a project selection method if it is to lead consistently to correct capital budgeting decisions. The method must consider (1) all cash flows through the entire life of the project and (2) the time value of money, such that dollars that come in sooner are valued more than later ones. In addition, when a method is being used to select from a set of mutually exclusive projects, it must (3) choose the project that will maximize the firm's value.

The payback method violates items (1) and (2) by not considering all cash flows and ignoring the time value of money. Both the NPV and the IRR provide appropriate financial accept/reject decisions for independent projects, but only the NPV method satisfies item (3) under all conditions.

Performing the Postaudit

An important aspect of the project cash/capital budgeting process is the postaudit, which compares actual results to those that were predicted in the project proposal, allowing for explanations of any differences. For example, many firms require their operating divisions to send a monthly report for the first six months after a project goes into operation and a quarterly report thereafter until the project's results meet expectations. From then on, reports on the project are handled like those of other operations.

Improved forecasts result when decision makers systematically compare their projections to actual outcomes, as conscious or unconscious biases can be identified and eliminated. Additionally, project managers tend to do better forecasting if they know that outcomes will be verified. New forecasting methods can also be sought as the need for them becomes apparent (e.g., as the business becomes more complex or as new methods of financial/business value analysis are developed).

Because each element of the cash flow forecast is subject to uncertainty, a percentage of all projects undertaken by any reasonably venturesome firm will necessarily be off target. This fact must be considered when appraising the performances of the operating managers who submit capital expenditure requests. Projects also sometimes fail to meet expectations for reasons beyond the control of the project managers and for reasons that could not be realistically anticipated. However, separating the operating results of one investment from those of the larger system can often be difficult. While some projects stand alone and permit ready identification of costs and revenues, the actual cost savings that result from some projects can be very hard to measure, because of the large number of other variables that can affects outcomes.

Results of the postaudit process must be used appropriately. If results are used punitively, managers mights be reluctant to suggest potentially profitable but risky projects in the future. Finally, the project managers who were actually responsible for a given project decision might have moved on by the time its results are known. Because of these difficulties, some firms tend to play down the importance of the

❖❖❖

postaudit. However, observations of both businesses and governmental units suggest that the best-run and most successful organizations are the ones that emphasize the postaudit process. Accordingly, the postaudit has become one of the most important elements in a good benefit-cost analysis cash/capital budgeting system.

⚙ Additional Readings ⚙

Adam, P., and R. Vande Water. 1995. "Benchmarking and the Bottom Line: Translating Business Reengineering into Bottom-Line Results." *Industrial Engineering,* February, pp. 24–26.

American Productivity and Quality Center. 1998. "What Is Benchmarking?" Brochure. Houston: APQC.

Brigham, Eugene F. 1986. *Fundamentals of Financial Management.* 4th ed. New York: Dryden Press.

Camp, R. C. 1989. *Benchmarking: The Search for Industry Best Practices That Lead to Superior Performance.* Milwaukee: ASQC Quality Press.

___. 1995. *Business Process Benchmarking: Finding and Implementing Best Practices.* Milwaukee: ASQC Quality Press.

Cleland, David I., ed. 1998. *Field Guide to Project Management.* Milwaukee: ASQ Quality Press.

___. 1998. "Stakeholder Management." In *Project Management Handbook,* ed. Jeffrey Pinto. San Francisco: Jossey-Bass, pp. 55–72.

Duncan, W. R. 1994. *A Guide to the Project Management Body of Knowledge.* Upper Darby, Pa.: Project Management Institute, 1994.

Evans, Dorla A., and William E. Souder. 1998. "Methods of Selecting and Evaluating Projects." In *Project Management Handbook,* ed. Jeffrey Pinto. San Francisco: Jossey-Bass, pp. 119–37.

Frame, J. D. 1994. *The New Project Management.* San Francisco: Jossey-Bass.

Gee, Glenn, Wesley Richardson, and Bill Wortman. 1996. *CQM Primer.* West Terre Haute, Ind.: Quality Council of Indiana.

Graham, Robert J., and Randall L. Englund. 1997. *Creating an Environment for Successful Projects: The Quest to Manage Project Managers.* Milwaukee: ASQ Quality Press.

Hutchins, Greg. 1996. *The Quality Book.* Portland, Ore.: QPE.

Martin, J. D., et al. 1991. *Basic Financial Management.* 5th ed. Englewood Cliffs, N.J.: Prentice Hall.

Meredith, J. R., and S. J. Mantel Jr. 1995. *Project Management: A Managerial Approach.* New York: John Wiley & Sons.

Micklewright, M. J. 1993. "Competitive Benchmarking: Large Gains for Small Companies." *Quality Progress,* June, p. 67.

Robbins, S. P., and M. Coulter. 1966. *Management.* 5th ed. Upper Saddle River, N.J.: Prentice Hall.

Schoeffler, Sidney, Robert D. Bizzell, and Donald F. Heany. 1974. "Impact of Strategic Planning on Profit Performance." *Harvard Business Review* (March–April) Vol 52: pp. 137–45.

Spendolini, M. J. 1992. *The Benchmarking Book.* Milwaukee: ASQC Quality Press.

Stamatis, D. H. 1997. *TQM Engineering Handbook.* New York: Marcel Dekker.

Swanson, R. 1993. "Quality Benchmark Deployment." *Quality Progress,* December.

Wheelen, T. L., and J. D. Hunger. 1995. *Strategic Management and Business Policy.* 5th ed. New York: Addison-Wesley.

Wideman, R. Max. 1998. "Project Risk Management." In *Project Management Handbook,* ed. Jeffrey Pinto. San Francisco: Jossey-Bass.

Chapter 32

Implementation

❖ *This chapter should help you*

- ◆ Understand requirements for obtaining management support and for managing resistance to change
- ◆ Become familiar with the relationship between project implementation and short-term (tactical) plans
- ◆ Understand the importance of cross-functional collaboration and continuous review and enhancement of the quality process
- ◆ Become familiar with different requirements and approaches for communicating progress during and after project implementation

---

Pinto and Slevin list 10 major issues that project managers should keep in mind to improve the probability of a project's success:

- ◆ keep the mission in the forefront
- ◆ balance cost consciousness with project performance
- ◆ communicate openly and continuously with clients
- ◆ be certain that the technology to succeed exists
- ◆ set up and maintain a scheduling system
- ◆ select the right people for the project team
- ◆ confirm top management's support of the project
- ◆ prepare for contingencies by continually asking what-if questions
- ◆ do not be too hasty to judge a project as a success or failure
- ◆ remember that any project is only as good as its application[1]

Although a good project plan is vital to success, this list shows the important project management issues that must be continually addressed during project implementation.

MANAGEMENT SUPPORT AND ORGANIZATIONAL ROADBLOCKS

A primary role of management is not only to provide resources for new initiatives but also to ensure that projects are supported throughout their life. Projects can affect day-to-day operational issues as well as long-term strategy, organizational structure, and business processes. When problems arise, the project team's authority might be limited by the mission statement's scope, but top management retains the authority to span organizational boundaries to address barriers to project success.

Management Support: Overcoming Resistance

When management initially announces a new project, there might be a burst of enthusiasm. People might be hesitant to point out weaknesses or potential problems with ideas that have been presented by influential members of the organization. However, individuals or groups who did not raise objections at the beginning of a project might do so as the project progresses. Although the project team will usually include representative members of key stakeholder groups, resistance might still occur because of a particular individual not being directly involved. There is also a natural resistance to change, both biological and psychological, based on fear and differences in priorities or values.

Resistance can be in a passive form, whereby the project is simply not supported, or it can take more active forms, such as presentations to management as to why the project's goals should be changed or why the project should be terminated. Such resistance can be public or private, but it must be identified by the project team and considered by management for resolution. Of course, if the resistance is found to have merit, then some aspect of the project might need to be adjusted or the entire project canceled.

Some common ways of reducing resistance to change include the following:

◆ ensure that there is a common vision of change (e.g., communicate the mission and the importance of the project)

◆ understand the emotional impact of change

◆ understand the systems view—that is, be aware of how changing one process or part of the organization will affect other processes or parts

◆ communicate what will and what will not change

◆ model the behaviors that are desired

◆ provide effective feedback, rewards, and consequences

◆ be consistent in responding to resistance

◆ be flexible, patient, and supportive[2]

In the case of critical projects, resistance can be overcome early in a project by giving absolute authority to the project team. During the Persian Gulf War, a team of U.S. Army officials were given written authority and the necessary military equipment to develop a successful new bomb that could penetrate reinforced concrete before exploding. If not for the war, the project authority would have been much more limited, and the product development process might have been tied up in red tape for years.

Management support is typically provided in the form of an upper-level manager who acts as the project's sponsor. This person does not have to be at the highest level of the organizational hierarchy but must be knowledgeable about the organization as a whole as well as being familiar with both formal and informal lines of authority. A good sponsor can identify the opinion leaders in the informal network whose support the project must have. This helps the project leader enlist the support of key people toward the goal. The sponsor should know how to address people, procedural, or other roadblocks, including working in a persuasive fashion that does not engender a climate of favoritism. The sponsor might also work as a mentor to the project manager by helping the manager gain a more complete understanding of the organization and its functioning as well as providing assistance in comprehending the in-depth dynamics of project management and change management.

Organizational Roadblocks: Internal

Resistance is often created by a functional design. Managers often have strong authority in their operational areas but might apply a narrow perspective to a particular project. The task of running their own organizational units as efficiently as possible can create conflict with the goals or processes of the project.

Another source of problems is the perception of how scarce resources and funding are allocated and whether the allocation process appears to favor some types of projects or people. Although the reasons for sanctioning one project over another might be based on excellent rationale, people can misinterpret or fabricate their own version of the reasons for a particular decision if the decision-making process is not well communicated.

Fear of loss of power, jobs, or competence is also a common internal roadblock that can be more difficult to identify and resolve because it involves subsurface feelings.

Organizational Roadblocks: External

External roadblocks to a project can be the result of international, national, state, local, or industry regulatory issues that often can add significant time and cost to projects. Regulations are usually set in place in reaction to past mistakes but often are criticized because the process of meeting them can be extremely time consuming. A project team must have adequate knowledge of applicable regulatory issues and be able to interface with the bodies responsible for carrying them out.

Suppliers can also be a source of problems, especially when resources are constrained, project timing is changed from what was originally set, or differences occur in the interpretation of contracts. Financial institutions that provide loans for project funding also have their own approval cycle that might not be optimized for project timing, and subsequent changes to the project might be met with concern about the organization's ability to perform. Economic downturns that can occur during a project's life can also cause suppliers to reorganize their own priorities, with a resulting impact on the project.

Product liability, malpractice lawsuits, special interest groups' agendas, and competitors' countermoves have also created a need for organizations to more carefully plan and execute projects. These sources of roadblocks are not only more difficult to predict and plan for, but are also ones against which management has much less leverage.

❖❖

SHORT-TERM (TACTICAL) PLANS

Short-term plans are the course of action developed to achieve a milestone within the overall project. They are used to achieve the goals set out in short- and long-term strategic plans or projects. The strategic plan states what is to be done, whereas the tactical plan states how it will be accomplished. The project team has the job of breaking down the "what" into the many "hows" and then carrying the plan to completion.

For example, a strategic plan might include a goal of reducing the overall cost of quality as part of an overall cost reduction effort. A specific project, then, might be to reduce quality costs associated with the supplier base. The tactical plan might include one step for performing assessments of suppliers to determine the better candidates with which to work and another step for working with selected suppliers to help them improve their internal processes. It might be expected that this will lead to reduced incoming inspection costs, less on-line scrap, and decreased downtime. However, implementing the assessment process itself will require the selection and/or training of qualified assessors, definition and documentation of the assessment criteria, and scheduling and performing the assessments. Budgets would need to be allocated for the travel expenses for both the assessors and those who will work with the suppliers on the process improvements.

A project, then, is a series of actions, and the completion of a series of actions achieves a milestone on the project chart. The project team's task is to break down the project into the smallest action units possible. The team will create tactical plans for each portion of the project, and some portions of a very large project might merit their own project managers. Each part will have a budget and a timetable for status reports and must meet completion requirements. Contingency plans might be developed for some tasks, especially those on the critical path.

CROSS-FUNCTIONAL COLLABORATION

Because many projects cross organizational boundaries (e.g., departments, facilities, divisions, and companies), forming a team of people who do not normally work together or who do not work in close proximity is a significant issue in project management. Regardless of where the project team members are located, they must have a common understanding of the goals, action plans, and their responsibilities in the project. Knowledge of team building and conflict management methods is a valuable addition to a project manager's toolkit.

Cross-functional collaboration is being aided more and more by technological tools such as e-mail, group software, and video conferencing. These technologies allow the group to remain in close contact even though team members might not be able to meet physically on a frequent basis. This trend will become even greater in the future as project teams become more widespread in their geographical locations. This means that project team members will be selected mainly on the basis of their skills as opposed to their geographical location.

CONTINUOUS REVIEW AND ENHANCEMENT OF QUALITY PROCESS

Continuous review and enhancement of the quality process is achieved by frequent checks on project status and acting on the findings. Reviews should look not only at the project's status but also at what has been learned about project management or the particular process change being addressed by the project. A final review should take place at the end of the project as well.

Sharing information with others outside of the project team ensures that management and other stakeholders are aware of the project's status. Well-documented status reports can usually perform this role, especially when supported by informal communication on an as-needed basis. Communicating what has been learned is important; various channels, including departmental meetings or time set aside specifically for shared learnings, are appropriate.

Project management allows a project to be treated as a separate organizational entity, depending on its own merits. Those responsible for the project should be held accountable and rewarded as appropriate. It is easy to implement measurements to judge timeliness, return on investment, and overall success; other aspects of projects are more difficult to manage.

Some common quality errors in project implementation include the following:

◆ accepting responsibility for a project without a clearly defined goal and written authority

◆ starting a project before reviewing the financial viability

◆ starting a project without identifying and obtaining input from stakeholders

◆ starting a project without a management-approved action plan

◆ starting a project without an agreed-to reporting method and schedule

◆ starting a project without a commitment of resources

◆ failing to report slippages in the hope of making them up

◆ surprising management in a negative fashion

◆ ignoring inconvenient rules, regulations, and permits

◆ counting on budget approval after the fact

◆ not having defined metrics that judge success

Perhaps the worst mistake of all is assembling a team and then not letting it do its job. If a project team will not be allowed to fully utilize members' skills to accomplish what the organization has determined to be a worthwhile goal, then the team should not be created.

DOCUMENTATION AND PROCEDURES

Methodologies for how project planning and implementation is to be carried out within the organization should be documented (e.g., procedures and forms). Each project should then be documented, utilizing the methodology that has been defined. The methodology should include the following:

- project mission statement
- project plan
- project plan approval
- project plan updates or revisions
- performance results, including expenses

Inexpensive project management software has become increasingly available and allows project tracking and reports to be maintained throughout the life of the project.

The use of formal, written communications in project management ensures that records are permanent and complete, that background materials exist for use in future projects, and that the concerns of all parties have been addressed. Informal, verbal communications are also useful because they are inexpensive as well as quick and easy to prepare and use. However, informal communications are more likely to be incomplete or misinterpreted and do not allow transfer of a consistent methodology.

Additional Readings

"Cross-functional Management: Research Report #90-12-01." 1990. Methuen, Mass.: GOAL/QPC.

Darnall, R. W. 1996. *The World's Greatest Project: One Project Team on the Path to Quality.* Upper Darby, Pa.: Project Management Institute.

Kerzner, H. 1995. *Project Management: A Systems Approach to Planning, Scheduling, and Controlling.* 5th ed. New York: Van Nostrand Reinhold.

Leavett, J. S., and P. C. Nunn. 1994. *Total Quality Through Project Management.* New York: McGraw-Hill.

MacLean, Gary E. 1993. *Documenting Quality for ISO 9000 and Other Industry Standards.* Milwaukee: ASQC Quality Press.

Okes, Duke W. 1991. "Developing Effect Change Agent Skills Workshop," 32nd Annual Quality Clinic, Knoxville, Tenn., March.

Parker, G. M. 1994. "Cross-Functional Collaboration." *Training and Development,* October, p. 49.

Pinto, Jeffrey K., and Dennis P. Slevin. 1988. "Critical Success Factors." In *Project Management Handbook,* ed. Jeffrey Pinto. San Francisco: Jossey-Bass, pp. 379–95.

Stamatis, D. H. 1994. "Total Quality Management and Project Management." *Project Management Journal,* September, pp. 48–54.

Part 5 Endnotes

Chapter 31

1. D. H. Stamatis, *TQM Engineering Handbook* (New York: Marcel Dekker, 1997), p. 364.
2. David I. Cleland, "Stakeholder Management," in *Project Management Handbook,* ed. Jeffrey Pinto (San Francisco: Jossey-Bass, 1998), p. 84.

3. R. Max Wideman, "Project Risk Management," in Pinto, ed., *Project Management Handbook,* p. 291.

4. American Productivity and Quality Center, "What Is Benchmarking?" Brochure; Thomas J. Cartin and Donald J. Jacoby, *A Review of Managing Quality and a Primer for the Certified Quality Manager Exam* (Milwaukee: ASQ Quality Press, 1997), p. 270.

5. Greg Hutchins, *The Quality Book* (Portland, Ore.: QPE, 1996), pp. 7–39.

6. Glenn Gee, Wesley Richardson, and Bill Wortman, *CQM Primer* (West Terre Haute, Ind.: Quality Council of Indiana, 1996), p. VI-35.

7. Hutchins, pp. 7–39.

8. Ibid., pp. 7–40.

9. Gee et al., p. VI-36.

10. Sidney Schoeffler, Robert D. Bizzell, and Donald F. Heany, "Impact of Strategic Planning on Profit Performance," *Harvard Business Review* (March–April 1974).

11. Dorla A. Evans and William E. Souder, "Methods of Selecting and Evaluating Projects," in Pinto, ed., *Project Management Handbook,* p. 233.

Chapter 32

1. Jeffrey K. Pinto and Dennis P. Slevin, "Critical Success Factors," in *Project Management Handbook,* ed. Jeffry Pinto (San Francisco: Jossey-Bass, 1998) p. 390.

2. Duke W. Okes, "Developing Effective Change Agent Skills Workshop," 32nd Annual Quality Clinic, Knoxville, Tenn., March 1991.

Part 6
Continuous Improvement

◆◆◆

Chapter 33

Tools

◆◆◆

❖ *This chapter should help you*

  ◆ Become familiar with quality control tools and their applications
    in problem solving
  ◆ Become familiar with quality management tools and their applications
    in problem solving
  ◆ Understand Shewhart's PDCA cycle and Deming's PDSA cycle

APPROACHES TO PROBLEM SOLVING

Regardless of the quality system in place, room for improvements always exists. Bringing competent people together to make improvements project by project is an excellent method for assessing and enhancing the current system. When the weakness(es) in a system that led to a problem is determined and controls are implemented to prevent a recurrence of that problem and other problems like it, the entire organization benefits. A systematic approach should be used to understand problems and to identify their causes; only when these causes are uncovered and properly understood can they be eliminated.

The following example illustrates the sequence of steps performed in one scenario:

A monthly analysis of a quality cost report reveals that a particular work center has high scrap rates and that the problem appears to be getting progressively worse. The manufacturing manager and the supervisor in the department where the problem is occurring agree that several possibilities exist to explain the causes of the problems. First, three of eight workers have been in the department only a couple of months and are still learning their jobs. Second, two machines are considerably older than the others and break down more frequently. Finally, this department was the bottleneck in the production system the previous month, so it is rushing to push extra product through.

Once an understanding of the problem exists, steps must be taken to correct it. The supervisor forms an improvement team of both new and experienced people from the department that is experiencing the problem: a manufacturing engineer, a maintenance person, and several setup technicians. The supervisor further studies the issues and recommends possible short-term actions to lessen the problem's impact immediately and works with the team to formulate and implement longer-range measures.

❖❖

The situation and management's actions are reported to the Continuous Improvement Steering Committee so that the team's actions can be supported and coordinated with the ongoing work of the company's other improvement teams. Launching the team without advance approval from the committee is justifiable because the problem is serious and complex enough to merit a team approach and because this area is likely to become the company's most prominent bottleneck. The Committee agrees with the assessment and assigns a team mentor.

This brief scenario introduces many concepts relating to the methods for achieving continuous improvement within an organization. Employees often are brought together in small teams either for special, temporary assignments such as the one described above previously, or in permanent "quality circles" to assist with the smooth running of the systems under their stewardship. Employee teams usually employ a systematic problem-solving approach, the core steps of which are to (1) define the problem, (2) gather and analyze data, (3) propose and test viable solutions, (4) implement a solution, and (5) follow up to ensure that the problem has been solved and that the solution has not created new problems. The scientific approach can be conducted on a company-wide basis, or a project approach that focuses on one manageable project after another might be more feasible than a massive overall improvement campaign.

The scientific approach and other problem-solving and analytical tools are applied to discover the cause(s) of problems so that appropriate measures can be taken to eliminate those causes from the system or process. In the previous scenario, the employee team used problem-solving and analytical tools to accumulate valid data about the problems. Management, in turn, used these tools to prioritize problems so that necessary resources could be allocated and a plan formulated for the continuous application of methods to improve service and reduce costs.

Once existing problems have been solved, many companies focus on problem prevention by undertaking additional analysis to discover why root causes were not detected or acted on until they caused waste and delays. Such root causes spread rapidly when fueled by lack of knowledge or management inattention (e.g., to maintenance, training, education, process control, or the overall system).

Often, what is initially determined to be causing a problem or defect (e.g., a specific machine, department, component, or person) may simply be a symptom of a much larger difficulty. Typically, problems are caused not by a single uninformed or careless person but because of a chain of events and contributing conditions that offer several unrealized opportunities to discover and prevent the shortcoming.

Some problem-solving tools demand a rigorous mathematical approach, while others can be mastered quickly. However, even the simplest analytical tool is ineffective if used in the wrong circumstances or if the data that are gathered are not interpreted correctly. For example, three months of decreasing sales may indicate flagging performance by the sales department but more likely is the result of normal random variation of a process over which the sales department controls only some of the important inputs. Punishing or rewarding people for the random swings in a process is a sure way for management to lose credibility.

Auto mechanics need to accurately diagnose and quickly fix engine problems, not simply replace components until the problem part is found (a lengthy and costly method). Likewise, problem solvers need a systematic approach that consists of examining the symptoms with believable data and facts, performing a valid diagnosis, and experimenting with solutions until the optimum one is discovered, implemented, and proven to endure without negatively affecting other aspects of the system.

A systematic approach to attacking problems on a project-by-project basis works for several reasons:

- Resource allocation improves the chances of success.

- Using facts and data improves problem-solving efficiency and effectiveness by ensuring that improvement efforts focus on the proper areas.

- Other areas of the process or system benefit. For example, in the opening scenario the problem with the machines might help the company develop a maintenance program to improve the long-term performance of all similar machines and even other equipment.

- If problem-solving tools are used methodically and well, a finite number of problems exists.

Main reasons that the problem-solving process fails include the following:

- insufficient data (jumping from an analysis to a solution too quickly)

- inaccurate data (not knowing the difference between subjective and objective data and/or collecting data in such a way that human error occurs)

- no closed loop (i.e., failing to test the solution before implementing it)

- solving the wrong problem (mistaking a symptom of the problem for the actual problem)

- failing to include the right people in the problem-solving process

QUALITY CONTROL TOOLS

Diagnostic tools are used to dissect a system, gather data and facts, and, through the process of elimination, discover and implement the action(s) that will relieve the condition. Seven problem-solving tools, often called the seven quality control tools, are discussed in the following sections. These are cause-and-effect analysis, the checksheet, control charts, flowcharts, histograms, Pareto analysis, and scatter diagrams. Many other tools exist to assist with problem solving, but these seven are considered by many to be the mainstays of the continuous improvement toolkit.

Cause-and-Effect Analysis

Developed by Dr. Kaoru Ishikawa of Japan, cause-and-effect (C-E) analysis is sometimes referred to as the Ishikawa, or fishbone, diagram. In a C-E diagram, the problem (the effect) is stated in a box on the right side of the chart, and likely causes are listed around major headings (bones) that lead to the effect. People, machinery, methods, and materials are the most commonly used broad categories of problem

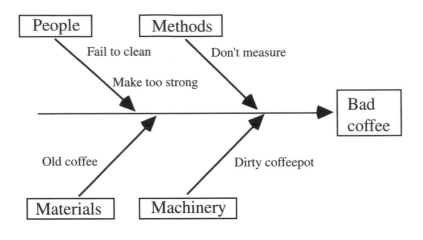

◆ **Figure 33.1.** Cause-and-effect diagram.

sources for manufacturing problems, although other useful general headings, such as environment or measurements, are sometimes added.

Cause-and-effect diagrams assist in organizing the contributing causes to a complex problem. Figure 33.1 uses bad coffee as an example of a problem. This illustration lists some obvious causes of bad coffee, sorted into the major categories suggested previously. The next step might be to ask "Why?" for each of those causes. As new reasons are stated, continue to ask "Why?" until all possible explanations are listed. Each new question brings the several root causes one step closer.

The C-E diagram is a very popular tool for project improvement teams because it facilitates an orderly discussion of a complex topic. When the team has completed a brainstorming exercise (discussed shortly), it might be appropriate, depending on the purpose of the session, to use the output to build the "skeleton" of a C-E chart. Cause-and-effect analysis ensures that possible causes of a problem are further investigated. Often, each "bone" is assigned to a team member for action or additional data-gathering or analysis.

Checksheet

The checksheet (or tally sheet), is often the first tool taught to employee teams because it is simple, it initiates the process of information gathering, and it encourages the use of facts instead of opinions in communicating about problems. The checksheet is easy to use, fits almost anywhere, takes very little time to set up and maintain, can be taught to anyone in just a few minutes, and immediately provides data to be used in the troubleshooting process.

Checksheets are used to measure the frequency of events or defects over short time intervals, ranging from hours to weeks. The checksheet in Figure 33.2 illustrates at a glance what the largest problems are in terms of frequency of occurrence. It is often helpful to see data arranged so that the most costly problems are obvious. An average-cost-per-incident column is often included in a checksheet to facilitate the translation of data to a Pareto chart (discussed shortly). As people gain familiarity

Switch Assembly   Op 236   Plastic footer   Operator_____

Chart began July 12, 1995

	Week 1						Totals
Burns	III	ℍ⊢					
Misrun		III	II				
Bad finish	ℍ⊢						
porosity		I					
flash	ℍ ℍ⊢ I	IIII I					
color							

◆ **Figure 33.2.**   Checksheet.

with the procedure, they can easily learn to estimate costs, lost time, or other useful measures. Because the primary purpose of the checksheet is to gather data, it is used in almost every stage of a problem-solving project that involves data gathering.

Checksheets often reveal problems that are caused by problems in another area. Therefore, data might not be used directly within the department to fix problems but might be handed to the supplying department to assist in their problem-solving efforts. The substitution of data for opinions about problems often transforms a request for help from "just another gripe" into a helpful discussion of business issues.

Control Charts

A control chart serves two vital purposes as a data-gathering tool: (1) it discerns when a process is being influenced by unnatural forces or special causes, creating an out-of-control condition, and (2) it tells how a process is behaving over time.

Control charts should be examined for any visible nonrandom patterns in data points. An analysis of a nonrandom pattern might indicate what is causing a process to behave a certain way. The pattern might reveal problems with the process, such as wildly fluctuating values, sudden process jumps or shifts, and increasing variation. The pattern might also reveal an improvement in a process, such as decreasing variation, and therefore is a useful control measure for the problem solver.

Four guidelines can be used as a basic test for randomness in control charts:

1. The points should have no visible pattern.
2. Most of the points should be close to the centerline.
3. Some points should be close to the outer limit (called *control limits* in statistical process control, or SPC).
4. An approximately equal number of points should fall above and below the centerline.

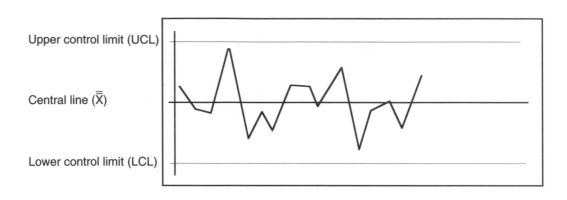

◆ **Figure 33.3.** Control chart.

If all four criteria are met, then the process is likely to be "in control." A control chart is shown in Figure 33.3.

A control chart is used to determine whether a process is stable (which leads to predictable performance). By monitoring the output of a process *over time,* a control chart can be used to assess whether the application of process changes or other adjustments have resulted in improvements and whether these effects are permanent. If the process produces measurable parts, the average of a small sample of measurements, not individual measurements, should be plotted.

Flowcharts

The flowchart is a map of each step of a process, in the correct sequence, showing the logical sequence for completing an operation. The flowchart is a good starting point for a team seeking to improve an existing process or attempting to plan a new process or system. The picture helps the team understand what it takes to accomplish a specific task, and if there are problems with a process, the flowchart might make the missing or erroneous steps apparent. In addition to providing basic reference points, flowcharts can contain additional information (depending on the reasons for the project), such as times, tools, and responsibilities. Flowcharts are one of the most universal and flexible tools taught to teams. A flowchart is shown in Figure 33.4.

The flowchart is the logical starting point for many kinds of problem-solving projects. Often, the evolution of a process is detrimental rather than helpful, as steps are discarded because people are too busy, forgetful, or improperly trained. Therefore, the flowchart is useful as a diagnostic tool when a process is being examined as a possible source of cost savings. When the corrections are made, the flowchart becomes a simple road map—a coordinating procedure that helps people understand what the best practice looks like.

Histograms

It is helpful to display data in a pictorial format that indicates the frequency with which certain events occur. The histogram provides a graphical picture of the frequency distribution of a measured quality characteristic, such as temperature, time,

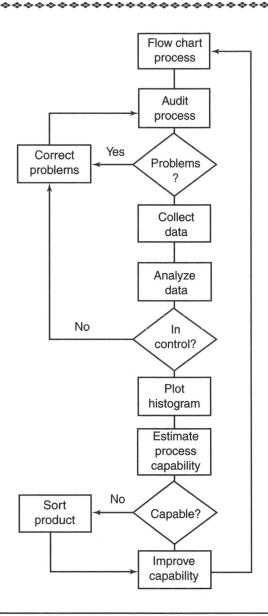

◆ Figure 33.4. Flowchart. Source: Quality Publishing. Used with permission.

and height. An important diagnostic tool, the histogram makes the variation in a group of data readily apparent. A histogram assists in an analysis of how the data are distributed by illustrating how the measures of process dispersion and central tendency relate to process specifications. A histogram is shown in Figure 33.5.

The shape of the histogram allows the user to make predictions about the performance of a process or product, as fluctuations can warn of a lack of control and a lack of predictability. The wider the spread of data, the greater the variation. For a normal (bell-shaped) distribution, the most frequently appearing value (mode) is

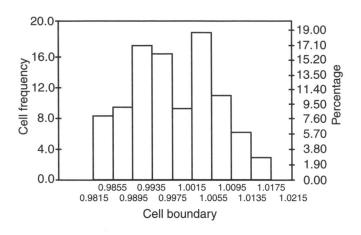

◆ **Figure 33.5.** Histogram. Source: Quality Publishing. Used with permission.

centered with data appearing equally on either side. If data extend beyond the specification limits, the process or product might be out of tolerance.

Pareto Analysis

Vilfredo Pareto, an Italian economist in the 1800s, is noted for his observation that 80 percent of the wealth in Italy was held by 20 percent of the population. Juran later applied this "Pareto principle" to other applications and found that 80 percent of the variation of any characteristic is caused by only 20 percent of all the possible variables. It is now accepted that when a list of defects is sorted by the frequency of occurrences, relatively few causes account for the majority of defects.

The Pareto principle can be applied to most quality improvement efforts. By focusing consistently on the small number of problems that cause the disproportionate share of quality-related issues, management can attack the largest problems by expending the smallest effort. The Pareto principle automatically prioritizes quality improvement projects so that the nonconformances making up the majority of costs can be determined easily.

A Pareto analysis identifies the sources that contribute to a problem. These sources can then be depicted on a bar graph (a Pareto chart). A Pareto chart makes apparent the "vital few" contributors to a problem so that management can concentrate resources on correcting the major contributors to the problem.

In this chapter's opening scenario, Pareto analysis sent the manager to a specific work center—one in which time delays and large amounts of waste were present. Pareto analysis also enabled the department manager to pinpoint two machines and three new operators as the key sources of trouble. Figure 33.6 shows how the team can use a Pareto chart to determine whether any specific parts, materials, configurations, tools (or any other breakdown of the data) are contributing disproportionately to the scrap problems. Money often is the measurement used on the *y*-axis, as it is not the *frequency* of the problem but the *cost* of the problem that is of vital interest. The Pareto chart is one of the problem solver's most useful tools because it is useful

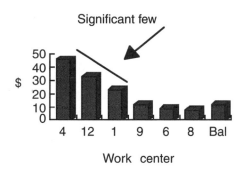

◆ **Figure 33.6.**   Pareto analysis.

at every stage of data analysis. In addition, personal computers and easy-to-use software such as spreadsheets have made the automation of graphics in Pareto charts easier and more practical for problem solvers.

Scatter Diagrams

A scatter diagram shows the relationship between two variables, either input (independent) or output (dependent) variables. Often the scatter diagram is used only to establish the presence or absence of a correlation, not necessarily a cause-and-effect relationship, between two variables.

If it appears that values for one of the variables are caused (explained) by the value of another variable, the values for the dependent variable should be plotted along the *y*-axis. In the example in Figure 33.7, the shear strength of a glue joint has been plotted along the *x*-axis and the curing temperature along the *y*-axis. In this example, the shear strength of this joint increases with an increase in cure temperature, within the normal processing limits. If the data points were to fall onto a single, straight line, the variation in glue strength would be fully explained by the value of the cure temperature. In most cases, there is deviation from a straight line, indicating the existence of other sources of variation in the process.

If the slope of the plots is generally upward, as in this example, a positive correlation exists between values. That is, as one variable increases, the other variable increases correspondingly. Other possible correlations are negative, weak, or none. A negative correlation line slopes downward; this means that as one of the variables increases, the corresponding value for the second variable decreases. If no visible pattern appears to exist in the plotted points, the variables are not correlated to one another.

Three additional factors should be considered when using the scatter diagram. First, *not all relationships between variables are linear.* If the range of temperatures were extended in Figure 33.7, it is likely that a peak strength in the glue joint would be reached, after which increasing the cure temperature would damage the joint and reduce its strength. Therefore, the relationship between the two variables is not really a straight line but rather a curve that climbs upward, peaks, and then descends.

❖❖❖

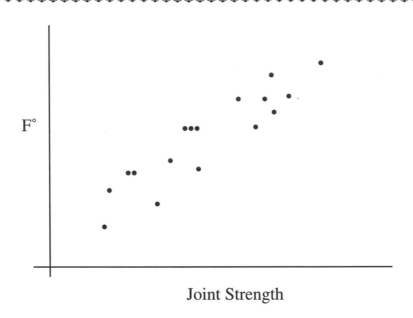

◆ Figure 33.7.   Scatter diagram.

A second consideration is that *the slope of the line does not provide any information on a graph of this type* because the scale can be expanded or compressed on either axis to change the slope at will.

The third consideration, and probably the most important is that *a direct and strong correlation does not necessarily imply a cause-and-effect relationship.* An often used example to make this clear is "The volume of ice cream sold per day is strongly correlated to the daily number of fatalities by drowning." Obviously, neither of these variables is the cause of the other, and the most likely explanation is that each of these variables is caused by and is strongly correlated to a third variable: the outside temperature.

When it is desirable to understand the relationship between two variables or to determine whether a relationship exists, the scatter diagram is a quick and easy way to make any relationship visible.

QUALITY MANAGEMENT TOOLS

The problem-solving tools discussed in the previous sections are taught to and used *by teams* to identify and analyze problems and possible solutions. The management and planning tools discussed in this section are used *by managers,* who frequently need to organize issues, ideas, time, and words rather than materials, machines, and tools. Developed specifically for managers, the following seven management and planning tools are just a few of the many devices used to assist managers in the prioritization and scheduling of the resources needed to solve complex or ongoing problems. These tools are the activity network diagram, the affinity diagram, the interrelationship digraph, the matric diagram, the priorities matrix, the process decision program charts, and the tree diagram.

As with the seven problem-solving tools, these management and planning tools are used to develop an understanding of the processes and related problems that

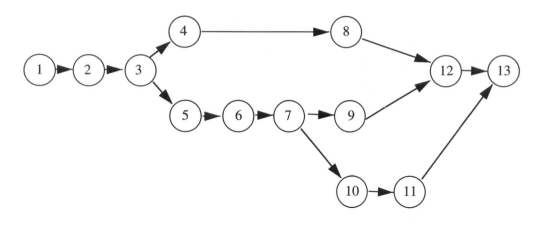

◆ Figure 33.8.   Activity network diagram.

will likely be assigned to an improvement team. The desired outcome should be considered when choosing team members. Members should have a stake in the success of the project, have expertise in the areas to be covered, have sufficient time to participate, and should be able to function well in a group environment. Team members should be trained in the use of the management and planning tools discussed in the following sections. These tools are sophisticated and powerful yet simple enough to be mastered in a reasonable amount of time. Training should include a brief exposure to each tool that explains how and when the tool is used, discusses how it relates to the other tools, and demonstrates the use of each tool more thoroughly.

Activity Network Diagram

Developed by the Rand Corporation in support of complex and large Air Force contracts, the activity network diagram (AND) is a simplified version of the program evaluation and review technique (PERT) and the critical path method (CPM) familiar to project managers. The PERT and CPM techniques typically include specific references to start and stop times, resource usage, costs, cash flows, priorities and slack time, and so on and therefore and thus are more complicated and require more expertise to use. The AND is a picture that shows who is going to do what and when. Arrows are drawn to show what must be done in series and what can be done in parallel so that areas for action can be identified if the overall time estimate is too high to meet goals.

In the AND shown in Figure 33.8, each numbered node represents one task that must be completed as a part of a project. In this example, Task 2 must be completed before Task 3 begins. Tasks 4 and 5 can begin simultaneously as soon as Task 3 is completed. Both Task 8 and Task 9 must be completed before Task 12 can begin. Tasks 11 and 12 must be completed before Task 13 can be started.

The AND is used when a task is complex and/or lengthy, and because of schedule constraints it is desirable to determine which activities can be done in parallel. The AND is used often as a planning aid for construction projects and for large manufacturing contracts that are best handled as projects.

Affinity Diagram

The affinity diagram, a modification of the traditional brainstorming method, encourages people to develop creative solutions to problems rather than to react automatically from the logic of "this is the way we've always done it." A list of ideas is created, then individual ideas are written on small note cards that are placed face up on a horizontal surface. Team members study the note cards and categorize ideas by moving the note cards into groups. No discussion is allowed during this activity; a dissenting opinion is indicated simply by moving a card back to its original location or into another or new grouping. Once a consensus has been reached on the groupings, each category is labeled with an appropriate title written on a new note card, and discussion can begin.

The affinity diagram is a logical way to achieve order out of the chaos that can be created during a freewheeling brainstorming session. An affinity diagram is an excellent method to use when beginning a new project in the following cases: (1) when the ideas about an issue are not clear, are not well understood, or are not well organized and (2) when a team is facing a project that appears too big or too complex.

Interrelationship Digraph

In planning and organizing, it is not enough just to create a huge collection of ideas. The affinity diagram organizes and makes visible the initial relationships in a large project, but the interrelationship digraph (or relationship diagram) pinpoints logical patterns of cause and effect between those ideas.

For example, a small company desiring to grow could use one of the following strategies to support that objective: increased or more aggressive advertising, increasing the sales budget, increasing inventory, improving quality, or increasing capacity. The organization might focus on one or more of these items and would expect a return (growth) for investment in the factors that cause growth. This is where the picture ends for many organizations.

However, problems occur because life is not a simple straight-line collection of causes and effects but a "system" with consequences that are not always apparent. The previous example does not consider competitors' actions during the same time frame. Rather than watching their profits erode, competitors are likely to take actions (e.g., increasing advertising, cutting prices, or using aggressive sales tactics) that will diminish the small company's returns. Many management plans and actions create and stimulate their own systems of resistance.

The interrelationship digraph helps management recognize the patterns, symptoms, and causes of this naturally emerging resistance. For example, the production manager who is responsible for accelerating output with diminishing resources is not likely to be thrilled when an ever-growing number of employees are committed to team meetings in the face of critical deadlines. A natural (and appropriate) response is to pressure the teams to postpone, shorten, delay, and/or cancel their meetings. This resistance produces frustration and anger in team members. When management is able to recognize the sources and causes of resistance, it can undertake measures

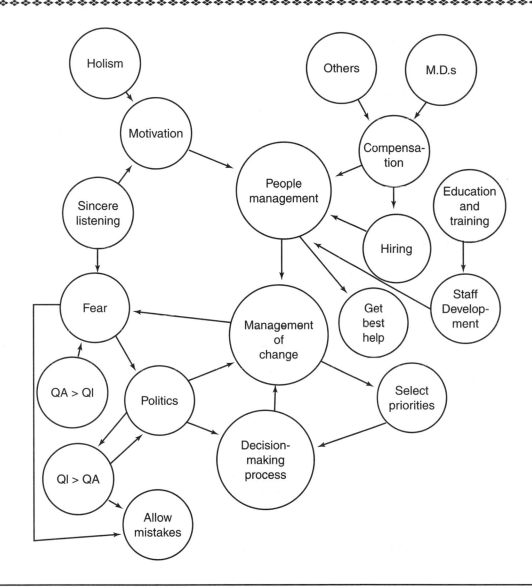

Figure 33.9.   Interrelationship digraph. Source: Quality Publishing. Used with permission.

that force the resistance to collapse on itself. A completed interrelationship digraph is shown in Figure 33.9.

The interrelationship digraph is constructed when the group creates a note card for each planned action, lays all the notes on a horizontal surface, and draws arrows to show links between the actions. The question that should be asked about each planned action is, "If I do this, what will happen?"

The interrelationship digraph is used to simplify a network or cycle of problem causes. It effectively pinpoints the root cause(s) of problems that appear to be connected symptoms.

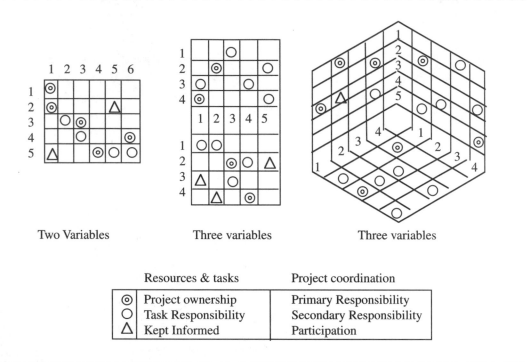

Two Variables   Three variables   Three variables

Resources & tasks	Project coordination
⊙ Project ownership	Primary Responsibility
○ Task Responsibility	Secondary Responsibility
△ Kept Informed	Participation

❖ **Figure 33.10.** Matrix diagrams at various stages of completion.

Matrix Diagram

The matrix diagram is probably the most widely used of the seven management tools because of its versatility and ease of use. It answers two important questions when sets of data are compared: Are the data related? and How strong is the relationship? For example, a matrix diagram might be used when management is faced with a large and complex objective and a collection of departmental resources. The horizontal axis of the matrix diagram would be labeled with the tasks required to complete the objective and the vertical axis with the names of different departments available to perform the work. For each of the required tasks, the matrix diagram would show which departments were in charge, which had some involvement, and which had no involvement in the performance of these tasks.

The quality function deployment (QFD) House of Quality (shown in Chapter 24) is a matrix diagram that lists customer needs on one axis and the in-house standards on the second axis. A second matrix diagram is then developed to show the in-house requirements on one axis and the responsible departments on the other. The QFD process might use an entire series of matrix diagrams to pin down service or design options, product options, training possibilities, objectives, functional responsibilities, and so on. Figure 33.10 shows a number of clever ways to show relationships between up to four sets of variables.

The matrix diagram is created for two reasons. First, surprising patterns often become visible in diagrams. For example, an organization might discover that it does not have a departmental responsibility for key segments of the tasks considered vital to mission accomplishment. Secondly, the completed matrix diagram is an extremely useful checklist for ensuring that tasks are being completed on time and within budget constraints and also serves as a reminder of which individuals are responsible for accomplishing these tasks.

Priorities Matrix

The priorities, or prioritization, matrix introduces an entire series of planning tools built around the common matrix chart, usually with significant information on two axes. Matrix tools, which have existed for many years under various names, have capitalized on clever ways to use many axes, such as the QFD House of Quality matrix, which bristles with useful information all around the core (central) matrix.

The priorities matrix works when there are more tasks than available resources—a common enough condition to merit serious consideration in most organizations. It assists a manager or team in choosing between several viable options that have many useful characteristics, not all of which are present in the same choice.

The relative merits of each available course of action and their related effects create a complicated picture that is difficult to prioritize. For example, how does a person choose between two automobiles, one of which offers average gas mileage, four-wheel drive, and a fully automated set of window and seat controls, and another that has a superior sound system, a significantly smoother ride, and better fuel economy? For one driver, four-wheel drive might be a must-have option that dominates all other considerations, but another driver might value fuel economy above all other options. The priorities matrix does not ignore emotional needs but uses an evaluation process to lend a measure of objectivity to decision making.

A priorities matrix is created and used according to the following steps:

1. A matrix is created to help prioritize decision criteria. All factors affecting the final choice are listed along both the horizontal and vertical axis of the matrix. Criteria are compared and assigned a weighted score on the basis of the perceived importance of each criterion.

2. Possible choices are compared to see how well they align with each criterion. A new matrix is created for each criterion being evaluated. Each possibility is compared with all other choices and is evaluated in terms of how well it conforms to the most heavily weighted decision criteria. The priorities matrix in Figure 33.11 rates automobiles according to the reliability of their transmissions, considered the top criteria in this case.

3. The final matrix, shown in Figure 33.12, lists the possible choices on the left axis and the decision criteria along the top. The conformance score is multiplied by the criteria weight to fill the matrix. The scores for each option (each automobile model in Figure 33.11) are totaled, and the option with the highest score is likely to be selected.

Although the priorities matrix appears complicated, a group can be taught the method in a very short time. This tool provides some objectivity to what could

	1	2	3	4	Tot	%
1		10	5	5	20	48.8
2	1/10		5	10	15.1	36.8
3	1/5	1/5		5	5.4	13.1
4	1/5	1/10	1/5		.5	1.2

Total   41.0

1: Equally reliable transmissions
5: Much more reliable   1/5: Much less reliable
10: Overwhelmingly more reliable   1/10: Overwhelmingly less reliable

◆ **Figure 33.11.**   Priorities matrix: Evaluating options against decision criteria.

	a	b	c	d	TOT	%
a		5	1/10	1/10	5.2	10.2
b	1/5		1/5	1/10	.5	1.0
c	10	5		1/10	15.1	30.1
d	10	10	10		30	59.8

Column total   50.8

1: Equally important
5: Much more important   1/5: Much less important
10: Overwhelmingly more important   1/10: Overwhelmingly less important

◆ **Figure 33.12.**   Priorities matrix: Assigning a utility index to criteria.

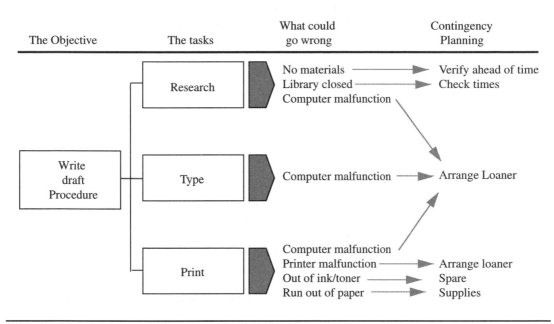

The Objective | The tasks | What could go wrong | Contingency Planning

Figure 33.13. Process decision program chart.

otherwise be an emotional decision. When numerous possibilities exist and the selection criteria are many and complicated, this tool permits a group to systematically discuss, identify, and prioritize the criteria that should have the most influence on the decision and to then evaluate all the possibilities while keeping a complete picture in mind.

Process Decision Program Chart

No matter how well planned an activity is or how well prepared employees are, management knows that things do not always turn out as expected. Therefore, contingency plans often must be developed. One type of contingency plan, the process decision program chart, resembles the reliability engineering tools of failure modes and effects analysis (FMEA) and fault tree analysis. The actions to be completed are listed, then possible scenarios are developed about problems that could occur; management then decides in advance which measures will be taken to solve those problems if and when they do occur. A plan must exist to ensure the availability of the resources that might be needed to correct a problem and to minimize the damage resulting from the problem. Figure 33.13 shows a process decision program chart.

This process decision program chart is especially useful when a procedure is so new that experience cannot suggest what might go wrong. It also is useful as a checklist when a project is large or complex.

Tree Diagram

The tree diagram identifies the tasks and methods needed to solve a problem and reach a goal. It lays out in great detail and in an orderly manner the complete range

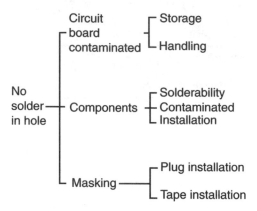

◆ **Figure 33.14.** Tree diagram. Source: Quality Publishing. Used with permission.

of tasks, from the broad to the very specific, that need to be accomplished to achieve a primary goal. A completed tree diagram is shown in Figure 33.14. The tree diagram is a logical follow-up to either the affinity diagram or the interrelationship digraph.

OTHER CONTINUOUS IMPROVEMENT TOOLS

Many other tools are useful for generating or analyzing information to be used as an organization strives for continuous improvement. These include brainstorming/nominal group technique and force-field analysis (in the following sections), QFD (discussed in Chapter 24), and process mapping (discussed in Chapter 38).

Brainstorming/Nominal Group Technique

The brainstorming technique is a simple and orderly way for a group to generate theories about possible problems and their solutions. Because brainstorming encourages creative thinking, the group leaders must avoid deliberately channeling or structuring ideas in any way. A brainstorming session proceeds according to the following steps. The brainstorming topic is agreed on and written in clear terms in full view of everyone in the group. The meeting leader then solicits ideas from the group. Members are asked to contribute every thought that occurs to them and are free to build on previous contributions. Ideas are written down, without correction, modification, censoring, ridicule, or any other expression of judgment about their validity. The creative phase of brainstorming builds on divergent thinking; that is, it attempts to uncover new thoughts through the freewheeling sparks that participants get from one another.

When the flow of ideas shuts down, all the ideas that were written down must be processed and turned into actionable thoughts. This stage, called convergent thinking, consists of arranging the results of the previously described exercise. One popular way of accomplishing this is through the nominal group technique, which consists of the following steps:

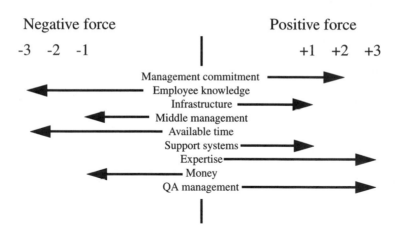

Negative force   Positive force

-3   -2   -1   +1   +2   +3

Management commitment
Employee knowledge
Infrastructure
Middle management
Available time
Support systems
Expertise
Money
QA management

◆ **Figure 33.15.**   Force–field analysis chart.

1. Generating a list of ideas (brainstorming).

2. Combining, simplifying, explaining, and condensing ideas to make the generated list complete and clear but not repetitive.

3. Asking each participant to choose silently a specific number (e.g., from one to three or up to a third) of all the ideas that they think merit further discussion and/or action.

4. Recording each participant's votes either through a voice polling or by using pieces of paper. At this point, if there are still too many ideas to make prioritization easy or obvious, the process can be repeated as many times as necessary.

Brainstorming often leads to consensus about problem causes and creative problem solving, especially when process experts are in the group. The resulting collection of ideas can be moved to, for example, the C-E diagram, as brainstorming is a natural lead-in to many types of problem-solving efforts.

Force-Field Analysis

When an organization wants to make major changes, it usually encounters significant resistance to the project. For example, many organizations strive to attain ISO 9000 registration. Although management might agree that such a goal is desirable, the people involved in a project of this magnitude should examine the company for sources of weakness. In Figure 33.15, force-field analysis begins with the identification of those factors that are considered essential to achieving the desired goal: ISO registration. A brainstorming session would begin with the question, "What must happen to overcome our current state of equilibrium and move our organization into a state of readiness for ISO registration?" At the conclusion of the brainstorming exercise, the list of ideas might include factors such as management commitment, employee knowledge, available time, planning skills, ISO expertise, favorable middle-management climate, support systems, and infrastructure.

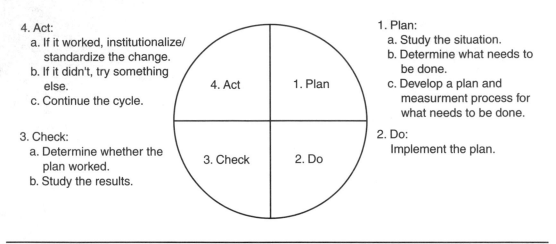

4. Act:
   a. If it worked, institutionalize/
      standardize the change.
   b. If it didn't, try something
      else.
   c. Continue the cycle.

3. Check:
   a. Determine whether the
      plan worked.
   b. Study the results.

1. Plan:
   a. Study the situation.
   b. Determine what needs to
      be done.
   c. Develop a plan and
      measurment process for
      what needs to be done.

2. Do:
   Implement the plan.

◆ **Figure 33.16.** PDCA/PDSA cycle.

A quick look at this chart shows that the group performing the analysis feels that the overall strengths in reaching the goal include the level of management commitment and the knowledge and ability in the quality assurance area. Areas of potential concern include a lukewarm middle-management climate and cash problems as well as serious problems with employee training and time availability for a project of this magnitude. Individuals' ratings for each area will vary, so the best approach is to poll team members through an anonymous rating on index cards and then average the results to reach a final rating.

The force-field analysis chart presents a team with a good picture of any preparation or "preselling" that should be undertaken before serious resources are delegated to the project. The development of the analysis and the pursuant discussion might help some groups reach a consensus.

THE PDCA/PDSA CYCLE

The Plan-Do-Check-Act (PDCA) cycle for learning and improvement was developed by Shewhart to show how improvement takes place. It was subsequently popularized and renamed the Plan-Do-Study-Act (PDSA) cycle by Deming. In either case, someone initiates the process by developing a plan to stimulate an improvement. Then the plan is put into action, preferably on a small scale.

In the next stage, the results of the action are examined critically. Did the action produce the desired results? Were any new problems created? Was the action worthwhile in terms of cost and so on? The knowledge gained in the third step is acted on. Possible actions include changing the plan, adopting the procedure, abandoning the idea, modifying the process, amplifying or reducing the scope, and then beginning the cycle all over again. Shown in Figure 33.16, the PDCA/PDSA cycle, as simple as it is, truly captures the spirit of *continuous improvement*. When employees are empowered through self-control, the PDCA/PDSA cycle can be used to manage performance at the process level and the work level. Information for analysis at the process level includes summaries of basic data for specific products and processes over a specified period of time. By comparison, information for analysis at the work level includes individual measurements for specific events at the time of their occurrence.

Continuous improvement hinges on application of the PDCA/PDSA cycle at the work level, the process level, and the company level. Trend analysis is a vital part of the PDCA/PDSA process in evaluating or checking actual performance against planned or expected performance outcomes.

🏠 Additional Readings 🏠

Asaka, T., and K. Ozeki. 1990. *Handbook of Quality Tools: The Japanese Approach.* Portland, Ore.: Productivity Press.

Barnett, A. J., and R. W. Andrews. 1994. "Are You Getting the Most out of Your Control Charts?" *Quality Progress*, November, pp. 75–80.

Hume, Hitoshi, ed. 1987. *Statistical Methods for Quality Improvement.* Milwaukee: ASQC Quality Press.

Ishikawa, Kaoru. 1989. *Guide to Quality Control.* Milwaukee: ASQC Quality Press.

Joiner Associates. 1995. *Introduction to the Tools: Everything You Need to Know About the Basics but Are Too Busy to Ask.* Madison: Joiner Associates.

PQ Systems, Inc. 1996. *Total Quality Tools.* Miamisburg: PQ Systems, Inc.

Pyzdek, Thomas. 1994. *Pocket Guide to Quality Tools.* Tucson, Ariz.: Quality Publishing.

Smith, Gerald F. 1998. *Quality Problem Solving.* Milwaukee: ASQ Quality Press.

Stamatis, D. H. 1997. *TQM Engineering Handbook.* New York: Marcel Dekker.

Tague, N. R. 1995. *The Quality Toolbox.* Milwaukee: ASQC Quality Press.

Chapter 34

Cost of Quality

❖ *This chapter should help you*

- ◆ Understand quality cost categories
- ◆ Understand the importance of measuring the cost of quality
- ◆ Understand how to implement a cost of quality program

WHAT IS COST OF QUALITY?

Cost of quality is a management term used by many manufacturing and service companies to correlate the financial impact of quality activities to specific business goals. Attaching a dollar amount to a condition or an occurrence helps management easily see whether that circumstance would be favorable. Once recognized, workforce education can exploit the benefits of favorable circumstances. Likewise, workforce training can minimize the negative implications of unfavorable conditions.

In the 1950s, Dr. Armand Feigenbaum, a General Electric engineer, saw the value in a management reporting program that focused on quality costs, their causes, and their effects. During the same period, Dr. Joseph Juran, the well-known quality expert, began writing about the importance of measuring quality in the terms best understood by upper management: dollars. These concepts were the basis of what has evolved into the popular corporate "cost of quality programs." No one method exists for collecting and reporting an entity's quality cost drivers because each company's accounting system collects and reports costs differently. However, by applying the logic of quality cost, any corporate accounting or quality manager should be able to design a meaningful measurement tool used to report on and highlight their quality issues and undertake meaningful quality improvement activities.

Cost-of-quality reporting is one of the best tools available to raise an organization's awareness of quality issues. Management's approach to quality must underscore the importance of ongoing learning and self-improvement. Cost of quality is a learning tool itself and requires education to be used effectively. Management should not only support this education but also participate in it to emphasize its importance. Through this education, employees will better understand how to fulfill the responsibility of achieving quality work in their jobs and will learn how what they do affects both internal and external customers. Workers who understand how costs are collected and reported realize how their work influences their department's budget performance and, it is hoped, their company's total performance.

❖❖

Collection and analysis of quality cost help employees understand the activities that truly drive their organization. Management has a much better chance of focusing on the significant cost drivers when it understands the activity bases from which costs are generated. Once the drivers are understood, overall employee awareness can be raised, and the company is better able to identify problem costs and take corrective action.

DESIGNING A COST-OF-QUALITY PROGRAM

The design of a cost-of-quality program can be viewed as a three-step process: (1) categorizing costs, (2) focusing on problem prevention, and (3) establishing and tracking measurements.

Categorizing Costs

There are three major categories of quality costs: appraisal, prevention, and failure. In his book *Quality IS Free,* Phil Crosby asserted that quality does not cost money; rather, it is the *absence* of quality (the nonconformances and failures) that swells total costs. Crosby popularized the terms *cost of poor quality* or *cost of nonquality* and recognized that to avoid these bad costs, money would have to be spent up front on prevention and appraisal. Crosby's categories are used regularly in many organizations for cost-of-quality analyses.

When designing a cost-of-quality program and setting up the natural expense accounts to track the elements, attention must be given to the "buckets" into which costs fall. Two basic areas of cost exist: conformance costs, or "good" costs, and nonconformance costs, or "bad" costs. Conformance costs include prevention and appraisal, whereas nonconformance costs include internal and external failures. Because the cost of quality can often be 20 percent to 30 percent of sales, these dollars must be traced to their sources to understand their cause-and-effect relationships.

Quality costs apply to all departments and should not be confined to those associated with production. Often, the costs generated within the support functions are substantial and represent a significant slice of the quality cost pie. They are often hidden within standard costs. In addition, labor expenses might be reported with an overhead allocation for benefits and other indirect expenses, just as material might be reported at the invoice, or "fully loaded," price. The existence of such pitfalls dictates that considerable skill be applied to properly determine true and comparable costs.

Conformance Costs. The phrase *price of conformance* (POC) actually describes the costs of ensuring that a company's day-to-day activities are being performed correctly, that is, that the customer's requirements are being met. Conformance costs can be further categorized as prevention costs and appraisal costs.

Prevention costs are the costs associated with activities specifically designed to prevent poor quality in products or services. Examples include new-product review, quality planning, supplier capability surveys, process capability evaluations, quality improvement team meetings, quality improvement projects, and quality education and training. Appraisal costs are those costs associated with measuring, evaluating, or auditing products or services to ensure conformance to quality standards and performance requirements. They include the costs of incoming and source inspection/test of purchased materials; validation, verification, and checking activities; in-process and final inspection/test; product, service, or process audits; calibration of measuring and testing equipment; and the cost of associated supplies and materials.

Nonconformance Costs. Nonconformance costs are those that result when products and services do not conform to requirements or customer/user needs; that is, they are the costs resulting from poor quality. The price of nonconformance (PONC) has extensive and long-lasting consequences for customers. In this sense, the word *customer* refers not only to the end user but also to all persons affected by the product or process. Companies pay for not initially doing things correctly, and the costs of the additional activities required for not meeting the customer's specified requirements ultimately must be passed on to consumers and shareholders. These inefficiencies apply to both internal and external customers and can increase the total cost of the product or service enough to make a company uncompetitive.

Internal failure costs occur *before* the product is delivered to the customer. Examples are costs of rework and repair, reinspecting and retesting of product, material downgrading, inventory shrinkages or pickups, unscheduled downtime, and internal miscommunications that result in delays. External failure costs occur *after* delivery of products or while furnishing a service to the customer. Examples include the costs of processing customer complaints, field service, customer returns, warranty claims, product recalls, and product liability lawsuits.

Focusing on Problem Prevention

Long experience with managing quality costs has taught that a relatively modest investment in prevention can lead to significant reductions in failure costs and ultimately lower inspection costs as well. Although solving manufacturing, design, or service problems is a worthwhile goal of a cost-of-quality program, preventing those problems from occurring is the ultimate goal. An approach that emphasizes problem prevention is best because a customer's perception of an operation's performance often dictates whether the business relationship will continue. A prevention-based system should identify and address potential issues quickly, before they become serious. The earlier in the process those situations are prevented from occurring, the more cost savings can be realized.

It is natural to resort to "easy fixes" to solve problems as they occur. Unfortunately, this behavior is inconsistent with today's theory in the quality profession and is very costly for the organization. For example, increasing the number of inspectors is the easiest way to keep problems from being shipped out the door, but it is also the most costly! This solution is neither expedient nor consistent with the foundations of total quality management, which is fixing the problem at the root cause. It is better to spend resources on avoiding problems (conforming to existing requirements) than on solving problems, as greater resources are required to repair problems after they have occurred.

Establishing and Tracking Measurements

Before you can move in a meaningful direction, you must know where you are now. Data are needed to measure improvements in the system. Changes in performance can be measured by first selecting the standard on which to base the appraisal and then by tracking the improvement trend over time.

Quality improvement cannot exist without measurements that give a starting point as well as a finishing line and capture all the performance data in between. To decide what needs improving and to weigh the benefits against the expense, meaningful quantitative and qualitative measures must be available. These empirical, fact-based data should be used to make operating decisions.

Quantitative evaluations (measurements) help the manager identify improvement opportunities by documenting and quantifying the degree to which work areas need improvement. They also help evaluate the efficacy of changes by tracking improvement, from the past history and proximity to the goal, by reporting on the consequences of the efforts and by weighing the potential gains of improvements against the expense of implementing solutions. One cannot manage what one cannot or does not measure.

Undeniably, the most frequently used measure of quality is dollars. Tracking labor hours, floor space, or other activity bases are other options, but hard dollar figures are best understood and remembered by top management. Therefore, it is important to involve accountants in designing a cost-of-quality program. Cost accountants can combine knowledge of the manufacturing process with an understanding of the company's financial reporting systems to choose the most appropriate elements for a meaningful quality report. The accountants can work with process engineers to properly evaluate the technical aspects of the process. The accountant is responsible for transforming the perception of the process into a value traceable to, and compliant with, nationally recognized financial reporting standards.

The collection system must be comprehensive if it is to be effective. It also must be practical and therefore must fit in with the company's regular cost system. In developing the details of the quality cost system, there are two important criteria to follow: (1) recognize that quality cost is a tool to justify improvement actions and measure their effectiveness and (2) realize that including insignificant activities is not essential.

If large elements of quality cost are not identified in the regular cost system (e.g., scrap, rework, and redesign costs), the system may have to be redesigned. Estimates should be used until the system can be adjusted. Redesigning a company's cost system is a major undertaking with many ramifications. This is discussed further in the American Society for Quality's basic reference on the subject, *Principles of Quality Costs*, third edition (1999), edited by Jack Campanella, which should be consulted for more detailed information.

For process measurements to be implemented throughout the organization, it is vital to gain the support not only of management but also of workers closest to the process. The employees doing the tasks to be measured should have a role in developing the most meaningful measurements because they will be the ones taking the measurements and will be asked to offer solutions to the problems. For effective measurements, the general rule is to keep them simple. The simpler the measures, the more they will appeal to groups of workers.

Departmental measures must be such that all employees clearly understand goals. For example, measures that most anyone can relate to are the number of telephone calls that "rolled over" to voice mail, the quantity of incorrect entries on a form, or the number of customer complaints received during a specified period. These measures identify the sources of errors, simplify problem-solving efforts, and provide feedback to the people doing the work. If process control requirements increase, the employees will already be familiar with simple measures, and adding more complex measures will not be difficult.

To establish a meaningful cost of quality program, an organization must select the activities that are most problematic. Employees in various departments should participate in identifying the most significant business issues. The underlying rule is not to lay blame on individuals but rather to focus on preventing defects and eliminating inefficiencies.

Identifying Value-Added and Non-Value-Added Activities

In addition to identifying areas of nonconformance, the organization may want to identify and categorize the most important value-added and non-value-added tasks. The value-added activities contribute to the individual's ability to meet the requirements of internal and external customers. They often include activities such as providing supplier responses, meeting with clients, and conducting employee coaching and training sessions. Non-value-added activities are not absolute business necessities. These can be found by looking for duplicate efforts between departments, unnecessary slack time between activities, and unnecessary administrative requirements. Some authorities consider these costs of nonconformance.

Activities to be measured include the number of discrepant units or output from a process, at what point in the process the defects occur, or the types of external factors introduced when the discrepancies occurred. The items should be ranked in order of their overall significance, with the largest problems listed first. Nonconformance costs are frequently displayed on a Pareto chart. Those items that are easiest to correct and that yield measurable results should be dealt with first. This is an important initial step because it will help the group receive recognition for "quick wins" (success stories). This will help build morale levels early in the process and provide much-needed momentum just as employee commitment begins to wane.

The line workers and frontline administrative staff are best able to assess the quality levels of the work produced because they are closest to it and the most familiar with the deliverables. The people closest to the process best know what to measure and are the most appropriate people to conduct the measurement studies. Ownership of the measurement process must be given to employees who work with those processes on a daily basis because it is they who will have the greatest impact on making changes.

Quality measurements require a group effort with adequate time to do a thorough job. This is a very consequential activity, so agreement must be reached on which measurements will be useful. Peer meetings should be held to identify the

❖❖

various cost-driving elements; individuals should be assigned data collection tasks in a predetermined format (developing this format might take a few days), and regular meetings should be held to measure progress.

Measurement charts can be displayed in high-traffic areas so that "process owners" can answer others questions about the data. This increases their stake in the process by ensuring that they will get drawn in deeper and increases their awareness about the effects of the work of other groups on their numbers. Formally posting departmental measures provides performance information to others in the organization. It also sends the message that the process being examined is important and that management is interested in the results. Just the fact that a process is measured will usually result in increased performance. The workers pay more attention because they know that the eyes of others are on them. It is human nature to strive for acceptance and to do a good job. All workers want to showcase their talents and successes.

IMPLEMENTING A COST-OF-QUALITY PROGRAM

Nothing is more important to the success of a cost-of-quality program than management's demonstrated commitment to the program. Management should obtain monthly cost reports and use them to make decisions. This action sends a strong company-wide message about the importance of using quality-related data in running the business.

The cost-of-quality report, a dynamic document produced at least once a year, expresses to management (in dollars) how well the organization is performing from a quality perspective. If proper workforce education and training are taking place, if management is participating in the process, and if the company's awareness level has been raised, the trend should show a shift away from expensive detection-oriented activities and a migration toward cost-saving prevention activities. As managers are taught to use cost-of-quality reports as valuable devices to identify cost drivers, they will also develop an understanding of how certain processes drive the business in ways they have never before imagined. This is the greatest payoff from cost-of-quality work.

Historically, management has focused on production quantities or the high cost of rework. Recently, however, the focus seems to be shifting to other-cost-of-sales areas, such as warranty expense and customer retention costs. Management uses cost reports to ensure that appropriate investments are made in prevention expenses, such as design engineering.

Management must make an adequate effort to plan the cost-tracking system so that value will be harnessed. Costs can be collected via the existing natural expense accounts in the corporation's general ledger. Most manufacturing organizations track costs in accounts such as scrap, inspection, rework, overtime, and premium freight expense. However, the true value of the reports depends on their structure and level of detail. Reports can be arranged to accrue costs on a work order or project basis (job accounting) or can be continuously cumulative (process accounting).

If management does not demonstrate that the reports are valuable and are being used, staff members cannot be expected to use the reports. Breakthrough process changes are much more likely to take place when the environment is supportive, so management must lead by example.

The most effective and easiest way to express costs associated with activities is simply to count the number of times the specific incident arose and graphically depict the situation on a chart. Pareto charts, control charts, and histograms are generally the easiest formats for most people to understand. Data must always be presented with the least skilled person in mind. Only the simplest charts are effective for communicating information to groups of people with diverse experience and education levels.

Finally, no operational decisions should be made arbitrarily or in a vacuum. Changes should be based on qualitative information and objective evidence. It is too easy to rush to a conclusion before all the data are analyzed. The root cause will be found by tracing decisions to facts, not feelings.

🏛 Additional Readings 🏛

Atkinson, Hawley, John Hamburg, and Christopher Ittner. 1994. *Linking Quality to Profits: Quality-Based Cost Management.* Milwaukee: ASQC Quality Press.

Campanella, Jack 1999. *Principles of Quality Costs: Principles, Implementation and Use.* 3rd ed. ASQ Quality Costs Committee. Milwaukee: ASQ Quality Press.

___. 1989. "Quality Cost: Principles and Applications." in *Quality Cost: Ideas and Applications,* vol. 2. Milwaukee: ASQC Quality Press, pp. 460–66.

Chang, Richard. 1994. *Step-by-Step Problem Solving.* Irvine, Calif.: Richard Chang Publications Division.

Crosby, Philip B. 1990. *Leading: The Art of Becoming an Executive.* New York: McGraw-Hill.

——. 1979. *Quality Is Free.* New York: McGraw-Hill.

Juran, Joseph M. 1988. *Planning for Quality.* New York: Macmillan/The Free Press.

Chapter 35

Process Improvement

❖ *This chapter should help you*

- ◆ Identify possible failure mechanisms for process improvement teams
- ◆ Explain the role of the team facilitator
- ◆ Explain the role of the team leader
- ◆ Describe the possible role of a steering committee for process improvement teams
- ◆ Understand the mechanisms for identifying and implementing process improvements

Basic to the process improvement philosophy is the recognition that improvement never ends: It is a continual moving forward, whether in quantum leaps or minor gains. Because most business problems are process-related rather than employee-related, businesses must realize the importance of focusing on processes for business improvement. On the other hand, employees should not be ignored—they should be given the best possible working conditions and provided with ongoing education, and their individual problems should be addressed as they occur.

One obvious benefit of process improvement is long-term survival. As competition continually intensifies and external customers become increasingly selective, corporations can no longer blindly pump out products and services to an eager mass audience content to get almost anything with minimal regard to quality. This situation, which existed after World War II, is definitely not the case today. Quality is no longer a luxury—it is a necessity to get and keep an organization in the marketplace.

Quality alone is not enough to deliver total customer satisfaction. Other factors contributing to customer satisfaction include on-time delivery and an acceptable price. Process improvements should reduce cycle time, increase throughput, reduce unnecessary inventories, and, where appropriate, reduce operating expenses. Process improvement should also consider policy constraints as well as physical constraints. Following well-defined process improvements that take a global focus can lead the organization to increased profitability, company growth, and long-term viability.

❖❖

IDENTIFYING AREAS FOR IMPROVEMENT

Because a system is an interconnected set of processes, improving specific processes can greatly enhance overall system performance. However, organizations should not begin improving all their processes blindly because this can result in suboptimization from an overall system perspective. The process to be redesigned should be selected carefully to achieve the maximum return on the effort invested and to ensure that it is important to long-term strategies or current operational deficiencies.

Often, it is better to improve or reengineer key processes (those with the greatest potential for improving value to stakeholders) first because these enhancements will usually result in better quality, quicker throughput, and increased profitability. Effort should not be expended to improve processes that will not improve profitability or solve serious quality problems. Efforts in total quality management often fail because of the inability to show management the resulting benefits in financial terms.

Another factor to consider is that short-term fixes, although well intentioned, can ultimately result in unforeseen long-term problems. In addition, the best time for an organization to improve is when it is strong; however, many endeavor to improve only when potential disaster is imminent.

FORMING PROCESS IMPROVEMENT TEAMS

Improving a selected process generally involves the establishment of a process improvement team. This team might report progress to a steering committee or executive group on progress on an ongoing basis during the process improvement effort.

Corporate and Team Goals

The steering committee often identifies processes most in need of improvement and initiates teams to address the opportunities. They might do project selection on the basis of customer satisfaction data, cost-of-quality reports, or other strategic or operational performance measures (e.g., capacity, throughput, and cycle time).

The goal of each process improvement team should be clearly delineated and understood by all involved. Without such goals, it is easy for the team to begin working on something that might be of interest to them but that will not optimize the overall system. This does not mean that a given goal is fixed. With the steering committee's approval, a new goal might be developed on the basis of new knowledge that is gained during the improvement effort.

One of the key purposes for the steering committee is to ensure that all teams are working cohesively toward the enterprise's strategic goals. Without such direction, the goals of one team can conflict with those of another team. Additionally, the steering committee has the power to approve budgetary outlays for new equipment, software, and so on.

The steering committee also has the power to approve the team's recommendations, and the authority to enforce their implementation. Teams can work hard to improve a process, only to find their final report gathering dust on the corporate shelves. Such inaction results in the belief that management is not serious about process improvement, and employees might be reluctant to become involved in future efforts.

Team Structure

How a team is structured will depend on the scope of the process on which they will be working. A cross-functional team is most widely used for process improvement, as it is usually necessary to cover the range of job functions that the process affects. Team membership should also consider the team dynamics that will affect their development and performance (see Chapters 39, 40). Process improvement teams will consist of a team leader, team members, and often a facilitator.

Team Leader. The team leader is responsible for setting the meeting times, creating meeting agendas, directing the team (including making team homework assignments), and reporting progress to the steering committee. Ultimately, the team leader will coordinate implementation of the team's approved recommendations. The team leader should have a strong vested interest in the process and is often a process owner who is responsible for the results of the process. The team leader must have strong organization skills and should be strong, compassionate, and sensitive at the appropriate times.

Team Facilitator. The team facilitator has the responsibility of keeping the team moving smoothly. The facilitator can play devil's advocate by asking questions to spur looking at the process from differing points of view. It is critical that the team facilitator understand quality management theory. In particular, he or she should recognize the importance of individual and group psychology in accomplishing the process redesign. The facilitator is also available to assist the team with the technical aspects of improvement, such as process mapping, selecting data collection strategies, using relevant analysis tools, and ultimately developing a project plan to carry out improvement recommendations.

It is recommended that the team facilitator be a person knowledgeable in quality methods and not a part of the organization (or at least a major department) involved in the redesign. These requirements are necessary to ensure that the process is properly analyzed and to provide an independent, objective view. The facilitator should ensure that broader issues, such as customer requirements and cost of quality, are taken into consideration.

Other Team Members. Other team members are those involved with the process to be improved and often include internal or external customers and suppliers. Technical experts and outsiders with no vested interest in the process are sometimes added to help provide additional knowledge, objectivity, or creativity. The team members will generally have action items to be carried out apart from the team meetings. Education is sometimes needed at the team level to make all members aware of the quality-based process to be followed in analyzing and/or redesigning the process to be improved.

❖❖❖

GUIDELINES FOR PROCESS IMPROVEMENT

A macro synthesis of the focus of the Baldrige Award provides a useful set of criteria for guiding process improvement efforts:

◆ *Leadership.* Senior executives should oversee the process.

◆ *Strategic.* Improvements should be targeted primarily at those processes that will provide a strategic gain or advantage.

◆ *Involvement.* Because of their knowledge and responsibility, people who work in the process should be the ones doing the analysis and improvement.

◆ *Process.* Approach all projects from the view that what is to be improved is a process that transforms inputs (from suppliers) into outputs (for customers).

◆ *Data.* Decisions such as what processes to improve and what to change to make it better should be based on data, when possible.

◆ *Customer.* Process changes should take into account the impact on, and feedback from, the customers.

◆ *Prevention.* Because the idea is to create processes that are able to meet or exceed requirements, actions taken should keep process problems from recurring.

ANALYZING THE CURRENT PROCESS

The methods for analyzing and improving a process are many, and the approach to be used depends on the particular situation. If the purpose of the team is to alleviate a recurring problem (e.g., get an unstable process under control by eliminating assignable/special causes of variation), then a detailed study of current performance and what contributes to the specific problems that are occurring will typically be required. If the purpose is to improve overall capability of a process that is unable to meet requirements (e.g., a stable process with inadequate capability) or to enhance the capability through an incremental improvement, then a broader understanding of the process will be required. If the purpose is to totally redesign the process (e.g., a reengineering approach), looking at the details of the current process might be of little value.

A normal way of analyzing the current process is to first look at it from a macro view:

◆ Who are the suppliers and what inputs do they provide?

◆ What are the outputs of the process and who are the customers to whom they are sent?

◆ How can the performance of the inputs and outputs be measured (e.g., measures of quality, time lines, and cost)?

◆ How is the process currently performing on these measures?

◆ What changes in performance are desired?

◆   What are the variables (inputs and process controls) that contribute to performance?

◆   What process changes could be made to improve performance?

Evaluation of the current process is normally a useful step, as it helps everyone gain the same perspective and often enlightens those who did not previously have a broad understanding. It also provides a baseline of knowledge from which to build. Of course, too much time should not be spent analyzing the current process, as this can cause analysis paralysis, loss of enthusiasm, and upper management's frustration with progress. The time required depends on the complexity of the process and the availability of data. "Low hanging fruit" improvements should be implemented immediately rather than waiting for a full process analysis/redesign.

Common ways to analyze the current process include flowcharting and process mapping (see Chapter 38), studying past data to determine the validity of the process, and examining customer–supplier relationships.

Historical Data. Historical data are often available to illustrate the performance of the process; if not, baseline data might need to be collected. Control charts are an excellent source of information, as they not only will provide information over a time period but can also differentiate between assignable causes and common causes of variation (see Chapter 16), which will require different types of actions.

Customer–Supplier Relationships. By studying and documenting the requirements of all internal and external customers and suppliers, team members will help ensure that the new process addresses their needs. The specifications of internal customers and suppliers frequently are not documented. The process team should develop operational definitions of these requirements and then determine whether documented specifications should be created. These might also include items such as the tests to be performed and format of the resulting data.

CREATIVE THINKING VERSUS ANALYTICAL THINKING

The process of improvement often requires analysis of the process, breaking it down into discrete parts, and understanding how each part is performing and contributes to the overall process. Many of the tools used (see Chapter 33) provide a means of performing this analysis, either by representing the process (e.g., through a flowchart or cause-and-effect diagram) or showing how it is performing (e.g., through a Pareto chart of the problem or a control chart of the trends). Therefore, analytical thinking is an important part of process improvement.

Equally important is the part of improvement that requires coming up with new ideas. Brainstorming possible causes of a problem (before determining what is actually the cause) or potential solutions to a problem (before settling on one to try) is not an analytical process. It requires creativity and openness.

Analytical and creative thinking are sometimes seen as opposites because they use different sides (hemispheres) of the brain. Because individuals usually have a dominant way of thinking, team membership and facilitation can have a significant

❖❖❖

impact on the improvement process because of the challenge of allowing both analytical and creative thinkers to work within the same group.

TEAM DEVELOPMENT

Just as individuals develop over their life span (e.g., infant, adolescent, teenager, adult, and senior), groups tend to change over time. In *The Team Handbook,* Scholtes discusses the stages of team development—forming, storming, norming, and performing (discussed in Chapter 43)—and provides guidelines for helping teams progress through these stages. The development phase can also be enhanced by making sure that team members have a basic understanding of how to (1) interact in positive ways, (2) deal with difficult people or situations, (3) contribute to accomplishing the team's goals, and (4) give or receive feedback. *The Team Memory Jogger,* by GOAL/QPC Joiner Associates, can be a useful resource for team members in this regard.

For all the potentially negative aspects of working in teams, there are many benefits. Because the decisions reached are multidisciplinary, they usually are more readily accepted and will therefore solve the problems better than conventional approaches. As Senge points out in *The Fifth Discipline,* if the team really gels, the resulting experience can be a highlight of one's career. Senge provides a framework of organizations from a standpoint of their learning that can also provide useful insights for improving the team process.

The result of some process improvement efforts is that people from previously separate functional areas now work together in a newly designed process. These types of changes require much more significant attention to organizational change issues, helping a new organizational entity focus on the mission. For example, in administrative processes, significant time delays often occur at the hand-off points between departments (e.g., see the IBM example covered in Hammer's *Reengineering the Corporation* whereby the net time required to process a loan application decreased from one week to four hours). In Hammer's subsequent book, *Beyond Reengineering,* he recognizes the importance of managing change in the building of process-centered organizations.

Some organizations also do process improvement through an accelerated team process, often called a *kaizen event* or *kaizen blitz.* These teams spend three to five days focusing on a particular work area and implement changes within the time period. Gains on the order of 50 percent (e.g., increase in productivity and reduction in changeover time) are not uncommon. In these cases, the team development process is accelerated by providing the facilitator with more authority than is done with most teams.

IMPLEMENTING AND MONITORING PROCESS IMPROVEMENT

After the team has implemented the improved process design (which might require approval from management, depending on the level of authority), the team must evaluate the impact of the change. If the desired improvement was achieved, then the new method should be standardized (e.g., everyone is properly trained in the new process, and appropriate procedures or standards are revised to reflect the new design). If the change did not have the desired effect or had a negative one, then the team must review what did not go well. Causes could be that the implementation was not done well or that the solution did not address the correct issues.

Assuming that the desired impact was achieved, monitoring of the process should be done for some time to ensure that the change has been institutionalized.

COMMON MISTAKES AND BARRIERS TO SUCCESS IN PROCESS IMPROVEMENT

Some common mistakes that result in failure of a process improvement effort are described here.

Unclear Goals

If a process improvement team is chartered without establishing a clear mission or goal, then the team will either do nothing or will go in the direction that it believes is best. The team must understand the purpose of the team and how it fits into corporate objectives. The team goal should be documented in specific terms and then reviewed by the team leader and/or team members for clarity and understanding. One way to test the understanding is to ask, "What will you measure to determine whether the goal has been accomplished?"

Inadequate Training

Team members need to be properly trained in process improvement methods; often including both technical and social skills. A facilitator can be made available as an alternative, but this should not be the long-term solution.

Insufficient Analysis of the Process

The process improvement team usually needs to study the existing process. Without a proper understanding of customer needs, the steps used to meet them, and the cause-and-effect relationship between process controls and process results, improvement efforts become a "shotgun" approach—trying different things until something works.

Inadequate Monitoring of the Project

Teams can quickly become frustrated if they are not making progress. Management should be tracking progress to identify problems, such as people not attending meetings or other departments failing to provide the necessary support, or to identify a short-term need for specialized technical knowledge.

Additional Readings

Adams, Scott. 1996. *The Dilbert Principle*. New York: HarperBusiness.

Bemowski, Karen, and Brad Stratton, eds. 1998. *101 Good Ideas: How to Improve Just about Any Process*. Milwaukee: ASQ Quality Press.

Deming, W. Edwards. 1994. *The New Economics*. 2nd ed. Cambridge: Massachusetts Institute of Technology, Center for Advanced Engineering Study.

❖❖

——. 1986. *Out of the Crisis.* Cambridge: Massachusetts Institute of Technology, Center for Advanced Engineering Study.

Dettmer, H. William. 1996. *Goldratt's Theory of Constraints: A Systems Approach to Continuous Improvement.* Milwaukee: ASQC Quality Press.

——. 1995. "Quality and the Theory of Constraints." *Quality Progress,* April, pp. 77–81.

GOAL/QPC and Joiner Associates. 1995. *The Team Memory Jogger.* Methuen, Mass.: GOAL/QPC.

Goldratt, Eliyahu M. 1992. *The Goal.* 2d ed. Great Barrington, Mass.: North River Press.

——. 1994. *It's Not Luck.* Great Barrington, Mass.: North River Press.

Hammer, Michael. 1996. *Beyond Reengineering.* New York: HarperBusiness.

Hammer, Michael, and James Champy. 1993. *Reengineering the Corporation: A Manifesto for Business Revolution.* New York: HarperBusiness.

Latzko, William J., and David M. Saunders. 1995. *Four Days with Dr. Deming.* New York: Addison Wesley.

Ledbetter, Dean. 1995. "The Five Most Hated Words in Design Engineering: 'Your Product Does Not Work.'" *The Quality Management Forum* 21, (Winter) No. 4. p. 5.

Scharf, Alan. 1995. "Five Steps to Breakthrough Thinking Success." *The BT Facilitator Newsletter,* no. 1, October 20.

Scholtes, Peter R. 1988. *The Team Handbook.* Madison, Wisc.: Joiner Associates.

——. 1995. "Teams in the Age of Systems." *Quality Progress,* December, pp. 51–58.

Senge, Peter M. 1990. *The Fifth Discipline: The Art and Practice of the Learning Organization.* New York: Currency Doubleday.

Shingo, Shigeo. 1986. *Zero Quality Control: Source Inspection and the Poke-Yoke System.* Portland, Ore.: Productivity Press.

Stein, Robert E. 1994. *The Next Phase of Total Quality Management: TQM II and the Focus on Profitability.* New York: Marcel Dekker.

Chapter 36

Trend Analysis

❖ *This chapter should help you*

◆ Understand the concepts involved in trend analysis

◆ Distinguish between short- and long-term trend analysis

◆ Understand the barriers to successful trend analysis

MANAGEMENT BY FACT

Modern business management systems depend on measurement, data, information, and analysis. This concept is embodied in *management by fact*, a core value of the Baldrige Award criteria. The following excerpt from the 1999 award criteria describes the use and analysis of measurement data to drive improvements in performance:

> Businesses depend upon the measurement and analysis of performance. Such measurements must derive from the organization's strategy and provide critical data and information about key processes, outputs, and results. Many types of data and information are needed for performance measurement and improvement. Performance areas included are: customer, product, and service; operations, market, and competitive comparisons; and supplier, employee, and cost and financial. Analysis refers to extracting larger meaning from data and information to support evaluation, decision making, and operational improvement within the organization. *Analysis entails using data to determine trends, projections, and cause and effect—that might not be evident without analysis* [emphasis added]. Data and analysis support a variety of purposes, such as planning, reviewing overall performance, improving operations, and comparing performance with competitors or with "best practices" benchmarks.[1]

ESTABLISHING MEASUREMENT POINTS

To measure the performance of a given process, it is important to establish strategic measurement points. These points should be selected in accordance with the nature and importance of the process being evaluated. A process flow diagram that shows the progression of events, such as the one shown in Figure 36.1 will help determine the measurement points. *First-time-yield* and *Final-yield* of a process are key measurements that help determine process performance and improvement opportunities.

❖❖❖

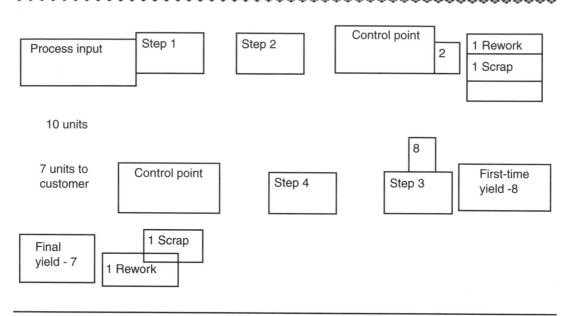

❖ **Figure 36.1.** Measurement points in a process flow diagram.

In the process shown in Figure 36.1, 10 units of input are processed through the first two steps, and that output is monitored for acceptance at a control point at which two nonconforming products are identified. One is scrapped, whereas the other is reworked and added at the appropriate step. The first time yield of the process is calculated as 80 percent (10 – 2 = 8). The reworked unit passes the second time through, raising the total number processed through control point 1 from 7 to 8. After the remaining two steps are completed, two more nonconforming products are detected. The final yield is calculated as 70 percent (8 – 2 + 1 = 7). Data collected from each measurement point make it possible to determine improvement opportunities for each step in the process. This method of measurement and analysis can be used for manufacturing as well as service processes. Measurement and data collection is a useless activity if the results are not analyzed and used to implement improvements.

As discussed in Chapter 16, understanding the theory of variation is vital in making appropriate fact-based decisions. The distinctions between common-cause variation and special-cause variation, summarized in Table 36.1, must be recognized and used in determining which actions to take to either control or improve performance. The general consensus is that the majority of all variation—an estimated 85 percent—is due to common causes.

Managing variation has a significant impact on daily quality management activities. Successful managing of common-cause variation is key to continuous improvement of any process. Because common-cause variations are inherent in the process and resources used, a long-term strategic approach is necessary. This will involve a company-wide commitment and vision to quality management because common causes of variation affect company-wide strategic plans, policies, and budgets and must be managed on a daily basis. By contrast, special cause variation is sporadic and easily identifiable and often can be managed on an occasional basis

TABLE 36.1.   Common- versus Special-Cause Variation

Common Cause	Special Cause
Inherent in the process	External to process
Present always	Isolated; dependent on individual situation
Impact varies with ambient conditions	May or may not depend on ambient conditions
Individually slight but collectively can be significant	Individually larger variation than common cause variation
Resultant is stable under normal conditions	Unstable; appears without any previous indication
Process tend to be predictable or within statistical control under normal conditions	Unstable and statistically out of control
Solution	Solution
Cannot be eliminated or minimized without strategic planning and adequate resources; often higher management intervention needed	Can be eliminated or minimized with minimum resources Usually no higher management intervention needed

using relatively minimal resources. The key to minimizing any variation is to identify the particular factor that caused the variation and then eliminate it.

USING MEASUREMENT DATA TO DETECT TRENDS

A trend is defined both as a "line of general direction or movement" and as the "general movement in the course of time of a statistically detectable change." Analysis of trends is an activity that is preceded by the establishment of a measurement system. Measurement systems provide performance feedback for monitoring actual performance against a target level. Trends in actual performance might indicate declining, sustained, or improving performance when compared to a target level.

By itself, measurement data do not result in continuous improvement. Having data organized in a manner that supports analysis is vital.[2] Analytical tools that organize data and are helpful in trend analysis include Pareto charts, checksheets, histograms, control charts (all discussed in Chapter 33), and run charts, which are plots of data arranged chronologically. Run charts can be analyzed to determine the presence of patterns that can be attributed to common causes of variation or special causes of variation, if present.

"A further distinction in controls is whether they provide information before, during, or after operations."[3] Leading indicators are measures that can be used to predict the outcome of future events on the basis of trend analysis of past and current results. For example, market research might precede product development. Lagging indicators depict actual trends against expected performance levels. Warranty claims are an example of a lagging indicator. "A well-balanced system of executive reports makes use of leading indicators as well as summaries which lag behind operations."[4]

Measurement data must also be reliable, accurate, and accessible to be useful in detecting the need for corrections. Those who analyze results and are empowered to make course corrections should be trained to do so; this reduces the likelihood of human error. "Quality control is greatly simplified when operating people are in a state of self-control. . . . Ideally, the quality planning for any job should put the employee into a state of self-control. When work is organized in a way which enables a person to have full mastery over the attainment of planned results, that person is said to be in a state of self-control and can therefore properly be held responsible for the results. . . . To put people into a state of self-control, several fundamental criteria must be met. People must be provided with:

◆ Knowledge of what they are supposed to do (e.g., the budgeted profit, the schedule, and the specification).

◆ Knowledge of what they are doing (e.g., the actual profit, the delivery rate, the extent of conformance to specification).

◆ Means for regulating what they are doing in the event that they are failing to meet the goals. These means must always include the authority to regulate and the ability to regulate by varying either (a) the process under the person's authority or (b) the person's own conduct."[5]

USES AND TYPES OF TREND ANALYSIS

Trend analysis uses measurement data to identify favorable and unfavorable patterns or trends in actual performance as compared to any identified indicator, such as goals, specifications, standards, or past results. First, trend analysis is beneficial in recognizing emerging patterns in performance results. Such patterns are often not evident or are so gradual that they cannot be detected unless measurements of events are examined periodically. Second, when changes are planned to improve performance, trend analysis is used to assess the effects of implementing corrective actions by comparing past to present performance. Finally, trend analysis is an important activity for ensuring that improvement gains are sustained over time. Trend analysis can be long or short range.

Long-Range Trend Analysis

Long-range trend analysis, the examination and projection of overall performance over an extended time period, is used mainly for strategic planning and management of overall progress in achieving company-wide performance goals.[6] At the *company level*, measurement data, including corporate summaries of financial and nonfinancial performance, are analyzed to help management understand the company's performance and prioritize improvement actions on the basis of performance trends. Performance trends also can be compared to those of competitors as a tool for setting priorities for improvement actions.

Strategic planning consists of setting targets for key performance indicators. Long-term targets are usually considered to be those that are expected to be attained in three to five years, whereas short-terms targets are expected to be attained within one year. Long-term targets are selected in direct correlation with the company's objectives and strategic plans. The progress of plans are reviewed periodically with the objective of improving incremental trends in performance over time. Typical performance indicators measured and trended as part of the strategic planning process include market share, time to market, customer satisfaction and quality ratings, and service cycle time. A specific projected improvement trend, such as "to attain a 5 percent gain in market share within the next 12 months and a 15 percent gain in market share within the next 36 months," would be monitored to assess actual performance goals. Managerial summaries of process-level performance often are used to review and analyze performance results.

Short-Range Trend Analysis

Various forms of trend charts are used to trigger process adjustments or systems improvements when conducting short-range trend analysis at the process level or the work-unit level.[7]

Process Level. At the *process level*, analysis of measurement data provides both departmental and cross-functional understanding of the system's performance over time. Often, company policy defines the frequency for the trending and reporting of performance results together with criteria that define adverse trends and recommended actions for establishing or restoring control.

Well-designed quality systems include provisions for self-control monitoring and assessment. For example, an equipment calibration program typically describes requirements for conducting routine calibrations and for making adjustments to units in which out-of-tolerance results are observed. Self-control monitoring and assessment of the calibration system's efficacy is achieved through use and analysis of the calibration measurement data. This includes the performance history of each unit that is calibrated and each unit's rating as compared to others. Trending of data is used to set frequencies for performing calibrations, including the identification of equipment that repeatedly requires adjustment at the end of each calibration period as well as equipment that is stable and operates within the required limits of use. Guidelines for performing trend analysis and remedial actions to improve performance should be stated in the calibration policy.

Work-Unit Level. At the *work-unit level*, the process operator analyzes measurement data and adjusts the process to eliminate special causes of variation. To accomplish this, the operator might use a measurement system, such as a control chart, that includes definitions of what constitutes a trend. This type of trending is based on the interpretation of a series of events that are closely related in time with the objective of sustaining process control.

Through the use of quality control tools that are incorporated into work processes as work instructions, process operators are able to monitor the performance of key process characteristics. Work instructions for measuring data, analyzing

❖❖

trends in data, and making and recording process adjustments are documented as part of the quality system.

BARRIERS TO SUCCESSFUL TREND ANALYSIS

The barriers to success in conducting long-range trend analysis differ from the barriers related to short-range trend analysis. One such example is emphasis on absolute values. For short-range trend analysis of a series of events closely related in time, absolute values are more critical for establishing the existence of a trend. For example, the utility of a variables control chart depends on the accuracy of the measurements taken to detect gradual changes that occur over a short period of time. For long-range trend analysis, emphasis on absolute values does not add value in the ability to recognize a gradual drift or sudden shift in performance at the company level. Long-range trend analysis is useful in evaluating a general direction or movement, not a statistically detectable drift.

Another example includes the ways in which data are organized to support analysis. Because quality control tools are frequently incorporated within a set of given work instructions at the work-unit level, the manner in which the data are reported and analyzed is standardized. At the process level, and especially at the company level, the way in which measurement data are organized and reported can be influenced by whomever is given the responsibility for providing updates on progress. Selective reporting of data, or reporting incomplete information to bias the analysis, is evidenced in organizations in which fear is a driver in the workplace. On the other extreme, exception reporting can inflate the meaning of the data or give false indications that a sudden shift has occurred.

Common barriers to success in conducting effective short- and long-range trend analysis include the following:

◆ Lack of rapid access to valid data in order to maintain a state of control or to prevent nonconformances.

◆ Lack of self-control capability because the process itself is inadequate or because one or more of the criteria for maintenance of self-control are not met.

◆ Lack of understanding the theory of variation, leading to poor decision making when evaluating decision alternatives and projecting results. Without understanding the basis for common-cause versus special-cause variation, the tendency is to blame individuals for problems instead of recognizing that system deficiencies exist and must be eliminated.

In *The Fifth Discipline,* Senge discusses the learning disabilities related to trend analysis that plague corporations and threaten their survival. In each case, these disabilities reflect the absence of a systematic approach for assessing performance to key business indicators. The goal is to evaluate results for evidence of trends so that corrective or preventive action can be taken before it is too late.

Senge believes that managers often are so concerned with individual events that they are precluded from recognizing longer-term patterns (or trends) of change that lie behind the events and from understanding the causes of the patterns. Senge uses the parable of the boiled frog to illustrate this lack of managerial self-control in being able to recognize and respond to gradual changes that often post the greatest threats to survival:

> If you place a frog in a pot of boiling water, it will immediately try to scramble out. But if you place the frog in room temperature water, and don't scare him, he'll stay put. Now, if the pot sits on a heat source, and if you gradually turn up the temperature, something very interesting happens. As the temperature rises from 70 to 80 degrees F., the frog will do nothing. In fact, he will show every sign of enjoying himself. As the temperature gradually increases, the frog will become groggier and groggier, until he is unable to climb out of the pot. Though there is nothing restraining him, the frog will sit there and boil. Why? Because the frog's internal apparatus for sensing threats to survival is geared to sudden changes in his environment, not to slow, gradual changes.[8]

The U.S. automobile industry succumbed to this phenomenon in the 1960s when it did not view Japan as a threat to survival as the Japanese share was less than 4 percent of the automobile market. Automakers in the United States failed to react as the Japanese market share gradually climbed toward 15 percent by 1974. It was not until the 1980s that attention was given to a trend that had reached an epidemic level of more than 20 percent. By 1989, the Japanese market share had climbed to nearly 30 percent. The U.S. automobile industry had been caught off guard by failing to recognize that a trend had been developing over a period of years.

Attempts to fix one problem often trigger another one. As time passes, it becomes more difficult to identify this sort of pattern. This is what happens when the consequences of an action are not immediately apparent and do not become visible until the distant future or in a distant part of the larger system within which people operate.

Managers should be on the alert regarding short- and long-term trends. Response to trended results must be made in compliance with company policies, objectives, and strategic plans. When the Plan-Do-Check-Act (PDCA) cycle is not executed at various levels within a company, nonsystems or non-fact-based decision making occurs, and problems such as the ones discussed previously can result and threaten the company's survival.

🏮 Additional Readings 🏮

Brassard, Michael. 1989. *The Memory Jogger Plus*. Methuen, Mass.: GOAL/QPC.

Campanella, Jack, ed. 1999. *Principles of Quality Costs*. 3rd ed. ASQ Quality Costs Committee. Milwaukee: ASQ Quality Press.

Juran, Joseph M., and Frank M. Gryna, eds. 1988. *Juran's Quality Control Handbook*. 4th ed. New York: McGraw-Hill.

The Malcolm Baldrige National Quality Award: 1999 Criteria for Performance Excellence. Gaithersburg, Md.: National Institute of Standards and Technology.

Senge, Peter. 1990. *The Fifth Discipline*. New York: Doubleday.

❖❖

Chapter 37

Measurement Issues

❖❖

❖ *This chapter should help you*

- ◆ Become familiar with the concepts of reliability and validity
- ◆ Understand how to choose and use sampling plans and other statistical analysis techniques
- ◆ Become familiar with specifications, calibration, and process capability

---

RELIABILITY AND VALIDITY

The term *reliability engineering* was first used in its modern technical sense by Major General Leslie E. Simon as director of ordnance research and development in connection with the Nike missile program. Other early pioneers were E. L. Grant, L. F. Bell, and E. G. D. Paterson in articles published in *Industrial Quality Control,* the forerunner of *Quality Progress.*

Reliability is the *probability* that an item or product will perform its intended function in a given environment for a predetermined amount of time in a satisfactory manner. Validity is the *test proof* that an item or product will perform its intended function in a given environment for a predetermined amount of time in a satisfactory manner. Consider the following statement:

An automobile engine has a .95 probability of running an automobile 100,000 miles in 10 years in the open environment of the continental United States.

This statement implies that the manufacturer's recommended maintenance schedule will be followed and that the vehicle will be operated in a legal manner. However, when building the engine, the manufacturer must take into account that not all users will adhere to these guidelines.

There are four phases in planning a reliable product: designing, manufacturing, testing (validation), and maintaining. These stages are discussed here as they would pertain to the design and subsequent manufacture of a new automobile model.

Designing

Before any work begins on a new car model, the designer needs to determine which perceived customer needs the new design is trying to meet. In many cases, performing surveys or actually meeting with identified potential customers helps the designer in this product conceptualization phase. How much engine power does the customer require in this type of car? How often does the customer plan to provide maintenance? At this point, up to 35 percent of the expected life cycle costs are identified.

Next, in the product design/development phase, the customer's needs are regarded as they mesh with the issues of safety, maintainability, and ergonomics (How does the human body fit into the car? Are special wrenches required for maintaining the engine?). Approximately 90 percent of the life cycle costs are identifiable at this point. The following factors will be taken into account.

Cost Cost factors relate to the perceived needs of the customer. To achieve best-in-class status, the manufacturer must exceed the customer's expectations at a lower cost while meeting the requirements of others, such as regulatory agencies.

Environmental. Environmental factors refer to two separate characteristics. First, environment refers to the individual components that must function within the system. In this case, environment refers to the functioning physical relationships. For example, what type of wear would a hard steel piston produce in the cylinder? Second, environment might refer to the physical place within which the system as a whole must function. For example, an engine designed for the continental United States might not perform well north of the Arctic Circle.

Human. The characteristics of humans must be taken into account. Can the mechanic remove the oil filter from the engine without a special tool?

Redundancy. Often, more than one means of achieving a given level of performance exists so that all paths must fail before the system will fail. This is usually achieved by adding parallel elements (e.g., jet planes can fly even when one engine stops working).

Derating. Derating is the assignment of a product to operate at stress levels below its normal rating (e.g., a capacitor rated at 300 volts is used in a 200-volt application).

Fail-Safe. When the consequences of design failure are severe, such as the loss of life or substantial financial loss, a fail-safe design should be adopted if possible. For example, the failure of the cooling pumps in a nuclear plant could shut down the entire system.

Produceability/Maintainability. Can the design be produced at the desired quality level? If engine performance depends on a manufacturing tolerance that cannot be met, then performance becomes moot. The same is true of maintenance.

A good design exists when the above conditions have been met. All components conform to mandatory and voluntary requirements, function and costs meet or exceed the desired level, and a prototype indicates that the item can actually be built and used as intended.

Manufacturing

Manufacturing is the full-scale development phase. This applies to production items or build-and-install (one time). The design is basically complete, and prototype runs are occurring. Changes are very costly at this stage and usually do not occur because of cost or time constraints.

Testing (Validation)

Previously, product testing was performed in the design phase to see whether a prototype built with the design parameters performed within the reliability constraints (probability of functioning in a given environment for a given time.) This activity is validation of the prototype. Checking out one unit would be a test. After manufacturing, testing will occur to see whether the product was built as designed. At this time, the entire design and the production process will be validated by a much larger scale designed experiment. At the prototype stage, three engines might be run on the test bed for 100,000 miles; after the operational phase, 100 cars might be road driven for 200,000 miles. Even though validation can be costly and time consuming, it often prevents the greater losses that could occur in the event of failure.

Maintaining

The maintenance stage of the product life cycle begins with field use of the item. At this point, ease of use and maintenance design affect the reliability of the product (e.g., the specially built air filter for our engine that cost 10 times as much as most air filters might get blown clean and reused). Finally, some products must be disassembled at the end of their useful lives. In making a product that can be disassembled, it is important that performance not be degraded. A glass furnace must be taken down every three to five years because the ceramic bricks deteriorate. In designing for its disassembly, it is not desirable to shorten its life span.

SYSTEM EFFECTIVENESS

The effectiveness of a system is assessed against three characteristics: availability, dependability, and capability. Availability refers to the system's ability to be in an operable and committable state at the start of mission when the mission will start at an unknown point of time (Will the engine start at random times, not just on Mondays?). Dependability refers to the probability that the system will enter its operational mode (Will the engine start every time?). The probability that the system will function given the conditions is its capability (Will the engine start in the rain?).

Failure Modes and Mechanisms

When investigating and diagnosing causes of failure, the time in service and mode of failure must be considered along with the mechanism of the failure. Three mechanisms normally are involved in failure: infant mortality, the constant failure rate, and wear-out.

Infant mortality refers to premature failure and usually is due to faulty components or poor workmanship. The constant failure rate is an extended period during which failure can occur sporadically and thus refers to random failures. Each component has a distribution associated with its life span, but the point of failure of individual units cannot be known. However, the performance of the class of units as a whole can be predicted, and when the product is unable to satisfy basic performance goals or when it is no longer cost effective to repair the item, failure results. Wear-out refers to a product that has lasted for at least the minimum time for which it was

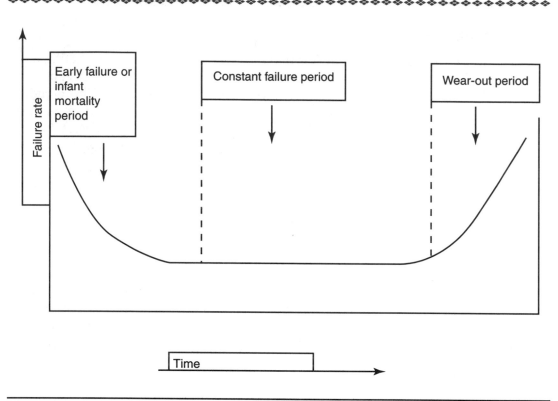

designed. At this point, cost or state of the output has limited the life of the unit. As the upper limit is approached, component degradation and fatigue occur, and the failure rate increases to the point at which it might not be practical to continue operating the system.

Life cycle commonly is portrayed by the Weibull distribution, also known as the bathtub curve. During the infant, or burn-in, phase, failure rates drop sharply. They remain constant during operation and then rise sharply during wear-out. The Weibull distribution is illustrated in Figure 37.1.

Reliability Statistics

$$\text{Failure rate} = \frac{\text{Number of items failed}}{\text{Total test time}}$$

$$\text{Mean time between failures} = \frac{\text{Total test time}}{\text{Number of items failed}}$$

Failure Control

Failure mode and effects analysis (FEMA) is a system of looking at potential problems and their causes and predicting undesired results. FMEA is normally used to predict product failure from past part failure, although it is occasionally used to analyze future system failures. This method of failure analysis is generally performed for design and process.

The fault tree analysis method starts with undesired events and looks for solutions and is often used in the health and safety fields. Fault tree analysis looks at parts that can be responsible for product failure.

SAMPLING PLANS AND OTHER STATISTICAL ANALYSIS TECHNIQUES

Sampling plans and other statistical analysis techniques are used to identify the level of nonconformance *after* a product is made. Most sampling plans should be used only as an interim step while process control is achieved so that "after the fact" actions are avoided. Prior to the advent of process control, the quality control group was often regarded as those who "wait until the battle is over and then shoot the wounded."

Sampling is performed on a population to establish whether the lot, group, or batch of material meets or exceeds a given level of nonconformance, whereas statistical analysis estimates the level of nonconformance.

Sampling is based on the work of Dodge, Romig, and the standards group that developed MIL-STD 105 during World War II. Also known as the ABC Standard (American, British, and Canadian Standard), MIL-STD 105 was of great help in the mass production of the war effort. It has now been replaced by ANSI/ASQC Z1.4 (discussed shortly).

Sampling assumes that if a nonconformance is random throughout a lot, a random sampling taken and expressed in proportions can determine whether a given level of nonconformance is exceeded. Because sampling occurs *after* production, it is a defensive measure. Whether sampling is the correct technique for assessing a lot depends on lot size, lot frequency, nonconformance levels, and acceptable risks. For example, pencils received from an office supply house normally are not sampled because the risk associated with defective pencils is minimal. In contrast, medical devices might be subjected to extensive sampling or even 100 percent inspection because of the enormous consequences that could result in the event of failure.

A break point exists beyond which it is logical to sample or not sample. In the past, the obvious candidate for sampling was the supplier that submitted frequent lots. Today, however, that supplier may be an obvious candidate for a supplier certification program in which no sampling is required.

When properly applied over a period of time, sampling can keep nonconformances below a predetermined level. Compared with 100 percent inspection, sampling is more economical (saves labor and time), requires less handling of the product, and is often more accurate because it causes less fatigue. However, sampling plans do have some drawbacks: They can be used to avoid process control, they are less economical than process control, and they yield less information on the true state of nonconformance than do 100 percent inspection or statistical analysis.

None of the many sampling plans available yield 100 percent detection of nonconformances. Because of this situation and possible legal issues, some industries do not use sampling plans, as census conducted by sampling plan might yield a result that is misleading.

Two types of errors can occur in sampling. The alpha (α), or producer, risk refers to the possibility that good product will be rejected. The beta (β), or consumer, risk refers to the possibility that bad product will be accepted.

❖❖

CHOOSING AND USING A SAMPLING TABLE

The first decision to be made when selecting a sampling table is which plan to use from the family of plans. To enter and use a sampling plan, one piece of arbitrary information is needed: the acceptable quality level (AQL), which is the level of non-conformance that will be accepted and is usually spelled out in a specification or contract. ANSI/ASQC Z1.4 defines AQL as "the maximum percent nonconforming per hundred units that, for purposes of sampling inspection, can be considered satisfactory as a process average."[1] Because AQLs are arbitrary, a feasible explanation should exist for why that number was chosen.

The lot or batch size is a fact that needs to be known. The most well known plan, MIL-STD 105 (which has been replaced by ANSI/ASQC Z1.4-1993), assigns "code letters" to ranges of lot sizes for use within the sampling tables. ANSI/ASQC Z1.9-1993, which replaces MIL-STD 414, is another commonly used sampling plan for variables.

Dodge–Romig tables are effective attribute plans for sampling inspection when the process average is known. The operating characteristic (OC) curve shows, for a given acceptance control chart configuration, the probability of accepting a process as a function of the process level. The OC curve is a graph of the percentage defective in a batch versus the probability that the sampling plan will accept that batch.

The first decision to make is which level of sensitivity to choose in a sampling plan. ANSI/ASQC Z1.4-1993 (Z1.4) contains four special levels and three general levels. Special levels (S1 through S4) are used when the sample size is small and large risks of error are acceptable. The destructive testing of prototype locomotive engines is an example of an item that might fall into this category. General level I requires smaller samples and is used when the process is known to produce a "good" quality level. It is not to be confused with reduced inspection under the switching rules (see the following discussion). Level II is the normal starting point for most processes when no prior knowledge of quality levels exists. Level III is used when the process is known to produce a "marginal" quality level. If it is a "bad" level, the process should be corrected! Level III should not be confused with tightened inspection under the switching rules.

Once the inspection level has been determined, the table with the batch or lot size is used to identify the code letter to use when entering the sampling table. Next, a choice must be made to use single-, double-, or multiple-sampling plans. In single sampling, lots are inspected, and the decision to accept or reject is based on the acceptance number (c) for that sample size (n), as shown in Figure 37.2. In double sampling, lots are inspected, and the decision to accept or reject is based on the acceptance number (c) for the combined sample size ($n1 + n2$). In double-sampling plans, the first sample will have an accept number, a "zone of continuing sampling," and a reject number. If process quality is good, most lots will be accepted on the first sample, thereby reducing sampling cost. The inspector also can feel that the lot is being given a second chance if a second sample must be drawn.

In multiple sampling, lots are inspected, and the decision to accept or reject is based on a maximum of seven samples of (n). Multiple plans work the same as

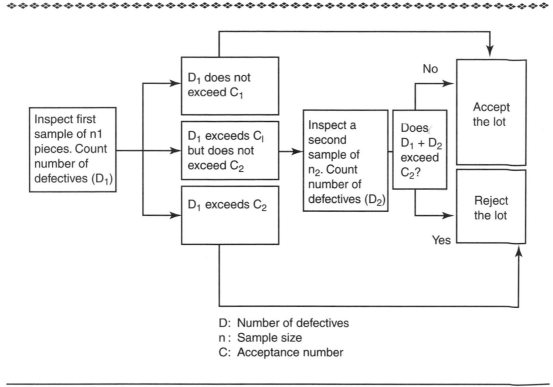

D: Number of defectives
n : Sample size
C: Acceptance number

◆ **Figure 37.2.**   Sampling decisions.

double plans but use up to seven "draws" before final resolutions. This is the most discriminating of plans but is also most susceptible to inspector abuse.

Z1.4 contains "switching" rules that go into effect when quality levels prove to be continuously good (reduced sampling) or deteriorating (tightened sampling). If the switching rules are not used, then Z1.4 is not being used. When a single lot is sampled under one of the sampling plans, the acceptable outgoing quality level (AOQL) tables and OC curves are not applicable.

Z1.4 also contains a "discontinue of sampling" clause. When a given number of lots is rejected, sampling by the plan must stop, and the company must decide what to do. In the case of military contracts, 100 percent inspection is the next step.

OTHER METHODS OF STATISTICAL ANALYSIS

Sampling plans can be used only when a given population meets given criteria. When using attribute plans, the only information gained is "yes" or "no" with a given degree of probability. The actual "shape" of the population remains unknown. In these circumstances, several basic techniques can estimate the true condition of the lot or batch under question.

Frequency histograms present numerical data in a pictorial form. Data are grouped and plotted so that the distribution of the data becomes apparent. The "picture" formed is easier to comprehend than a column of numbers and makes

❖❖

statistics easy to discern. The term *distribution* refers to the shape of the data in a histogram. The following distributions are commonly noted in histograms:

Normal. Observations of the data set are concentrated around the average and it is equally likely that observations will occur above and below the average. In such cases, variation is usually the result of many small causes.

Exponential. Observations are more likely to occur below the average than above.

Weibull. Describes a wide variety of patterns of variation, including departures from the normal and exponential.

Binomial. Defines the probability of *r* occurrences in *n* trials of an event that has a probability of occurrence of *p* on each trial.

Negative Binomial. Defines the probability that *r* occurrences will require a total of *r* + *s* trials of an event that has a probability of occurrence of *p* on each trial (note that the total number of trials, *n*, is *r* + *s*).

Poisson. Resembles binomial but is especially applicable when there are many opportunities for occurrence of an event but a low probability (less than 0.10) on each trial.

Hypergeometric. Defines the probability of *r* occurrences in *n* trials of an event when there are a total of *d* occurrences in a population of *N*.

The arithmetic mean is the average of all data in the sample. The median is the middle number in the data set. The mode is the number that occurs most frequently in the data set. The range is the difference between the maximum and the minimum value in the data set. A more general measure of variation is the sample standard deviation. The square of sample standard deviation is called variance.

The formula to calculate sample standard deviation is as follows:

$$s = \sqrt{\frac{\Sigma(X - \bar{x})^2}{n - 1}}$$

where Σ = summation, X = individual observation, $\bar{x}$ = sample mean, and n = number of observations. The formula for variance is as follows:

$$s^2 = \sqrt{\frac{\Sigma(X - \bar{x})^2}{n - 1}}$$

SPECIFICATIONS, CALIBRATION, AND PROCESS CAPABILITY

This section deals with specifications, calibration, and process capability.

Specifications

A specification is a detailed precise presentation of something or of a plan or proposal for something. As used in this book, specification can refer to a product, process, or system. Product specifications include tolerance specifications (the total allowable variation around a level or state, i.e., the upper limit minus the lower limit) and limit specifications, which are boundaries created by visual extremes on physical samples (attributes). The term *process specification* refers to work methods and process conditions, such as temperature, pressure, and time cycles. A system specification refers to the designation of formally defined plans for quality systems, such as ISO 9001, 9002, or 9003; criteria for the Baldrige Award; or industry-specific plans, such as QS-9000. A capability study should be performed before specifications are set or accepted.

Calibration

Calibration is the set of operations which establish, under specified conditions, the relationship between values indicated by a measuring instrument or measuring system, or values represented by a material measure or a reference material, and the corresponding values of a quantity realized by a reference standard. When data has been obtained from a calibrated instrument or system, its accuracy is ensured, and it can be used in decision making.

Accuracy, precision, and bias are the associate factors of equipment calibration. The American Society for Testing Materials (ASTM) has long studied these issues in general and for applications to specific materials. Accuracy is a generic concept of exactness related to the closeness of agreement between the average of one or more test results and an accepted reference value. Precision is a generic concept related to the closeness of agreement between test results obtained under prescribed like conditions from the measurement process being evaluated. Bias is a generic concept related to a consistent or systemic difference between a set of test results from the process and an accepted reference value of the property being measured.

ANSI/ASQC Q9001-1994 states that a calibration program should consist of the following general requirements:

The supplier shall establish and maintain documented procedures to control, calibrate, and maintain inspection, measuring, and test equipment (including test software) used by the supplier to demonstrate the conformance of product to the specified requirements. Inspection, measuring, and test equipment shall be used in a manner which ensures that the measurement uncertainty is know and is consistent with the required measurement capability.

Where test software or comparative references such as test hardware are used as suitable forms of inspection, they shall be checked to prove that they are capable of verifying the acceptability of product, prior to release for use during production, installation, or servicing, and shall be rechecked at prescribed intervals. The supplier shall establish the extent and frequency of such checks and shall maintain records as evidence of control.

Where the availability of technical data pertaining to the measurement equipment is a specified requirement, such data shall be made available, when required by the customer or customer's representative, for verification that the measuring equipment is functionally adequate.

Control procedure: The supplier shall:

a. determine the measurements to be made and the accuracy required, and select the appropriate inspection, measuring, and test equipment that is capable of the necessary accuracy and precision;

b. identify all inspection, measuring, and test equipment that can affect product quality, and calibrate and adjust them at prescribed intervals, or prior to use, against certified equipment having a known valid relationship to internationally or nationally recognized standards. Where no such standards exist, the basis used for calibration shall be documented;

c. define the process employed for the calibration of inspection, measuring, and test equipment, including details of equipment type, unique identification, location, frequency of checks, check method, acceptance criteria, and the action to be taken when results are unsatisfactory;

d. identify inspection, measuring, and test equipment with a suitable indicator or approved identification record to show the calibration status;

e. maintain calibration records for inspection, measuring, and test equipment;

f. assess and document the validity of previous inspection and test results when inspection, measuring, and test equipment is found to be out of calibrations;

g. ensure that the environmental conditions are suitable for the calibrations, inspections, measurements, and tests being carried out;

h. ensure that the handling, preservation, and storage of inspection, measuring, and test equipment is such that the accuracy and fitness for use are maintained;

i. safeguard inspection, measuring, and test facilities, including both test hardware and test software, from adjustments which would invalidate the calibration setting.

A common mistake made in calibration is the failure to record both "as found" conditions and the "recalibrated condition" of an instrument.

Process Capability

Process capability establishes the limits within which a tool or process operates based on minimum variability as governed by the prevailing circumstances. Knowing the spread of the process on any given attribute allows for intelligent decision making when accepting a specification or a component fit.

Several formulas are used to describe the capability of a process when comparing the distribution of the process to the specification limits required:

$$\text{Process capability ratio (PCR, or } C_p) = \frac{\text{Total tolerance}}{6\sigma}$$

Where total tolerance = product specification width and 6σ = 6 sigma spread of the process. The symbol C_p is more commonly used. The symbol C_{pk} is used to denote the process capability ratio, accounting for the location of the process mean. This is accomplished by computing the distance to the nearest specification limit as follows:

$$C_{pk} = \text{the smaller of} \quad \frac{\text{USL} - \bar{X}}{3\sigma} \quad \text{or} \quad \frac{\bar{X} - \text{LSL}}{3\sigma}$$

where USL = upper specification limit, LSL = lower specification limit, X = process mean, and σ = process standard deviation. Generally:

C_{pk} > 1.33 (capable)
C_{pk} = 1.00 – 1.33 (capable with tight control)
C_{pk} < 1.00 (not capable)

In practice, sigma (σ) must be estimated from the data. The sample standard deviation is the most common estimator. The biggest mistake made with process capability is paying no attention to the data after collecting it.

Process capability studies should be performed as early as possible in the new product phase and then revisited during the life cycle of the process. (Run the study to know where you are at and as the process ages run it routinely to spot wear.)

🏮 Additional Readings 🏮

Juran, Joseph M., and Frank M. Gryna. 1993. *Quality Planning and Analysis.* 3rd ed. New York: McGraw-Hill, Inc.

ISO 10012-1. *Quality Assurance Requirements for Measuring Equipment.*

American Society for Quality Control/Statistics Division. 1996. *Glossary and Tables for Statistical Quality Control.* 3rd ed. ASQC Statistics Division. Milwaukee: ASQC Quality Press.

ANSI/ISO/ASQC Q9001-1994 Quality Systems. Model for Quality Assurance in Design, Development, Production, Installation, and Servicing. Milwaukee: ASQC Quality Press.

ANSI/ISO/ASQC A8402-1994 Quality Management and Quality Assurance— Vocabulary.

Grant, E.L. and Richard S. Leavenworth. *Statistical Quality Control.* 7th ed. New York: McGraw-Hill, Inc.

Besterfield, Dale H. 1994. *Quality Control.* 4th ed. Milwaukee: ASQC Quality Press.

Chapter 38

Concurrent Engineering
and Process Mapping

❖ *After reading this chapter, you should*

◆ Understand the concept of concurrent engineering

◆ Understand how process mapping is used to analyze and communicate complex business operations

---

CONCURRENT ENGINEERING AND PROCESS MAPPING DEFINED

Concurrent engineering is a strategic approach that organizations adopt to remain competitive in a global economy. Process mapping is a technique used to analyze and communicate complex business operations and is often used in conjunction with concurrent engineering.

Concurrent engineering refers to a company's coordinated efforts to focus on product development simultaneously in a team approach versus independently by function. Instead of performing work sequentially, departments, when possible, perform work in parallel to eliminate slack time. Integrating efforts and streamlining cooperation among marketing, engineering, fulfillment, and other functional departments creates business processes that are effective, efficient, and responsive. The term *concurrent engineering* is used mainly in manufacturing environments; however, the same approach is used in other work settings, which often refer to "self-managed" or "cross-functional" work teams.

Many definitions exist for the terms *process* and *mapping*. *Process* is defined, referred to, and interpreted differently, depending on the user, purpose, subject, profession, industry, and even geographic location. When business employees describe the stages for how several departments in a manufacturing company pick, pack, and ship a product, Europeans or those familiar with ISO 9000 usually refer to these stages as a "procedure" or "interdepartmental procedure." Asians or those familiar with structured communications methods for learning are likely to refer to these stages as a "process" while referring to a set of work instructions performed by one person as a "procedure."

A process generally refers to a particular method of how something happens, beginning with an input and ending with an output. Because a process involves two or more stages or operations over time, it might show change, relationships, cause and effect, movement, and/or actions. In the context of work, processes typically show how people (or departments) interrelate to accomplish tasks over time. A work process is usually a part of a work system that also includes a combination of people, equipment, materials, methods, and environment that produces added value.

Mapping (or charting) refers to the presentation of data or information graphically. Charting techniques are either action or nonaction oriented. Process mapping, a diagramming technique that describes work flows for a variety of purposes, including as an aid in concurrent engineering, is an action-oriented charting technique because users begin reading at a specific point and continue in a sequential way. Therefore, the reading process is dynamic or action oriented. Charting tools and techniques have been created to assist in communicating, evaluating, and understanding complex work processes because they can be significantly more efficient in communicating complex information effectively than prose-based (narrative) and list-based formats.

A process map (or chart) is a diagram showing which tasks, activities, functions, and/or decisions need to be performed and, where applicable, by whom (participant). Because concurrent engineering involves two or more participants, process mapping is an appropriate technique for illustrating concurrent engineering. The communication in a process map is not how to perform tasks or make decisions but rather *to describe* what happens. Communicating *how* to perform a task is usually referred to as a work instruction. An example of a process could be how a sales order is handled among a variety of departments in a company. Specifically how a sales clerk enters the order in the computer database would be more of an instruction within the sales order handling process.

APPROACHES TO PROCESS MAPPING

To adequately understand the two approaches used in process mapping today, it is helpful to examine them from a historical context.

Industrial Era

During the industrial era (the end of the 19th century), the traditional management approach focused on the specialization of work performance according to functional hierarchies. Each area performed its piece of work, "tossed it over the wall" to the next functional department, and then "washed its hands" of the work. Departments were independent entities that served another department's needs, often with little or no knowledge of the final customer's needs. Large organizations were managed by top-, middle-, and line-level managers, in a hierarchial, centrally controlled military-type structure.

Beginning in the late 19th century, industrial engineers used flowcharts focusing on time, location, and movement of materials and parts for work simplification. By the mid-1920s, the term "flowcharting" had entered the dictionary in America. Early experts recognized in process charting for work simplification of blue-collar jobs were such industrial engineers as Frank B. Gilbreth, Lillian Gilbreth, and Allan Mogensen. Later experts, recognized in process charting for work simplification in office systems improvement focusing on paperwork jobs, were Ben Graham Sr. and his son Dr. Ben S. Graham Jr.

Information Era

With the maturation of the information era (the middle of the 20th century) and the increasing availability of information technology to the workforce, the evolving management approach tends to focus on concurrent work performance efforts. Functional departments "team" to manage and control their own performance by collectively seeking to satisfy the end user's needs. In many cases, the organization's hierarchical structure remains in place; however, the focus is on the process of meeting the customer's needs through collective participation. Therefore, communication becomes less vertical and more horizontal.

Concurrent performance approaches can result in shortened cycle times, reduced design costs, and fewer engineering changes. These improvements can help bring a product to market more quickly and ultimately ensure a better product. Also, allowing employees to participate more fully greatly increases their sense of contribution, value, and confidence. Over the past decade, many small companies have outpaced large companies in meeting customer needs. Concurrent engineering can be an attractive strategic approach for large companies seeking to retain or regain their share in competitive markets.

The symbology used in the information systems processing industry resulted in another method of process mapping. Historically, this method has been used by computer specialists and other technically related disciplines to document and communicate the processing of information manually and electronically. The American National Standards Institute (ANSI) created and in 1960 published "Flowcharting Symbols and Their Usage in Information Processing," a standard that was last updated in 1970. This method's symbology is widely adapted to other uses, including process mapping, because it is maturely established and used widely in business systems analysis.

Although selected parts of the ANSI standard are adapted for non-information systems processing uses (e.g., for communicating instructions for human performance in business operations and training manuals), no formal methods are *widely* recognized for analyzing or communicating processes with flow diagrams. Such methods tend to be new and informal and used primarily for analytical purposes. More rare are formal methods used for performance-based communications purposes.

Since the mid- to late 1980s, an increased interest in process mapping has been sparked as organizations rethink their purpose in such activities as concurrent engineering, reengineering, total quality management, and the need to communicate processes as a performance-based intervention to self-managed work teams.

Because of the large number of companies following the ISO 9000 standards and the availability of affordable software packages, creating process maps to convey procedural and process information has become the technique of choice for many quality assurance professionals. Process mapping is used to express activities in every department, from truck scheduling and delivery routes to the proper sequencing of heart valve actuators.

USES OF PROCESS MAPS

Process maps are used to communicate information about work processes for analytical, learning, or auditing purposes. It is not uncommon to use or redevelop a process map to serve all three purposes. For example, a process map could be used to analyze the stages and timing for selecting suppliers and possibly improve the supplier selection process. The finalized process map could then be stated in procedures and training manuals to inform employees of the standard supplier selection process. Finally, an auditor could use the process map to determine whether the participants using the process are in compliance with the documented supplier selection process.

Analytical Purposes

Process maps for analytical purposes can be prepared to assist in planning a process, improving an existing process, or understanding why problems are occurring (such as in nonconformance outputs). Process maps for analytical purposes are often rough, quick sketches since in these instances the process map is not intended to be published for use by many individuals.

In concurrent engineering, a process map developed for improving a process to take action on output is referred to as a *past-oriented, problem-management* strategy. A process map developed for analytical planning purposes to affect output is referred to as a *future-oriented, problem-prevention* strategy.

Learning Purposes

Process maps developed for learning purposes seek to be performance-based communication and are typically published in an organization's standard operating practices manual. Process maps also can be published in organizational training manuals to introduce the "big picture" of the work process to new employees before specific details are provided. Employees need to understand how they fit into the overall operating scheme, and a properly drawn process map can lead them there quickly. Finally, process maps for learning purposes might be published and distributed as a job aid, that is, as a handy reference for the worker.

Auditing Purposes

Process maps developed for auditing purposes serve to document the process so that the auditor can determine (verify) whether the process is being performed accordingly. Process maps for auditing purposes have become increasingly popular in such industries as energy, aerospace/defense, environmental, heath care, information systems, and manufacturing. Government agencies and professional associations, such as the National Committee for Quality Assurance in managed health care and the International Organization of Standards, require that work practices be documented and followed accordingly.

DEVELOPING A PROCESS MAP

Process mapping is an art and technique in the analysis, communication, and design of work and information. The technique takes practice to master, and there are a variety of sources available on mapping with different interpretations. Common development stages to the two process mapping methods mentioned previously include

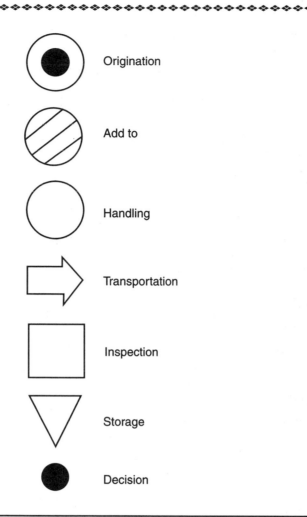

Origination

Add to

Handling

Transportation

Inspection

Storage

Decision

◆ **Figure 38.1.**   Process mapping symbols.

defining the work process, diagramming the process according to the symbology of the method selected, and, if necessary, determining ways to improve the process.

Defining the Work Process

In defining a work process it is important to identify, at a minimum, the following elements: the inputs, outputs, customers (internal and/or external), customer requirements of the outputs, process participants, process owner, process stakeholders, and the first and last operations in the process.

Diagramming the Process

The earliest process mapping method, developed for work simplification, uses the symbols shown in Figure 38.1. In this method, each symbol is supplemented with written descriptions (four or five words), usually placed below the symbol, as shown

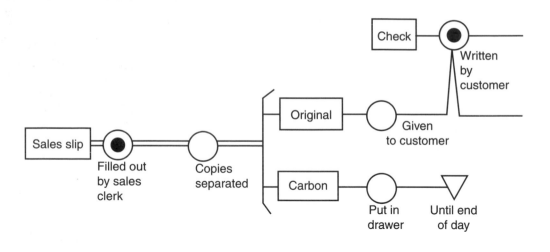

◆ **Figure 38.2.** A simple process map.

Symbol's Name	Symbol's Shape	Symbol's Purpose
Operation, stage, or step	Rectangle	Indicates action to take in steps or describes action taken in stages or events
Decision	Diamond	Indicates branch to possible paths
Terminal	Oval	Orients reader in and out of flow
Flow line	Line with arrowhead	Indicates direction for reading the flowchart
Connector	Small circle	Indicates transfer of flow line to/from another location

◆ **Figure 38.3.** ANSI symbols.

in Figure 38.2. This method has principles for applying the symbols and designing the chart's layout. The method also has a worksheet for recording data about occurrences in the process in order to assess improvement potential.

When using the geometric symbols adapted from the ANSI standard, "Flowcharting Symbols and Their Usage in Information Processing," it is best to limit the selection of symbols to a maximum of five types. The recommended symbols are shown in Figure 38.3. With the affordability of personal computing and graphics packages, designers are increasingly using pictorial symbols (icons, sketches, and computer clip art), either with or without the ANSI geometric-like symbols, in process maps.

Organizational processes usually involve two or more participants (individuals and/or groups, such as a department or organizational unit). Therefore, the process map should indicate which participant is responsible for actions depicted in the

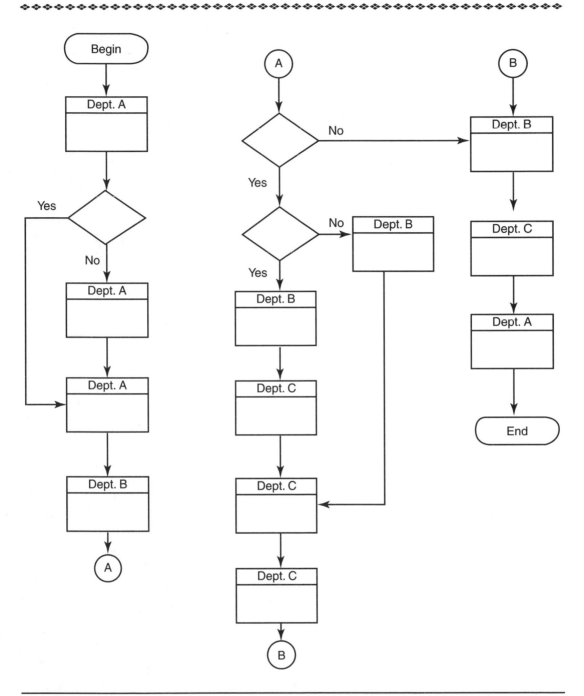

◆ Figure 38.4.   Flowchart: Nongrid format.

process. In Figure 38.4 a nongrid format using the *striping* technique in the rectangles, is used to present the process flow and to identify the participants. Figure 38.5 shows the same information in a grid format that lays out the flowchart in columns represented by the respective participant. This type of chart is also called a cross-functional flowchart or deployment chart.

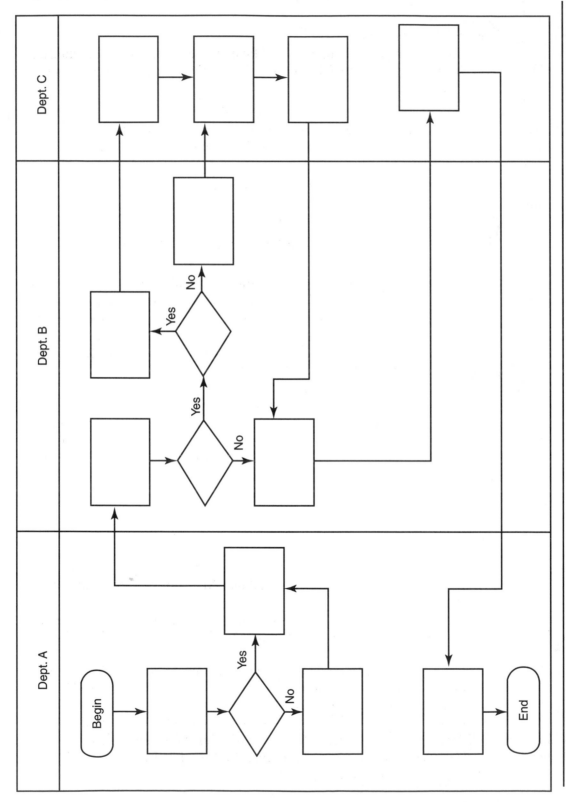

◆ **Figure 38.5.** Flowchart: Grid format.

Determining Ways to Improve the Process

Once the process map has been drawn, it should be evaluated to determine whether it reflects actual events. Common problems with developing effective process maps include the following:

◆ Difficulty in identifying processes and subprocesses from beginning to end. This includes a common understanding of what a process consists of and determining the parameters of the processes in the context of the work environment.

◆ Difficulty in identifying alternative paths, inspection points, and ways to improve a process.

◆ Difficulty in applying principles and techniques for effective communication regarding quantity of information, formats, styles, layout, wording, and titles to the process map.

A major barrier to success in process mapping is the unavailability of widely recognized formal methods for process mapping. Likewise, formal learning sources (seminars, workshops, and publications) to develop process mapping talents are lacking. Business and industry are at an early stage of implementing concurrent engineering and other process management approaches in their environments. Also, no formal authority mandates the standardization of the symbols and their applications.

The impact on success in using concurrent engineering and process mapping is best realized by monitoring statistical performance before and after the process has been modified. Data which may be measured when monitoring statistical performance include completion time, number of units produced, number of people or departments involved, amount of value-added steps, number of defects, and the degree of confidence in workers' performance.

🏠 Additional Readings 🏠

American National Standards Institute. 1970. *"Flowcharting Symbols and Their Usage in Information Processing"* (X3.5-1970). New York: ANSI.

Fleischer, Mitchell, and Jeffrey Liker. 1997. *Concurrent Engineering Effectiveness: Integrating Product Development Across Organizations.* Milwaukee: ASQ Quality Press.

Galloway, Dianne. 1994. *Mapping Work Processes.* Milwaukee: ASQC Quality Press.

Graham, Ben S., Jr. 1990. *Professional Work Simplification Techniques Workshop.* Tipp City, Ohio: The Ben Graham Corporation.

——. 1990. "Work Simplification: From Bricklayer to Microcomputer." In *Templates.* Business Forms Management Association. Columbus, Ohio: Vol. 8 pp. 10–13.

Hartley, J. R. 1992. *Concurrent Engineering.* Cambridge, Mass.: Productivity Press.

Horn, Robert E. 1991. "Processes." In *Participant's Manual for Developing Procedures, Policies and Documentation.* Waltham, Mass.: Information Mapping, p. 29.

Hurley, H., and C. Loew. 1996. "A Quality Change for New Product Development." *Quality Observer* January, pp. 10–13.

Turino, J. 1991. "Concurrent Engineering: Making it Work Calls for Input from Everyone." *IEEE Spectrum* July, p. 91.

Urgo, Raymond E. 1994. "Flowcharting Performance-Based Processes and Procedures." In *42nd Annual Conference Proceedings.* Arlington, Va.: Society for Technical Communication, p. 459.

——. 1996. *Participant's Manual for Flowcharting Performance-Based Processes and Procedures.* Los Angeles: Urgo and Associates.

——. 1994. "Process and Procedure Flowcharts for Job Aids." In *32nd Annual Conference Proceedings.* Washington, D.C.: National Society for Performance and Instruction, p. 336.

🦋 Part 6 Endnotes 🦋

Chapter 36

1. *The Malcolm Baldrige National Quality Award: 1999 Criteria for Performance Excellence* (Gaithersburg, Md.: National Institute of Standards and Technology, 1999), p. 3.
2. Jack Campanella, ed., *Principles of Quality Costs,* 2nd ed., ASQC Quality Costs Committee (Milwaukee: ASQC Quality Press, 1990), p. 28.
3. Joseph M. Juran and Frank M. Gryna, eds., *Juran's Quality Control Handbook,* 4th ed. (New York: McGraw-Hill, 1988), p. 8.11.
4. Ibid., p. 8.12.
5. Ibid., pp. 6.32, 6.19.
6. Campanella, p. 28.
7. Ibid.
8. Peter Senge, *The Fifth Discipline.* (New York: Doubleday, 1990) p. 247.

Chapter 37

1. ANSI/ASQC Z1.4 (1981).

Part 7

Human Resource Management

Chapter 39

Leadership Roles and Responsibilities

❖ *This chapter should help you*

◆ Define the primary purpose, roles, and responsibilities of personnel holding leadership positions within an organization

◆ Understand how those roles and responsibilities are related to quality and organizational performance

◆ Relate the key issues of conflict management and ethical conduct to the role of leadership

◆ Describe a model for selecting a method for addressing a particular conflict situation

◆ Understand the relationship between the ASQ code of ethics and the role of a quality manager

WHAT DOES A LEADER DO?

As changes in organizations' structures, processes, and priorities have occurred, so too have the roles and characteristics of an effective leader evolved significantly during the past two decades. Many writers have defined the difference between management and leadership as being the amount of autocratic control exercised over people. For example, Kouzes and Posner define leadership as a shared responsibility and state the difference as "managers . . . get other people to do, but leaders get other people to want to do."[1] Others have recognized that the type of leader needed is dependent on the particular situation, such as the organization, its mission and competitive environment, and the makeup of the individuals being led.[2]

Other issues that make leadership not only difficult to define but also difficult to learn include the following:

◆ The fact that leadership is often an appointed role (e.g., president or department manager) but frequently is a role taken on by different people who are working together on a particular project. For example, the leadership role at any particular point during a project might be taken on by a person who has the skills necessary during that project phase.

◆ The increase in "knowledge work," where the person being "led" often has more knowledge of the tasks to be accomplished than the individual who is formally defined as the leader.

◆ The increase in virtual teams, in which a group of individuals is jointly responsible for a particular outcome but team members are not in face-to-face contact, such as when phone, e-mail, video conferencing, and other technologies are used to communicate.[3]

Schein described the multiple paradoxes involved in leadership by stating that leaders of the future will be persons "who can lead and follow, be central and marginal, be hierarchically above and below, be individualistic and a team player, and, above all, be a perpetual learner."[4]

Leaders must ensure that particular activities are carried out. For example, a key role of executive leadership is to provide strategic direction, resources, and information that will enable the organization to accomplish its current mission. Leaders also have the responsibility of developing the organization and its members, products/services, and business processes such that future business needs will be met. Deming emphasized the latter by stating that the job of a leader is to transform the organization.[5]

Another role of leaders is to ensure that the organization works effectively with respect to the interaction among individuals, groups, and business units both within and outside the organization and that behaviors meet accepted standards for business ethics. The quality manager's role often includes the special challenge of representing customers during complaint processing or organizational/product changes to ensure that customers' interests are taken into account.

Requirements for good leadership are similar regardless of the functional department a manager oversees. However, some specific requirements for quality managers in leadership roles include the following:

◆ personal commitment to both product and organizational quality

◆ a strong sense of value for others' managerial work and leadership

◆ skilled application of the broad base of knowledge of the quality field and an understanding of how to apply this knowledge in each functional area of the organization

◆ wisdom about both people and things and an understanding of how to integrate them to get work accomplished (in other words, being a change agent)

◆ absence of temperamental or emotional characteristics that would interfere with the ability to work with others

Some critical personal attributes that leaders in the quality management area should exhibit include creativity, patience, flexibility, and self-discipline. Good listening skills, excellent coaching and training skills, sensitivity to customer and employee issues, and a personal commitment to excellence are also essential. Finally, a leader must be a mentor, capable of managing change, and willing to empower subordinates.

Resolves Conflict

One of the most important things a leader does on a continual basis is make decisions. These decisions must take into account the long-term effects of an action on the organization and its stakeholders. Because of the multiple considerations that must be accounted for, conflict management often plays a major role in decision making. Therefore, conflict management is an important skill for a leader.

Conflict occurs when two or more strategies selected to achieve a goal or objective appear to be mutually exclusive. That is, each strategy is capable of satisfying only particular aspects of a desired outcome. Generally, conflict can be defined as the perceived absence of a prominent alternative.[6] Conflicts cannot be dissolved (a term preferable to "resolved") when two or more parties believe that what each wants is incompatible with what the other wants.

Conflict situations in organizational settings can involve any combination of individuals or groups and internal or external parties. For example, conflict within a team could be between individuals or subgroups, conflict inside an organization might be between two departments, and conflict between organizations might involve customers, suppliers, or regulatory bodies.

However, conflict is increasingly being viewed as a vital, energizing force in an organization. The management and resolution of differences between individuals and groups unlocks the creativity of an organization, allowing it to innovate, change, and grow. "Contrary to conventional wisdom, the most important single thing about conflict is that it is good for you. While this is not a scientific statement of fact, it reflects a basic and unprecedented shift in emphasis—a move away from the old human relations point of view where all conflict was basically seen as bad. In brief, in our new frontier environment, conflict is the order of the day."[7]

When people take a "What's in it for me?" approach to decision making, conflicts proliferate in various forms and intensities. The benefits of conflict management, achieved through negotiation based on principles that result in win-win collaborations, are immense. Some crucial benefits to the organization are the following:

◆ *Provides a unified direction.* This provides a platform for achieving the organization's goals and objectives in the most effective and efficient manner.

◆ *Results in employee satisfaction.* This in turn produces customer satisfaction.

◆ *Improves the health and safety of employees.* This occurs as more de-escalators are employed (e.g., active listening and finding alternatives).

Following are some components of an approach for resolving a conflict to the mutual benefit of all involved parties:

◆ define the conflict as a mutual problem

◆ identify goals that are common to all parties

◆ find creative alternatives that satisfy all parties

◆ ensure that all parties understand their own needs and communicate them clearly

◆ attempt to equalize power by emphasizing mutual interdependence (as opposed to independence or dependence)

◆ be certain that contacts are on the basis of equal power

◆ communicate needs, goals, positions, and proposals openly, honestly, and accurately

◆ state needs, goals, and positions in the opening offer

◆ empathize with and understand others' positions, feelings, and frames of reference

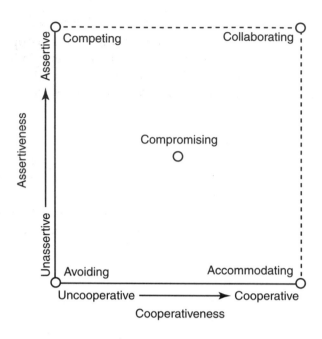

◆ Figure 39.1.   Conflict-handling modes. Source: Marvin D. Dunnette. Used with permission.

◆   reduce defensiveness by avoiding threatening, harassing, and inconveniencing other parties

Conflicts can never be successfully resolved when one party does the following:

◆   defines the conflict as a win-lose strategy

◆   pursues his or her own goals or hidden agenda

◆   forces the other party into submission

◆   increases its power by emphasizing its independence of the other party and the other party's dependence on it

◆   tries to arrange contacts where its power is greater

◆   uses inaccurate or misleading communication to further its needs, goals, position, and proposal

◆   overemphasizes its needs, goals, and position in the opening offer

◆   avoids all empathy and understanding of others' positions, feelings, and frames of reference

◆   would rather both parties lose (lose-lose) than have the other party get its way

Thomas and Kilman have developed a model defining five conflict-handling modes. It is based on the two dimensions of (1) assertiveness, the extent to which the party attempts to satisfy his or her own concerns, and (2) cooperativeness, the extent to which the party attempts to satisfy the other party's concerns.[8] The resulting matrix, shown in Figure 39.1, has been developed into an instrument that can be used to assess one's conflict-handling style. The interpretation portion of the instrument emphasizes that each conflict mode might be appropriate for a particular situation. Quality managers, because of their increased role in facilitating cross-functional cooperation for strategic alignment and continuous improvement, should be aware of and develop their conflict handling abilities.

Adheres to Professional Ethics

People need to know what behaviors are and are not acceptable. Therefore, a critical role of leadership is to ensure that the organization has defined those behaviors or the principles behind them as clearly as possible. This is often done by documenting the values and principles to be used as guidance in the pursuit of the organization's vision and mission. However, another way employees learn is by observing the actions of persons in leadership, influential, or powerful positions. Therefore, it is important that a leader's actions be congruent with the stated principles and values.

For some business fields, professional societies have defined a code of practice to be followed by their membership. Figure 39.2 shows the Code of Ethics for quality professionals established by the American Society for Quality (ASQ).

Fundamental Principles:

◆ Will be honest and impartial, and will serve with devotion my employer, my clients and the public.

◆ Will strive to increase the competence and prestige of the profession.

◆ Will use my knowledge and skills for the advancement of human welfare, and in promoting the safety and reliability of products for public use.

◆ Will earnestly endeavor to aid the work of the Society.

Relations with the Public:

◆ Will do whatever I can to promote the reliability and safety of all products that come within my jurisdiction.

◆ Will endeavor to extend public knowledge of the work of the Society and its members that relates to the public welfare.

◆ Will be dignified and modest in explaining my work and merit.

◆ Will preface any public statements that I may issue by clearly indicating on whose behalf they are made.

Relations with Employers and Clients:

◆ Will act in professional matters as a faithful agent or trustee for each employer or client.

◆ Will inform each client or employers of any business connections, interests or affiliation which might influence my judgement or impair the equitable character of my services.

◆ Will indicate to my employer or client that adverse consequences to be expected if my professional judgement is overruled.

Code of Ethics

To uphold and advance the honor and dignity of the profession, and in keeping with high standards of ethical conduct I acknowledge that I:

Fundamental Principles

- Will be honest and impartial, and will serve with devotion my employer, my clients, and the public.
- Will strive to increase the competence and prestige of the profession.
- Will use my knowledge and skill for the advancement of human welfare, and in promoting the safety and reliability of products for public use.
- Will earnestly endeavor to aid the work of the Society.

Relations With the Public

1.1 Will do whatever I can to promote the reliability and safety of all products that come within my jurisdiction.
1.2 Will endeavor to extend public knowledge of the work of the Society and its members that relates to the public welfare.
1.3 Will be dignified and modest in explaining my work and merit.
1.4 Will preface any public statements that I may issue by clearly indicating on whose behalf they are made.

Relations With Employers and Clients

2.1 Will act in professional matters as a faithful agent or trustee for each employer or client.
2.2 Will inform each client or employer of any business connections, interests, or affiliations which might influence my judgment or impair the equitable character of my services.
2.3 Will indicate to my employer or client the adverse consequences to be expected if my professional judgment is overruled.
2.4 Will not disclose information concerning the business affairs or technical processes of any present or former employer or client without his consent.
2.5 Will not accept compensation from more than one party for the same service without the consent of all parties. If employed, I will engage in supplementary employment of consulting practice only with the consent of my employer.

Relations With Peers

3.1 Will take care that credit for the work of others is given to those whom it is due.
3.2 Will endeavor to aid the professional development and advancement of those in my employ or under my supervision.
3.3 Will not compete unfairly with others; will extend my friendship and confidence to all associates and those with whom I have business relations.

◆ **Figure 39.2.**   ASQ Code of Ethics.

◆ Will not disclose information concerning the business affairs or technical processes of any present or former employer or client without his consent.

◆ Will not compensation from more than one party for the same service without the consent of all parties. If employed, I will engage in supplementary employment of consulting practice only with the same consent of my employer.

Relations with Peers:

◆ Will take care that credit for the work of others is given to those to whom it is due.

◆ Will endeavor to aid the professional development and advancement of those in my employer under my supervision.

◆ Will not compete unfairly with others; will extend my friendship and confidence to all associates and those with whom I have business relations.

One of the more important responsibilities of leadership is taking action on the basis of how well employees meet ethical guidelines. Employees who demonstrate ethical practices, especially during difficult situations, must be commended for their actions, whereas those who do not act ethically must be dealt with appropriately.

Additional Readings

Bridges, William. 1996. "Leading the De-Jobbed Organization." In *The Leader of the Future,* ed. Frances Hesselbein, Marshall Goldsmith, and Richard Beckhard. San Francisco: Jossey-Bass, pp. 11–18.

Deming, W. Edwards. 1994. *The New Economics.* Cambridge: Massachusetts Institute of Technology.

Handy, Charles. 1996. "The New Language of Organizing and Its Implications for Leaders." In *The Leader of the Future*, ed. Frances Hesselbein, Marshall Goldsmith, and Richard Beckhard. San Francisco: Jossey-Bass, pp. 3–9.

Kelly, Joe. 1970. "Making Conflict Work for You." *Harvard Business Review* (July–August). Vol. 48: p. 6.

Kouzes, James M., and Barry Z. Posner. 1987. *The Leadership Challenge.* San Francisco: Jossey-Bass Publishers.

Schein, Edgar H. 1996. "Leadership and Organizational Culture." In *The Leader of the Future*, ed. Frances Hesselbein, Marshall Goldsmith, and Richard Beckhard. San Francisco: Jossey-Bass, pp. 59–69.

Thomas, Kenneth. 1996. "Conflict and Conflict Management." In *The Handbook of Industrial and Organizational Psychology,* ed. Marvin Dunnette. Chicago: Rand McNally, pp. 889–935.

Thomas, Kenneth W., and Ralph H. Kilmann. 1974. *Thomas-Kilmann Conflict Mode Instrument.* Tuxedo, N.Y.: XICOM.

Zeleny, Milan. *Multiple Criteria Decision Making.* New York: McGraw-Hill.

Chapter 40

Quality Staffing Issues

❖ *This chapter should help you*

- ◆ Understand the comprehensive nature of the process of managing the human resources required for supporting the quality mission
- ◆ Define techniques for and potential problems with the selection of new employees
- ◆ Explain why performance evaluations can be a useful tool for improving organizational performance
- ◆ Understand the necessity of ongoing professional development for all employees
- ◆ Relate the role of goals and objectives to the quality staffing function

---

Although a product's or service's quality requirements often determine the company's organizational structure for quality, in many organizations the function is overseen by a separate department that coordinates and controls quality-related activities. An effective quality organization should do the following:

- ◆ provide leadership in company-wide quality planning
- ◆ analyze and report quality information to top management
- ◆ perform quality auditing and surveillance activities
- ◆ monitor for process improvement and waste identification
- ◆ train and consult on quality technologies
- ◆ identify or develop new quality methodologies and transfer them to line management.

A key role of a plant-level quality manager is to ensure that adequate personnel and skills are available to support ongoing order fulfillment operations as well as to prepare for new product, organizational, or technological initiatives. This role requires understanding the skills and number of personnel needed, maintaining these levels as they are affected by promotions and turnover, and applying the concept of continuous improvement to these human resources. Titles of the positions that the quality manager might oversee include quality engineering, quality technicians, quality analysis, quality system and process auditors, metrology personnel, and inspection personnel (e.g., product audits).

Depending on the size of the organization, a division- or corporate-level quality manager might have many of these same responsibilities. However, someone at this level of the organization is also likely to be involved in defining new strategic initiatives, integrating and standardizing quality methods across the organization, and transferring new technologies. They will often provide policy input to the plant-level quality function but might not actually have a staff reporting to them. Plant quality managers often report as a solid line to the general plant manager, with a dotted-line relationship to the division/corporate manager.

SELECTING STAFF

To know what staff is necessary, an organization must first understand the tasks to be performed and the skills necessary. On the basis of the company's product and process technology, management philosophy, and desired organizational structure, the requirements can then be organized into specific job functions/titles, each of which will have a description of the primary responsibilities. Job descriptions also state any educational and/or experience requirements of a person qualified to fill the position as well as the level of accountability and authority allocated to the position.

Quality department candidates must possess an aptitude for quality, including appropriate mathematical and analytical skills. Additionally, candidates must be able to establish credibility through their integrity, rapid learning, and application of their knowledge and skills. Because quality personnel are part of the staff rather than line function, they must be viewed as adding value and should be customer oriented (both external and internal).

Personnel to fill job openings in the quality function can be selected by internal promotion or by external recruitment. Internally promoted employees have the advantage of dealing with a known entity and, depending on their knowledge of the company's products and processes, might be productive more immediately. A disadvantage of hiring from within the company is the possibility that past relationships or performance can affect others' view of the individual and therefore hinder their ability to influence. Hiring from outside also has the advantage of bringing in potentially new concepts and ideas.

A list of potential candidates must be created as the first step when a position needs to be filled. This might be done through advertising the position both internally and externally, by contacting a recruiter, or by working with placement personnel from educational, professional, or other institutions. Applicants are then screened through a review of resumes; those applicants whose resumes generate the most interest are then invited to interview for the position. Although special skills and experience might be necessary for some positions (e.g., metrology), organizations sometimes consider candidates who are believed to have the attitude and flexibility for change and the ability to learn, as specific skills can be developed once a person is hired.

Human resources personnel specially trained in interviewing techniques, as well as the department manager, will typically perform the interview. Depending on the position to be filled and the work design of the organization, peers and customers of the position to be filled might also participate in the interview process.

Employers are increasingly turning to various forms of preplacement testing. Tests might check for cognitive ability, intelligence, physical ability, personality, and interests. Any test administered must be proven valid and reliable and appropriate for the position for which the testing is done to avoid possible liability or discrimination claims.[1] Checking candidate references is also a valuable step in the hiring process, but legal issues are applicable in this area as well.

Once the best candidate has been identified, an offer is made regarding pay and benefits. If it is declined, the next suitable candidate will be offered the position. When the offer has been accepted, the individual must be oriented as to company facilities, people, and practices.[2] The quality manager should ensure that the company's quality policies and procedures are included in such orientations.

One mistake often made by managers is putting their staffing considerations in a reactive mode, responding only as positions become vacant. A more proactive view is that of having a succession plan that looks at key positions and individuals in the organization over time.[3] Developing people who will be able to move into other positions makes the organization more responsive to change. Quality managers should ensure that positions critical to quality, especially their own, are considered for succession planning.

EVALUATING PERFORMANCE

Accurately evaluating staff performance is part of the continuous improvement of an organization. Performance evaluation involves reviewing personnel performance against expectations, identifying strengths and weaknesses, and creating a development plan. Performance evaluations are also considered for promotion and salary decisions and as input into disciplinary actions.

To be fair, performance evaluations must be continuous, fact based, and founded on clear, established, and communicated expectations. They must result in the identification of areas for improvement and/or corrective action. Performance evaluations should evaluate only areas deemed to be important; they will lose credibility if they focus on trivial matters.

Performance evaluations usually involve scoring the individual's performance against predefined criteria and often include narrative comments. A common problem with performance evaluations is either that ratings are often forced into a normal distribution or that everyone is rated about the same. An additional source of information for evaluation is a record of critical incidents maintained by the manager. This involves keeping a log of behaviors (good or bad) that the employee used when facing a significant or difficult situation.[4]

A good performance evaluation system can increase an organization's efficiency and effectiveness. It can motivate employees and improve morale as well as identify areas for employee skill building and training. Continuous improvement of people skills can result in higher customer satisfaction.

A fair performance appraisal system exists when the following criteria are met:[5]

◆ Expectations are clearly identified and guidelines for output are established.

◆ The format for the evaluation is established and regular, and periodic meetings are scheduled.

◆ A "contribution plan" for the subordinate is established and monitored directly and through peers.

◆ Notes of performance, both good and bad, are made and retained.

◆ A scheme for just-in-time training and coaching should be in place for when things are not going as planned (to address inadequate performance).

◆ Resources should be allocated and tasks redefined to overcome deficient performance.

◆ Disciplinary action should rarely occur as a result of the appraisal. If disciplinary action is taken, an appeals system must be readily available.

◆ Assessment of performance should be based on factors such as consistency of output, the presence of favorable or unfavorable environmental conditions, the ability to do a better job, the use of discretion (within limits), and the ability to work as part of a team (e.g., in problem-solving teams, or quality circles).

◆ Finally, an evaluation should express whether the subordinate grasped fully the quality aspects of the job and to what degree the supervisor's expectations were met.

When the performance evaluation system is improperly applied, the following mistakes can occur:

◆ When appraisal is not done on a continuous or frequent basis, the performance review will result in some employees receiving unfair evaluation because of inaccuracies. Infrequent appraisals also fail to allow employees to rectify deficient performance in a timely manner.

◆ Annual reviews might be performed late and done as a routine step to satisfy "the higher ups" in the organization.

◆ Difficulties in differentiating between personal effectiveness and performance accountabilities can interfere with evaluations.

◆ Managers might not be able to give or accept feedback.

A more recent development in performance evaluation is the involvement of more than a manager and the individual being evaluated. Known as *360-degree feedback,* these systems solicit feedback from peers, subordinates, and internal and external customers.

An important role of the quality manager in the performance evaluation process is to ensure that the criteria used for evaluating personnel include measures that are related to product and organizational quality.

Many, including Deming, have expressed concerns about the use of performance appraisal systems. Deming stated that because the individual is part of a system, it is impossible to differentiate between the contribution of the individual versus the contribution of the system to the resulting performance.[6]

ENCOURAGING PROFESSIONAL DEVELOPMENT

The objective of professional development is to improve employees' performances in their current positions as well as to prepare them for future roles or positions.[7] Most successful companies recognize the importance of the continuous professional development of employees, as witnessed by the number of companies who now operate corporate universities.

The need for professional development is closely linked to the organization's goals and objectives, individual employee's goals and objectives, and the organization's current performance. Employee development should include the active involvement of both the employee and the manager with a focus on individual and business performance. Opportunities for development are often identified during the performance evaluation process.

In order to keep professional development aligned with business needs, it is important that everyone know where the business is going (e.g., mission and strategy) and what skills will be needed in the future. However, the personal interests of each employee should be taken into account as well. Management must be cognizant of employees' skills and abilities and be able to ascertain whether these skills and abilities are sufficient for meeting the organization's current or future needs. Timely plans can then be created to define skills to be developed, explain how this will be done, and ensure the provision of adequate resources.

Development of employees can be done many ways. Internal mechanisms include training courses, special assignments, and mentoring, whereas external methods include workshops, college courses or degrees, conferences, and self-study. The Internet and corporate intranets will likely become major resources for future developmental efforts.

The quality manager has two primary responsibilities regarding professional development. The first is to ensure that the skills being developed throughout the organization include those that will allow other functions to perform their duties well. Another is to develop the personnel within the quality department, including him- or herself. The American Society for Quality's certification programs and professional development courses are a valuable resource for developing quality-related skills.

An organization that encourages professional development of its employees has a greater opportunity to become a "learning organization," thereby increasing its efficiency and effectiveness. Organizational change can also become easier as employees become more knowledgeable. Opportunities available for career development and the organization's efforts to support that development also influence employee satisfaction. The resulting increase in employee satisfaction often leads to greater customer satisfaction.

If management does not recognize that employees expect the organization to provide developmental opportunities, those employees who are more learning oriented might become dissatisfied with the organization or seek employment elsewhere. The same is true when management gives lip service to development without providing adequate resources. Employee development must be a high priority for all organizations in the age of knowledge.

GOALS AND OBJECTIVES

Ultimately, the goal of any organization is to satisfy stakeholders, including customers, employees, suppliers, regulatory agencies, and the community. The precise definition of these goals and how they will be measured should be communicated to appropriate shareholders. One way of accomplishing this is to define and communicate the vision, mission, values, and principles that are to guide the organization. Each business unit or department might also create its own mission statement that supports the organizational mission.

The business planning process defines the long-term plans and annual goals and objectives as well as the strategies used to achieve them and measures to be used to monitor success. Again, these need to be communicated to appropriate stakeholders (e.g., if an increase in product reliability is targeted, suppliers of critical components should be made aware of these plans so that their own business plan can include activities to support the goal). Each organizational unit or department needs to set and align its own goals with those at the aggregate level. Having departmental goals helps managers better define the skills, personnel, and other resources necessary to achieve the goals. Acquiring, enabling, measuring, and improving human resources within a span of control is what human resources is all about.

To be useful for an organization, goals should meet the following criteria:

◆ *They should be acceptable.* Involvement in goal setting is one way of ensuring acceptance and often involves a catchball process in which goals are set by one level of the organization and reviewed/revised by the next level until all have reached agreement.

◆ *They should be precise.* Goals must be defined in terms that are sufficiently clear but not overly constraining.

◆ *They should be attainable.* Difficult goals can help to motivate people; goals perceived as impossible can have the opposite effect.

◆ *They should be congruent.* Goals throughout the organization should not conflict with one another or with defined organizational values.[8]

An ongoing goal of the quality department is to communicate, coordinate, and facilitate organization-wide quality requirements as established by top management. The quality department is responsible for assessing and reviewing the effectiveness of the quality program and providing timely and requisite information for managerial decision making. Other important functions include providing the necessary skills and training for professional growth of its employees, serving as members of various types of quality teams, and becoming knowledgeable of customer, stakeholder, and employee needs.

The quality department is involved in supporting the organizational goals and objectives through improvement in and training for the processes included in the company's quality manual. Training might also include how to perform broad-based organizational assessments, how to plan and conduct internal quality system audits, and how to use statistical process control and problem-solving tools as well as other pertinent tools of quality. Quality department staff might also facilitate continuous improvement teams.

❖❖

After the quality department has established concise and attainable goals and objectives, it must measure and review performance against the plan. The quality department should be a role model for other departments in showing how the Plan-Do-Check-Act (PDCA) process works to implement continuous improvement.

🏛 Additional Readings 🏛

Albanese, Robert. 1985. "Objectives and Goals." In *Handbook for Professional Managers,* ed. Lester Bittel and Jackson Ramsey. New York: McGraw-Hill, pp. 617–22.

Aldrich, John W. 1994. "Staffing Concepts and Principles." In *Human Resources Management and Development Handbook,* ed. William R. Tracey. New York: AMACOM, pp. 181–89.

Buckner, Marilyn, and Lynn Slavenski. 1994. "Succession Planning." In *Human Resources Management and Development Handbook,* ed. William R. Tracey. New York: AMACOM, pp. 561–75.

Deming, W. Edwards. 1994. *The New Economics.* Cambridge: Massachusetts Institute of Technology.

Dessler, Gary. 1996. *Human Resource Management.* 7th ed. Englewood Cliffs, N.J.: Prentice-Hall.

Jacques, Elliot, and Stephen D. Clement. 1994. *Executive Leadership.* Malden, Mass.: Basil Blackwell and Cason Hall.

Juran, Joseph M. 1988. "Organizing for Quality." In *Juran's Quality Control Handbook,* 4th ed., ed. Joseph M. Juran and Frank M. Gryna. New York: McGraw-Hill.

McCullough, Richard C. 1987. "Professional Development." In *Training and Development Handbook,* ed. Robert L. Craig. New York: McGraw-Hill, pp. 35–64.

Chapter 41

Quality Responsibilities in Job/Position Descriptions

❖ *This chapter should help you*

◆ Understand how job descriptions can aid in deploying quality responsibilities

◆ Describe what information should be included in a job description

◆ Define some of the quality responsibilities that should be included in job descriptions

---

RESPONSIBILITIES FOR QUALITY

One way to ensure that a quality department and each staff position within the quality department understand their responsibilities for quality is to document responsibilities with respect to quality performance. Job descriptions are one usual way of documenting these responsibilities. If performance evaluations are then based on the job content defined in the job descriptions, the importance of each employee's role with respect to quality will be emphasized.

For existing positions, job descriptions would ideally be developed jointly between the manager and employee. The document should include the following:

◆ position title
◆ basic job functions
◆ to whom the individual reports
◆ titles of positions reporting to the individual
◆ knowledge and skill requirements (including educational and experience qualifications when applicable)
◆ limits of authority (e.g., maximum dollar limits with respect to decision making)
◆ specific job functions
◆ performance standards[1]

Organizations typically also include any special physical requirements for the job (e.g., ability to lift 20 kilograms) to reduce the likelihood of legal action regarding discrimination under the Americans with Disabilities Act.

The range of quality activities within an organization is large and is somewhat dependent on the industry. However, following is a list of typical job titles and activities:

Vice president of quality: Establishes the direction for the development and administration of the company's quality programs. Consults with peers on the attitudes and practices of quality throughout the organization to develop an environment of continual improvement in every aspect of the company's products and services. Acts as a champion for quality.

Director of quality: Coordinates all aspects of the company's quality program, such as developing and administering the program, training, coaching employees, and facilitating change throughout the organization. Responsible for establishing strategic plans, policies, and procedures at all levels to ensure that the quality program will meet or exceed internal and external customers' needs and expectations.

Quality manager: Ensures the administration of the company's quality program within a defined segment of the organization. Might be responsible for dealing with customers and suppliers on quality-related issues.

Quality engineer: Designs, installs, and evaluates quality process sampling systems, procedures, and statistical techniques; designs or specifies inspection and testing mechanisms and equipment; analyzes production and service limitations and standards; recommends revision of specifications when indicated; formulates or helps formulate quality policies and procedures; conducts training on quality concepts and tools; and interfaces with all other engineering components within the company and with customers and suppliers on quality-related issues.

Quality specialist: As the primary assignment, performs a specific quality-related function with the company's quality program (e.g., quality training, auditing, or reliability testing). Has either received direct training or has been performing the activity for a number of years. Shows a very high degree of skill performing the activity.

Quality supervisor: Administers the company's quality program within a defined department of the organization. Has direct reports that implement some aspect of the policies and procedures of the quality program.

Quality analyst: Initiates and/or coordinates quality-related data from production and service activities and reports these data using statistical techniques.

Quality coordinator: Collects, organizes, monitors, and distributes any information related to the functions of the quality department. Might also communicate information on the latest standards, procedures, and requirements related to the company's products or services. Typically generates reports using computer skills and distributes these reports to various users in the organization, customers, or suppliers.

Quality technician: Performs basic quality techniques to track, analyze, and report on materials, processes, and products to ensure that they meet the company's quality standards. Might calibrate tools and equipment.

Quality inspector: Inspects, audits, and reports on materials, processes, and products using variable or attribute measuring instruments and techniques to ensure conformance with the company's quality standards.[2]

Job descriptions must also be regularly reviewed and revised on the basis of organizational changes and continuous improvement.

Additional Readings

Aldrich, John W. 1994. "Staffing Concepts and Principles." In *Human Resources Management and Development Handbook,* ed. William R. Tracey. New York: AMACOM, pp.181–89.

Bemowski, Karen. 1998. "1998 Salary Survey." *Quality Progress,* November, pp. 25–94.

Clemmer, Jim. 1995. *Pathways to Performance: A Guide to Transforming Yourself, Your Team, and Your Organization.* New York: Macmillan.

Jacques, Elliot, and Stephen D. Clement. 1994. *Executive Leadership.* Malden, Mass.: Basil Blackwell and Cason Hall.

Juran, Joseph M., and Frank M. Gryna. 1993. *Quality Planning and Analysis.* New York: McGraw-Hill.

❖❖

Chapter 42

Employee/Team Empowerment

❖❖

Put everybody in the company to work to accomplish the transformation. The transformation is everybody's job.

Dr. W. Edwards Deming, from his 14-step strategy

❖ *This chapter should help you*

- ◆ Define empowerment and how it affects organizational and personal performance
- ◆ Understand the major issues, positive and negative, usually encountered when empowering employees and teams

---

To meet increased competitive challenges of a global economy and a heightened focus on customer service, traditional management practices have undergone a transformation over the past two decades. Employee empowerment, participative management, and team-based problem solving and decision making have become part of everyday business language.

WHAT IS EMPOWERMENT?

Empowerment is based on the belief that employees have the ability to take on more responsibility and authority than has traditionally been given them and that heightened productivity and a better quality of work life will result. Different words and phrases are used to define empowerment, but most are variations on a theme: to provide employees with the means for making influential decisions. Juran defined empowerment as "conferring the right to make decisions and take action."[1]

Empowerment is difficult to define because its meaning takes on the flavor of the organization or individual attempting to implement it. However, it is based on the organization design/development concepts of job enlargement and job enrichment.

For maximum performance, organizations need to fully utilize the human resources employed rather than only a part of the person. Empowerment means giving up some of the power traditionally held by management and shifting knowledge and responsibilities to persons who actually operate the business processes. This means that management must themselves take on new roles, knowledge, and responsibilities.

Empowerment does not mean that management relinquishes all authority, totally delegates decision making, and allows freedom from boundaries or self-management without accountability. It requires development of mutual trust, attention to individuals' capabilities, and a clear agreement about roles, responsibilities, risk taking, and boundaries. Boundaries are set on the basis of factors such as company values and goals, ethical standards, customer needs, and organizational capabilities.

Empowerment applies to both individuals and teams. The increasing growth of knowledge workers in business makes teamwork a critical component. "Knowledge workers function on the job as part of a team. Almost 85% work as team members."[2] Self-directed teams and high-performance work systems are labels often used for more empowered organizational designs. The Baldrige Award recognizes empowerment as an important issue in its Human Resource Focus category.

IMPLEMENTING EMPOWERMENT

Empowerment is difficult to implement because it is a major change from past ways of working. It involves behavioral change of all members of the organization: management, operations personnel, and support staff. Therefore, it is critical that the organization lay the appropriate groundwork. To start, an organization should develop an operational definition of empowerment and communicate a strong commitment to it, starting with top management. It should develop a time-phased implementation plan and build the necessary organizational systems to support it.

A clear implementation plan takes into account all aspects of empowerment and is essential to its success. To be included are the phases and scope of implementation and a description of responsibilities and expectations. A clear consideration of barriers and concerns should be addressed in its development. Assigning a person or team to oversee the implementation plan is a key factor in achieving a smooth transition.

Empowerment takes time. To be fully empowered, employees must have the skills, knowledge, authority, willingness, and resources to make accurate and timely decisions about their work in the best interests of the customer and the organization. Senior management must provide five critical elements for an organization to realize full empowerment:

◆ access to critical business information

◆ training in how to effectively use the information

◆ authority and discretion to take appropriate action

◆ opportunity to make valuable contributions and key decisions

◆ recognition for accepting and exercising the responsibility necessary to get their jobs done as well as assisting others to do their jobs

Empowerment must be implemented with the customer in mind. The intent is for frontline personnel to have the decision-making capability to "delight" customers. For example, Xerox developed a customer obsession program that includes delegating downward some key policy decisions previously made at higher levels. Empowering service personnel to resolve customer problems is a key strategy for Xerox.[3]

Making ongoing improvements to work processes is also a key attribute of empowerment. Business literature is replete with examples of how teams have reduced costs and increased the quality of organizational processes. Successful suggestion programs also encourage individual employees to make process improvements.

Restructuring the Organization

Restructuring the organization can also help initiate and foster empowerment. Ken Somers indicates that process-focused and flatter organizations lend themselves better to empowerment since they allow employees to better focus on the customer, as opposed to traditional hierarchies that encourage employees to focus on the manager.

Empowerment is often viewed as an inverted triangle of organizational power. In the traditional view, management is at the top while customers are on the bottom. In an empowered environment, customers are at the top while management is in a support role at the bottom. Figure 42-1 illustrates these two organizational structures.

Transferring Authority

Empowering personnel requires the transfer of authority with a clear agreement about expectations, responsibilities, and boundaries. This process takes place over a period of time as both managers and subordinates become comfortable with the concepts and implications of empowerment. In the book *The Leadership Challenge,* four principles that foster this transition are noted:

◆   Give people important work to do on critical issues.

◆   Give people discretion and autonomy over their tasks and resources.

◆   Give visibility to others and provide recognition for their efforts.

◆   Build relationships by finding them sponsors and mentors.[4]

For empowerment to be successfully implemented, the leader's role must shift from that of a traditional manager to that of an enabler. Leaders must balance their need for personal control with the ability to provide freedom for others to act on their own authority. This is a mind-set as well as a negotiated agreement between leaders and their subordinates. Empowering leaders creates an environment in which this balance can take place. They involve their subordinates in planning, delegate responsibility, clarify the scope of authority, delineate boundaries, encourage, motivate, and reward accomplishments.

Training Personnel

Because empowerment requires new skills and knowledge, training personnel at all levels is essential. The management team needs to understand the key concepts of empowerment and how best to initiate and support it. Frontline managers need to understand how to implement the process and how to transition from a traditional role to that of an empowering leader. Nonmanagement employees need to be trained in the management/administrative aspects of their new roles. Everyone needs to understand what empowerment entails from them and from the organization as a whole. Specific skills training will depend on the types of additional responsibilities

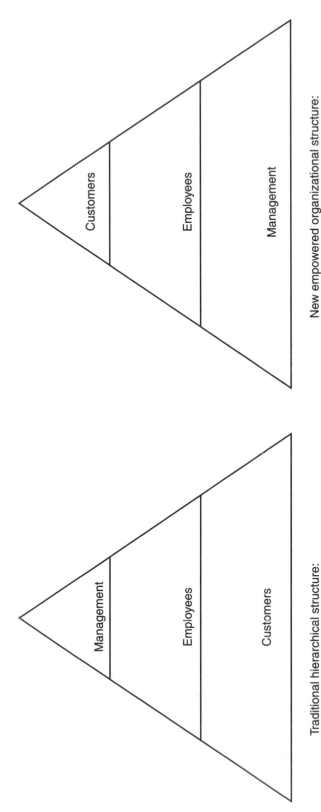

Figure 42.1. Traditional versus empowered organizational structure.

The diagram shows two triangles:

Left triangle (point to the left): Traditional hierarchical structure: With management at the apex, employees below, and customers below them. (Sections labeled Management, Employees, Customers)

Right triangle (point to the left): New empowered organizational structure: With customers on top, employees below, and a smaller group of management at the bottom supporting everyone above. (Sections labeled Customers, Employees, Management) that each person will be taking on. Changes in the performance evaluation and reward systems are also usually required to reinforce the training and desired behavioral changes.

BENEFITS OF EMPOWERMENT

Aubrey and Felkins reported a survey administered in several companies to evaluate the perceived benefits of employee involvement. It indicated significant improvements in attitudes and behavior. For example, results showed an increase in individual self-respect, increased respect for employees by supervisors, increased employee understanding of management, reduced conflict, and increased employees awareness of why many problems are not solved quickly. A similar survey administered to management indicated that employee involvement seemed to increase productivity.[5]

Numerous publications report the positive financial results achieved by teams in organizations that provided them with appropriate support and decision-making authority. For example, one article stated that two Mayo Clinic teams completed their objectives in five to six weeks, resulting in cost savings of more than $300,000 each.[6]

Customer satisfaction also typically improves when personnel is given the authority to make decisions directly related to customer problems or needs. For example, AT&T Universal Card Service reported that through its employee empowerment program, delighting the customer helped to propel the organization to the number-two spot in the bank credit card industry and helped it win the Baldrige Award. Other Baldrige Award winners (e.g., Xerox, IBM, and Motorola) report similar results.

COMMON MISTAKES AND BARRIERS TO EMPOWERMENT

Empowerment has become the buzzword of the 1990s, yet it remains an elusive concept. Several barriers hinder its effective implementation:

◆ *Lack of a clear commitment.* To succeed, top management must clearly communicate its support. Without this commitment, empowerment will be impossible to implement.

◆ *Failure to define empowerment.* Failing to develop an operational definition of empowerment results in confusion and inconstant implementation. Many managers do not understand the term and can unwittingly block its effective implementation by sending conflicting messages.

◆ *Failure to implement appropriate incentives.* People who have been rewarded for behavior that serves a traditional hierarchical system will resist transitioning to a new role unless incentives to encourage change are in place.

◆ *Lack of an implementation plan.* Empowerment takes time, resources, and up-front costs for training and organizational support systems. An implementation plan is essential to prepare this groundwork. An organization that does not think through all the implications sets up serious barriers to success.

❖ *Inability to modify organizational culture.* Many traditional organizations will hinder empowerment by virtue of their hierarchical structures, reward processes, and cultural values. Unless appropriate changes are made, empowerment will fail.

⬛ Additional Readings ⬛

Aubrey, Charles A., and Patricia K. Felkins. 1988. *Teamwork: Involving People in Quality and Productivity Improvement.* Milwaukee: ASQC Quality Press.

Buffa, Dudley, and Michael Hais. 1996. "How Knowledge Workers Vote." *Fast Company,* October–November, pp. 70–71.

Godfrey, Blanton. 1996. "Blitz Teams." *Quality Digest,* October, p. 15.

Juran, Joseph M. 1993. *The Last Word: Lessons of a Lifetime in Managing for Quality.* Wilton, Conn.: Juran Institute.

Kouzes, James M., and Barry Z. Posner. 1987. *The Leadership Challenge.* San Francisco: Jossey-Bass.

Xerox Business Produces and Systems. 1989. *Leadership through Quality Processes and Tools Review.* Rochester, N.Y.: Author.

Chapter 43

Team Formation and Evolution

Never doubt that a small group of thoughtful, committed citizens can change the world; indeed, it is the only thing that ever has.

Margaret Mead

❖ *This chapter should help you*

◆ Understand why team work designs are being widely applied in business settings

◆ Define several different types of teams being used

◆ Distinguish between the purposes of different types of teams

◆ Communicate some primary mechanisms for helping teams succeed

---

WHAT IS A TEAM?

A team is a group of people performing interdependent tasks who work together toward a common goal. Some teams have a limited life (e.g., a process improvement team organized to solve a particular problem), whereas others are ongoing (e.g., a departmental team that meets at a regular frequency to review their goals, activities, and performance). This definition of teams can encompass many types of groups, but this chapter's focus is on team structures currently prevalent in U.S. businesses. As the understanding of interrelationships between organization processes and their potential impact on quality, productivity, and cost increases, team formation has become an increasingly popular method used to address various business concerns. Although the team approach to business management is considered a powerful one, the ability to leverage the full potential of teams is still evolving.

The word *team* is believed to have evolved from the Indo-European word *deuk*, which means "to pull." The fuller meaning of this word was "to pull together." The modern sense of *team* emerged in the 16th century.[1]

When implementing teams in the American business environment, difficulties often arise over our culture's emphasis on individual accomplishments versus the need to share responsibility and successes with others in a team environment. American industry was initially built around Frederick Taylor's approach of dividing work into singular activities performed by teams in the factory setting. Some of the related organizational support structures developed during this era have persisted

❖❖

into modern time. For example, many reward systems reinforce individual performance. It has been only recently that teamwork has received formal recognition and special rewards. For example, formal gainsharing programs that financially reward individuals on the basis of performance of the company, division, facility, and/or product line of which they are part help reinforce the need for working cooperatively toward a common mission.

Many of today's concepts of teams were initiated through the implementation of quality circles during the 1970s. However, most early efforts to use a team approach in the United States were not successful because they duplicated Japanese-type quality circles rather than being designed on the basis of American culture and because they did not integrate the teams with other organizational philosophies and systems (e.g., the need for changes in leadership roles and comparison systems). Team work designs have since evolved into a multidimensional concept that includes many different types of teams formed for various purposes. Three major categories of teams are discussed later; team development phases that are applicable to all are presented next.

TEAM DEVELOPMENT PHASES

Teams go through stages of growth and maturity as the members work together. Understanding these team development phases is critical to the effective management of the team process. The stages can vary in intensity and duration, depending on the type of team, the environment in which it works, and the individuals who constitute it. A generic model for the phases of team development, described by Tuckman in 1965, is shown in Figure 43.1. This model is still in use today to train team leaders, facilitators, and members.

Stage I: Forming

When people first come together to form a team, they bring with them their individual identities and imprints of their separate environments. Each team is a new experience, even for those who have been members of previous teams. Individuals enter this situation cautiously, feeling uncertain of what their role and performance will be in the new experience. During the forming stage, the team usually embarks on defining its purpose, identifying roles for each member, and clarifying responsibilities and acceptable behavior.

Stage II: Storming

During this phase, the reality of the team's task sinks in. Team members still think primarily as individuals and might attempt to form decisions on the basis of their individual experiences rather than pooling information with other members. Collaboration has not as yet become the norm as team members fluctuate in their attitude about the team's chances for success. The behaviors exhibited during this time can involve arguing, testing the leader's authority, attempting to redefine goals, and defensiveness and competition.

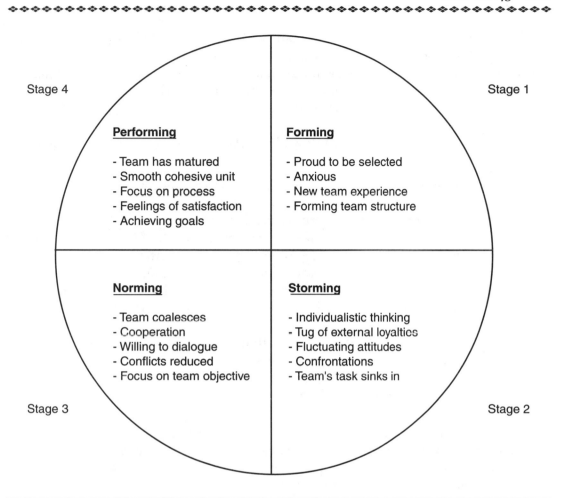

◆ **Figure 43.1.**   Team development phases.

Stage III: Norming

In this phase, individuals coalesce into a team by shifting their focus from internal, personal concerns to that of meeting team-related challenges. Interpersonal conflicts and the tug of external loyalties is reduced. Team members are willing to discuss differences for the sake of the team, resulting in more cooperation and dialogue.

Stage IV: Performing

At this stage, the team has matured to the point where it is working as a smooth cohesive unit. Team members have a better understanding of one another's strengths and weaknesses and are able to work through group problems. There is a better appreciation of the team's processes and a general satisfaction with team membership. During this phase, the team is making significant progress in achieving its goals.

Although the four stages of development indicate a logical sequence that occurs over time, the actual progress made by each team will vary. For example, a team that has progressed to stage III or IV might fall back to stage I or II if they learn that some of their previous assumptions about one another or the issues on which they were working are not true or as team membership is modified because of retirements or job transfers. Some teams might never progress beyond an earlier stage because of limited project time duration or poor team leadership or facilitation of group dynamics.

TYPES OF TEAMS

To be successful, a team needs to have a clear understanding of its purpose and how that purpose is linked to and supports the organization's strategic plans. This is often a formal, written statement that is mutually agreed to by all team members and by management. This statement, referred to as a *mission statement* or a *statement of purpose,* is contained in a charter that legitimizes the team's effort and provides a tacit agreement from management to provide whatever support is necessary to sustain the team. The document should include a clear description of the team's purpose, its responsibility, its scope of work, its relationship to other teams or projects, its reporting relationships within the organization, and the expected deliverables.

Three primary types of teams used within the business environment—process improvement teams, work groups, and other self-managed teams—are discussed in the following sections.

Process Improvement Teams

Process improvement teams are project teams that focus on improving a specific business process. These project teams come together to achieve a specific goal, are guided by a well-defined project plan, and have a negotiated beginning and end. Such teams are typically cross-functional in nature.

An organization should define criteria for selecting processes for improvement. Scholtes recommends the following: "The process should have a direct impact on customers, the impact of improvements can be experienced in a relatively short period of time, the process should not be undergoing major transitions or be involved in another study, it should be relatively simple, and a substantial group of managers should agree that it is important to the company and its customers."[2] Chapter 35 dealt with this phase of process improvement.

Individuals should be selected on the basis of their knowledge about the process under study, their interpersonal skills, their willingness to work as a team member, and their sense of ownership for the outcome of the project. In addition, team leaders should have good leadership qualities, be familiar with team processes and group dynamics, know the basics of project management, and be well versed in a process improvement methodology.

The team's effort should be well planned before the initial team meeting occurs. The team's purpose, scope, and responsibility must be fully agreed on. The team leader and team members should be preselected and their time allocations negotiated. A team sponsor to champion the team's effort and troubleshoot problems should be selected from the management ranks. Assigning a team facilitator is also beneficial. A team's estimated completion date and deliverables should be agreed on. A detailed project plan and schedule should be developed to ensure success of the team's effort.

The first team meeting can set the tone for the entire team effort. Therefore, it is important to plan the event well. The following are several guidelines:

◆ include key decision makers and have them emphasize the importance of the project

◆ ensure that all have a full understanding (and buy-in) of the team's purpose and scope

◆ allow team members to get acquainted

◆ clarify team members' roles

◆ work out decision-making issues

◆ set meeting ground rules

◆ review project plan and schedule

◆ establish the structure of future meetings

The team will then utilize a process improvement methodology/model to guide analysis of the project under study, creativity tools to identify potential improvement actions, and project management skills to implement decided actions.

Work Groups

Work groups are teams of employees who have responsibility for a particular process (e.g., department or product/process line) and who work together in a participative relationship. The degree of authority and autonomy can range from relatively limited to full self-management, depending on the organizational culture. The participative approach is based on the belief that employees will be more productive if they take responsibility for their work. The group leader is usually the individual responsible for the work area (e.g., supervisor or team leader).

Work groups are usually structured similar to quality control circles, in which department personnel meet weekly to review performance of their process. They utilize a systems view of their processes, suppliers, and customers and monitor performance measures that indicate how well they are doing. These teams focus on making continual, incremental improvements to their work processes. In some ways they are similar to the process improvement teams discussed previously, the key differences being that work teams are neither cross-functional nor temporary. A facilitator is usually available to teams in the event they desire additional support.

A work group is both a physical structure and a set of beliefs. In order for work groups to achieve good results, it is critical that the organizational systems and values support the effort. Certain basic elements should be considered when attempting to initiate work groups[3]:

◆ support of upper management

◆ clearly defined communication lines

◆ incremental improvement goals

◆   training for management and work group participants

◆   well-defined work group structure and expectations

◆   appropriate skills mix

◆   revised compensation and performance-appraisal systems

Also needing to be addressed are issues such as the following:

◆   scope of responsibility

◆   autonomy

◆   degree and rate of maturation

◆   type and source of administrative information needed

◆   decision-making processes

◆   types of goals and measures of success

◆   recognition and rewards

◆   development of skills

◆   selection of leaders or facilitators

◆   new-hire orientation process

◆   agreed-to values for creativity, risk taking, and problem solving

It is best to develop an implementation plan and build the support systems before initiating such groups, and a pilot to test the approach is highly recommended.

Other Self-Managed Teams

Self-managed, or self-directed, teams are groups of employees involved in directly managing the day-to-day operation of their particular process or department. They are empowered to make decisions on a wide range of issues (e.g., safety, quality, maintenance, scheduling, and personnel). Many of their responsibilities include those traditionally held by managers. These can range from allocation of assignments to goal setting and conflict resolutions to performance evaluations. The role of a manager in this type of situation transitions to that of facilitator or coach. Leadership of these teams is selected internally and in most cases is rotated among team members. These types of teams are also called *self-directed teams* or *high-performance work systems.*

If one envisions work groups on a sliding scale of empowerment and autonomy, then self-managed teams would fall on the upper scale of these attributes. All the elements that apply to work groups as delineated previously also apply to self-managed teams. However, self-directed work teams take more concerted up-front planning, preparation of support structures, and nurturing as the teams go through a maturation process. The transition will usually take a significant time period and needs consistent and patient support from management.

Several key implementation lessons that apply to the startup effort of a self-managed team were captured during a study completed in a financial organization:

◆   Put into place a well-thought-out structure to design and guide the implementation process, for example, a steering committee, a design team, and a pilot effort.

◆   Special training and guidance should be given to managers and supervisors to make the transition from their current role to their new support roles.

◆   The new team structure will cause changes that might be threatening to all involved. Some individuals might see themselves as losers in the change. A careful plan to manage people through the transition is required.

◆   The time needed for a team's maturation is long and energy consuming. Therefore, it is important to set realistic expectations.[4]

Comprehensive training is also critical. For example, one Fortune 500 company provides training in the following areas:

◆   customer focus

◆   development of a common vision and mission that is integrated with the larger organization's mission

◆   clear understanding of roles and operating guidelines

◆   skills for working together to make decisions, plan work, resolve differences and conduct meetings

◆   empowerment concepts and strategy

◆   setting goals and solving problems for continuous improvement[5]

Self-managed teams are frequently more successful when they are set up along with a new facility ("green-field site") than when an organization attempts to transition from a traditional work design at an old facility ("brown-field site"). Existing facilities sometimes begin the transition to self-managed teams by using cross-functional process improvement teams and/or work teams as learning mechanisms.

FOSTERING GOOD TEAMWORK

A team's growth is a responsibility both of individual team members and of the organization. As shown in Figure 43.2, both must contribute their unique elements to create the cultural synergy that makes teams productive.

Elements of Organizational Support

For teams to be effective, the value for supporting them must be integrated into the core of the organizational culture. This becomes the foundation on which all policies, processes, roles, and interactions are built. The creation of an organizational vision and mission that is heartfelt and inspiring is an important ingredient. An explanation of how to develop this type of vision can be found in Senge et al.'s, *The Fifth Discipline Fieldbook.*

A new type of leadership is necessary to provide teams with the authority they need to be successful. This requires a transformation from the old type of autocratic leadership to the new facilitating/coaching/participative approach. Several attributes for the new style of leader are described in Kouzes and Posner's *The Leadership Challenge,* including being imaginative, honest, supportive, fair minded, forward looking, broad minded, inspiring, cooperative, and caring.

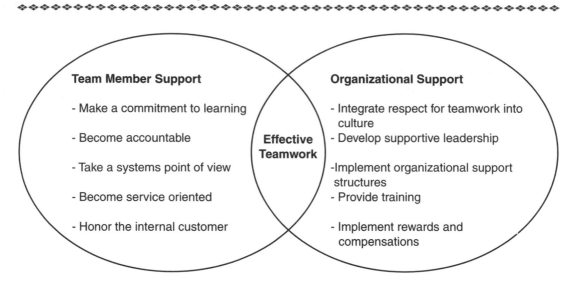

Team Member Support

- Make a commitment to learning

- Become accountable

- Take a systems point of view

- Become service oriented

- Honor the internal customer

Effective Teamwork

Organizational Support

- Integrate respect for teamwork into culture
- Develop supportive leadership

-Implement organizational support structures
- Provide training

- Implement rewards and compensations

◆ **Figure 43.2.** Supporting factors for effective teamwork.

Items to be considered in the development of support structures is the implementation of advisory groups, sponsors, planning efforts, availability of necessary information, and monitoring for improvement and feedback cycles. Some guidelines for the integration of teamwork into organizational structures and how to evaluate its success are covered in Aubrey et al.'s *Teamwork*.

Team members and managers at all levels need to be trained in all aspects of the team concept. This needs to include team dynamics, project management, process improvement methodology, empowerment, managing people through transitions and organizational change, attributes of the new leader and the transformation process, and how to motivate and reward efforts. It is generally better to have this type of specialized training provided from outside the organization.

Finally, the organization can show its support for teams by implementing a system for rewarding and compensating team members for their work (further discussed in Chapter 44).

Elements of Team Member Support

Transitioning to team membership takes new skills. Each individual must first understand that new skills and information are required and then proactively seek to obtain and apply them. Learning can occur both informally and formally. If formal training is not offered by the organization, individuals should either seek it externally or petition the organization to provide it internally. Individuals should also seek informal information from their peers who have more experience as well as from reading, observing, and being open to on-the-job learning. Project teams need to learn team dynamics, process improvement methodology, project management, and creative problem solving. In addition, self-managed teams need to obtain all the administrative skills and knowledge necessary to manage themselves.

Fostering effective teams includes a set of skills as well as a set of values. These values must be accepted by all team members in order to promote healthy teamwork. Such values include cooperation, sharing information, honoring the internal customer, taking responsibility, accepting empowerment, respecting boundaries, commitment to team goals, and the willingness to negotiate. In short, it requires responsibility for the team's success as well as for one's own role in facilitating that success.

Gaining a full appreciation for the integration that exists between all elements of an organization is to gain an understanding of cause-and-effect cycles. Being sensitive to how a team's decisions and relationships affect other aspects of the organization will promote the effectiveness of the whole. An in-depth discussion of a systems point of view is found in Senge's *The Fifth Discipline*.

Meeting and exceeding customer satisfaction is the definitive goal of the quality movement. Reduced cost, reduced time to market, and increased quality are all aimed at satisfying customers. A focus on satisfying the internal customer will form strong links in a chain that ultimately will provide exceptional service to the external customer. To a team this means treating one another as well as non–team members in the organization as valued customers.

THE BENEFITS OF TEAMS

Teams benefit both the organization that fosters them and individual team members. Some of the frequently cited benefits are discussed in the following sections.

Benefits to Team Members

The benefits of team membership to individuals on process improvement teams include the following:

- gain problem-solving skills
- learn about team dynamics and teamwork
- promote cross-functional understanding
- expand learning outside the area of expertise
- provide training ground for leadership
- allow opportunity to stretch
- obtain a network of contacts after the team effort ends

Members of work groups and self-managed teams can expect to receive the following benefits:

- enhanced acceptance of empowerment principles
- a gain in status and power
- increased span of knowledge

- increased quality of work life
- feelings of satisfaction and commitment
- increased innovation and creative problem solving
- incorporation of worker's values into the work system

Benefits to Organizations

Process improvement teams offer the following benefits to the organization:

- concentration of diverse sets of knowledge
- synergy in problem solving
- objective analysis of problem or opportunity
- visibility to broader issues
- cost savings realized from improvements
- promotion of cross-functional understanding

Work groups and self-managed teams are beneficial to the organization for the following reasons:

- improved quality and productivity
- greater innovation
- reduced operating costs
- increased interconnectivity of functions
- increased commitment to organizational mission
- more flexible response to changes
- feelings of ownership and stewardship
- reduced turnover and absenteeism

One report indicated that self-managed work teams are 30 percent to 50 percent more productive than conventional organizational structures. AT&T reported an increase in quality of operator service by 12 percent. Federal Express cut errors by 13 percent, and Johnson & Johnson decreased inventory by $6 million. 3M's Hutchinson facility increased production by 300 percent.[6]

COMMON MISTAKES AND BARRIERS TO SUCCESS

Team approaches fail to reach their full potential for many reasons. Some of the more typical ones are discussed in the following sections.

Process Improvement Teams

A survey to determine why quality improvement teams took a long time to complete their assignments revealed the following reasons. When diagrammed in a Pareto chart, they fell in the following order of impact:

❖ Time is lost when team members are unable to dedicate sufficient time to the project because process improvement team efforts are typically superimposed on regular work schedules.

❖ Management failed to confront resistance to changes that were implied by the team's solution. This resulted in barriers to obtaining access to needed information.

❖ There was a lack of preexisting process-related data. In some cases, teams needed to develop the required measurements and collect the data on their own.

❖ The purpose, or mission, of the teams were not well defined at the beginning.

❖ Some teams wandered off course.[7]

Work Groups and Self-Managed Teams

Numerous reasons have been noted in literature on the reasons why these types of teams fail to reach their full potential. A summary follows:

❖ failing to integrate the concept into the organizational culture

❖ lack of structured organizational support systems

❖ minimal up-front planning

❖ failure to prepare managers for their changing roles

❖ failure to prepare team members for their new roles

❖ inappropriate reward and compensation systems

❖ limited integration with the rest of the organization

❖ inadequate training

❖ impatience with the length of time needed for maturation

❖ incomplete understanding of group dynamics

🏠 Additional Readings 🏠

Aubrey, Charles A., and Patricia K. Felkins. 1988. *Teamwork: Involving People in Quality and Productivity Improvement.* Milwaukee: ASQC Quality Press.

Gilmore, Steve, Ed Rose, and Ray Odom. 1993. "Building Self-Directed Work Teams." *Quality Digest*, December, pp. 29–32.

Godfrey, Blanton. 1996. "Blitz Teams." *Quality Digest*, October, p. 15.

Kouzes, James M., and Barry Z. Posner. 1987. *The Leadership Challenge: How to Get Extraordinary Things Done in Organizations.* San Francisco: Jossey-Bass Publishers.

Manz, Charles C., and Henry P. Sims Jr. 1993. *Business without Bosses: How Self-Managed Teams Are Building High-Performance Companies.* New York: John Wiley & Sons.

Scholtes, Peter R., et al. 1988. *The Team Handbook.* Madison, Wisc.: Joiner Associates Consulting Group.

❖❖

Senge, Peter. 1990. *The Fifth Discipline: The Art and Practice of the Learning Organization.* New York: Doubleday Currency.

Senge, Peter, et al. 1994. *The Fifth Discipline Fieldbook.* New York: Doubleday.

Tuckman, Bruce W. 1965. "Developmental Sequence in Small Groups." *Psychological Bulletin* 63, (Nov–Dec) no. 6: 384–99.

Williams, Ron. 1995. "Self-Directed Work Teams: A Competitive Advantage." *Quality Digest,* November, pp. 50–52.

Chapter 44

Team Management

There has never been a greater need for mastering team learning in organizations than there is today.

Peter M. Senge, *The Fifth Discipline*

❖ *This chapter should help you*

◆ Define the major issues involved with managing team performance

◆ Understand the roles of team members and others in supporting teams

◆ Describe some ways team performance can be evaluated

◆ Communicate methods for recognizing and rewarding team efforts

MANAGING A TEAM

There are two major components in managing a team: task-type activities and maintenance-type activities. Task-type activities are those that keep a team focused and moving toward its goal, whereas maintenance-type activities are focused on maintaining the well-being of the dynamics of team member interaction.

Task-Type Activities

Some key components of keeping a team focused on its goals are the following:

◆ having and staying on an agenda during team meetings

◆ agreeing on and utilizing a technical process (e.g., a specific problem-solving model or method) to guide progress toward the goal

◆ using decision-making techniques appropriate to the situation

◆ defining and holding team members accountable for action items and responsibilities

Maintenance-Type Activities

Team dynamics are difficult to describe. To the casual observer, a team's efforts are only those things involved with meeting its goals. Such items as meetings, project plans, status reports, and deliverables are easy to point to as evidence of teamwork. Not so easily observed are the undercurrents, or team dynamics, that inevitably are a part of and have an impact on team performance. Individuals

399

come to a team situation with separate values, needs, and loyalties, and these need to be recognized in order for a team to function effectively.

The primary sources of information on team dynamics are fields such as sociology, psychology, anthropology, organizational development, and political science. Group behavior in these fields has been studied in working, living, academic, and therapeutic environments. Issues such as communication, leadership styles, social interactions, types of participation, and group member roles have been studied. Some of the more prevalent studies were done in the 1950s and 1960s, when sensitivity-training groups (often referred to as T-groups or encounter groups) became popular. These experiences resulted in a rich storehouse of knowledge about group processes.[1]

FACILITATION TECHNIQUES

A facilitator is a person whose focus is on helping the group manage the task and maintenance processes. Typically, a facilitator does not get involved in the content—the technical aspect of what the team is working on. The specific responsibilities of a facilitator have been summarized as follows:

- cultivates an unbiased and impartial environment
- ensures that a full examination and discussion of issues take place
- provides an objective framework
- maintains focus so that purposeful discussion does not deteriorate
- offers a method for organizing diverse and multiple viewpoints
- regulates interruption to allow fair access to everyone
- diffuses destructive behaviors
- supplies a visual and verbal tracking of ideas

Typical facilitator activities include the following:

- encouraging reluctant participants to speak
- helping to resolve conflict between team members
- providing feedback to the leader and/or team
- ensuring that ground rules (agreed-to group norms) are followed
- ensuring that members are listening to and understanding others
- legitimizing everyone's perceptions and feelings
- verbalizing what is going on
- checking for agreement
- maintaining or regaining focus on the meeting agenda or topic of discussion
- ensuring consensus
- periodically summarizing results

Maintaining the Team Process

Team members are most productive in an environment in which others are responsive and friendly, encourage contributions, and promote a sense of worth. Team ground rules should be laid out to clarify standards of behavior, define the decision-making process, and specify meeting logistics. Problems that frequently occur with teams were summarized by Scholtes in *The Team Handbook*. Examples of types of problems that can interfere with the team process are listed in the following, as are suggestions of the recommended action:

Floundering: Difficulty in starting or ending an activity.

What to do: Redirect team to the project plan and written statement of purpose.

Overbearing participants: Team members attempt to use influence on the basis of their position of authority in the organization.

What to do: Talk to the authority off-line; ask for cooperation and patience.

Dominating participants: Participants who talk too much.

What to do: Structure meeting so that everyone is encouraged to participate (e.g., have members write down their opinions, then discuss them in the meeting one person at a time).

Reluctant participants: Participants who rarely speak.

What to do: Practice gatekeeping by using phrases such as "John, what's your view on this?" or divide tasks into individual assignments and have all members report.

Unquestioned acceptance of opinions as facts: Participants who make opinions sound like facts.

What to do: Do not be afraid to ask whether this is an opinion or a fact. Ask for supporting data.

Rush to accomplishment: Rushing to get to a solution before the problem-solving process is worked through.

What to do: Remind the group that rushing can hurt the quality of the team's work.

Attribution: Attempting to explain other members' motives.

What to do: Check it out by encouraging dialogue.

Discounts and "plops": Ignoring or ridiculing another's values or not acknowledging a statement made during the meeting.

What to do: Train in listening skills. Support the discounted person.

Digression and tangents: Meandering and unfocused conversations.

What to do: Use written agenda with time estimates. Continually direct the conversation back on track. Remind team of its mission.

Feuding team members: Conflict involving personal matters.

What to do: Request that these types of conflict be taken off-line. Reinforce ground rules.

Solutions to conflicts should be in the best interest of the team. Team members should be nonjudgmental, listening to team discussions and new ideas. Group feelings should be verbalized by periodically surfacing undercurrents or by giving feedback.

❖❖

Providing Constructive Feedback

One of the most important skills to have in working with a team is the ability to provide constructive feedback during and/or at the end of a meeting. It is also an important vehicle to help the team mature. This feedback can be provided by the facilitator or by team members.

There are two types of feedback: motivational and coaching. Motivational feedback must be constructive, that is, specific, sincere, clear, timely, and descriptive of what actually occurred in the meeting. Coaching, or corrective, feedback specifically states the improvements that need to be made. Scholtes provides the following guidelines for providing constructive feedback:

◆ be specific

◆ make observations, not conclusions

◆ share ideas or information, not advice

◆ speak for yourself

◆ restrict feedback to known things

◆ avoid using labels

◆ do not exaggerate

◆ phrase the issue as a statement, not a question[2]

Determining the Decision-Making Process

It is important to determine what decision-making processes the team will use. The "consensus" decision-making process is recommended for major decision points. This approach is time consuming and demanding but provides the most thorough and cohesive results. It allows the team to hammer out different points of view on an issue and come to a conclusion that is acceptable.

A definition of consensus is that the decision is acceptable enough that all team members can *live* with it. To achieve this state, all team members should express their views and objectively listen to the views of others. The decision issue should be dialogued and alternatives discussed and considered. This process needs to continue until everyone can support the final decision.

MEMBER ROLES AND RESPONSIBILITIES

A team is comprised of various roles that work synergistically to make it an effective team. Some of these are permanent, whereas others rotate among team members. Typical team roles are sponsor, team leader, facilitator, scribe, recorder, timekeeper, and team members. The roles and responsibilities of each are described in the following sections.

Sponsor

A sponsor can be an individual or a team of advisers. The sponsor (often the process owner) should be at a level high enough in the organization to be able to overcome any organizational difficulties encountered by the team. A sponsor's responsibility includes helping to initiate the team effort by authorizing the activity; coordinating the front-end planning; helping to select a leader, facilitator, and team members; defining the purpose and scope of the team; and negotiating resources. During the team effort, the sponsor monitors progress, troubleshoots when there are problems, acts as a liaison to upper management or other departments/teams, helps obtain necessary information and resources, and acts as a coach.

Team Leader

The team leader is responsible for the team's success. Responsibilities include the following:

- managing team meetings
- developing (in conjunction with the sponsor) and monitoring a project plan
- keeping the effort on track
- providing status updates to management
- helping the facilitator with group dynamics
- serving as a liaison between the team and the organization
- helping to resolve problems
- handling administrative duties and keeping team records

A team leader is also responsible for contributing to the team's content, although the leader must be careful that his or her comments do not receive greater status than those of other team members.

Scribe and Recorder

A scribe is responsible for recording the team's discussions/decisions on a board, flip chart, or overhead projector (e.g., when brainstorming or when needed to visually capture information). This role can be performed by a facilitator, team leader, or team member. A recorder is responsible for capturing information from the team meeting in a record of meeting minutes and distributing them appropriately. Both functions are often rotated among team members (e.g., at each meeting or at regular intervals).

Timekeeper

Efficient meetings begin on time and end on time. Assigning a timekeeper helps a team meeting stay on track. Meeting agendas often indicate how much time is allocated for each meeting activity. Therefore, the role of the timekeeper is to monitor the agenda and alert the team when the time has come to move to the next activity. This function generally is rotated among team members. At times, the team facilitator might take on this responsibility.

Team Members

Each individual who is a team member is responsible for bringing with and utilizing their unique mix of skills, knowledge, and information and to be jointly responsible for the team's outcome. This requires attending meetings, being accountable for contributions, communicating clearly and honestly, attempting to reach consensus, and sharing the responsibilities of the leader and facilitator by participating in both task- and maintenance-types of activities. This also means completing on time whatever tasks are assigned between team meetings.

Self-Facilitation

Roles and responsibilities of the facilitator were discussed previously. An external facilitator can be a valuable resource to a team. However, if performance of the team remains dependent on the facilitator, then the facilitator has not done an effective job of helping the team to develop. A highly developed team should have the knowledge and ability to deal with problems that might arise, such a detour from the agenda, interpersonal conflict, or ineffective decision making—in effect, to become self-facilitating.

PERFORMANCE EVALUATION

The measuring and communicating effectiveness of a team provides it with important feedback about progress and therefore can help promote necessary changes and stimulate improvement. It is also important as feedback to management to indicate the degree to which a team is meeting its objectives. Both objective and subjective data can be used, although the former are more difficult to obtain than the latter.

A team should take responsibility for self-evaluation. One way to do this is to select the criteria for evaluation using team member training materials as a source of input as well as the team's list of behavioral norms. A list of questions, along with a rating scale, can then be used by the team at the end of each meeting to monitor how well they are performing. The evaluation criteria can also evolve over time as the team develops. Standard instruments, such as the Team Effectiveness Profile, can also be used for team self-evaluation.

Questionnaires or interviews can also be administered to outside personnel, such as internal and external customers, other teams, or management. These types of metrics can capture perceived progress on such attributes as relationship building, effectiveness of the team's progress, and efficiency of the team's process. Capturing and evaluating lessons learned can also be an excellent evaluation and feedback tool.

Objective measures/metrics for evaluating final team performance can also be established prior to or as part of initiating a team. For example, tangible results in quality and productivity can be measured to determine how much the team has saved the organization.

RECOGNITION AND REWARD

Teams, like individuals, deserve recognition for their efforts, and this recognition can also provide encouragement to support future progress and success. In an organization that is just beginning to use the team process, this might be the single most important factor for sustaining momentum. The following suggestions for rewards and recognition are described by Aubrey and Felkins:

- supportive comments and helpful suggestions provided by management during team presentations

- public recognition through professional societies, or through publication of results in such journals as *Quality Progress* or *Quality Digest* as well as company newsletters and bulletins

- performance appraisals that reflect employees' personal growth and contribution as a team member

- material rewards such as certificates, pins, coffee mugs, and lunches

- "gain sharing," or distributing some of the cost savings or revenue enhancements to team members

- bonuses or other monetary rewards[3]

In addition to external recognition, it is important that team leaders provide internal recognition to their members as they progress through established milestones. Recognition might also be given by the team leader or team members to individuals whose contributions are exceptionally over or above expectations.

Formal recognition for team-based improvement efforts often involve ceremonies at that key leaders recognize teams which have made significant contributions (e.g., excellent project outcomes and/or significantly enhanced organizational learning). The recognition might also involve a symbolic award (usually not financially based). Formal efforts to reward team performance are likely to include a modification of performance evaluation criteria to include the new behaviors desired, with a resulting increase in financial compensation or other desired job opportunities being a possible outcome for good performers.[4]

BENEFITS OF GOOD TEAM MANAGEMENT

Much has been published on the benefits of effective team management. Some of the more frequently cited ones follow:

- a training ground for leadership and facilitator skills

- quicker and more effective team results

- more efficient use of time and energy

- increased discipline in project planning and management

- increased quality of communication

- elimination or shortening of the "storming" phase of team development

- reinforcing the positive image of teams in organizations

Key requirements to make this possible include the following:

- a well-defined purpose and mission

- the support of management, who allocates appropriate resources

- a well-defined project and/or implementation plan

- training in leadership, facilitation, project planning, team management, problem-solving methodology, and effective meeting skills

❖❖

- ◆ selection of a strong team leader and experienced facilitator
- ◆ understanding of team dynamics and how to enhance them
- ◆ availability of accurate data and pertinent/timely information
- ◆ team members dedicated to reaching their team objectives

🏛 Additional Readings 🏛

Aubrey, Charles A., and Patricia K. Felkins. 1988. *Teamwork: Involving People in Quality and Productivity Improvement.* Milwaukee: ASQC Quality Press.

Dyer, William G. 1987. *Team Building: Issues and Alternatives.* Reading, Mass.: Addison-Wesley.

Juran, Joseph M. 1988. "Upper Management and Quality." In *Juran's Quality Control Handbook,* ed. Joseph M. Juran and Frank Gryna. 4th ed. New York: McGraw-Hill pp. 8.1–8.25.

Schmidt, Warren H., and Jerome P. Finnegan. 1993. *TQ Manager: A Practical Guide for Managing in a Total Quality Organization.* San Francisco: Jossey-Bass.

Scholtes, Peter R. 1988. *The Team Handbook.* Madison, Wisc.: Joiner Associates Consulting Group.

Zimmerman, A. L., and Carol J. Evans. 1993. *Facilitation . . . From Discussion to Decision.* East Brunswick, N.J.: Nichols Publishing.

📑 Part 7 Endnotes 📑

Chapter 39

1. James M. Kouzes and Barry Z. Posner, *The Leadership Challenge* (San Francisco: Jossey-Bass, 1987), pp. 27, 135.

2. William Bridges, "Leading the De-Jobbed Organization," and Edgar H. Schein, "Leadership and Organizational Culture," in *The Leader of the Future,* ed. Hesslebein (San Francisco: Jossey-Bass, 1996).

3. Charles Handy, "The New Language of Organizing and Its Implications for Leaders," in Hesselbein et al., eds., *The Leader of the Future.*

4. Edgar H. Schein, "Leadership and Organizational Culture," in Hesselbein et al., eds., *The Leader of the Future.*

5. W. Edwards Deming, *The New Economics* (Cambridge: Massachusetts Institute of Technology, 1994), p. 116.

6. Milan Zeleny, *Multiple Criteria Decision Making* (New York: McGraw-Hill, 1977), p. 117.

7. Joe Kelly, "Making Conflict Work for You," *Harvard Business Review* (July–August 1970) Vol. 48: 6.

8. Kenneth W. Thomas and Ralph H. Kilmann, *Thomas-Kilmann Conflict Mode Instrument* (Tuxedo, N.Y.: XICOM, 1974).

Chapter 40

1. Gary Dessler. 1996. *Human Resource Management* 7th ed. (Englewood Cliffs, N.J.: Prentice-Hall), p. 174.
2. John W. Aldrich, "Staffing Concepts and Principles," in *Human Resources Management and Development Handbook,* ed. William R. Tracey. (New York: AMACOM, 1994), p. 185.
3. Marilyn Buckner and Lynn Slavenski, "Succession Planning," in Tracey, ed., *Human Resources Management and Development Handbook,* p 562.
4. Dessler, p. 351.
5. Elliot Jacques and Stephen D. Clement, *Executive Leadership* (Malden, Mass.: Basil Blackwell and Cason Hall, 1994).
6. W. Edwards Deming, *The New Economics* (Cambridge: Massachusetts Institute of Technology, 1994).
7. Richard C. McCullough, "Professional Development," in *Training and Development Handbook,* ed. Robert L. Craig (New York: McGraw-Hill, 1987), p. 37.
8. Robert Albanese, "Objectives and Goals," in *Handbook for Professional Managers,* ed. Lester Bittel and Jackson Ramsey (New York: McGraw-Hill, 1985).

Chapter 41

1. John W. Aldrich, "Staffing Concepts and Principles," in *Human Resources Management and Development Handbook,* William R. Tracey, ed. (New York: AMACOM 1994), p. 182.
2. Karen Bemowski, "1998 Salary Survey," *Quality Progress,* November 1998, p. 25.

Chapter 42

1. Joseph M. Juran, *The Last Word: Lessons of a Lifetime in Managing for Quality* (Wilton, Conn.: Juran Institute, 1993), p. 332.
2. Dudley Buffa and Michael Hais, "How Knowledge Workers Vote," *Fast Company,* October–November 1996, p. 78.
3. Xerox Business Products and Systems, *Leadership through Quality Processes and Tools Review* (Rochester, N.Y.: Author, 1989).
4. James M. Kouzes and Barry Z. Posner, *The Leadership Challenge* (San Francisco: Jossey-Bass, 1987).
5. Charles A. Aubrey and Patricia K. Felkins, *Teamwork: Involving People in Quality and Productivity Improvement* (Milwaukee: ASQC Quality Press, 1988).
6. Blanton Godfrey, "Blitz Teams," *Quality Digest,* October 1996, p. 15.

❖❖

Chapter 43

1. Peter M. Senge et al., *The Fifth Discipline Fieldbook* (New York: Doubleday, 1994).
2. Peter R. Scholtes et al., *The Team Handbook* (Madison, Wisc: Joiner Associates Consulting Group, 1988), p. 240.
3. Steve Gilmore et al., "Building Self-Directed Work Teams," *Quality Digest,* December 1993, p. 26.
4. Charles C. Manz and Henry P. Sims Jr., *Business without Bosses: How Self-Managed Teams Are Building High-Performance Companies* (New York: John Wiley & Sons, 1993).
5. Ibid.
6. Ron Williams, "Self-Directed Work Teams: A Competitive Advantage," *Quality Digest,* November 1995, p. 38.
7. Blanton Godfrey, "Blitz Teams," *Quality Digest*, October 1996, p. 15.

Chapter 44

1. William G. Dyer, *Team Building: Issues and Alternatives* (Reading, Mass.: Addison-Wesley, 1987).
2. Peter R. Scholtes et al., *The Team Handbook* (Madison, Wisc.: Joiner Associates Consulting Group, 1988).
3. Charles A. Aubrey and Patricia K. Felkins, *Teamwork: Involving People in Quality and Productivity Improvement* (Milwaukee: ASQC Quality Press, 1988).
4. Joseph M. Juran and Frank M. Gryna, eds., *Juran's Quality Control Handbook* (New York: McGraw-Hill, 1998), pp. 8.6–8.7.

Part 8
Training and Education

Chapter 45

Importance of Top-Down Support and Strategic Planning for Quality Training

❖ *This chapter should help you*

◆ Understand that justification for training is linked to the key drivers in an organization's strategic plans

◆ Distinguish between problems or needs due to a performance deficiency and those due to a deficiency of knowledge and/or skills

◆ Understand why training does not solve a performance problem

◆ Appreciate that training should be done only when it will produce a desirable and measurable outcome (e.g., specific skills and value added to the organization)

DISTINGUISHING BETWEEN TRAINING AND EDUCATION

Technical training has been a part of human activity since the earliest times when survival depended on learning how to find food and use tools for agriculture and hunting. During the Middle Ages, the Roman Catholic Church rose to prominence by educating clerics and aristocrats. Likewise, merchant guilds provided education and apprenticeships to children of guild members who in turn became guild members and worked in the profession. The industrial revolution of the 18th and 19th centuries changed education and technical training approaches. Colleges and universities were formed to provide public education and industries began to provide apprenticeships independent of the guilds.

Frederick W. Taylor's scientific management techniques matched individuals to particular jobs and identified the optimal way in which a job could be performed, therefore increasing production output and efficiency. Henry Ford used these methods to create an assembly line. Using this approach, a person could be trained for a particular, defined job, precluding the need for a broader education. This was a departure from the previous "master craftsman" model, in which a worker was expected to understand all aspects of the job.

Today, increasingly complex technology, more comprehensive management systems, accelerated change, and global competition require more and more employees to have formal education in addition to technical training. The terms *education* and *training* are often used interchangeably, but education can be thought of as the process of acquiring knowledge and information, usually in a formal manner. Some examples are the study and understanding of human behavior, team dynamics, and the principles of statistics. On the other hand, training is the process of acquiring proficiency in some skill or skills. Some examples are team leadership and facilitation and the application of the seven quality control tools.[1] Education equips students to acquire new knowledge by teaching them how to think. In contrast, training emphasizes maintaining or improving skills needed to perform a specific job, or acquiring new job skills.

Figure 45.1 compares two workers with relatively equal basic skills and abilities. What differences will emerge if, over a period of time, education is provided to one and training to the other? If the education process is successful, the worker receiving education will have broadened his or her knowledge base, therefore expanding his or her thinking processes. The worker receiving training will have received specific instruction in how to do an aspect of his or her job. The outcome of education can be measured only by testing comprehension and knowledge retention. On the other hand, training is measured by the learner's ability to demonstrate the learned skill by producing desired outcomes (e.g., by correctly conducting self-inspection of part completed to decrease defects). To easily differentiate "education" from "training," answer the following question: If your grade-school-age son or daughter brought home a school notice requesting you to choose between two new course offerings for your child, would you choose "Sex Education" or "Sex Training"?

Education typically involves little or no "training" (other than learning how to study and take tests). Training usually involves some "education" in the theory or principles underlying the development and need for the skill. Taking a refresher course in preparation for the Certified Quality Manager examination combines learning some skills in test taking with much assimilation, or reawakening, of knowledge in a broad range of subjects.

Debate continues as to whether "quality" in "quality management" should be considered a noun (as in management of a quality control/assurance department or a quality initiative) or an adjective (as in quality *of* management throughout the organization). To be a quality (with a big Q) professional manager suggests a need to continually reeducate oneself as well as to continue to acquire new skills and sharpen proven skill sets. "In this sense, perhaps, the whole notion of certification must be recast. It is not so much a testament to a body of knowledge that one has learned as it is a demonstration that one has attained a foundation on which to continue building."[2] The very concept of total quality implies new and continual education and training. Quality management is reinventing itself to include everyone in the organization with quality responsibilities. This trend translates to the need for new knowledge and skills, reeducation, and training.[3]

With the rapid increase in and importance of "knowledge work," there is a need for continual education/training. Often the competency (the sum of knowledge, skills, attitude, and experience) of the workforce can be a factor that differentiates world-class, learning organizations from their competitors.

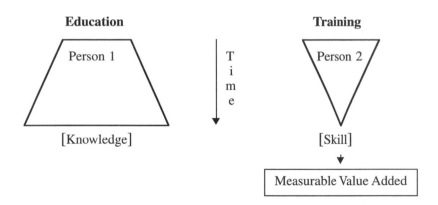

Education — Person 1 — [Knowledge]

Time

Training — Person 2 — [Skill]

Measurable Value Added

◆ **Figure 45.1.**   Training versus education.

Empowering workers to be responsible for the quality of their work has become routine in many industries. Inspection can be eliminated when controlling the process and/or preventing defects is emphasized. This requires broader worker capabilities and effective training so that workers will know when and how to react to changing conditions.

TOP-DOWN SUPPORT AND STRATEGIC PLANNING IN QUALITY TRAINING

For most organizations, training is a significant budget item. During downturns in business, it is often the first place top management looks to reduce costs. Therefore, it is imperative that top-management views training as a strategic, cost-justified investment. It is the cost of *not* training (analogous to the "cost of quality" versus the "cost of nonquality" issue) that needs to be addressed by the investment in training. Training is most beneficial to the organization when top management understands and supports the training program's role in achieving the goals and objectives of the organization's strategic plans. Top-management commitment is necessary to ensure that strategic plans, which should include a need for training, are appropriately planned and budgeted.

Juran and Gryna suggest the consideration and customization of the following six issues when planning for training:

1. the quality problems and challenges faced by the organization
2. the knowledge and skills needed to solve these problems and meet these challenges
3. the knowledge and skills actually possessed by the jobholders
4. the training facilities and processes already in existence
5. the prevailing climate for training in the organization, based on the record of past programs
6. what needs to be done differently to achieve the desired quality[4]

❖❖

Top management's failure to support training efforts can result in the following:

◆   the inadequate integration of training into business planning as a quality-inducing process

◆   poor or absent role models for deploying and reinforcing the daily use of quality principles throughout the organization

◆   the inability of trainees to grasp the intended connection between what they are to learn and the strategic objectives (e.g., continuous improvement, customer focus, product and service quality, productivity, profit, and employee training and development) of the organization

◆   distrust in management's exhortations about quality if workers receive little or no training to do their jobs but are criticized for not meeting unknown expectations

◆   a failure to recognize training as important enough to build training skills as a requisite skill set for all management and team leaders

◆   ineffective training design and delivery (e.g., classroom training when on-the-job training would be more appropriate and lectures when hands-on demonstration and practice would be best)

◆   a lack of, or inconsistency in, on-the-job recognition

◆   a failure to reinforce the use of posttraining skills (when managers and supervisors do not understand their role as a "coach")

◆   treatment of training as just an expense and therefore potentially expendable when business takes a downturn

◆   lack of application of benefits-to-cost analysis to justify training and to measure results of training (Many training programs or training departments could have survived an economic downturn if the value/payoff of training in improving bottom-line factors had been established, measured, and proven. If a dollar-return-on-training investment cannot be attributed to training, training should not be done.)

◆   the failure of training practitioners to adequately study, assess, and address the needs of the organization's mainline operations

◆   a failure to measure the training's effectiveness in terms of the improved outcomes of organization affected by the training (In more successful organizations, trainers establish a partnering relationship with the line operation they serve.)

◆   sustaining the premise (and the resulting conflict) that the training department decides who is to be trained, what is to be the training content, and how and when it is to be delivered, for example, everyone at once versus one individual just in time (Often, line management is expected to "send" their employees to the prescribed training on the training department's schedule. Also, training might be designed to address quality tools and techniques to the exclusion of addressing the needs of the organization, such as when all employees are taught detailed statistical process control techniques when only certain individuals need this skill or when only specific techniques fit the organization's needs.)

◆ a failure to recognize that a superbly trained workforce is a unique and important selling point because it is part of the core competency that differentiates an organization in the marketplace

◆ a failure to realize that what gets measured gets done, so training will be neglected if it is not measured or if it is not high on the list of priorities for resource allocation

At the daily operational level, education might be prescribed or individually requested to introduce new concepts or principles, for example, the concept of cycle time reduction and its impact on quality or the principles of performance management. Training might be prescribed to build new skill sets, to refresh faded skills, or to qualify individuals to a prescribed standard. Such education and training, at the operating levels, must still be traceable to the organization's strategic plans and objectives.

A proposed training program can be initially evaluated through a benefit-cost analysis. The resulting budget should be supported by top management as it identifies the trade-offs between the cost of, and the benefits that are realized by doing, the training. Depending on the detail desired, the training costs can include trainee salaries, production lost, facilities, training materials, and trainer or consultant costs. With a focus on the results expected from the training, benefits can include improved customer satisfaction, better product or service quality, improved productivity, increased employee retention and improved employee morale, and a more flexible workforce.

From the perspective of the organization's strategic plans, education and training are means for supporting organization objectives, for example, building a new or updated core competency to address a threatening competitive situation, introducing a state-of-the-art technological change, or increasing customer satisfaction by reducing order response time. Organizations that use a systemic mechanism for translating the strategic plans and associated training objectives to the lowest levels of the organization, such as those using hoshin planning (discussed in Chapter 14), will have the best chances for success. This process is valuable because it helps everyone in the organization better understand training goals.

WHAT TRAINING CAN AND CANNOT DO

An organization should be aware that training will not solve all its problems. At times, organizations attempt to use training to solve a problem when lack of skill is not the issue. "Poor performance is rarely caused by a skill deficiency correctable by training."[5] Training cannot remedy a situation caused by poor performance or other root causes that are not skill related. Mager and Pipe's *Analyzing Performance Problems* offers a diagnostic process for analyzing and correcting performance problems.

The first consideration, before committing any resources, is to clearly differentiate whether the operating problem or situation is a performance deficiency or a knowledge/skill deficiency. It is often stated in the training field that "whenever a

❖ TABLE 45.1.   Deficiency Analysis

Analysis of Problem/Situation	Answer	Potential Change
Does TI* have time to do job well?	No	Add resources? Change methods?
Does TI have proper facilities in which to work?	No	Add resources?
Does TI have the proper tools to do the work?	No	Add resources?
Does TI have proper procedures, instructions job aids?	No	Add resources? Train methods?
Does TI know what they are supposed to do?	No	Provide feedback? Train?
Has TI ever done the job correctly?	Yes	Add positive consequences?
Could TI do the job properly if their lives depended on it?	Yes	Add positive consequences?
If TI could do the job in an exemplary way, would they?	No	Remove negative consequences?
Are there more negative than positive consequences in doing the job?	Yes	Adjust balance toward positive?
Does TI know when they are not performing as supervisor expects?	No	Provide feedback?
Do supervisors of TI have requisite knowledge/skills?	No	Train supervisors to coach?

*TI = targeted individuals.

manager says that a training problem exists, 80% of the time the problem is found to be something in the system, not the people." Questions to help determine where the problem originates are listed in Table 45.1. Correcting deficiencies in job execution is best achieved by changing resources, by providing more objective feedback, or by adding or removing behavioral consequences. For example, if an individual is not performing the job but could do so if his or her life depended on it, retraining is not the answer.

When training is determined to be the best solution to the problem or situation, the next step is to determine training needs. (Training needs assessment is covered in detail in Chapter 47.) Some items to consider when establishing these needs are the following:

◆   Is the need mandated by a regulatory body (e.g., safety, hazardous materials, or sexual harassment awareness)?

◆   Is the need mandated by management in support of a specific strategic objective (e.g., customer contact skills or ISO 9000 quality system)?

◆   Is the need directed toward correcting a knowledge/skill deficiency? If so, who are the affected individuals? How many individuals are affected? Where are they located? What do they need to learn to do? What do they presently know about how to do what they are expected to do? What is the expected outcome of the training? Within what time frame must the individuals be trained? Need all individuals affected be trained at one time, together, or just in time?

◆   What training delivery method is most appropriate for the needed training (e.g., instructor-led classroom training, on-the-job training, or other)?

◆   What facilities, training methods/programs, trainers, materials, and so on are available? What presently unavailable resources are needed to achieve the training objective? Does a benefits-to-cost analysis justify the training? How will the training be funded (e.g., budgeted, appropriation, grant or subsidy, or other)?

◆   How should the training effectiveness be measured and evaluated (e.g., demonstration of skills learned, on-the-job performance improvement, or return-on-training investment)?

◆   What top management commitment and personal involvement is necessary to successfully execute the training plans?

A training design determination can be established once needs have been established, the number of individuals to be trained has been determined, the availability of personnel and facilities for training has been confirmed, and so on. (Training tools are described in more detail in Chapter 49.) The needs, timing, resources available, funding, and operating constraints will affect the method of training delivery selected. For example, two newly hired workers who need basic safety, housekeeping, and ISO 9000 quality system training on reporting for work might be asked to watch three videos and successfully complete a quiz to demonstrate assimilation of the learning points. In the case of all machine operators needing to learn how to use a new onboard statistical process control (SPC) computer terminal to be installed at their machines just before the new system goes on-line, appropriate training might consist of just-in-time, instructor-led classroom training with each individual demonstrating the requisite skills to complete the training. In yet another example, one-to-one on-the-job training by a skilled operator is one solution in which an experienced machine operator is transferred to a new work cell where unfamiliar machinery is in use. Another solution in the same situation might be to send the operator to a course offered by the machinery manufacturer. As these examples show, the variety of designs and the media available for training is extensive. For a large percentage of training needs, the use of on-the-job training by a skilled trainer/supervisor and the introduction of a "job aid" (e.g., checklists, work instructions, and diagrams) might be an effective solution.

❖❖

Fade-out, the diminishment of the learned skill as time elapses between training delivery and use of the learned skill, is a significant issue in training. For this reason, it is best to schedule training just prior to participants' need for the training on the job. Likewise, when a skill is infrequently used, fade-out occurs and refresher training might be needed

🏠 Additional Readings 🏠

Anderson, John C., Kevin Dooley, and Manus Rungtusanatham. 1994. "Training for Effective Continuous Quality Improvement." *Quality Progress,* December, pp. 57–61.

Boyett, Joseph H., and Henry P. Conn. 1988. *Maximizing Performance Management.* Lakewood, Colo.: Glenbridge Publishing.

Brown, Mark Graham, Darcy E. Hitchcock, and Marsha L. Willard. 1994. *Why TQM Fails and What to Do about It.* New York: Irwin Professional Publishing.

Cartin, Thomas J., and Donald J. Jacoby. 1997. *A Review of Managing Quality and a Primer for the Certified Quality Manager Exam.* Milwaukee: ASQ Quality Press.

Gunter, Berton H. 1998. "Gunter's Last Column." *Quality Progress,* April, p. 111.

——. 1996. *Making Training Work: How to Achieve Bottom-Line Results and Lasting Success.* Milwaukee: ASQ Quality Press.

Juran, Joseph M. 1989. *Juran on Leadership for Quality.* New York: The Free Press.

——. 1992. *Juran on Quality by Design.* New York: The Free Press.

Juran, Joseph M., and Frank M. Gryna, eds. 1998. *Juran's Quality Control Handbook.* 4th ed. New York: McGraw-Hill.

Mager, Robert. 1988. *Making Instruction Work.* Belmont, Calif.: David S. Lake Publishers.

Mager, Robert F., and Peter Pipe. 1984. *Analyzing Performance Problems or "You Really Oughta Wanna."* 2nd ed. Belmont, Calif.: David S. Lake Publishers.

Main, Jeremy. 1994. *Quality Wars: The Triumphs and Defeats of American Business.* New York: The Free Press.

Nopper, Norman S. 1993. "Reinventing the Factory with Lifelong Learning." *Training,* May, pp. 55–58.

Phillips, Jack J. 1997. *Return on Investment in Training and Performance Improvement Programs.* Houston: Gulf Publishing.

Weaver, Marcia. 1996. *Empowering Employees through Basic Skills Training.* Milwaukee: ASQC Quality Press.

Chapter 46

Training Subgroups and Topics

❖ *This chapter should help you*

- ◆ Appreciate the breadth and depth of quality-related content in both management training and nonmanagement training
- ◆ Understand the role and importance of on-the-job training (OJT) and some of the difficulties in conducting effective OJT
- ◆ Understand the role of and training required for effective facilitators

---

MANAGEMENT TRAINING

Having management learn first, then instruct their direct reports, and so on is a method used by many successful companies to cascade knowledge down throughout the organization. It is an excellent way for management to demonstrate support, become personally involved, and better comprehend the subject matter.

As the Body of Knowledge for the ASQ Certified Quality Manager examination suggests, managing requires an eclectic repertoire of skills (e.g., technical skills for the responsibility managed, planning and organizing skills, staffing and people management skills, project management skills, and training, coaching, and mentoring skills). In addition, managers need to develop skills in managing conflict and negotiations as well as build a solid understanding of variation and the use of measurements.

In most organizations, the quality manager is the in-house expert on quality issues and, as such, is expected to be involved in identifying the quality subject training needs for other managers. The quality manager should ensure that the technical content of a course meets the training needs.

It is not enough simply for training to be conducted; it is extremely important that follow-up activities require the manager to use the knowledge or skill gained in the training session. If a manager is not required to employ the new skill immediately, only a small portion of the training is likely to be retained. Additionally, a manager must be given the opportunity to apply the new skill in the environment in which it is expected to be used. The training should be reinforced and evaluated periodically to ensure that the concepts are understood and the skills are practiced.

Training for managers differs from that for other employees because managers often are not expected to actually *do* the things that are the subject of the training but rather are expected to be able to *oversee* proper application of the training. A simple

❖❖

example might be training in statistical process control (SPC). An operator would be expected to actually use the training to record the data and control the process. To do this, the operator would need to understand control chart rules and what action to take when "out-of-control" conditions are shown on the chart. However, a manager additionally needs to interpret the data at a higher level. Are the average or range chart control limits so broad that action is required on the machine to improve capability even when the process is in control? This might be determined from customer complaints, are reviewed by the manager but not normally reviewed with the machine operator.

Trainers need to understand that the learner is always in control of what is learned. For a training program or an on-the-job learning experience to be fully effective, the learners need to see clearly how what is being taught will benefit them and fulfill a "felt need" in them.[1] This is true of both managers and other employees, but because managers have the authority to set directions, a failure to recognize this fact can effectively nullify the training efforts.

A training program should address its benefits in terms of the trainee's needs. The information presented must be reinforced with actual hands-on application of the concepts. Although hands-on activities can be simulated in a classroom setting, it is better to actually do these activities in the work environment, as described in the following example:

> A training program for teaching internal quality auditing to employees would consist of several steps. First, the training establishes the purposes and benefits of internal auditing to the participants and to the organization. Second, training examines the elements of auditing and explains how to establish an audit schedule, prepare a checklist, conduct an opening meeting, perform the audit, hold the closing meeting, report audit results, and follow up on any problems detected. Classroom training could be supplemented with exercises and role-playing to demonstrate and reinforce the skills presented. The procedures the organization follows in preparing for an actual audit, for example, preparing a checklist, should be followed exactly. Training should continue with employees demonstrating competence in all the skills learned by performing an audit of the organization. The trainer(s) should supervise and coach participants in the entire auditing process, including the issuance of the audit report and concluding with audit follow-up activities.

Relevant topics to address when educating management in the principles, concepts, and techniques of quality management include the following:

◆ planning strategically and tacitly supporting organizational strategic plans and objects

◆ process/system thinking and concepts of internal customers

◆ planning, organizing, staffing, directing, and controlling a quality initiative and principles and practices of project planning and management

◆ quality of management in marketing and sales, product design and development, procurement, production, delivery systems, and support services

- customer focus: deploying the voice of the customer throughout the organization

- overview of quality-related standards and practices, for example, criteria for the Baldrige Award (and similar state awards), ISO 9000 series (and derivatives such as QS-9000 and AS 9000), and current good manufacturing practices (cGMP)

- tools and techniques (e.g., the seven basic tools of quality management and the seven basic tools of quality control), design of experiments (DOE), failure mode and effects analysis (FMEA), cost of quality (COQ), benchmarking, process mapping, problem solving/decision making, and statistical thinking

- continuous improvement concepts, principles, and practices as promulgated by acknowledged quality gurus (e.g., Deming, Juran, Feigenbaum, Ishikawa, Crosby, and others)

- other organizational change/improvement methodologies, for example, process reengineering, agile/lean manufacturing, and cycle time reduction (just-in-time systems, single minute exchange of dies, or SMED), balanced scorecard, activity-based costing, Internet and intranet communications, supplier partnering, customer partnering, and self-assessments

- training and development of a customer- and quality-focused workforce

- linkages with other systems, for example, environmental management, safety, financial, compensation and benefits, employee recognition and rewards, legal, and community relations

- managing little "q": a quality assurance unit, a quality control unit, and a quality auditing unit

- fundamental concepts and practices of managing an organization-wide quality management system (QMS): management's responsibilities, establishing a quality policy and plans, structuring a QMS, controlling the design process, capturing and deploying customers' requirements, controlling the QMS documents, ensuring procurement of quality materials from qualified suppliers, controlling all processes and the quality of output, establishing and fostering use of timely corrective actions and preventive actions for continuous improvement, ensuring that objective evidence of quality management is maintained, continually monitored and assessed, ensuring that personnel are qualified for the work they do, ensuring that quality management extends to postproduction servicing, and employing appropriate statistical methods to facilitate continuous improvement

Management education/training is ineffective without top management's commitment to the need, content, and use of the techniques learned. For example, training in technical tools, such as full or fractional factorial design of experiments, is of no value unless there are worthwhile projects being conducted in the organization that make use of this knowledge and skill. Also, some organizations mistakenly measure training progress by the number of training programs conducted or people that flow through a classroom rather than by how effectively the training is used to achieve the organization's strategic objectives.

❖❖❖

EMPLOYEE TRAINING

The ISO 9000 quality systems standards have heightened awareness of the need for training and qualifying personnel who conduct activities pertaining to quality, as defined in the organization's quality plan, procedures, and practices. Typical basic training topics for training all employees might include quality principles and practices, problem-solving methods, the basic seven quality tools, working as a team member, team protocols, and interpersonal skills. Training might also need to be done on the technical aspects of a job.

Skills required in day-to-day activities can be acquired through formal training in procedures and concepts or through on-the-job training (OJT). When practical, employee training might be more effective when formal training is combined with OJT. Both formal training and OJT need a defined structure, clear objectives, and a method for demonstrating competency. Regardless of the training system used, the trainer must be qualified to teach the topic/skill to be trained (including underlying concepts and the reason for training), must know how to properly use requisite tools and references (including any equipment used to deliver training), and should be aware of how to best train adults. Knowles delineated theories of learning and teaching for adults in *The Adult Learner: A Neglected Species.*

Nonmanagerial employees tend to have more specific OJT than do managers. On-the-job-training can be highly effective because the training is conducted in the actual work environment—on the same equipment and using the same processes used in day-to-day activities.[2] Historically, OJT normally has been conducted by a manager or other employee familiar with job requirements. However, especially in organizations that face rapid rates of change and thus have difficulties keeping current with technology, outsourcing training to external training providers has become a popular trend.

Johnson presents six principles of OJT:

1. Usually used for skills training.
2. Useful for individuals or small groups.
3. Without a solid OJT program, there is a strong possibility that people are learning incorrect techniques from trial and error or their teammates.
4. TQM requires OJT in the workplace, whether it be shop floor, computer, or a sales call.
5. OJT must have a plan even though it may not be as formal as those used in the lecture method.
6. Teaching process:
   A. Tell them
   B. Show them
   C. Have them show you
   D. Repeat until performance is satisfactory[3]

Like all training programs, OJT programs require a needs analysis, training objectives, clear statement of responsibilities, the procedures and work instructions for the specific job/task, and the basis for measuring job/task mastery. ISO 9000 quality systems standards require the training to be documented. This can be as simple as the trainer and trainee both signing a training plan to signify that training has been completed and was effectively demonstrated.

The most common problem with an OJT system arises when it is not structured in the same manner as are formal training programs. For example, it is common in OJT for an employee who is familiar with the job to train another employee without objectives or a planned system. Job inconsistencies can result in the manner in which employees perform their duties. In addition, the lack of structure can cause bad habits to be included in the training. Another problem occurs when a relatively inexperienced employee is responsibility for training others. The employee might know how to do the job, but, as anyone who has done training knows, it is much more difficult to teach someone to do a job than to do it.

When a supervisor/manager conducts the training, training can be ineffective, abbreviated, and cursory because of the following:

◆ The time that a manager can devote to the training effort might be limited.

◆ The supervisor/manager might lack the competency to conduct training.

◆ Training is often unplanned.

◆ Time for training is normally not a high priority.

◆ Managers/supervisors do not do the job routinely and might lack firsthand knowledge of all the things that must be done to do a job successfully.

Because up to 75 percent of all training is estimated to be on-the-job, OJT is potentially the most powerful training tool that an organization can use. It offers immediate feedback on the training's success and is considered practical because "it's the job."[4] Performance improvement is virtually assured when planned, structured OJT is combined with formal training and positive reinforcement.

FACILITATOR TRAINING

Facilitator training is important to the success of a quality team. Facilitators should be trained in meeting facilitation and conflict resolution. Other topics covered in facilitator training may include: instructing and coaching skills, interpersonal skills in a dynamic group environment, basic behavior management skills, quality management principles and practices, and appropriate use of quality tools. The role of the facilitator is to act as the following:

◆ a guide to circumvent the minefields and pitfalls of special applications not covered in textbooks

◆ a catalyst to assist in developing a plan and to provide follow-up to all management levels, thus maintaining continuity

◆ an objective evaluator and auditor of team progress, identifying any roadblocks to success and opportunities to improve performance[5]

Facilitators are needed less as the team becomes more seasoned and mature. Initially, the facilitator is more of a coach and referee in the team process and therefore requires good communications skills in addition to some technical knowledge of the subject, meeting facilitation skills, and the ability to resolve conflict among team members when it occurs. Because of the skills and specialized training required, skilled facilitators are rarely found in most organizations.

A well-trained facilitator is a valuable asset in any situation being addressed by a team-based approach. A combination of formal training and OJT with an experienced facilitator will produce the best results. Conflict resolution training especially lends itself to this method.

Finally, problems invariably surface when facilitators without training in conflict resolution and meeting management are appointed to teams. Also, some managers prefer to facilitate meetings themselves in order to manipulate a team toward an action on which the manager has previously decided.

SUMMARY

Regardless of the group being trained, training is a process. Whether training is conducted one-to-one, on-the-job, or in a classroom, there is a process cycle. Briefly, the process is as follows:

◆ determine training needs

◆ obtain funding and approval

◆ design the training content and sequence of instruction

◆ select/design the training delivery method(s)

◆ develop, test, and modify the training as needed

◆ deliver the training

◆ evaluate the effectiveness of the training

◆ apply the training

◆ measure the improvement

🏠 Additional Readings 🏠

Camp, Robert C. 1995. *Business Process Benchmarking: Finding and Implementing Best Practices*. Milwaukee: ASQC Quality Press.

Carnevale, Anthony P., Leila J. Gainer, and Ann S. Meltzer. 1990. *Workplace Basics: The Essential Skills Employers Want*. San Francisco: Jossey-Bass.

Hammer, Michael, and James Champy. 1993. *Reengineering the Corporation*. New York: HarperBusiness.

Hradesky, John L. 1995. *Total Quality Management Handbook*. New York: McGraw-Hill.

Johnson, Richard S. 1993. *Quality Training Practices*. Milwaukee: ASQC Quality Press.

Kelly, Leslie, ed. 1995. *The ASTD Technical Skills and Training Handbook*. New York: McGraw-Hill.

Knowles, Malcolm. 1973. *The Adult Learner: A Neglected Species*. Houston: Gulf Publishing.

Mohrman, S. A., S. G. Cohen, and A. M. Mohrman. 1995. *Designing Team-Based Organizations.* San Francisco: Jossey-Bass.

Rummler, Geary A., and Alan P. Brache. 1991. *Improving Performance: How to Manage the White Space on the Organization Chart.* San Francisco: Jossey-Bass.

Schaffer, Robert H. 1988. *The Breakthrough Strategy: Using Short-Term Successes to Build the High Performance Organization.* New York: HarperBusiness.

Schuman, S. P. 1996. "What to Look for in a Group Facilitator." *Quality Progress,* June.

Stolovitch, Harold D., and Erica J. Keeps, eds. 1992. *Handbook of Human Performance Technology: A Comprehensive Guide for Analyzing and Solving Performance Problems in Organizations.* San Francisco: Jossey-Bass.

Tracey, William R., ed. 1994. *Human Resources Management and Development Handbook.* 2d ed. New York: AMACOM.

Chapter 47

Training Needs Analysis

❖ *This chapter should help you*

◆ Realize that planning is critical for training to achieve its intended outcome

◆ Understand that assessment data, when analyzed, should pinpoint the desired training outcomes vital to structuring, delivering, and ultimately evaluating training

◆ Recognize that many techniques and tools exist for assessing and analyzing training needs

---

PURPOSES OF A NEEDS ASSESSMENT AND ANALYSIS

Training might be indicated for one or more of the following reasons:

◆ to comply with new or changed regulatory and/or customer requirements

◆ to address new or changed systems, processes, procedures, methods, equipment, or tools

◆ to add skills to an employee's present skill set in preparation for a new assignment

◆ to refresh previous training to ensure maintenance of a specific skill set

◆ to qualify and/or certify an individual to a specific workmanship standard

◆ to correct a skill deficiency noted in an individual's performance appraisal

In addition, there might be needs to satisfy that are not strictly "training" (see Chapter 45 for a discussion of the difference between education and training). These might include the following:

◆ to provide company orientation for new or transferred employees

◆ to provide knowledge of theories and concepts pertinent to the organization's products or services and practices, such as theory pertaining to electrical currents and transmission

◆ to provide knowledge of required and/or acceptable behaviors, for example, the avoidance of behavior that could be construed as sexual harassment

◆ to mentor an individual in personal development and/or career advancement

❖❖

ASSESSING TRAINING NEEDS

An assessment of training needs can range from a company-wide periodic (annual, in this example) assessment in which the analysis provides data for an annual training plan and budget to a simple observation that a given employee does not know how to perform an assigned task. Many companies address their training needs by matching people to jobs on the basis of education and then training them in the specific requirements of the job. For this to be successful, the needs assessment should begin with top management and the organization's strategic plan.

The following issues are applicable when beginning a top-down needs assessment:

What are the organizational goals, business objectives, strategic plans, and action plans? What major changes are anticipated in the short and long term?

What products or services do the clients produce? What technologies do they use to do this?

What is the organizational structure? Who are the decision makers? What are the political realities? What are the microcultures and policies of each client business unit?

How are budgets approved? What is the financial health of the larger organization?

What core competencies to employees already have? What core competencies do they need currently or in the future?

What is the history of technical training in the organization?

Who are the organization's main customers? What are the organization's marketing plans? What are competitors doing?

What industry issues or regulations affect technical training?[1]

A proper assessment of needs helps prioritize resources to ensure that they are available to address the most critical training needs. Assessment data forms the basis for designing training program content. Finally, the needs assessment must be deployed to each business unit, which in turn cascades this downward until the training needs of individual employees are addressed.

There are two dozen or more techniques or tools for determining training needs and for separating out nontraining needs. Data obtained from most of these needs assessment and analysis tools provide information for designing training program content as well as provide a baseline for evaluating training. (Training evaluation is discussed in Chapter 48.)

A few of these tools or techniques include the following:

❖ *Job analysis* consists of breaking a job down to levels of increasing specificity. Outputs are a sequenced task listing by level and job inventories.

❖ *Task analysis* involves the specification of all overt and covert behaviors pertinent to the performance of a job. Outputs can be stimulus-response tables, flowcharts, time and motion studies, and behavior observation tables.

❖ *Front-end analysis* can be accomplished through many techniques, for example, a performance audit, root cause analysis, or a competency analysis. The outputs provide data in a myriad of formats, usually a matrix.

◆ *Organizational diagnosis*, for an entire organization examines relationships and communication, vertically, horizontally and diagonally. The output is a summary of findings and conclusions and recommended actions.

◆ *Instruments for analysis* can include tests, questionnaires, surveys, checklists, simulations, games, and self-completing assessments.

◆ *Techniques involving personal interaction* can include observations of work being performed, individual or group interviews, brainstorming, focus groups, and needs analysis by walking around (NABWA).

◆ *Qualitative data analysis techniques* can be used to analyze collected data, such as numbers, words, phrases, and paragraphs.

For a simple approach to determine needs at the individual level, Kirkpatrick suggests five ways:

1. Ask the participants.
2. Ask the bosses of the participants.
3. Ask others who are familiar with the job and how it is being performed, including subordinates, peers, and customers.
4. Test the participants.
5. Analyze performance appraisal forms.[2]

DESIGNING THE TRAINING PROGRAM

After conducting a needs assessment and analysis, the next step should be to design a cost-effective training program to fill the gaps detected by the assessment. A cost-effective program is one that produces the desired outcomes at the least expenditure of resources. Figure 47.1 shows a training system modeled to support the goals and objectives of an organization's strategic plan.

A training program can be as simple as planning for one-to-one, on-the-job training for an individual to as involved as training large groups of employees in the use of a new process or equipment. Regardless, there should be a defined training plan and documented evidence that the training was successfully completed.

The major factors to consider in designing a training program are the following:

◆ *Who* needs the training (participants)? How many? Where located?

◆ *Why* do they need the training? What are they doing now? At what skill level are they now?

◆ *What* do they need to learn? How much of what they need is *knowledge* and how much is pure *skill* attainment?

◆ *What* measurement(s) will best indicate participants can do the tasks to which they are assigned (apply the skill set)?

◆ *What* basis will be used to evaluate the success of the training program (see Chapter 48)?

◆ *What* method is best for delivering the training within the organization's resource constraints (e.g., classroom, on-the-job, or outside training provider)?

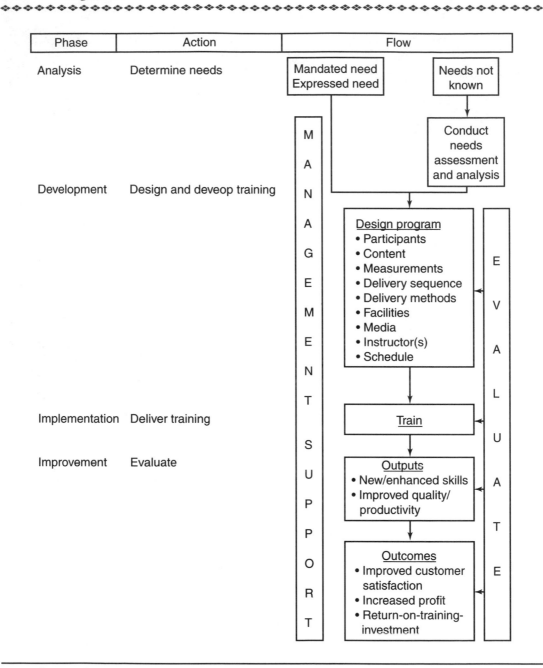

Figure 47.1. A training system model.

- *Where* can the training best be delivered (which facility, what room, or at or away from the workplace)?
- *What* media is best to use in delivering the training (e.g., audio, visuals, video, print, intranets, or the Internet; see Chapter 49)?
- *Who* should deliver the training? What trainer qualifications are needed? If not a qualified trainer or facilitator, will training of trainer be needed? How many trainers are needed?

Relative to Target Population (TP)	J	T	F	C
TABLE 47.1. Distinguishing between Performance and Skill/Knowledge Issues				
Does TP have time to do job well?	X	X		
Does TP have proper facilities in which to work?	X			
Does TP have the proper tools to do the work?	X			
Does TP have proper procedures, instructions, job aids?	X			
Does TP know what they are supposed to do?		X	X	
Has TP ever done the job correctly?		X	X	
Could TP do the job properly if their lives depended on it?		X		X
If TP could do the job in an exemplary way, would they?				X
Are there more negative than positive consequences in doing the job?				X
Does TP know when they are not performing as supervisor expects?			X	
Do supervisors of TP have requisite knowledge/skills?		X	X	X

◆   *When* should training best be done? What is the best schedule, considering workplace demands?

◆   *What* is the projected return-on-training-investment (ROTI)? Is the training, as planned, worth the investment?

IMPROVING JOB-RELATED BEHAVIOR (JOB PERFORMANCE)

When conducting a needs assessment, the problem that surfaces is sometimes a performance problem. Conducting a training program is not a viable solution when job behavior (and attitude) is the cause of poor performance. If it is suspected that performance rather than lack of knowledge and skill is the issue to be resolved, apply the test questions listed in Table 47.1. From answers to the questions in Table 47.1, select a *job* solution (J) if the problem is the way the task is organized or if the tools and so on are inadequate. The skill might not be needed at all if the job/task can be eliminated. If the employee(s) lack the requisite knowledge/skills, select a *training* solution (T). If the problem is that the employee(s) do not know what is expected of them, select a solution that improves performance *feedback* (F). If the employee(s) is capable of doing the work but fails to do it, take action to change the *consequences* (C) of doing the job. Frequently, workers know how to get the job done but receive more negative than positive consequences for doing so and really do not know what is expected of them. The solution is to train supervisors in how to provide performance feedback and positive consequence for work done well. Of course, a situation might

❖❖

be detected in which both a knowledge/skill deficiency and a performance problem exist. The performance problem probably should be resolved first so that training efforts are not wasted.

SUMMARY OF CAVEATS

A number of factors can unhinge a training program. Most of these factors result from a poor assessment of the organization's needs. The following problems often occur when a proper assessment is neglected:

◆ training without consideration of the goal

◆ training without application

◆ training without near term application

◆ training to the wrong problem

◆ single-level training, such as the tendency to train managers at the exclusion of other organizational levels

◆ poorly prepared training, trainers, or participants

◆ the wrong training or trainers

◆ inadequate background knowledge of participants

◆ an expensive packaged training plan that does not fit

◆ the tendency to quickly begin training and abandon it when it is not the miracle cure that was desired[3]

If the value to be gained by training does not exceed the cost, a less expensive training method should be used or the training should not take place. People should not be trained until there is an immediate way for them to use the skill. Most of the skills acquisition process should focus on learning by doing, but sequencing learning activities in the order they are performed on the job is not always best. Building from simpler to more complex tasks may be a better aid in achieving mastery.

The skill level of the intended training participants should be assessed so that training can be structured to build on present skill levels. People should not be trained in a skill they already can demonstrate. Finally, if there is a performance problem and if lack of skill is not an issue, some other solution is indicated.

🏠 Additional Readings 🏠

Blank, William E. 1982. *Handbook for Developing Competency-Based Training Programs.* Englewood Cliffs, N.J.: Prentice-Hall.

Clark, Ruth Colvin. 1989. *Developing Technical Training.* Reading, Mass.: Addison-Wesley.

Gael, Sidney. 1983. *Job Analysis: A Guide to Assessing Work Activities.* San Francisco: Jossey-Bass.

Gilbert, Thomas F. 1978. *Human Competence.* New York: McGraw-Hill.

Johnson, Richard S. 1993. *Quality Training Practices.* Milwaukee: ASQC Quality Press.

Kelly, Leslie, ed. 1995. *The ASTD Technical Skills and Training Handbook.* New York: McGraw-Hill.

Kirkpatrick, Donald L. 1994. *Evaluating Training Programs: The Four Levels.* San Francisco: Berrett-Koehler.

Laird, Dugan. 1985. *Approaches to Training and Development.* 2d ed. Reading, Mass.: Addison-Wesley.

Lee, William W., and Kenneth H. Roadman. 1991. "Linking Needs Assessment to Performance Based Evaluation" *Performance & Instruction* (July) Vol 30: 4–6.

Levinson, Harry. 1972. *Organizational Diagnosis.* Cambridge, Mass.: Harvard University Press.

Mager, Robert F. 1988. *Making Instruction Work or Skillbloomers.* Belmont, Calif.: David S. Lake Publishers.

Rossett, A. 1987. *Training Needs Assessment: Techniques in Training and Performance Development Series.* Englewood Cliffs, N.J.: Educational Technology Publications.

Westcott, Russell T. 1995. "A Quality System Needs Assessment." In *In Action: Conducting Needs Assessment (17 Case Studies),* ed. Jack J. Phillips and Elwood F. Holton III. Alexandria, Va.: American Society for Training and Development. p. 235

Zemke, Ron. 1988. "How to Do a Needs Assessment When You Think You Don't Have Time." *Training,* March, pp. 38–44.

Zemke, Ron, and Thomas Kramlinger. 1982. *Figuring Things Out: A Trainer's Guide to Needs and Task Analysis.* Reading, Mass.: Addison-Wesley.

❖❖

Chapter 48

Posttraining Evaluation and Reinforcement

❖❖

❖ *This chapter should help you*

- ◆ Understand that a needs assessment develops baseline data for the design, delivery, and evaluation of training
- ◆ Appreciate the relative value of the five levels of training evaluation
- ◆ Gain a fundamental exposure to reinforcement principles and understand why training without reinforcement might not achieve the desired behavior
- ◆ Understand that training that will not produce a measurable benefit to the organization should not be done

---

EVALUATING THE QUALITY TRAINING PROCESS

As indicated in the training model in Chapter 47, all phases of the training process should be evaluated, as posttraining evaluation is essential in determining whether the training program meets the objectives of the training plan. Posttraining evaluation includes the following:

- ◆ verification of the design (e.g., subject content and delivery methods)
- ◆ facilities, equipment and tools, and media to be used
- ◆ qualifications of the trainer
- ◆ selection of the participants
- ◆ measures to be used to assess training effectiveness (validation)
- ◆ measures to be used to assess outcomes resulting from training (validation)

Technical training effectiveness can be greatly enhanced by four key considerations: appropriate preparation of the training facilities, appropriate timing of the training relative to when performance is required, appropriate sequence of training relative to skills mastery, and appropriate feedback indicating performance difficulties and progress.

Figure 48.1 lists and describes five levels for evaluating training. Kirkpatrick is credited with defining the first four levels (reaction, learning, behavior, and results)

No.	Level	Questions	Comments
1	Reaction	Were the participants pleased with the training?	The typical "smile" sheets collected at the end of a program, session, or module.
2	Learning	Did the participants learn what was intended for them to learn?	Were the training objectives met? Typically determined from some kind of test.
3	Behavior	Did participants change their behavior on the basis of what was taught?	Typically determined from an assessment of how learned behaviors are applied on the job.
4	Results	Was there a positive affect on the organization resulting from participants' changed behavior?	Typically measured from pretraining versus posttraining analysis of the organization's outcomes. Usually a "quantity" type measure (increased: production, lower rejects, no. of time periods without a customer complaint, etc.).
5	ROTI	Was there a measurable net dollar payback for the organization, resulting from participants' application of learned behavior?	Return-on-training-investment (ROTI) is based on the dollar valued added by the investment in the training.

◆ **Figure 48.1.** Levels of training evaluation.

for evaluating training.[1] Kirkpatrick subsequently added a fifth level, return on investment (ROI).

Robinson and Robinson expanded level three to distinguish between Type A (are participants applying the skills and behavior as taught?) and Type B (are participants applying nonobservable, (e.g., mental skills, learning to the job?) learning.[2]

Level 5 in Figure 48.1, ROTI, is a perspective addressed by Westcott.[3] Phillips also addresses all five levels of evaluation.[4] In Figure 48.2, Phillips presents a matrix comparing each level of evaluation to value of information, power to show results, frequency of use, and difficulty of assessment. For example, the Reaction level provides

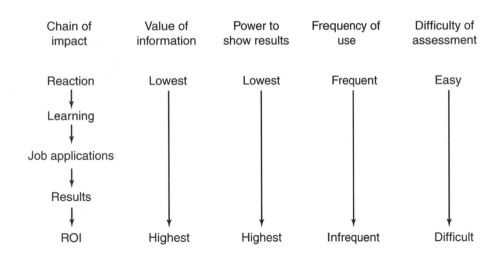

Chain of impact	Value of information	Power to show results	Frequency of use	Difficulty of assessment
Reaction	Lowest	Lowest	Frequent	Easy
Learning				
Job applications				
Results				
ROI	Highest	Highest	Infrequent	Difficult

◆ **Figure 48.2.** Characteristics of evaluation levels. Source: © 1996, J.J. Phillips, *The ASTD Training and Development Handbook,* McGraw–Hill. Used with permission.

the lowest-value information and results and is frequently and easily used; the ROI level offers the highest-value information and results and is infrequently used and difficult to assess. Quality training programs that score high at all levels are likely to be successful. The failure of a quality training program is likely to be linked to one or more of the following causes:

◆ cultural resistance by line managers

◆ doubt as to usefulness of the training

◆ lack of participation by line managers

◆ technique versus problem orientation

◆ inadequacies of leaders

◆ mixing of levels of participants

◆ lack of application during the course

◆ language too complex

◆ lack of participation by the training function

◆ operational and logistical deficiencies[5]

Expanding on the second item in the previous list, doubt occurs when (1) no linkage exists with the strategic plans of the organization, (2) no apparent connection is evident between behaviors to be learned and application on the job, (3) no projected goals are established for posttraining improvement, and (4) the question of "What's in it for me?" is inadequately addressed for participants and their supervisors.

Problems that can arise, in addition to the ones listed previously, include the following:

◆ No or weak partnering among managers/supervisors, trainers, and participants mutually involved in achieving the training objectives.

◆ Training program poorly planned and delivered. Problems could include (1) inadequate needs assessment and analysis, (2) training content (objectives, subjects, media, and demonstrations) does not match needs, (3) lack of measures for evaluation, (4) overemphasis on theory and technique versus skill application, (5) lack of practice during the course, (6) inadequacies of trainers, and (7) ineffective selection of participants.

◆ Lack of or inadequate reinforcement for participants' success in learning and applying learning on the job.

RATIONALE FOR TRAINING EVALUATION

If the training is new or is a major revision to previous training, the following needs to be determined:

◆ From the design verification phase, are there projections indicating that the training program will be worth the resources to be expended, and that the outcomes will support the organization's strategic plans?

◆ Does it make sense to go further if the appropriate resources cannot be made available?

◆ Would it be more cost effective to continue with in-house design or to consider a training provider's product?

◆ If going forward with the design and delivery of the program appears feasible, which of the possible alternatives available have the greatest positive impact on the organization? Which have the greatest positive impact in the short term? In the long term?

During the delivery of training, the following should be frequently evaluated:

◆ Is the training achieving stated objectives?

◆ Are the right people attending the training?

◆ What parts of the training are yielding the most benefit to the participants? Which are yielding the least? Why?

◆ What modifications must be made "in-flight" to correct a problem or deficiency?

◆ If this or similar training is to be done again, what should be done differently? Why? How?

◆ Are there facility problems that need to be corrected immediately?

◆ Is the trainer succeeding in producing trained participants? If not, why?

After the training, the following questions should be asked:

◆ Are the participants satisfied? If not, why?

◆ Are the participants' organizations satisfied? If not, why?

◆ Have all the training plan requirements been met?

◆ How can the training design and delivery be improved?

◆ Did the training produce the desired outcomes?

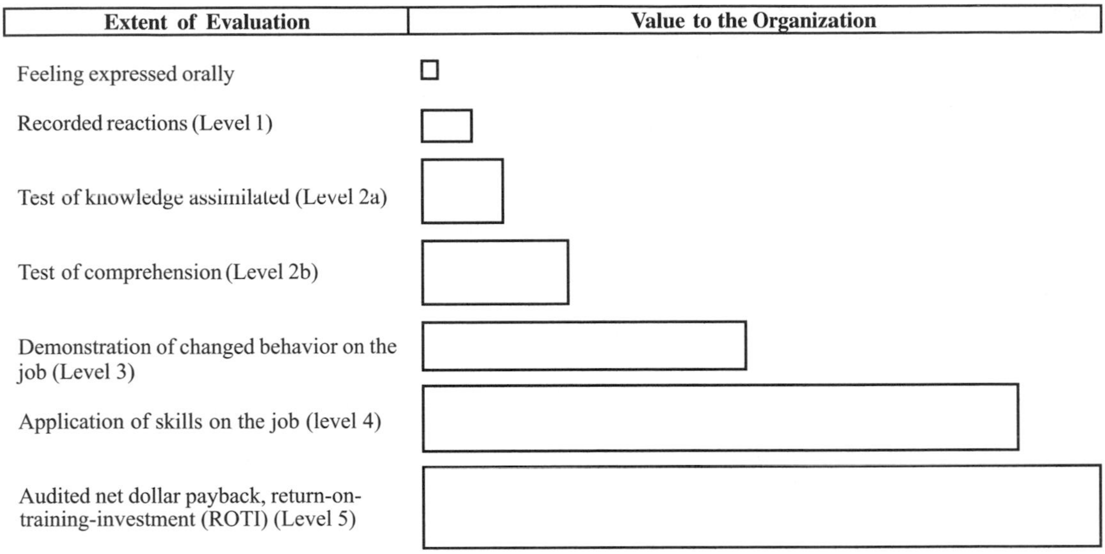

Extent of Evaluation	Value to the Organization
Feeling expressed orally	
Recorded reactions (Level 1)	
Test of knowledge assimilated (Level 2a)	
Test of comprehension (Level 2b)	
Demonstration of changed behavior on the job (Level 3)	
Application of skills on the job (level 4)	
Audited net dollar payback, return-on-training-investment (ROTI) (Level 5)	

◆ **Figure 48.3.**   Conceptual view of the relative value of evaluated training.

Figure 48.3 shows a conceptual view of the relative value of evaluating training.

REINFORCING QUALITY TRAINING

Numerous ways exist to reinforce quality training. Cash awards are of dubious value and are not recommended in connection with training in affluent societies. Positive reinforcement is used during the training to shape the participants' behavior and is vital when the trained person properly applies the skills learned on the job.

In most situations, a key to reinforcement is to provide more positive than negative consequences for appropriate behavior/performance. Another key point is to provide positive performance feedback to the participant immediately following an observation of work done well. The types and frequencies of consequences can be collected through an analysis of a job/task environment during the needs assessment phase. An analysis will often show that participants have, prior to training, received a negative balance of consequences. For example, a lathe operator might get raw material late or receive material of an inferior quality, causing excessive tool replacement. This in turn makes the operator's job more difficult and the output late, resulting in pressure (or criticism) from supervisors. Solution of this type of problem is up to management and should be resolved before any training is conducted. Training will not solve such a problem, and failure to solve such a problem ahead of time will likely detract from the training. In another example, first-line supervisors receive training in interpreting and taking action on the basis of control charts. On returning to the workplace, the next level of management fails to acknowledge the new skill and berates the supervisors for not pushing product out the door fast enough. More positively, supervisors could take special care to acknowledge their trained people with positive performance feedback when the learned skills are applied and the work is done properly. When properly given, performance feedback for work not up to expectation is a helpful rather than a punitive action.

Negative consequences to performance in a work environment can take many forms, including verbal abuse from supervisors or coworkers when a mistake is made, deduction from pay for rejects, inadequate training to do the job, inadequate instructions, poor working conditions, lack of proper tools, lack of adequate equipment and facility maintenance, no positive feedback when work is done well, and inadequate communication from management. Positive consequences are the removal of the previously mentioned types of negative conditions and the substitution of positive feedback for doing the job right in place of punishment for making mistakes.

Some pointers on reinforcement (behavior management) are the following:

◆ The proximity of positive reinforcement to a specific behavior and the degree of acceptability of the reinforcement by the performer affects the probability of recurrence of a behavior. (If something good happened the last time you did it right, probably something good will happen if you do it right again.)

◆ A performer is more likely to make small improvements than large ones. A small improvement positively reinforced will tend to make the next occurrence of the same behavior more probable. In a complex situation, if you wait until the performer learns the whole task perfectly before giving positive reinforcement, the performer might never reach the desired behavior. (This incremental reinforcement is called *shaping*.)

◆ If you observe the *absence of a desired behavior* and no consequences, and you want to *teach* that behavior, add positive consequences.

◆ If you observe a *desired behavior* and positive consequences, and you want to *increase* that behavior, add more positive consequences.

◆ If you observe *desired behavior* and positive consequences, and you want to *maintain* that behavior, be sure the balance of consequences are more positive than negative.

◆ If you observe a *desired behavior* and negative consequences, and you want to *increase or maintain* that behavior, add positive and remove negative consequences.

◆ If you observe *undesired behavior* and positive consequences, and you want to *stop or decrease* that behavior, remove positive consequences and/or ignore the behavior and/or add negative consequences (punish).

◆ If you observe *undesired behavior* and negative consequences, and you want to *stop or decrease* that behavior, add more negative consequences or remove negative consequences and positively reinforce another desired behavior.

This brief overview of some of the principles and practices for managing behavior is not, by itself, adequate to attempt to apply the principles to your work situation. Training and practice in applying the range of principles of behavior management to your specific situations is needed.

❖❖❖

Quality training should occur just-in-time (JIT); that is, immediately prior to the context in which it is to be used. The longer the time that elapses between the training and the opportunity to put the knowledge/skill gained into practice, the more likely the knowledge/skill gained will fade. In such cases, learning can be reinforced through a refresher course. A refresher course recaps previous learning in a shorter time period, at a faster pace, and in a more intense manner. Face-to-face instruction might not be required: The use of videotapes, audiotapes, or interactive CD-ROMs might be sufficient. The use of electronic means such as e-mail, company intranets, and Internet news groups in training are gaining in popularity. These formats allow the learning or reinforcement to take place in a casual environment and at the learner's pace.

Although many employers assume that employees will engage in training only if they receive an immediate tangible reward, research and experience indicate that most employees find value in training that helps them better achieve their personal, job, and career goals. Therefore, employees who are motivated to increase their proficiency are simultaneously working to improve their company's competitive advantage.

🏫 Additional Readings 🏫

Fournies, Ferdinand. 1978. *Coaching for Improved Performance.* New York: Van Nostrand Reinhold.

Juran, Joseph M., and Frank M. Gryna, eds. 1988. *Juran's Quality Control Handbook.* 4th ed. New York: McGraw-Hill.

Kirkpatrick, Donald L. 1959. "Techniques for Evaluating Training Programs," a four-part series beginning in the November issue of the *Training Director's Journal.*

Phillips, Jack J. 1996. *The ASTD Training and Development Handbook,* 1st ed. New York: McGraw-Hill.

——. 1997. *Return On Investment: In Training and Performance Improvement Programs.* Houston: Gulf Publishing.

Robinson, Dana Gaines, and James C. Robinson. 1990. *Training for Impact: How to Link Training to Business Needs and Measure the Results.* San Francisco: Jossey-Bass.

Westcott, Russell. 1994. "Applied Behavior Management Training." In *In Action: Measuring Return on Investment,* vol. 1, ed. J. Phillips. Alexandria, Va.: American Society for Training and Development, pp. 85–104.

——. 1994. "Behavior Management Training." In *Human Resources Management and Development Handbook.* 2d ed. New York: AMACOM, pp. 897–911.

——. 1994. "ROQI: Overlooked Quality Tool." *The Total Quality Review* (November/December): 37–44.

Chapter 49

Quality Training Tools

❖ *This chapter should help you*

◆ Understand that training adults requires different techniques than training youths

◆ Appreciate the critical linkage between training content and the methods of training delivery to build on what participants already know, provide ample opportunity to practice skills, and reinforce learning as it occurs, as mastery is achieved, and as the training is applied on the job

◆ Establish criteria for selecting the most appropriate and cost-effective training delivery methods and tools

---

TREND TOWARD LEARNING-CONTROLLED INSTRUCTION

Before an organization can select the appropriate methods and tools to use in quality training, it must first understand how adults learn. Adults in general exert more control over their lives than do younger people and this desire for control extends to the learning process as well.

Knowles identifies six factors that influence adult learning:

1. Adults have a need to know why they should learn something.

2. Adults have a deep need to be self-directing.

3. Adults have a greater volume and different quality of experience than youth.

4. Adults become ready to learn when they experience in their life situation a need to know or be able to do in order to perform more effectively and satisfyingly.

5. Adults enter into a learning experience with a task-centered (or problem-centered or life-centered) orientation to learning.

6. Adults are motivated to learn by both extrinsic and intrinsic motivators.[1]

Increasingly, newer technologies for delivering learner-controlled instruction (LCI), sometimes called self-directed learning (SDL), are becoming available. Working without an instructor and at their own pace, adult learners build toward ultimate mastery of the needed knowledge/skill. Learner-controlled instruction works well when there is only one person to train at any given time, when the learners are geographically distant, when training needs to occur at multiple sites simultaneously,

❖❖

	Advantages of LCI	Disadvantages of LCI
Trainee	• Available when trainee is ready • Individual choice of material • Immediate feedback • Work at own pace • No surprises • Provides review and reference	• Not accustomed to SDL • No instructor • No group interaction • Not comfortable setting objectives
Trainer-developer	• No constantly repeated classes • More time to develop • Less time on the road	• Difficult to develop properly • Must revise more frequently • More trainee preparation needed • Limited choice of media • Must sell concept to others
Corporation	• Multiple-site training • Fewer trainers • Reduced travel expenses • Reduced meeting room costs • Eliminates trainee travel costs • Reduced training downtime • Easier to schedule • Enables cross-training • Just-in-time training • Greater training consistency • Reduced training time in the aggregate	• Initial production costs higher • Higher reproduction costs • Higher distribution costs • Higher revision costs • Possible logistical problems

❖ TABLE 49.1.   Advantages and Disadvantages of LCI

Source: © 1996, J.J. Phillips, *The ASTD Training and Development Handbook,* McGraw-Hill. Used with permission when consistency of skill execution is a necessity, and when refresher training is needed.

The advantages and disadvantages of LCI should be considered. Piskurich lists the advantages and disadvantages of learner-controlled instruction in Table 49.1. The trend toward LCI reinforces the trend toward the use of technology-based training, as new technologies both stimulate and enable direct interaction between the individual and the material to be learned. Interactive CD-ROMs are a currently popular method for delivery of certain types of standardized training (e.g., computer application training).

The andragogical model requires that learners be actively involved in the process of evaluating their learning outcomes. Knowles proposes the following six questions:

- What procedures would I use with this particular group to bring into being the climatic conditions of mutual respect, cooperation rather than competition, supportiveness rather than judgmentalness, mutual trust, and having fun while learning?

- What procedures will I use to involve the learners continuously in planning?

- What procedures will I use in helping the participants diagnose their own learning needs?

- What procedures can I use for helping participants translate learning needs into learning objectives?

- What procedures can I use for involving the learners with me in designing and managing a pattern of learning experiences?

- What procedures can I use to involve the learners responsibly in evaluating the accomplishment of their learning objectives?[2]

INSTRUCTIONAL MODES

Quality training and education tools are used to support the concepts being taught. The wide variety of training tools can be categorized as traditional modes of instruction and computer-based instructional techniques.

Traditional Instructional Modes

Traditionally, instructional modes have included live instructors, printed handouts, and media aids, such as whiteboards, chalkboards, flip charts, felt-tip markers, and overhead projectors. Lectures, discussions, role plays, simple paper-based games, case studies, workbooks, videotape, audiotape, and self-directed learning with printed materials are often used. Lectures and role-playing date back to classical Greece, more than 2,000 years ago. In the past, lectures were the primary method of instruction, but creative instructors now use many other tools to enhance learning.

Lesson Plans. Lesson plans specify what material will be presented during a particular training session. Johnson lists the following guidelines for the successful development of lesson plans:

1. Lesson plans are crucial for training success.
2. Every subject must be adequately researched.

3. Develop twice as much material as you think you will need.
4. Ensure trainees know "what's in it for me" early on so they are motivated to learn.
5. Practice, practice, practice prior to presentation.
6. Use examples that pertain to the operation where possible.
7. Stimulate questions.
8. Use training aids.
9. Adapt the training to the group's level.
10. Never make excuses (e.g., "I've never taught this material before.").
11. Remain positive.
12. Follow your lesson plan.[3]

Johnson identifies four types of lesson plans: topical outline, manuscript, sentence, and key word.[4] The type of lesson plan developed depends on the instructor's experience and familiarity with the material, whether he or she has presented it previously, and the degree of formality desired in the presentation of the material.

Lectures and Presentations. A lecture is a one-dimensional, oral transmission of information to students by an instructor, either in-person or via electronic media. It is the most frequently used manner of conveying material to students and often is used in combination with other tools. Lectures are one type of presentation, but presentations can also include other oral, visual, and multimedia formats.

Coaching. Used on a one-on-one basis and conducted at the workplace, coaching is a

> teaching, learning, counseling relationship designed to develop job-related knowledge and skills and improve performance. It requires a continuous flow of instructions, comments, explanations, and suggestions from coach to employee—with the coach or tutor demonstrating, listening, questioning, relating learner's experiences, assisting, motivating, encouraging, and rewarding performance. The coaching option is used primarily to teach complex skills and operations, . . . when the number of trainees is small and the training is needed infrequently, and is a follow-on to other forms of employee training. It has the advantage of being flexible and adaptable. . . . Its disadvantages are that its success depends on the competence of the coach or supervisor and that it is limited to one trainee at a time.[5]

Coaching can be applied to work groups or teams, in which it more closely resembles the sports-team coach model.

Finnerty outlines the following steps for effective coaching:

◆ define performance goals
◆ identify necessary resources for success
◆ observe and analyze current performance
◆ set expectations for performance improvement

◆ plan a coaching schedule

◆ meet with the individual or team to get commitment to goals, demonstrate the desired behavior, and establish boundaries

◆ give feedback on practice and performance

◆ follow up to maintain goals[6]

Discussion Format. The discussion format allows participants freedom to present views, opinions, and ideas in an unrestrained environment. Roundtables and panel discussions are variations. These methods normally work best with a knowledgeable and experienced discussion leader. In presenting the ASQ Certified Quality Manager refresher course, a modified Socratic method of repeated questioning has been successfully used to elicit and share the accumulated knowledge and experience of course members.

Case Studies. Many different kinds of learning exercises fall under the heading "case studies." Case studies illustrate the application of study matter and show how different approaches can be used to solve problems. Case studies can serve to stimulate intense discussions and idea sharing.

Case studies can be developed in-house or purchased from a variety of sources. However, a form of mini case study, the *critical incident,* is often of greater value than a larger, more inclusive case study. The critical incident is usually derived from real situations within the organization for which the training is designed. A critical incident might consist of just a few sentences describing a specific type of event or condition without reference to names or locations. Critical incidents are usually "sprinkled" throughout the training to illustrate specific learning points. The advantages of critical incidents are the following:

◆ They are easier to prepare than a full-blown case study.

◆ Participants can usually identify with the situation (it is their company).

◆ Discussion is more targeted with less confusion generated than with the multifaceted case study.

◆ They take less discussion time and get to the learning points quickly.

The disadvantages of critical incidents are the following:

◆ Data used to compile critical incidents must be collected prior to course design, necessitating a plan to do so.

◆ A critical incident is a carefully crafted, succinct representation (usually written) designed to engender learning about how to respond to a specific event/situation/condition. A critical incident should not be confused with anecdotal material ("war stories") that are used extemporaneously to illustrate a point and/or to inject humor.

◆ Care must be taken to not target, purposely or accidentally, any person or work unit in the company. Data must be sanitized so as to appear anonymous.

Workbooks. Workbooks contain a collection of discussion topics, exercises, extra readings, and other reference material. They normally are used to supplement other materials provided during classroom presentations or as additional self-study materials. Workbooks can serve several purposes:

◆ *As a learning tool:* actively used during the presentation to encourage note taking (fill-in-the-blanks), as self-tests, as a supplement to material presented in class, as a more job-specific interpretation of material presented in a generic textbook, and as a reference to be used during class testing

◆ *Used to demonstrate mastery of each stage of the training:* specific notes or checklists kept by the participant and signed off on by the instructor

◆ *A guide to be used by the trained person back on the job:* might contain workmanship standards and other reference material

Workbooks can combine some or all of the features in the previous list. They can range from a binder for filing class handouts and making notes to a formal reference text.

On-the-Job Training. Most training occurs through on-the-job training. The learner is usually an employee who has been newly hired, transferred, or promoted into a position and lacks the knowledge and skill to perform some job component(s). A more experienced employee (peer or supervisor) is usually assigned to work with the trainee. Specific tasks are demonstrated and performed in the actual work environment to help the trainee gain the knowledge or skills previously lacking.

Instructional Games, Simulations, and Role Playing. Experience has shown that adult learners prefer to practice rather than just listen to lectures and that they prefer to interact with other learners when in a group learning environment.

Instructional games are activities designed to augment other training methods in order to focus the participants' learning toward specific training outcomes. Thiagarajan states, "Instructional games incorporate five characteristics: conflict, control, closure, contrivance, and competency base."[7] Simulations resemble instructional games but also include correspondence between some aspect of the game and reality. Role playing consists of spontaneously performing an assigned scenario.

Remote Learning. Correspondence schools and open learning programs at educational institutions are types of remote learning. Students at all levels of postsecondary enrollment can earn degrees in many fields without ever stepping into a classroom. This self-directed learning style consists of an instructor mailing (through traditional or electronic mail) a course syllabus and a list of assignments to students. Students complete the required work and send it to the instructor, who then returns the graded assignment. Remote learning is especially popular with nontraditional students who would not be able to attend classes in person. This type of learning requires a tremendous amount of self-discipline.

Computer-Based Instructional Techniques

Although most training continues to be conducted using the traditional techniques of lecture, discussion, and recitation, technology-based approaches are steadily growing and will continue to grow. The rapid development of computers, software, and audiovisual media has created dramatic new opportunities to enhance learning.

message if they are absorbed in taking notes. For this reason, the use of job aids should be considered both to augment initial training and to provide reinforcement on the job.

On-the-job skills training is best done by telling and showing how to do the task, having the trainee try, and then showing again the correct method. The trainer should positively reinforce improvement through as many iterations as necessary for the trainee to achieve mastery. Hands-on training can be supplemented with photos of properly completed tasks at each stage of production and/or videos of workers properly performing the tasks to enhance the learning experience. All training, even OJT, should be planned to ensure completeness, consistency, and correctness of instruction.

In skills training, the charisma of the trainer is less important than the ability of the trainer to transfer knowledge and skills to the participant that will, in turn, be demonstrable on the job. Training is not intended to be pure entertainment. This does not preclude the judicious use of humor and having fun learning.

🏠 Additional Readings 🏠

Alden, J., and J. Kirkhorn. 1996. "Case Studies." In *The ASTD Training and Development Handbook: A Guide to Human Resources Development*, ed. Robert L. Craig. New York: McGraw-Hill, pp. 497–516.

Brookfield, D. 1986. *Understanding and Facilitating Adult Learning.* San Francisco: Jossey-Bass.

Einsiedel, A. A. 1995. "Case Studies: Indispensable Tools for Trainers." *Training and Development*, August, pp. 50–53.

Finnerty, Madeline F. 1996. "Coaching for Growth and Development." In *The ASTD Training and Development Handbook: A Guide to Human Resources Development*, ed. Robert L. Craig. New York: McGraw-Hill, pp. 415–36.

Gery, Gloria. 1987. *Making CBT Happen: Prescriptions for Successful Implementation of Computer-Based Training in Your Organization.* Boston: Weingarten Publications.

Johnson, Richard S. 1993. *Quality Training Practices.* Milwaukee: ASQC Quality Press

——. 1993. *TQM: The Mechanics of Quality Processes.* Milwaukee: ASQC Quality Press.

Knowles, Malcolm S. 1996. "Adult Learning." In *The ASTD Training and Development Handbook: A Guide to Human Resources Development*, ed. Robert L. Craig. New York: McGraw-Hill, p. 253.

Knowles, Malcolm S., and David E. Hartl. 1995. "The Adult Learner in the Technical Environment." In *The ASTD Technical and Skills Training Handbook*, ed. Leslie Kelly. New York: McGraw-Hill, p. 486.

Nolan, M. 1996. "Job Training." In *The ASTD Training and Development Handbook: A Guide to Human Resources Development*, ed. Robert L. Craig. New York: McGraw-Hill, p. 747.

Piskurich, G. M. 1996. "Self-Directed Learning." In *The ASTD Training and Development Handbook: A Guide to Human Resources Development*, ed. Robert L. Craig. New York: McGraw-Hill, pp. 453–72.

A quality manager's activities in the area of technology include identifying the techniques available, understanding jargon so as to make wise selections, and serving on multifunctional teams that develop technology-based training packages.

The most common form of technology-supported training today are help files in computer software. Much of the training activity formerly done manually is now being done, just-in-time, electronically. Software is continually being upgraded to provide more help. Frequently, this help is invaluable in guiding the user toward more effective and efficient use of the software. Unlike with earlier packaged computer applications, now most software providers do not provide user manuals in print. A help screen might assist in solving a very specific problem, but not having a printed reference manual prevents the user from positioning the help instruction in the context of the entire system. A vast computer book publishing industry has been created and computer schools are flourishing to fill this gap.

Instruction delivered by computers does not rely on person-to-person interaction. Such computer-based instruction offers the user flexibility in training location and scheduling. Importantly, computer-based training allows the user to set their own pace. A major advantage for the organization is that computer-based training provides consistency of content presented and usually lower per participant training time and cost. Disadvantages of computer-based training include the cost of purchasing packaged programs and, when customized training is necessary, expensive program preparation and the lack of learning from other participants and the experience of an instructor. Combining self-paced, computer-based instruction with periodic group discussions enables learners the flexibility noted as well as an opportunity to get additional insights and/or get back on track.

Computers have been used in instruction for less than 50 years, but computer-based training techniques and methods continue to grow at a rapid pace. Computer networks, especially the Internet, are revolutionizing the learning process. Some have questioned the need for university classrooms in a computer-rich society in which expert knowledge from any field can be quickly disseminated to all interested parties. Learners using the Internet can share questions, answers, and ideas with each other very conveniently. Chat rooms, news groups, and list servers all promote learning when used for that purpose. Company intranets, CD-ROMs, computer games, interactive computer-based simulations, computer-based tutorials, and computer-directed testing are also available to assist in training and/or education.

The learning scenario can be greatly enriched by technology. There is literally no limit (except time and money) to the realism and dynamism provided by types of computer-based training. Virtual reality, a technology that allows the user to interface with a computer in three dimensions, stimulates all five senses to persuade the user that the images presented are in fact reality. When used in training, virtual reality provides a safe, repeatable, and cost-effective way to teach techniques or operations that are dangerous or expensive to perform in real life.[8]

Interactive multimedia training, one of the most valuable benefits offered by technology, can be integrated into computer systems used by workers so that small units of training can be delivered the moment they are needed to support job performance. Furthermore, if the learning requirement is of a technological nature, the use of technology itself adds realism and an appropriate context.

A common mistake in technology-based training is confusing the medium for the message. An organization can lose sight of its real needs if it gets hung up on the marvels of computer software, video images, and so on. Another serious mistake when dealing with technology is overspending. The technological approach is inherently costly up front, and once the designers of a technologically advanced training package begin the development process, it is easy to continue in that direction despite serious questions about cost effectiveness.

Finally, technical approaches to training risk the loss of important human interaction as learners become accustomed to interacting with technical devices: screens, buttons, keyboards, and joysticks. "Technology in and of itself does not innovate—people do; they are the key to successful implementation of new technology.[9] If training does not accompany new technology, the value of the technology to the organization is greatly diminished.

Other Training Techniques

Other options for providing training include the following:

- using external experts to deliver a "packaged" program or to custom-design and deliver a company-specific program
- training and qualifying in-house trainers to deliver an externally developed program
- augment training presented by in-house trainers with known subject-matter experts from outside the organization ("gurus")
- establish book reading discussion groups or forums focusing on material to be learned
- take guided and focused tours of other organizations
- participate in a benchmarking team
- invite more experienced people from other organizations to come in and talk
- send individuals to a manufacturer's technical training course
- partner with a local college or university to bring educational programs to the organization
- periodically reexamine the job(s) for ways to improve the processes and perhaps eliminate the need for training in a particular area or simplify the training needed
- establish a "buddy" system until the trainee has mastered the job
- periodically rotate jobs and cross-train workers to provide additional operation effectiveness and keep workers motivated
- partner with local organizations with common interests to share training costs and introduce a variety of experiences for all partners' employees

JOB AIDS

Job aids, as the name implies, are virtually any type of media that can either substitute for formal training and/or provide reinforcement or reference after training.

Often, providing a job aid can be the simplest and most cost-effective way to ¿ workers in doing their jobs. A few types of job aids are the following:

- procedure manual
- laminated checklist hung at a workstation
- message on a computer screen, a buzzer, or other physical/aural interruption warning of a missing step or incorrectly performed function
- nested (drop-down) computer help screens taking the learner to increasingly greater detail
- instructions printed on the back of the form giving detailed instructions for completing the form
- pertinent information included for each critical step described on a shop work order or traveler
- tool mounting board that has a clearly marked place for each type of tool
- diagnostic decision tree for solving a problem
- audiotape accessed by the learner wearing earphones that guides the learner through each task step at the sequence and pace expected on achieving mastery

Rossett and Gautier-Downes cite eight situations in which job aids are appropriate:

- when the individual cannot be expected to remember how to do a task because he or she is rarely required to do it
- to offer support for individuals who confront lengthy, difficult, and information-intensive challenges
- when the consequences of error are high
- when performance relies on a large body of information
- when performance is dependent on knowledge, procedures, or approaches that change frequently
- when turnover is high and the task is simple
- when employees are expected to act in an empowered way with emphasized or new standards in mind
- when there is little time or few resources for training[10]

KEYS TO EFFECTIVE TRAINING

When performing training, the trainer should remember to KISS (keep it simple, Sam or Sylvia). When the participants are so enthralled with the gadgets and gizmos that they forget the training message, the trainer went too far. A theme park type of production is seldom needed, practical, or economical in presenting training. Additionally, training technology that is difficult to use can detract from learning or even shut down the training in the event of equipment malfunction or user error if training delivery is totally dependent on the technology.

Training delivered by straight lecture, although a prevalent method, is often boring, and fades rapidly (if it "sticks" at all). Trainees might understand little of the

Rossett, A., and J. H. Gautier-Downes. 1991. *A Handbook of Job Aids.* San Diego: Pfeiffer & Company.

Stamatis, D. H. 1997. *TQM Engineering Handbook.* New York: Marcel Dekker.

Thiagarajan, S. 1996. "Instructional Games, Simulations, and Role Plays." In *The ASTD Training and Development Handbook: A Guide to Human Resources Development,* ed. Robert L. Craig. New York: McGraw-Hill, pp. 517–33.

Tracey, William R. 1994. "Selecting a Delivery System." In *Human Resources Management and Development Handbook,* 2d ed., ed. William R. Tracey. New York: AMACOM.

Wlodkowski, J. J. 1985. *Enhancing Adult Motivation to Learn.* San Francisco: Jossey-Bass.

Sources for Training Games and Simulations

Caroselli, Marlene. 1996. *Quality Games for Trainers: 101 Playful Lessons in Quality and Continuous Improvement.* New York: McGraw-Hill.

HRDQ Publisher, 2002 Renaissance Boulevard #100, King of Prussia, PA 19406-2756, 800-633-4533; www.hrdq.com.

Jossey-Bass/Pfeiffer, 350 Sansome Street, Fifth Floor, San Francisco, CA 94104; 800-274-4434.

Talico Incorporated, 2320 South Third Street, #5, Jacksonville Beach, FL 32250; 904-241-1721; www.talico.com.

Training House, P.O. Box 3090, Princeton, NJ 08543-3090; 609-452-1505.

Additional Readings

Burns, Anthony. 1997. "Multimedia as a Quality Solution." *Quality Progress,* February, pp. 51–54.

Chapman, Arlen D. 1998. "Training for Today's Quality Manager." *Quality Digest,* April, pp. 49–51.

Cocheu, Ted. 1988. "Training for Quality." *INFO-LINE* (publication of the American Society for Training and Development), May, p. 74.

Dawson, Graydon. 1992. "The Critical Elements Missing from Most Total Quality Management Training." *Performance & Instruction,* October, pp. 15–20.

Dusharme, Dirk. 1995. "Computer-Based Training: Hewlett-Packard's Learning Edge." *Quality Digest,* January, pp. 28–35.

Fournies, Ferdinand F. 1978. *Coaching for Improved Work Performance.* New York: Van Nostrand Reinhold.

Gordon, Jack, Ron Zemke, and Philip Jones, eds. 1988. *Designing and Delivering Cost-Effective Training.* Minneapolis: Lakewood Books.

Hawthorne, E. M. 1987. *Evaluating Employee Training Programs.* Westport, Conn.: Greenwood Press.

Kaufman, R., and A. M. Rojas. 1993. *Needs Assessment: A Users Guide.* Englewood Cliffs, N.J.: Educational Technology Publications.

Knowles, Malcolm. 1975. *Self-Directed Learning: A Guide for Learners and Teachers.* New York: Cambridge Book Co.

❖❖

Lowerre, J. 1994. "Training for Effective Continuous Quality Improvement." *Quality Progress*, December, pp. 57–61.

Miller, J. A. 1992. "Training Requirements to Support Total Quality Management." *CMA Magazine*, November, p. 29.

Nopper, Norman S. 1993. "Reinventing the Factory with Lifelong Learning." *Training*, May, pp. 55–58.

Santo, Susan A. 1991. *TQM Training: Lessons from World-Class Practitioners*. (A report prepared for the American Society for Training & Development), August, 66 pp.

Silberman, Mel. 1990. *Active Training: A Handbook of Techniques, Designs, Case Examples, and Tips*. Lexington, Mass.: Lexington Books.

Spiess, Michael E. 1993. "Four by Four: Finding Time for TQM Training." *Training and Development*, February, pp. 11–15.

☞ Part 8 Endnotes ☜

Chapter 45

1. Thomas J. Cartin and Donald J. Jacoby, *A Review of Managing Quality and a Primer for the Certified Quality Manager Exam* (Milwaukee, ASQ Quality Press, 1997), p. 230.
2. Berton H. Gunter, "Gunter's Last Column," *Quality Progress*, April 1998, p. 111.
3. Cartin and Jacoby, p. 229.
4. Joseph M. Juran and Frank M. Gryna, eds., *Juran's Quality Control Handbook*, 4th ed. (New York: McGraw-Hill, 1988), pp. 11.4–11.5.
5. Joseph H. Boyett and Henry P. Conn, *Maximizing Performance Management* (Lakewood, Colo.: Glenbridge Publishing, 1988), p. 8.

Chapter 46

1. Leslie Kelly, ed., *The ASTD Technical Skills and Training Handbook* (New York: McGraw-Hill, 1995), p. 214.
2. Richard S. Johnson, *Quality Training Practices* (Milwaukee: ASQC Quality Press, 1993), p. 179.
3. Ibid., pp. 191–92.
4. Ibid., p. 179.
5. John L. Hradesky, *Total Quality Management Handbook* (New York: McGraw-Hill, 1995), p. 57.

Chapter 47

1. Leslie Kelly, ed., *The ASTD Technical Skills and Training Handbook* (New York: McGraw-Hill, 1995), pp. 54–55.
2. Donald L. Kirkpatrick, *Evaluating Training Programs: The Four Levels* (San Francisco: Berrett-Koehler, 1994), p. 4.
3. Richard S. Johnson, *Quality Training Practices* (Milwaukee: ASQC Quality Press, 1993), p. 88.

Chapter 48

1. Donald L. Kirkpatrick, "Techniques for Evaluating Training Programs," a four-part series beginning in the November 1959 issue of the *Training Director's Journal*.
2. Dana Gaines Robinson and James C. Robinson, *Training for Impact: How to Link Training to Business Needs and Measure the Results* (San Francisco: Jossey-Bass, 1990), p. 168.
3. Russell Westcott, "Applied Behavior Management Training," in *In Action: Measuring Return on Investment;* "Behavior Management Training," in *Human Resources Management and Development Handbook,* 2d ed.; and "ROQI: Overlooked Quality Tool," in *The Total Quality Review.*
4. Jack J. Phillips, 1996. *The ASTD Training and Development Handbook,* 1st ed. New York: McGraw-Hill.
5. Joseph M. Juran and Frank M. Gryna, eds., *Juran's Quality Control Handbook,* 4th ed. (New York: McGraw-Hill, 1988), pp. 11.9–11.10.

Chapter 49

1. Malcolm Knowles, "Adult Learning" in *The ASTD Training and Development Handbook: A Guide to Human Resources Development,* 3rd ed., ed. Robert L. Craig (New York: McGraw-Hill, 1996), pp. 171–72.
2. Malcolm S. Knowles and David E. Hartl, "The Adult Learner in the Technical Environment," in *The ASTD Technical and Skills Training Handbook,* ed. Leslie Kelly (New York: McGraw-Hill, 1995), p. 12.
3. Richard S. Johnson, *TQM: The Mechanics of Quality Processes* (Milwaukee: ASQC Quality Press, 1993), pp. 147–48.
4. Ibid., p. 147.
5. William R. Tracey, "Selecting a Delivery System," in *Human Resources Management and Development Handbook,* 2d ed., ed. William R. Tracey (New York: AMACOM, 1994), p. 1191.
6. Madeline F. Finnerty, "Coaching for Growth and Development," in *The ASTD Training and Development Handbook: A Guide to Human Resources Development,* ed. Robert L. Craig (New York: McGraw-Hill, 1996), p. 423.
7. S. Thiagarajan, "Instructional Games, Simulations, and Role Plays," in *The ASTD Training and Development Handbook: A Guide to Human Resources Development,* ed. Robert L. Craig (New York: McGraw-Hill, 1996), pp. 519–20.
8. D. H. Stamatis, *TQM Engineering Handbook* (New York: Marcel Dekker, 1997), pp. 411–13.
9. P. Fernberg, "Learn to Compete: Training's Vital Role in Business Survival." *Managing Office Technology,* September 1993, pp. 14–16.
10. A. Rossett and J. H. Gautier-Downes, *A Handbook of Job Aids* (San Diego: Pfeiffer & Company, 1991).

Appendix A: CQM Body of Knowledge*

The following is an outline of the topics that constitute the Body of Knowledge for a quality manager.

- **I.** Quality Standards (8 questions)
    - **A.** Total Quality Management (TQM)
    - **B.** Continuous Process Improvement
    - **C.** Cycle Time Reduction
    - **D.** Supplier Management
    - **E.** Customer Service
    - **F.** Quality Awards/Quality Standards Criteria (e.g., Baldrige, ISO 9000)
- **II.** Organizations and Their Functions (12 questions)
    - **A.** Organizational Assessment
    - **B.** Organizational Structures (e.g., matrix, hierarchial)
    - **C.** Quality Functions within the Organization
    - **D.** Communication within the Organization
    - **E.** Change Agents and Their Effects on Organizations
    - **F.** Management Styles (e.g., by facts and data, by coaching/other leadership styles)
    - **G.** Business Functions
        - **1.** External: safety, legal and regulatory, product liability, environment, technology, process
        - **2.** Internal: human resources, engineering, sales and marketing, finance, R&D, purchasing
- **III.** Quality Needs and Overall Strategic Plans (18 questions)
    - **A.** Linkage between Quality Function Needs and Overall Strategic Plan
    - **B.** Linkage between Strategic Plan and Quality Plan
    - **C.** Theory of Variation (common and special causes)
    - **D.** Quality Function Mission
    - **E.** Priority of Quality Function within the Organization
    - **F.** Metrics and Goals That Drive Organizational Performance

*Reprinted from ASQ Certification Department, *Certified Quality Manager,* booklet (Milwaukee: American Society for Quality, 1998).

      G. Formulation of Quality Principles and Policies

      H. Requirements to Manage the Quality Function

IV. Customer Satisfaction and Focus (30 questions)

      A. Types of Customers (e.g., internal, external, end user)

      B. Elements of Customer-Driven Organizations

      C. Customer Expectations, Priorities, Needs and "Voice"

      D. Customer Relationship Management and Commitment (e.g., complaints, feedback, guarantees, corrective actions)

      E. Customer Identification and Segmentation

      F. Partnership and Alliances between Customers and Suppliers

      G. Communication Techniques (e.g., surveys, focus groups, satisfaction/ complaint cards)

      H. Multiple-customer Management and Conflict Resolution

      I. Customer Retention/Loyalty

V. Project Management (30 questions)

      A. Planning

         1. Integrated quality initiatives

         2. Short- and long-term quality plans and objectives

         3. Feedback loops

         4. Performance measures

            a. Timeliness

            b. Resources

            c. Methodology

         5. Relevant stakeholders

         6. Benchmarking

         7. Budgeting

         8. Benefit-cost analysis

      B. Implementation

         1. Management support and organizational roadblocks

         2. Short-term (tactical) plans

         3. Cross-functional collaboration

         4. Continuous review and enhancement of quality process

         5. Documentation and procedures

VI. Continuous Improvement (22 questions)

      A. Tools

         1. Quality control tools (charts and diagrams)

         2. Quality management tools (diagrams and matrices)

         3. PDCA (plan, do, check, act)

   B. Cost of Quality

   C. Process Improvement

   D. Trend Analysis

   E. Measurement Issues

    1. Reliability and validity

    2. Sampling plans and other statistical analysis

    3. Specifications, calibration, and process capability

   F. Concurrent Engineering and Process Mapping

VII. Human Resource Management (15 questions)

   A. Leadership Roles and Responsibilities

    1. Conflict resolution

    2. Professional ethics

   B. Quality Staffing Issues

    1. Selection

    2. Performance evaluation

    3. Professional development

    4. Goals and objectives

   C. Quality Responsibilities in Job/Position Descriptions

   D. Employee/Team Empowerment

   E. Team Formation and Evolution

    1. Process improvement teams

    2. Work groups

    3. Other self-managed teams

   F. Team Management

    1. Facilitation techniques

    2. Member roles and responsibilities

    3. Performance evaluation

    4. Recognition and reward

VIII. Training and Education (15 questions)

   A. Importance of Top-down Support and Strategic Planning for Quality Training

   B. Training Subgroups and Topics

    1. Management training—general quality principles

    2. Employee training—implementation of quality plans

    3. Facilitator training

   C. Training Needs Analysis

   D. Post-training Evaluation and Enforcement

❖❖❖

   E. Tools

      1. Lectures, workbooks, case studies, on-the-job training

      2. Use of technology in training (videos, computer-delivered instruction, etc.)

BODY OF KNOWLEDGE FOR CONSTRUCTED-RESPONSE PORTION (2 QUESTIONS)

Candidates will be presented with two open-ended questions selected from the following areas and will have 45 minutes in which to write responses to both problems or situations presented. Candidates may split their time spent on the problems as they like. Their responses will be graded on their knowledge of Quality Management, as it relates to the content areas listed below, as well as the following skills and abilities: communication skills; critical-thinking skills, including the ability to analyze and synthesize information; personnel management skills; and general management skills.

   A. Advise Management of the Role of Quality Systems

      1. Establish linkage between Quality initiatives and the organization's overall strategic and business plans

      2. Identify and prioritize areas where Quality initiatives and functions can be deployed within the organization

      3. Formulate Quality-related principles and policies (e.g., reward/recognition structures; continuous improvement)

      4. Identify ways of using Quality systems to meet customer needs

      5. Identify the resource requirements necessary for a Quality program

   B. Plan and Design Quality Projects and Procedures

      1. Plan, design, and prioritize integrated Quality initiatives that will result in continuous quality improvement

      2. Develop short- and long-term Quality plans

      3. Design assessment and tracking systems for Quality activities, including metrics and their applications

      4. Use internal and external customer expectations as a basis for specifying Quality system needs

      5. Involve relevant stakeholders (suppliers, customers, unions) in the design and implementation of Quality projects

      6. Design feedback loops to provide Quality information to the organization

   C. Implement Quality Initiatives

      1. Maintain organizational focus on Quality processes using motivational techniques and other approaches

      2. Create tactical implementation plans

      3. Optimize trade-off between Quality and resources

   D. Support Quality Training
   1. Identify Quality training needs
   2. Collaborate in the development, delivery, and evaluation of Quality training programs

   E. Assess Quality System Performance
   1. Develop and implement plans to evaluate the effectiveness of the Quality system
   2. Assess the effectiveness and efficiency of Quality projects and initiatives
   3. Use results of Quality assessments to improve processes

   F. Manage the Quality Function
   1. Define the mission of the Quality function
   2. Develop, review, reconcile/adjust budgets for the Quality function
   3. Evaluate and oversee the development of Quality staff
   4. Establish goals and objectives of the Quality function
   5. Develop Quality systems for supplier management processes
   6. Develop and implement supplier certification program
   7. Work with Human Resources to include Quality elements in position/job descriptions

Appendix B: Leading Contributors to the Quality Field
❖

This appendix lists the main tenets and summarizes the philosophies of leading contributors ("gurus") of the quality field. It is not meant to be an all-inclusive discussion of their ideas and work. Readers are encouraged to consult the references in the list of additional readings at the end of this appendix for more information.

W. EDWARDS DEMING

W. Edwards Deming was a prominent consultant, teacher, and author on the subject of quality. After he shared his expertise in statistical process control to help the U.S. war effort during World War II, the War Department sent Deming to Japan in 1946 to help that nation recover from its wartime losses. Deming published more than 200 works; the 14 points for transformation of management and the seven deadly diseases listed in *Out of the Crisis* are perhaps some of his best-known tenets.

Deming's 14 Points for Transformation of Management

1. Create constancy of purpose for improvement of product and service.
2. Adopt the new philosophy.
3. Cease dependence on mass inspection.
4. End the practice of awarding business on the price tag alone.
5. Improve constantly and forever the system of production and service.
6. Institute training.
7. Adopt and institute leadership.
8. Drive out fear.
9. Break down barriers between staff areas.
10. Eliminate slogans, exhortations, and targets for the workforce.
11a. Eliminate numerical quotas for the workforce.
11b. Eliminate numerical goals for people in management.
12. Remove barriers that rob people of pride of workmanship.
13. Encourage education and self-improvement for everyone.
14. Take action to accomplish the transformation.

The Seven Deadly Diseases

1. *Lack of constancy of purpose.* A company that is without constancy of purpose has no long-range plans for staying in business. Management is insecure, and so are employees.

2. *Emphasis on short-term profits.* Looking to increase the quarterly dividend undermines quality and productivity.

3. *Evaluation by performance, merit rating, or annual review of performance.* The effects of these are devastating—teamwork is destroyed, rivalry is nurtured. Performance ratings build fear and leave people bitter, despondent, and beaten. They also encourage defection in the ranks of management.

4. *Mobility of management.* Job-hopping managers never understand the companies they work for and are never there long enough to follow through on long-term changes that are necessary for quality and productivity.

5. *Running a company on visible figures alone.* The most important figures are unknown and unknowable—the "multiplier" effect of a happy customer, for example.

6. *Excessive medical costs for employee health care.* These increase the final costs for goods and services.

7. *Excessive costs of warranty.* These are often fueled by lawyers who work on the basis of contingency fees.

PHILIP B. CROSBY

Philip B. Crosby is the founder and chairman of the board of Career IV, an executive management consulting firm. He is most well known for introducing the idea of zero defects in 1961. Crosby defines quality as conformance to requirements; therefore, quality is measured by the cost of nonconformance. Using this approach means that one arrives at a performance goal of zero defects.

Crosby equates quality management with prevention. Therefore, inspection, testing, checking, and other nonpreventive techniques have no place in quality management. Crosby believes that statistical levels of compliance program people for failure. Furthermore, he maintains that absolutely no reason exists for having errors or defects in any product or service.

Companies should adopt a quality "vaccine" to prevent nonconformance. The three ingredients of this vaccine are determination, education, and implementation. Quality improvement is a process, not a program; it should be permanent and lasting. Crosby's 14 steps to quality improvement summarize his quality philosophy.

Crosby's 14 Steps to Quality Improvement

1. Make it clear that management is committed to quality.
2. Form quality improvement teams with representatives from each department.
3. Determine how to measure where current and potential quality problems lie.
4. Evaluate the cost of quality and explain its use as a management tool.
5. Raise the quality awareness and personal concern of all employees.
6. Take formal actions to correct problems identified through previous steps.
7. Establish a committee for the zero defects program.

8. Train all employees to actively carry out their part of the quality improvement program.

9. Hold a "zero defects day" to let all employees realize that there has been a change.

10. Encourage individuals to establish improvement goals for themselves and their groups.

11. Encourage employees to communicate to management the obstacles they face in attaining their improvement goals.

12. Recognize and appreciate those who participate.

13. Establish quality councils to communicate on a regular basis.

14. Do it all over again to emphasize that the quality improvement program never ends.

ARMAND V. FEIGENBAUM

Armand V. Feigenbaum is the founder and president of General Systems Co., an international engineering company that designs and implements total quality systems. He originated the concept of total quality control in his book *Total Quality Control,* published in 1951. Total quality control approaches quality as a strategic business tool that requires awareness by everyone in the company, just as cost and schedule are regarded in most companies today. Quality reaches far beyond defect management on the shop floor: It is a philosophy and commitment to excellence.

Quality is a way of corporate life, a way of managing. Total quality control has an organization-wide impact that involves implementation of customer-oriented quality activities. This is a prime responsibility of general management as well as the mainline operations of marketing, engineering, production, industrial relations, finance, and service and of the quality control function itself at the most economical levels. Feigenbaum defines total quality control as being excellence driven rather than defect driven.

An overview of Feigenbaum's approach is given in his "Three Steps to Quality" and "The Four Deadly Sins." These and other ideas are explored further in the "Nineteen Steps to Quality Improvement," derived from several of Feigenbaum's works.

Three Steps to Quality

Feigenbaum suggests that the quest for quality consists of three elements: quality leadership, modern quality technology, and organizational commitment.

Quality Leadership. Continuous management emphasis and leadership must exist in quality. Quality must be thoroughly planned in specific terms. This is an excellence-driven approach rather than the traditional failure-driven approach. Attaining quality excellence means keeping a constant focus on maintaining quality. This sort of continuous approach is very demanding on management. The establishment of a quality circle program or a corrective action team is not sufficient for its ongoing success.

Modern Quality Technology. The traditional quality department cannot resolve 80 percent to 90 percent of quality problems. In a modern setting, all members of the organization must be responsible for the quality of their product or service. This means integrating office staff into the process as well as engineers and shop floor workers. Error-free performance should be the goal. New techniques must be evaluated and implemented as appropriate. What might be an acceptable level of quality to a customer today might not be acceptable tomorrow.

Organizational Commitment. For quality to be achieved and continued, continuous motivation and more are required. Training that is specifically related to the task at hand is of paramount importance. In the United States, quality should be considered a strategic element of business planning.

KAORU ISHIKAWA

Professor of engineering at the Science University of Tokyo and president of the Musashi Institute of Technology in Tokyo, Ishikawa was an early student of Deming and a member of the Union of Japanese Scientists and Engineers (JUSE). He edited the *Guide to Quality Control,* prepared for training of foremen and middle managers in quality control and problem diagnostic tools and later published it as a textbook that was marketed in the United States. In 1943, Ishikawa developed the cause-and-effect diagram, also called the Ishikawa diagram or the fishbone diagram. In his book *What Is Total Quality Control? The Japanese Way,* he defines total quality control as follows:

◆ QC is the responsibility of all workers and all divisions.

◆ TQC is a group activity and cannot be done by individuals. It calls for teamwork.

◆ TQC will not fail if all members cooperate, from the president down to line workers and sales personnel.

◆ In TQC, middle management will be frequently talked about and criticized— be prepared.

◆ QC circle activities are a part of TQC.

◆ Do not confuse objectives with the means to attain them.

◆ TQC is not a miracle drug; its properties are more like those of Chinese herb medicine.

To achieve total quality control, a thought revolution must occur:

◆ Quality first—not short-term profit first.

◆ Consumer orientation—not producer orientation. Think from the standpoint of the other party.

◆ The next process is your customer—breaking down the barrier of sectionalism.

◆ Using facts and data to make presentations—utilization of statistical methods.

- Respect for humanity as a management philosophy—full participatory management.
- Cross-function management.

He advocates four types of audits:

- audit by the president
- audit by the head of the unit (e.g., division head or branch office manager)
- QC audit by the QC staff
- mutual QC audit

JOSEPH M. JURAN

Joseph M. Juran has pursued a varied career in management as an engineer, executive, government administrator, university professor, labor arbitrator, corporate director, and consultant. Specializing in managing for quality, he has authored hundreds of papers and a dozen books, including *Juran's Quality Control Handbook* (with Frank M. Gryna), considered by many to be the ultimate quality reference book.

Juran defines quality as consisting of two different but related concepts:

- One form of quality is *income oriented* and consists of those features of the product that meet customer needs and thereby produce income. In this sense, higher quality usually costs more.
- A second form of quality is *cost oriented* and consists of freedom from failures and deficiencies. In this sense, higher quality usually costs less.

Juran points out that managing for quality involves three basic managerial processes: quality planning, quality control, and quality improvement. (These processes parallel those long used to manage for finance.) His "trilogy" (from *Juran on Leadership for Quality* and *Juran's Quality Control Handbook,* among other publications) shows how these processes are interrelated.

Juran's Approach to Quality Improvement

For Juran, quality improvement comes first. His structured approach for this was introduced in his book *Managerial Breakthrough* (1964). This approach includes a list of nondelegable responsibilities for upper managers:

- Create awareness of the need and opportunity for improvement.
- Mandate quality improvement; make it a part of every job description.
- Create the infrastructure: Establish a quality council; select projects for improvement; appoint teams; and provide facilitators.
- Provide training in how to improve quality.
- Review progress regularly.
- Give recognition to the winning teams.
- Propagandize the results.

◆ Revise the reward system to enforce the rate of improvement.

◆ Maintain momentum by enlarging the business plan to include goals for quality improvement.

In Juran's view, a major, long-neglected opportunity for improvement lies in the business processes.

Juran's Approach to Quality Planning

As described in *Juran on Leadership for Quality*, quality planning should accomplish the following:

◆ meet customers' needs

◆ minimize product satisfaction

◆ avoid costly deficiencies (costly redoing of prior work)

◆ optimize company performance

◆ provide participation for those who are affected

Juran's quality planning roadmap, illustrated in Chapter 22 of this handbook, consists of the following steps:

◆ identify customers

◆ discover customers' needs

◆ translate (from their language, or needs, to your language, or product features)

◆ develop product

◆ develop process

◆ transfer to operations

Juran's Approach to Quality Control

Control takes place at all levels, from the CEO down to the workers, and all use the same feedback loop, which is the following:

◆ The sensor (which is "plugged into the process") evaluates actual performance.

◆ The sensor reports this performance to an umpire.

◆ The umpire also receives information on what the goal or standard is.

◆ The umpire compares actual performance to the goal. If the difference warrants action, the umpire energizes an actuator.

◆ The actuator makes the changes needed to bring performance in line.

To achieve control, the process must have numerical measures and adjustment capability. The goal of management should be to achieve what Juran calls "self-control" in all processes, wherein the process operator is capable of making all adjustments necessary to maintain control. Planning for control is part of the function of designing the process.

Juran identifies the ingredients of the Japanese quality revolution as follows:

- Upper managers took charge of managing for quality.
- They trained the entire hierarchy in the processes of managing for quality.
- They undertook to improve quality at a revolutionary rate.
- They provided for workforce participation.
- They added quality goals to the business plan.

Juran feels that the United States and other Western countries should adopt similar strategies to attain and retain world-class quality status.

Juran and Total Quality Management

Juran defines three levels of quality management:

- strategic quality management, which concerns itself mostly with policies
- operational quality management, which concerns itself with process management
- the workforce, which concerns itself with specifications and work procedures

A strong proponent of TQM, Juran defines TQM as a collection of certain quality-related activities:

- Quality becomes a part of each upper management agenda.
- Quality goals enter the business plan.
- Stretch goals are derived from benchmarking: Focus is on the customer and on meeting competition, and there are goals for annual quality improvement.
- Goals are deployed to the action levels.
- Training is done at all levels.
- Measurement is established throughout.
- Upper managers regularly review progress against goals.
- Recognition is given for superior performance.
- The reward system is revised.

WALTER A. SHEWHART

Walter A. Shewhart is referred to as the father of statistical quality control because he brought together the disciplines of statistics, engineering, and economics. He described the basic principles of this new discipline in his book *Economic Control of Quality of Manufactured Product*, the first statistics text focused on quality and a benchmark reference for more than a decade. Shewhart managed the Bell Laboratories, which pioneered the quality discipline and gave the profession some of its most capable experts. Mentor of both Juran and Deming, Shewhart did extensive research in statistics and probability and applied it to the Western Electric processes. He also invented control charts (the first control chart was a p chart) and pioneered the use of acceptance sampling as a lot-by-lot control.

❖❖

GENICHI TAGUCHI

Genichi Taguchi is the executive director of the American Supplier Institute, the director of the Japan Industrial Technology Institute, and an honorary professor at Nanjing Institute of Technology in China. Taguchi is well known for developing a methodology to improve quality and reduce costs, which, in the United States, is referred to as the *Taguchi methods*. He defines the quality of a product as "the (minimum) loss imparted by the product to society from the time the product is shipped." From this, he designed the Taguchi loss function, which translates any deviation of a product from its target parameter into a financial measure. The process of reducing the variation on the basis of designed experiments is called *parameter design*. Taguchi maintains that the goal is the most robust combination of product and process, that is, that the product that most consistently meets the customers' requirements by being most consistently produced by the process (not necessarily the most desirable product or the most efficient process but the most robust outcome of the combination of the two). The Taguchi loss function is a driver for continuous improvement.

🏮 Additional Readings 🏮

Crosby, Philip B. 1992. *Completeness: Quality for the 21st Century.* New York: Dutton/New American Library.

——. 1988. *The Eternally Successful Organization: The Art of Corporate Wellness.* New York: McGraw-Hill Book.

——. 1979. *Quality Is Free.* New York: New American Library.

——. 1996. *Quality Is Still Free: Making Quality Certain in Uncertain Times.* Milwaukee, Wis.: ASQC Quality Press.

——. 1984. *Quality without Tears: The Art of Hassle Free Management.* New York: McGraw-Hill.

——. 1986. *Running Things.* New York: McGraw-Hill.

Deming, W. Edwards. 1994. *The New Economics for Industry, Government, Education.* 2nd ed. Milwaukee: ASQC Quality Press.

——. 1986. *Out of the Crisis.* Cambridge: Massachusetts Institute of Technology, Center for Advanced Engineering Studies.

Dobyns, L., and C. Crawford-Mason. 1994. *Thinking about Quality: Progress, Wisdom, and the Deming Philosophy.* Milwaukee: ASQC Quality Press.

Feigenbaum, Armand V. 1991. *Total Quality Control.* 3rd ed., rev. New York: McGraw-Hill.

Ishikawa, Kaoru. 1982. *Guide to Quality Control.* Asian Productivity Organization. Distributed in U.S. by Unipub Ann Arbor, Mich.

——. 1985. *What Is Total Quality Control? The Japanese Way.* Englewood Cliffs, N.J.: Prentice Hall.

Juran, Joseph M. 1989. *Juran on Leadership for Quality.* New York: The Free Press.

——. 1992. *Juran on Quality Design: The New Steps for Planning Quality into Goods and Services.* Milwaukee, Wis.: ASQC Quality Press.

——. 1989. *Leadership for Quality.* Milwaukee: ASQC Quality Press.

——. 1995. *Managerial Breakthrough.* Rev. ed. Milwaukee: ASQC Quality Press.

——, ed. 1995. *A History of Managing for Quality: The Evolution, Trends, and Future Directions of Managing for Quality.* Milwaukee: ASQC Quality Press.

——. 1993. *Quality Planning and Analysis.* 3rd ed. New York: McGraw-Hill.

——, eds. 1988. *Juran's Quality Control Handbook.* 4th ed. New York: McGraw-Hill.

Latzko, William J., and David M. Sanders. 1995. *Four Days with Dr. Deming: A Strategy for Modern Methods of Management.* Milwaukee: ASQC Quality Press.

Lochner, R. H., and J. E. Matar. 1990. *Designing for Quality: An Introduction to the Best of Taguchi and Western Methods of Statistical Experimental Design.* Milwaukee: ASQC Quality Press.

Philip Crosby Associates. 1985. *Quality Improvement through Defect Prevention.* Winter Park, Fla.: Philip Crosby Associates.

Rosander, A. C. 1994. *Deming's 14 Points Applied to Services.* Milwaukee: ASQC Quality Press.

Scherkenback, W. W. 1991. *The Deming Route to Quality and Productivity: Roadmaps and Roadblocks.* Milwaukee: ASQC Quality Press.

Taguchi, Genichi. 1986. *Introduction to Quality Engineering.* Dearborn, Mich.: American Supplier Institute.

Walton, Mary. 1990. *Deming Management at Work.* Milwaukee: ASQC Quality Press.

Appendix C: Glossary

❖❖

A

ability test: an assessment device that measures a person's ability to learn or acquire skills (also referred to as an aptitude test).

acceptable quality level (AQL): when a continuing series of lots is considered, a quality level that, for the purposes of sampling inspection, is the limit of a satisfactory process average.

acceptance sampling: inspection of a sample from a lot to decide whether to accept or not accept that lot. There are two types: attributes sampling and variables sampling. In attributes sampling, the presence or absence of a characteristic is noted in each of the units inspected. In variables sampling, the numerical magnitude of a characteristic is measured and recorded for each inspected unit; this involves reference to a continuous scale of some kind.

acceptance sampling plan: a specific plan that indicates the sampling sizes and the associated acceptance or nonacceptance criteria to be used. In attributes sampling, for example, there are single, double, multiple, sequential, chain, and skip-lot sampling plans. In variables sampling, there are single, double, and sequential sampling plans. (For detailed descriptions of these plans, see the standard ANSI/ISO/ASQC A35342, *Statistics—Vocabulary and Symbols— Statistical Quality Control.*)

accreditation: certification by a duly recognized body of the facilities, capability, objectivity, competence, and integrity of an agency, service, or operational group or individual to provide the specific service or operation needed. For example, the Registrar Accreditation Board accredits those organizations that register companies to the ISO 9000 series standards.

accuracy: a characteristic of measurement which addresses how close an observed value is to the true value. It answers the question, "Is it right?"

ACSI: The American Customer Satisfaction Index, released for the first time in October 1994, is a new economic indicator, a cross-industry measure of the satisfaction of U.S. household customers with the quality of the goods and services available to them—both those goods and services produced within the United States and those provided as imports from foreign firms that have substantial market shares or dollar sales. The ACSI is cosponsored by the University of Michigan Business School and ASQC.

affinity diagram: a management and planning tool used to organize ideas into natural groupings in a way that stimulates new, creative ideas.

analysis: the first phase in the design of instruction in which data are gathered to identify gaps between actual and desired organizational performance.

❖❖

analysis of means (ANOM): a statistical procedure for troubleshooting industrial processes and analyzing the results of experimental designs with factors at fixed levels. It provides a graphical display of data. Ellis R. Ott developed the procedure in 1967 because he observed that nonstatisticians had difficulty understanding analysis of variance. Analysis of means is easier for quality practitioners to use because it is an extension of the control chart. In 1973, Edward G. Schilling further extended the concept, enabling analysis of means to be used with nonnormal distributions and attributes data where the normal approximation to the binomial distribution does not apply. This is referred to as analysis of means for treatment effects.

analysis of variance (ANOVA): a basic statistical technique for analyzing experimental data. It subdivides the total variation of a data set into meaningful component parts associated with specific sources of variation in order to test a hypothesis on the parameters of the model or to estimate variance components. There are three models: fixed, random, and mixed.

ANSI: American National Standards Institute

AOQ: average outgoing quality

AOQL: average outgoing quality limit

appraisal costs: costs incurred to determine the degree of conformance to quality requirements.

AQL: acceptable quality level

AQP: Association for Quality and Participation

arrow diagram: a management and planning tool used to develop the best possible schedule and appropriate controls to accomplish the schedule; the critical path method and the program evaluation review technique make use of arrow diagrams.

ASME: American Society of Mechanical Engineers

ASQ: a society of individual and organizational members dedicated to the ongoing development, advancement, and promotion of quality concepts, principles, and technologies. The Society serves more than 130,000 individuals and 1000 corporate members in the United States and 63 other countries.

ASTD: American Society for Training and Development

ASTM: American Society for Testing and Materials

attribute data: go/no-go information. The control charts based on attribute data include percent chart, number of affected units chart, count chart, count-per-unit chart, quality score chart, and demerit chart.

availability: the ability of a product to be in a state to perform its designated function under stated conditions at a given time. Availability can be expressed by the ratio: uptime being when the product is operative (in active use and in standby state) and downtime being when the product is inoperative (while under repair, awaiting spare parts, and so on).

❖❖

average chart: a control chart in which the subgroup average, X-, is used to evaluate the stability of the process level.

average outgoing quality (AOQ): the expected average quality level of outgoing product for a given value of incoming product quality.

average outgoing quality limit (AOQL): the maximum average outgoing quality over all possible levels of incoming quality for a given acceptance sampling plan and disposal specification.

award: something given in recognition of performance or quality.

B

benchmarking: an improvement process in which a company measures its performance against that of best-in-class companies, determines how those companies achieved their performance levels, and uses the information to improve its own performance. The subjects that can be benchmarked include strategies, operations, processes, and procedures.

bias: a characteristic of measurement that refers to a systematic difference.

big Q, little Q: a term used to contrast the difference between managing for quality in all business processes and products (big Q) and managing for quality in a limited capacity, traditionally in only factory products and processes (little q).

blemish: an imperfection that is severe enough to be noticed but should not cause any real impairment with respect to intended normal or reasonably foreseeable use (see also "defect," imperfection," and "nonconformity).

block diagram: a diagram that shows the operation, interrelationships, and interdependencies of components in a system. Boxes, or blocks (hence the name), represent the components; connecting lines between the blocks represent interfaces. There are two types of block diagrams: a functional block diagram, which shows a system's subsystems and lower-level products, their interrelationships, and interfaces with other systems, and a reliability block diagram, which is similar to the functional block diagram except that it is modified to emphasize those aspects influencing reliability.

brainstorming: a problem-solving tool that teams use to generate as many ideas as possible related to a particular subject. Team members begin by offering all their ideas; the ideas are not discussed or reviewed until after the brainstorming session.

breakthrough: a method of solving chronic problems that results from the effective execution of a strategy designed to reach the next level of quality. Such change often requires a paradigm shift within the organization.

BSI: British Standards Institute

business partnering: the creation of cooperative business alliances between constituencies within an organization or between an organization and its customers. Partnering occurs through a pooling of resources in a trusting

❖❖❖

atmosphere focused on continuous, mutual improvement (see also customer–supplier partnership).

business processes: processes that focus on what the organization does as a business and how it goes about doing it. A business has functional processes (generating output within a single department) and cross-functional processes (generating output across several functions or departments).

C

c chart: count chart (see also attribute data).

calibration: the comparison of a measurement instrument or system of unverified accuracy to a measurement instrument or system of a known accuracy to detect any variation from the required performance specification.

capability ratio (Cp): is equal to the specification tolerance width divided by the process capability.

cascading training: training that is implemented in an organization from the top down.

cause-and-effect diagram: a tool for analyzing process dispersion. It is also referred to as the Ishikawa diagram, because Kaoru Ishikawa developed it and the fishbone diagram, because the complete diagram resembles a fish skeleton. The diagram illustrates the main causes and subcauses leading to an effect (symptom). The cause-and-effect diagram is one of the seven tools of quality.

champion: an individual who has accountability and responsibility for many processes or who is involved in making strategic-level decisions for the organization. The champion ensures ongoing dedication of project resources and monitors strategic alignment (also referred to as a sponsor).

change agent: the person who takes the lead in transforming a company into a quality organization by providing guidance during the planning phase, facilitating implementation, and supporting those who pioneer the changes.

check sheet: a simple data-recording device. The check sheet is custom-designed by the user, which allows him or her to readily interpret the results. The check sheet is one of the seven tools of quality. Check sheets are often confused with data sheets and checklists (see also *checklist*).

checklist: a tool used to ensure that all important steps or actions in an operation have been taken. Checklists contain items that are important or relevant to an issue or situation. Checklists are often confused with check sheets and data sheets (see also check sheet).

chronic problem: a long-standing adverse situation that can be remedied by changing the status quo. For example, actions such as revising an unrealistic manufacturing process or addressing customer defections can change the status quo and remedy the situation.

CMI: certified mechanical inspector (ASQ)

coaching: a continuous improvement technique by which people receive one-to-one learning through demonstration and practice and that is characterized by immediate feedback and correction.

commercial/industrial market: refers to business market customers who are described by variables such as location, SIC code, buyer industry, technological sophistication, purchasing process, size, ownership, and financial strength.

common causes of variation: causes that are inherent in any process all the time. A process that has only common causes of variation is said to be stable or predictable.

company culture: a system of values, beliefs, and behaviors inherent in a company. To optimize business performance, top management must define and create the necessary culture.

competence: refers to a person's ability to learn and perform a particular activity. Competence generally consists of skill, knowledge, aptitude, and temperament components.

concurrent engineering: a process in which an organization designs a product or service using input and evaluations from business units and functions early in the process, anticipating problems, and balancing the needs of all parties. The emphasis is on upstream prevention versus downstream correction and maintaining customer requirements.

conformance: an affirmative indication or judgment that a product or service has met the requirements of a relevant specification, contract, or regulation.

conformance quality: occurs when a company focuses on conforming to requirements, doing things right the first time, and reducing scrap and rework.

consensus building: a decision-making approach in which a facilitator makes a decision only after ensuring that all team members support the decision.

constancy of purpose: occurs when goals and objectives are properly aligned to the organizational vision and mission.

consulting: a decision-making approach in which a facilitator talks to others and considers their input before making a decision.

consumer market customers: end users of a product or service.

consumer's risk: for a sampling plan, refers to the probability of acceptance of a lot, the quality of which has a designated numerical value representing a level that is seldom desirable. Usually the designated value will be the limiting quality level.

continuous probability distribution: means that the greatest number of observations fall in the center with fewer observations falling on either side of the average, forming a normal bell-shaped curve.

continuous process improvement: includes the actions taken throughout an organization to increase the effectiveness and efficiency of activities and processes in order to provide added benefits to the customer and organization. It is considered a subset of total quality management and operates according to the premise that organizations can always make improvements. Continuous improvement can also be equated with reducing process variation.

control chart: a basic tool that consists of a chart with upper and lower control limits on which values of some statistical measure for a series of samples or subgroups are plotted. It frequently shows a central line to help detect a trend of plotted values toward either control unit. It is used to monitor and analyze variation from a process to see whether the process is in statistical control.

corrective action: the implementation of solutions resulting in the reduction or elimination of an identified problem.

correlation: refers to the measure of the relationship between two sets of numbers or variables.

correlation coefficient: describes the magnitude and direction of the relationship between two variables.

cost of poor quality: the costs associated with providing poor-quality products or services. There are four categories of costs: internal failure costs (costs associated with defects found before the customer receives the product or service); external failure costs (costs associated with defects found after the customer receives the product or service); appraisal costs (costs incurred to determine the degree of conformance to quality requirements); and prevention costs (costs incurred to keep failure and appraisal costs to a minimum).

cost of quality (COQ): a term coined by Philip Crosby referring to the cost of poor quality.

count chart: a control chart for evaluating the stability of a process in terms of the count of events of a given classification occurring in a sample.

count-per-unit chart: a control chart for evaluating the stability of a process in terms of the average count of events of a given classification per unit occurring in a sample.

Cp: a widely used process capability index. It is expressed as

$$Cp = \frac{USL - LSL}{6\sigma}$$

Cpk: a widely used process capability index. It is expressed as

$$Cpk = \text{the lesser of} \left(\frac{USL - \mu}{3\sigma} \right) \text{or} \left(\frac{\mu - LSL}{3\sigma} \right)$$

CQA: certified quality auditor (ASQ)

CQE: certified quality engineer (ASQ)

CQI: continuous quality improvement (ASQ)

CQT: certified quality technician (ASQ)

CRE: certified reliability engineer (ASQ)

CSQE: certified software quality engineer (ASQ)

critical path: refers to the sequence of tasks that takes the longest time and determines a project's completion date.

❖❖

Critical Path Method (CPM): an activity-oriented project management technique that uses arrow-diagraming techniques to demonstrate both the time and cost required to complete a project. It provides one time estimate—normal time.

cross-functional team: a group organized by management and drawn from a variety of functional areas whose responsibility is to identify, analyze, and solve chronic problems that are beyond the scope of a quality circle's effort.

cumulative sum control chart: a control chart on which the plotted value is the cumulative sum of deviations of successive samples from a target value. The ordinate of each plotted point represents the algebraic sum of the previous ordinate and the most recent deviations from the target.

customer: see "external customer" and "internal customer"

customer delight: the result achieved when customer requirements are exceeded in ways the customer finds valuable.

customer satisfaction: the result of delivering a product or service that meets customer requirements, needs, and expectations.

customer service: refers to quality activities after the sale is made.

customer–supplier chain: a series of inputs, added value, and outputs that occur as employees are both customers and suppliers to one another.

customer–supplier partnership: a long-term relationship between a buyer and supplier characterized by teamwork and mutual confidence. The supplier is considered an extension of the buyer's organization. The partnership is based on several commitments. The buyer provides long-term contracts and uses fewer suppliers. The supplier implements quality assurance processes so that incoming inspection can be minimized. The supplier also helps the buyer reduce costs and improve product and process designs.

customer value: the market-perceived quality adjusted for the relative price of a product.

cycle time: refers to the time that it takes to complete a process from beginning to end and is a critical MBNQA criterion.

cycle time reduction: to reduce the time that it takes, from start to finish, to complete a particular business process.

D

data: facts presented in descriptive, numeric, or graphic form.

d chart: demerit chart

decision matrix: a matrix used by teams to evaluate problems or possible solutions. For example, after a matrix is drawn to evaluate possible solutions, the team lists them in the far-left vertical column. Next, the team selects criteria to rate the possible solutions, writing them across the top row. Then, each possible solution is rated on a scale of 1 to 5 for each criterion and the rating recorded in the corresponding grid. Finally, the ratings of all the criteria for each possible solution are added to determine its total score. The total score is then used to help decide which solution deserves the most attention.

defect: a product's or service's nonfulfillment of an intended requirement or reasonable expectation for use, including safety considerations. There are four classes of defects: Class 1, Very Serious, leads directly to severe injury or catastrophic economic loss; Class 2, Serious, leads directly to significant injury or significant economic loss; Class 3, Major, is related to major problems with respect to intended normal or reasonably foreseeable use; and Class 4, Minor, is related to minor problems with respect to intended normal or reasonably foreseeable use (see also "blemish," "imperfection," and "nonconformity").

delegation: a decision-making approach in which a facilitator shifts the responsibility for making a decision to someone else.

demerit chart: a control chart for evaluating a process in terms of a demerit (or quality score), i.e., a weighted sum of counts of various classified nonconformities.

Deming Cycle: see "plan-do-check-act cycle"

Deming Prize: award given annually to organizations that, according to the award guidelines, have successfully applied company-wide quality control based on statistical quality control and will keep up with it in the future. Although the award is named in honor of W. Edwards Deming, its criteria are not specifically related to Deming's teachings. There are three separate divisions for the award: the Deming Application Prize, the Deming Prize for Individuals, and the Deming Prize for Overseas Companies. The award process is overseen by the Deming Prize Committee of the Union of Japanese Scientists and Engineers in Tokyo.

demographics: variables among buyers in the consumer market, which include geographic location, age, sex, marital status, family size, social class, education, nationality, occupation, and income.

dependability: the degree to which a product is operable and capable of performing its required function at any randomly chosen time during its specified operating time, provided that the product is available at the start of that period. (Nonoperation-related influences are not included.) Dependability can be expressed by the ratio time available/time available + time required.

design: the second phase in the design of instruction in which decisions are made regarding course content, delivery methods, measurement, evaluation, and implementation. The outcome of this phase is a training plan.

design of experiments (DOE): a branch of applied statistics dealing with planning, conducting, analyzing, and interpreting controlled tests to evaluate the factors that control the value of a parameter or group of parameters. It is often used in conjunction with Quality Function Deployment (QFD).

designing in quality vs. inspecting in quality: see "prevention vs. detection"

desired quality: refers to the additional features and benefits a customer discovers when using a product or service which lead to increased customer satisfaction. If missing, a customer may become dissatisfied.

diagnostic journey and remedial journey: a two-phase investigation used by teams to solve chronic quality problems. In the first phase, the diagnostic journey, the team journeys from the symptom of a JOURNEY chronic problem to its cause. In the second phase, the remedial journey, the team journeys from the cause to its remedy.

discrete probability distribution: means that the measured process variable takes on a finite or limited number of values; no other possible values exist.

distribution: describes the amount of potential variation in outputs of a process; it is usually described in terms of its shape, average, and standard deviation.

Dodge–Romig sampling plans: plans for acceptance sampling developed by Harold F. Dodge and Harry G. Romig. Four sets of tables were published in 1940: single-sampling lot tolerance tables, double-sampling lot tolerance tables, single-sampling average outgoing quality limit tables, and double-sampling average outgoing quality limit tables.

E

education: refers to the knowledge employees need to learn to perform a future job or accept increased job responsibilities (see also training).

80-20: a term referring to the Pareto principle, which was first defined by J. M. Juran in 1950. The principle suggests that most effects come from relatively few causes; that is; 80 percent of the effects come from 20 percent of the possible causes.

employee involvement: a practice within an organization whereby employees regularly participate in making decisions on how their work areas operate, including making suggestions for improvement, planning, goal setting, and monitoring performance.

empowerment: a condition whereby employees have the authority to make decisions and take action in their work areas without prior approval. For example, an operator can stop a production process upon detecting a problem, or a customer service representative can send out a replacement product if a customer calls with a problem.

end users: external customers who purchase products/services for their own use or receive products/services as gifts; they are not employees of the organization supplying the product or service.

ethics: a code of conduct that is based on morals and defines what is fair for individuals and what is right for the public.

event: the starting or ending point for a group of tasks.

excited quality: the additional benefit a customer receives when a product or service goes beyond basic expectations. Excited quality "wows" the customer and separates the provider from the competition. If missing, the customer will still be satisfied.

expected quality: also known as basic quality, the minimum benefit a customer expects to receive from a product or service.

❖❖❖

experimental design: a formal plan that details the specifics for conducting an experiment, such as which responses, factors, levels, blocks, treatments, and tools are to be used.

external customer: a person or organization who receives a product, a service, or information but is not part of the organization supplying it (see also "internal customer").

external failure costs: costs associated with defects found after the customer receives the product or service.

F

facilitator: a team member who is responsible for creating favorable conditions that will enable a team to reach its purpose or achieve its goals by bringing together the necessary tools, information, and resources to get the job done.

factor analysis: a statistical technique that examines the relationships between a single dependent variable and multiple independent variations. For example, it is used to determine which questions on a questionnaire are related to a specific question such as "Would you buy this product again?"

failure mode analysis (FMA): a procedure to determine which malfunction symptoms appear immediately before or after a failure of a critical parameter in a system. After all the possible causes are listed for each symptom, the product is designed to eliminate the problems.

failure mode effects analysis (FMEA): a procedure in which each potential failure mode in every subitem of an item is analyzed to determine its effect on other subitems and on the required function of the item.

failure mode effects and criticality analysis (FMECA): a procedure that is performed after a failure mode effects analysis to classify each potential failure effect according to its severity and probability of occurrence.

feedback: the return of information in interpersonal communication; it may be based on fact or feeling and helps the party who is receiving the information judge how well he/she is being understood by the other party.

feedback and feedforward: terms defined by Feigenbaum to differentiate past quality traditions from today's strategic approach. Feedback is more reactive and is centered around the progression of an unsatisfactory product. Feedforward is more proactive and focuses on developing a satisfactory product in the first place.

fishbone diagram: see "cause-and-effect diagram"

fitness for use: a term used to indicate that a product or service fits the customer's defined purpose for that product or service.

flowchart: a graphical representation of the steps in a process. Flowcharts are drawn to better understand processes. The flowchart is one of the seven tools of quality.

❖❖❖

FMA: failure mode analysis

FMEA: failure mode effects analysis

FMECA: failure mode effects and criticality analysis

force-field analysis: a technique for analyzing the forces that aid or hinder an organization in reaching an objective. An arrow pointing to an objective is drawn down the middle of a piece of paper. The factors that will aid the objective's achievement, called the driving forces, are listed on the left side of the arrow. The factors that will hinder its achievement, called the restraining forces, are listed on the right side of the arrow.

formal communication: the officially sanctioned data within an organization, which includes publications, memoranda, training materials/events, public relations information, and company meetings.

14 points: W. Edward Deming's 14 management practices to help companies increase their quality and productivity. The 14 points are listed in Appendix B.

funnel experiment: an experiment that demonstrates the effects of tampering. Marbles are dropped through a funnel in an attempt to hit a flat-surfaced target below. The experiment shows that adjusting a stable process to compensate for an undesirable result or an extraordinarily good result will produce output that is worse than if the process had been left alone.

G

gap analysis: a technique that compares a company's existing state to its desired state (as expressed by its long-term plans) and determines what needs to be done to remove or minimize the gap.

Gantt chart: a type of bar chart used in process planning and control to display planned work and finished work in relation to time.

gauge repeatability and reproducibility (GR&R): the evaluation of a gauging instrument's accuracy by determining whether the measurements taken with it are repeatable (i.e., there is close agreement among a number of consecutive measurements of the output for the same value of the input under the same operating conditions) and reproducible (i.e., there is close agreement among repeated measurements of the output for the same value of input made under the same operating conditions over a period of time).

geometric dimensioning and tolerancing (GDT): a method to minimize production costs by showing the dimension and tolerancing on a drawing while considering the functions or relationships of part features.

goal: a nonquantitative statement of general intent, aim, or desire; it is the end point toward which management directs its efforts and resources.

go/no-go: state of a unit or product. Two parameters are possible: go conforms to specifications, and no-go does not conform to specifications.

H

hierarchy structure: describes an organization that is organized around functional departments/product lines or around customers/customer segments and is characterized by top-down management (also referred to as a bureaucratic model or pyramid structure).

high performance work: defined by the MBNQA criteria as work approaches systematically directed toward achieving ever higher levels of overall performance, including quality and productivity.

histogram: a graphic summary of variation in a set of data. The pictorial nature of the histogram lets people see patterns that are difficult to see in a simple table of numbers. The histogram is one of the seven tools of quality.

horizontal structure: describes an organization that is organized along a process or value-added chain, eliminating hierarchy and functional boundaries (also referred to as a systems structure).

hoshin planning: breakthrough planning. A Japanese strategic planning process in which a company develops up to four vision statements that indicate where the company should be in the next five years. Company goals and work plans are developed based on the vision statements. Periodic audits are then conducted to monitor progress.

House of Quality: a diagram (named for its house-shaped appearance) that clarifies the relationship between customer needs and product features. It helps correlate market or customer requirements and analysis of competitive products with higher-level technical and product characteristics and makes it possible to bring several factors into a single figure.

I

IEEE: Institute of Electrical and Electronics Engineers

imperfection: a quality characteristic's departure from its intended level or state without any association to conformance to specification requirements or to the usability of a product or service (see also "blemish," "defect," and "nonconformity").

in-control process: a process in which the statistical measure being evaluated is in a state of statistical control; i.e., the variations among the observed sampling results can be attributed to a constant system of chance causes (see also "out-of-control process").

informal communication: the unofficial communication that takes place in an organization as people talk freely and easily; it includes phone communication, e-mail, impromptu meetings, and personal conversations.

information: data transferred into an ordered format that makes it usable and allows one to draw conclusions.

inspection: measuring, examining, testing, and gauging one or more characteristics of a product or service and comparing the results with specified requirements to determine whether conformity is achieved for each characteristic.

intermediate customers: distributors, dealers, or brokers who make products and services available to the end user by repairing, repackaging, reselling, or creating finished goods from components or subassemblies.

internal customer: the recipient, person, or department of another person's or department's output (product, service, or information) within an organization (see also "external customer").

internal failure costs: costs associated with defects found before the customer receives the product or service.

interrelationship digraph: a management and planning tool that displays the relationship between factors in a complex situation. It identifies meaningful categories from a mass of ideas and is useful when relationships are difficult to determine.

intervention: an action taken by a leader to resolve an underlying conflict within a team or work group.

intervention focus: refers to how an intervention is directed: toward a group or toward a specific individual.

intervention intensity: refers to the strength of the intervention by the intervening person; intensity is affected by words, voice inflection, and nonverbal behaviors.

IQA: Institute of Quality Assurance

Ishikawa diagram: see "cause-and-effect diagram"

ISO: International Organization for Standardization

ISO 9000 series standards: a set of five individual but related international standards on quality management and quality assurance developed to help companies effectively document the quality system elements to be implemented to maintain an efficient quality system. The standards, initially published in 1987, are not specific to any particular industry, product, or service. The standards were developed by the International Organization for Standardization (ISO), a specialized international agency for standardization composed of the national standards bodies of 91 countries.

J

job description: a narrative explanation of the work, the work process, the work setting, and the organizational culture.

job specification: a list of the important functional and quality attributes (knowledge, skills, aptitudes, and personal characteristics) needed to succeed in the job.

Juran Trilogy: see quality trilogy

JUSE: Union of Japanese Scientists and Engineers

just-in-time manufacturing (JIT): an optimal material requirement planning system for a manufacturing process in which there is little or no manufacturing material inventory on hand at the manufacturing site and little or no incoming inspection.

❖❖

K

kaizen: a Japanese term that means gradual unending improvement by doing little things better and setting and achieving increasingly higher standards. The term was made famous by Masaaki Imai in his book *Kaizen: The Key to Japan's Competitive Success.*

Kano model: a representation of the three levels of customer satisfaction defined as dissatisfaction, neutrality, and delight.

L

ladder of inference: a mental model that explains how individuals have different interpretations about what happens in an organization. The model explains how people move beyond observable data and culturally understood meanings by adding their own meanings, assumptions, and theories.

leadership: an essential part of a quality improvement effort. Organization leaders must establish a vision, communicate that vision to those in the organization, and provide the tools, knowledge, and motivation necessary to accomplish the vision.

long-term goals: refers to goals that an organization hopes to achieve in the future, usually in three to five years. They are commonly referred to as strategic goals.

lot: a defined quantity of product accumulated under conditions that are considered uniform for sampling purposes.

lower control limit (LCL): control limit for points below the central line in a control chart.

M

macro processes: broad, far-ranging processes that often cross functional boundaries and are completed by more than one organization.

maintainability: the probability that a given maintenance action for an item under given usage conditions can be performed within a stated time interval when the maintenance is performed under stated conditions using stated procedures and resources. Maintainability has two categories: serviceability, the ease of conducting scheduled inspections and servicing, and repairability, the ease of restoring service after a failure.

Malcolm Baldrige National Quality Award (MBNQA): an award established by Congress in 1987 to raise awareness of quality management and to recognize U.S. companies that have implemented successful quality management systems. Two awards may be given annually in each of three categories: manufacturing company, service company, and small business. The award is named after the late Secretary of Commerce Malcolm Baldrige, a proponent of quality management. The U.S. Commerce Department's National Institute of Standards and Technology manages the award, and ASQ administers it. The major emphasis in determining success is achieving results.

management by policy: the organizational infrastructure that ensures that the right things are done at the right time.

managerial grid: a management theory developed by Robert Blake and Jane Mouton, that maintains that a manager's management style is based on his or her mind-set toward people; it focuses on attitudes rather than behavior. The theory uses a grid to measure concern with production and concern with people.

market-perceived quality: the customer's opinion of your products or services as compared to those of your competitors.

materials review board (MRB): a quality control committee or team, usually employed in manufacturing or other materials-processing installations, that possesses the responsibility and authority to deal with items or materials that do not conform to fitness-for-use specifications. An equivalent, error review board, is sometimes used in software development.

matrix chart: a management and planning tool that shows the relationships among various groups of data; it yields information about the relationships and the importance of task/method elements of the subjects.

matrix structure: describes an organization that is organized into a combination of functional and product departments; it brings together teams of people to work on projects and is driven by product scope.

maturity: the balance of courage and consideration that enables one to speak openly, give honest feedback, and demonstrate respect for the feelings of others.

mean: a measure of central tendency and is the arithmetic average of all measurements in a data set.

mean time between failures (MTBF): the average time interval between failures for repairable product for a defined unit of measure (e.g., operating hours, cycles, or miles).

measurement: refers to the reference standard or sample used for the comparison of properties.

median: the middle number or center value of a set of data when all the data are arranged in an increasing sequence.

micro processes: narrow processes made up of detailed steps and activities that could be accomplished by a single person.

mission statement: an explanation of purpose or reasons for existing as an organization; it provides the focus for the organization and defines its scope of business.

MIL-STD: military standard

MIL-Q-9858A: a military standard that describes quality program requirements.

MIL-STD-105E: a military standard that describes the sampling procedures and tables for inspection by attributes.

MIL-STD-45662A: a military standard that describes the requirements for creating and maintaining a calibration system for measurement and test equipment.

mode: the score that occurs most frequently in a data set.

multivariate control chart: a control chart for evaluating the stability or a process in terms of the levels of two or more variables or characteristics.

❖❖❖

N

n: sample size (the number of units in a sample)

NDE: nondestructive evaluation (see "nondestructive testing and evaluation")

NIST: National Institute of Standards and Technology

nominal group technique: a technique similar to brainstorming, used by teams to generate ideas on a particular subject. Team members are asked to silently come up with as many ideas as possible, writing them down. Each member is then asked to share one idea, which is recorded. After all the ideas are recorded, they are discussed and prioritized by the group.

nonconformity: the nonfulfillment of a specified requirement (see also "blemish," "defect," and "imperfection").

nondestructive testing and evaluation (NDT): testing and evaluation methods that do not damage or destroy the product being tested.

non-value-added: refers to tasks or activities that can be eliminated with no deterioration in product or service functionality, performance, or quality in the eyes of the customer.

NQM: National Quality Month

number of affected units chart (np chart): a control chart for evaluating the stability of a process in terms of the total number of units in a sample in which an event of a given classification occurs.

O

objective: a quantitative statement of future expectations and an indication of when the expectations should be achieved; it flows from goals and clarifies what people must accomplish.

off-the-job training: training that takes place away from the actual work site.

operating characteristic curve (OC curve): a graph used to determine the probability of accepting lots as a function of the lots' or processes' quality level when using various sampling plans. There are three types: Type A curves, which give the probability of acceptance for an individual lot coming from finite production (will not continue in the future); Type B curves, which give the probability of acceptance for lots coming from a continuous process; and Type C curves, which, for a continuous sampling plan, give the long-run percentage of product accepted during the sampling phase.

optimization: refers to achieving planned process results that meet the needs of the customer and supplier alike and minimize their combined costs.

out-of-control process: a process in which the statistical measure being evaluated is not in a state of statistical control, i.e., the variations among the observed sampling results can be attributed to a constant system of chance causes (see also "in-control process").

out of spec: a term used to indicate that a unit does not meet a given specification.

P

p chart: percent chart

parallel structure: describes an organizational module in which groups, such as quality circles or a quality council, exist in the organization in addition to and simultaneously with the line organization (also referred to as collateral structure).

pareto chart: a basic tool used to graphically rank causes from most significant to least significant. It utilizes a vertical bar graph in which the bar height reflects the frequency or impact of causes.

PDCA cycle: plan-do-check-act cycle

percent chart: a control chart for evaluating the stability of a process in terms of the percent of the total number of units in a sample in which an event of a given classification occurs. The percent chart is also referred to as a proportion chart.

performance appraisal: a formal method of measuring employees' progress against performance standards and providing feedback to them.

performance management system: a system that supports and contributes to the creation of high-performance work and work systems by translating behavioral principles into procedures.

performance plan: a performance management tool that describes desired performance and provides a way to assess the performance objectively.

performance test: an assessment device that requires candidates to complete an actual work task in a controlled situation.

personality test: an assessment device that measures a person's interaction skills and patterns of behavior.

plan-do-check-act cycle: a four-step process for quality improvement. In the first step (plan), a plan to effect improvement is developed. In the second step (do), the plan is carried out, preferably on a small scale. In the third step (check), the effects of the plan are observed. In the last step (act), the results are studied to determine what was learned and what can be predicted. The plan-do-check-act cycle is sometimes referred to as the Shewhart cycle because Walter A. Shewhart discussed the concept in his book *Statistical Method from the Viewpoint of Quality Control* and as the Deming cycle because W. Edwards Deming introduced the concept in Japan. The Japanese subsequently called it the Deming cycle.

point estimate: the single value used to estimate a population parameter. Point estimates are commonly referred to as the points at which the interval estimates are centered; these estimates give information about how much uncertainty is associated with the estimate.

poka-yoke: a term that means to foolproof the process by building safeguards into the system that avoid or immediately find errors. It comes from *poka*, which means "error," and *yokeru*, which means "to avoid."

population: a group of people, objects, observations, or measurements about which one wishes to draw conclusions.

precision: a characteristic of measurement that addresses the consistency or repeatability of a measurement system when the identical item is measured a number of times.

prevention costs: costs incurred to keep internal and external failure costs and appraisal costs to a minimum.

prevention vs. detection: a term used to contrast two types of quality activities. Prevention refers to those activities designed to prevent nonconformances in products and services. Detection refers to those activities designed to detect nonconformances already in products and services. Another term used to describe this distinction is "designing in quality vs. inspecting in quality."

primary: process that refers to the basic steps or activities that will produce the output without the "nice-to-haves."

probability: refers to the likelihood of occurrence.

probability distribution: a mathematical formula that relates the values of characteristics to their probability of occurrence in a population.

process: an activity or group of activities that takes an input, adds value to it, and provides an output to an internal or external customer.

process capability: a statistical measure of the inherent process variability for a given characteristic. The most widely accepted formula for process capability is 6σ.

process capability index: the value of the tolerance specified for the characteristic divided by the process capability. There are several types of process capability indexes, including the widely used C_p and C_{pk}.

process decision program chart (PDPC): a management and planning tool that identifies all events that can go wrong and the appropriate countermeasures for these events. It graphically represents all sequences that lead to a desirable effect.

process improvement: refers to the act of changing a process to reduce variability and cycle time and make the process more effective, efficient, and productive.

process improvement team (PIT): a natural work group or cross-functional team whose responsibility is to achieve needed improvements in existing processes. The life span of the team is based on the completion of the team purpose and specific goals.

process management: the collection of practices used to implement and process improve management and process effectiveness; it focuses on holding the gains achieved through process improvement and assuring process integrity.

process mapping: the flowcharting of a work process in detail, including key measurements.

process owner: the manager or leader who is responsible for ensuring that the total process is effective and efficient.

producer's risk: for a sampling plan, refers to the probability of not accepting a lot, the quality of which has a designated numerical value representing a level that is generally desirable. Usually the designated value will be the acceptable quality level.

product orientation: refers to a tendency to see customers' needs in terms of a product they want to buy, not in terms of the services, value, or benefits the product will produce.

product or service liability: the obligation of a company to make restitution for loss related to personal injury, property damage, or other harm caused by its product or service.

professional development plan: a career development tool created for an individual employee. Working together, the employee and his/her supervisor create a plan that matches the individual's career needs and aspirations with organizational demands.

profound knowledge theory: as defined by W. Edwards Deming, states that learning cannot be based on experience only; it requires comparisons of results to a prediction, plan, or an expression of theory. Predicting why something happens is essential to understand results and to continually improve.

program evaluation and review technique (PERT): an event-oriented project management planning and measurement technique that utilizes an arrow diagram or road map to identify all major project events and demonstrates the amount of time needed to complete a project. It provides three time estimates: optimistic, most likely, and pessimistic.

project life cycle: refers to the four sequential phases of project management: conceptualization, planning, implementation, and completion.

project plan: the blueprint for process improvement and the first step in changing a process. It includes a step-by-step description of how the process works, including current inputs, transformations, and outputs.

psychographic customer characteristics: variables among buyers in the consumer market that address lifestyle issues and include consumer interests, activities, and opinions.

Q

QA: quality assurance

QC: quality control

Q9000 series: refers to ANSI/ISO/ASQC Q9000 series standards, which is the Americanized version of the 1994 edition of the ISO 9000 series standards. The United States adopted the ISO 9000 series standards as the ANSI/ISO/ASQC Q9000 series.

QEIT: quality engineer in training (ASQ)

QIC: Quality Information Center of ASQ

QMJ: Quality Management Journal (ASQ)

QP: Quality Progress (ASQ)

❖❖

quality: a subjective term for which each person has his or her own definition. In technical usage, quality can have two meanings: (1) the characteristics of a product or service that bear on its ability to satisfy stated or implied needs and (2) a product or service free of deficiencies.

quality adviser: the person who helps team members work together in quality processes and is a consultant to the team. The adviser is concerned about the process and how decisions are made rather than about which decisions are made.

quality assessment: the process of identifying business practices, attitudes, and activities that are enhancing or inhibiting the achievement of quality improvement in an organization.

quality assurance/quality control: two terms that have many interpretations because of the multiple definitions for the words "assurance" and "control." For example, "assurance" can mean the act of giving confidence, the state of being certain, or the act of making certain; "control" can mean an evaluation to indicate needed corrective responses, the act of guiding, or the state of a process in which the variability is attributable to a constant system of chance causes. (For a detailed discussion on the multiple definitions, see ANSI/ISO/ASQC A35342, Statistics—Vocabulary and Symbols—Statistical Quality Control.) One definition of quality assurance is: all the planned and systematic activities implemented within the quality system that can be demonstrated to provide confidence that a product or service will fulfill requirements for quality. One definition for quality control is: the operational techniques and activities used to fulfill requirements for quality. Often, however, "quality assurance" and "quality control" are used interchangeably, referring to the actions performed to ensure the quality of a product, service, or process.

quality audit: a systematic, independent examination and review to determine whether quality activities and related results comply with planned arrangements and whether these arrangements are implemented effectively and are suitable to achieve the objectives.

quality circles: quality improvement or self-improvement study groups composed of a small number of employees—10 or fewer—and their supervisor.

quality control (QC): see "quality assurance/quality control"

quality costs: see "cost of poor quality"

quality cost reports: a system of collecting quality costs that uses a spreadsheet to list the elements of quality costs against a spread of the departments, areas, or projects in which the costs will occur and summarizes the data in exact accordance with plans for its use. The reports help organizations review prevention costs, appraisal costs, and internal and external failure costs.

quality culture: consists of employee opinions, beliefs, traditions, and practices concerning quality.

quality engineering: the analysis of a manufacturing system at all stages to maximize the quality of the process itself and the products it produces.

quality evidence audit: the final part of the data-gathering phase of a quality assessment in which data related to quality improvements is compiled, divided into key areas, and rated. The objective is to collect easily quantifiable data that can be clarified by follow-up interviews with select personnel.

quality function: the entire collection of activities through which an organization achieves fitness for use, no matter where these activities are performed.

quality function deployment (QFD): a structured method in which customer requirements are translated into appropriate technical requirements for each stage of product development and production. The QFD process is often referred to as listening to the voice of the customer.

quality loss function: a parabolic approximation of the quality loss that occurs when a quality characteristic deviates from its target value. The quality loss function is expressed in monetary units: The cost of deviating from the target increases quadratically the farther the quality characteristic moves from the target. The formula used to compute the quality loss function depends on the type of quality characteristic being used. The quality loss function was first introduced in this form by Genichi Taguchi.

quality metrics: numerical measurements that give an organization the ability to set goals and evaluate actual performance versus plan.

quality plan: the document setting out the specific quality practices, resources, and sequence of activities relevant to a particular product, project, or contract.

quality planning: the activity of establishing quality goals and developing the processes and products required.

quality principles: the rules or concepts that an organization believes in collectively. The principles have been formulated by senior management with input from others and are communicated and understood at every level of the organization.

quality score chart (Q chart): a control chart for evaluating the stability of a process in terms of a quality score. The quality score is the weighted sum of the count of events of various classifications in which each classification is assigned a weight.

quality system: the organizational structure, procedures, processes, and resources needed to implement quality management.

quality trilogy: a three-pronged approach to managing for quality. The three legs are quality planning (developing the products and processes required to meet customer needs), quality control (meeting product and process goals), and quality improvement (achieving unprecedented levels of performance).

quincunx: a tool that creates frequency distributions. Beads tumble over numerous horizontal rows of pins, which force the beads to the right or left. After a random journey, the beads are dropped into vertical slots. After many beads are dropped, a frequency distribution results. In the classroom, quincunxes are often used to simulate a manufacturing process. The quincunx was invented by English scientist Francis Galton in the 1890s.

❖❖

R

RAM: reliability/availability/maintainability (see individual entries).

random sampling: a sampling method in which every element in the population has an equal chance of being included.

range chart (R chart): a control chart in which the subgroup range, R, is used to evaluate the stability of the variability within a process.

ratio analysis: the process of relating isolated business numbers, such as sales, margins, expenses, and profits, to make them meaningful.

red bead experiment: an experiment developed by W. Edwards Deming to illustrate that it is impossible to put employees in rank order of performance for the coming year based on their performance during the past year because performance differences must be attributed to the system, not to employees. Four thousand red and white beads, 20 percent red, in a jar and six people are needed for the experiment. The participants' goal is to produce white beads because the customer will not accept red beads. One person begins by stirring the beads and then, blindfolded, selects a sample of 50 beads. That person hands the jar to the next person, who repeats the process, and so on. When everyone has his or her sample, the number of red beads for each is counted. The limits of variation between employees that can be attributed to the system are calculated. Everyone will fall within the calculated limits of variation that could arise from the system. The calculations will show that there is no evidence one person will be a better performer than another in the future. The experiment shows that it would be a waste of management's time to try to find out why, say, John produced four red beads and Jane produced 15; instead, management should improve the system, making it possible for everyone to produce more white beads.

Registrar Accreditation Board (RAB): a board that evaluates the competency and reliability of registrars (organizations that assess and register companies to the appropriate ISO 9000 series standards). The Registrar Accreditation Board, formed in 1989 by ASQ, is governed by a board of directors from industry, academia, and quality management consulting firms.

registration to standards: a process in which an accredited, independent third-party organization conducts an on-site audit of a company's operations against the requirements of the standard to which the company wants to be registered. Upon successful completion of the audit, the company receives a certificate indicating that it has met the standard requirements.

regression analysis: a study used to understand the relationship between two or more variables. Regression analysis makes it possible to predict one variable from knowledge about another. The relationship can be mathematically determined and expressed as a correlation coefficient.

reinforcement: the process of ensuring that the right knowledge and skills are being used; it has been described as catching people doing things right.

reliability: refers to the ability of a feedback instrument to produce the same results over repeated administration. It is the ability of an instrument to measure consistently and with relative absence of error. It is also the probability of a product performing its intended function under stated conditions for a given period of time (see also: mean time between failures).

resistance to change: the unwillingness to change beliefs, habits, and ways of doing things.

return on equity (ROE): the net profit after taxes, divided by last year's tangible stockholders' equity, and then multiplied by 100 to provide a percentage (also referred to as return on net worth).

return on investment (ROI): an umbrella term for a variety of ratios measuring an organization's business performance and calculated by dividing some measure of return by a measure of investment and then multiplying by 100 to provide a percentage. In its most basic form, ROI indicates what remains from all money taken in after all expenses are paid.

return on net assets (RONA): a measurement of the earning power of the firm's investment in assets, calculated by dividing net profit after taxes by last year's tangible total assets and then multiplying by 100 to provide a percentage.

right the first time: a term used to convey the concept that it is beneficial and more cost effective to take the necessary steps up front to ensure a product or service meets its requirements than to provide a product or service that will need rework or not meet customers' needs. In other words, an organization should engage in defect prevention rather than defect detection.

robustness: the condition of a product or process design that remains relatively stable with a minimum of variation even though factors that influence operations or usage, such as environment and wear, are constantly changing.

root cause analysis: a quality tool used to distinguish the source of defects or problems. It is a structured approach that focuses on the decisive or original cause of a problem or condition.

run chart: a form of trend analysis that uses a graph to show a process measurement on a vertical access against time, with a reference line to show the average of the data. A trend is indicated when a series of collected data points head up or down.

S

sample: a finite number of items of a similar type taken from a population for the purpose of examination to determine whether all members of the population would conform to quality requirements or specifications.

sample size: refers to the number of units in a sample randomly chosen from the population.

sample standard deviation chart (s chart): a control chart in which the subgroup standard deviation, s, is used to evaluate the stability of the variability within a process.

sampling: the process of drawing conclusions about the population based on a part of the population.

scatter diagram: a graphical technique to analyze the relationship between two variables. Two sets of data are plotted on a graph, with the y-axis being used for the variable to be predicted and the x-axis being used for the variable to make the prediction. The graph will show possible relationships (although two variables might appear to be related, they might not be: Those who know most about the variables must make that evaluation). The scatter diagram is one of the seven tools of quality.

self-inspection: the process by which employees inspect their own work according to specified rules.

self-managed team: a team that requires little supervision and manages itself and the day-to-day work it does; self-directed teams are responsible for whole work processes and schedules with each individual performing multiple tasks.

seven tools of quality: tools that help organizations understand their processes in order to improve them. The tools are the cause-and-effect diagram, check sheet, control chart, flowchart, histogram, Pareto chart, and scatter diagram (see individual entries).

Shewhart cycle: see "plan-do-check-act cycle"

signal-to-noise ratio (S/N ratio): a mathematical equation that indicates the magnitude of an experimental effect above the effect of experimental error due to chance fluctuations.

situational leadership: a leadership theory that maintains that leadership style should change based on the person and the situation, with the leader displaying varying degrees of directive and supportive behavior.

six-sigma quality: a term used generally to indicate that a process is well controlled, i.e., process limits ±3 sigma from the centerline in a control chart, and requirements/tolerance limits ±6 sigma from the centerline. The term was initiated by Motorola.

slack time: the time an activity can be delayed without delaying the entire project; it is determined by calculating the difference between the latest allowable date and the earliest expected date (see project evaluation and review technique).

special causes: causes of variation that arise because of special circumstances. They are not an inherent part of a process. Special causes are also referred to as assignable causes (see also "common causes").

specification: the engineering requirement, used for judging the acceptability of a particular product/service based on product characteristics, such as appearance, performance, and size. In statistical analysis, specifications refer to the document that prescribes the requirements with which the product or service has to perform.

sporadic problem: a sudden adverse change in the status quo that can be remedied by restoring the status quo. For example, actions such as changing a worn part or handling an irate customer can restore the status quo.

stages of team growth: refers to the four stages defined by Peter Scholtes: forming, storming, norming, and performing. The stages help team members accept the normal problems that occur on the path from forming a group to becoming a team.

❖❖❖

stakeholders: people, departments, and organizations that have an investment or interest in the success or actions taken by the organization, but are not directly involved in the customer–supplier chain.

standard: a statement, specification, or quantity of material against which measured outputs from a process may be judged as acceptable or unacceptable.

standard deviation: a calculated measure of variability that shows how much the data are spread out around the mean.

statement of work (SOW): a description of the actual work to be accomplished. It is derived from the work breakdown structure and, when combined with the project specifications, becomes the basis for the contractual agreement on the project (also referred to as scope of work).

statistical process control (SPC): the application of statistical techniques to control a process. Often the term "statistical quality control" is used interchangeably with "statistical process control"

statistical quality control (SQC): the application of statistical techniques to control quality. Often the term "statistical process control" is used interchangeably with "statistical quality control" although statistical quality control includes acceptance sampling as well as statistical process control.

storyboarding: a technique that visually displays thoughts and ideas and groups them into categories, making all aspects of a process visible at once.

strategic fit review: a process by which senior mangers assess the future of each project to a particular organization in terms of its ability to advance the mission and goals of that organization.

strategic planning: a method to set an organization's long range goals and observations.

structural variation: variation caused by regular, systematic changes in output, such as seasonal patterns and long-term trends.

supplier: any other-company provider of goods and services whose goods and services may be used at any stage in the production, design, delivery and use of a company's products and services. Suppliers include businesses, such as distributors, dealers, warranty repair services, transportation contractors, and franchises, and service suppliers, such as health care, training, and education. Internal suppliers provide materials or services to internal customers.

supplier audits: reviews that are planned and carried out to verify the adequacy and effectiveness of a supplier's quality program, drive improvement, and increased value.

supplier certification: the process of evaluating the performance of a supplier with the intent of authorizing the supplier to self-certify shipments if such authorization is justified.

supplier quality assurance: confidence that a supplier's product or service will fulfill its customers' needs. This confidence is achieved by creating a relationship between the customer and supplier that ensures the product will be fit for use with minimal corrective action and inspection. According to J. M. Juran, there are nine primary activities needed: (1) define product and program quality requirements, (2) evaluate alterative suppliers, (3) select suppliers, (4) conduct joint quality planning, (5) cooperate with the supplier during the execution of the contract, (6) obtain proof of conformance to requirements, (7) certify qualified suppliers, (8) conduct quality improvement programs as required, and (9) create and use supplier quality ratings.

SWOT analysis: an assessment of an organization's key strengths, weaknesses, opportunities, and threats. It considers factors such as the organization's industry, the competitive position, functional areas, and management.

system: a network of connecting processes that work together to accomplish the aim of the system.

systems approach to management: a management theory that views the organization as a unified, purposeful combination of interrelated parts; managers must look at the organization as a whole and understand that activity in one part of the organization affects all parts of the organization (also known as systems thinking).

T

tactical plans: short-term plans, usually of one- to two-year durations, that describe actions the organization will take to meet its strategic business plan.

tactics: the strategies and processes that help an organization meet its objectives.

Taguchi methods: the American Supplier Institute's trademarked term for the quality engineering methodology developed by Genichi Taguchi. In this engineering approach to quality control, Taguchi calls for off-line quality control, on-line quality control, and a system of experimental design to improve quality and reduce costs.

tampering: action taken to compensate for variation within the control limits of a stable system. Tampering increases rather than decreases variation, as evidenced in the funnel experiment.

team: a set of two or more people who are equally accountable for the accomplishment of a purpose and specific performance goals; it is also defined as a small number of people with complimentary skills who are committed to a common purpose.

team-based structure: describes an organizational structure in which team members are organized around performing a specific function of the business, such as handling customer complaints or assembling an engine.

theory of knowledge: a belief that management is about prediction, and people learn not only from experience but also from theory. When people study a process and develop a theory, they can compare their predictions with their observations; profound learning results.

theory x and theory y: a management theory developed by Douglas McGregor that maintains that there are two contrasting management styles, each of which is based on the manager's view of human nature. Theory X managers take a negative view of human nature and assume that most employees do not like work and try to avoid it. Theory Y managers take a positive view of human nature and believe that employees want to work, will seek and accept responsibility, and can offer creative solutions to organizational problems.

theory z: coined by William G. Ouchi, refers to a Japanese style of management that is characterized by long-term employment, slow promotions, considerable job rotation, consensus-style decision making, and concern for the employee as a whole.

360-degree feedback process: an evaluation method that provides feedback from the perspectives of self, peers, direct reports, customers, and suppliers.

top-management commitment: participation of the highest-level officials in their organization's quality improvement efforts. Their participation includes establishing and serving on a quality committee, establishing quality policies and goals, deploying those goals to lower levels of the organization, providing the resources and training that the lower levels need to achieve the goals, participating in quality improvement teams, reviewing progress organization-wide, recognizing those who have performed well, and revising the current reward system to reflect the importance of achieving the quality goals.

total quality management (TQM): a term initially coined by the Naval Air Systems Command to describe its Japanese-style management approach to quality improvement. Since then, total quality management (TQM) has taken on many meanings. Simply put, TQM is a management approach to long-term success through customer satisfaction. TQM is based on the participation of all members of an organization in improving processes, products, services, and the culture they work in. TQM benefits all organization members and society. The methods for implementing this approach are found in the teachings of such quality leaders as Philip B. Crosby, W. Edwards Deming, Armand V. Feigenbaum, Kaoru Ishikawa, and J. M. Juran.

traditional organizations: those organizations not driven by customers and quality policies. Also refers to organizations managed primarily through functional units.

training: refers to the skills that employees need to learn in order to perform or improve their performances of their current jobs or tasks.

tree diagram: a management and planning tool that shows the complete range of subtasks required to achieve an objective. A problem-solving method can be identified from this analysis.

trend analysis: refers to the charting of data over time to identify a tendency or direction.

type I error: an incorrect decision to reject something (such as a statistical hypothesis or a lot of products) when it is acceptable.

type II error: an incorrect decision to accept something when it is unacceptable.

❖❖❖

U

u chart: count per unit chart

upper control limit (UCL): control limit for points above the central line in a control chart.

V

validity: refers to the ability of a feedback instrument to measure what it was intended to measure.

value-added: refers to tasks or activities that convert resources into products or services consistent with customer requirements. The customer can be internal or external to the organization.

values: statements that clarify the behaviors that the organization expects in order to move toward its vision and mission. Values reflect an organization's personality and culture.

variables data: measurement information. Control charts based on variables data include average (X-) chart, range (R) chart, and sample standard deviation (s) chart.

variable sampling plan: a plan in which a sample is taken and a measurement of a specified quality characteristic is made on each unit. The measurements are summarized into a simple statistic, and the observed value is compared with an allowable value defined in the plan.

variation: a change in data, a characteristic, or a function that is caused by one of four factors: special causes, common causes, tampering, or structural variation (see individual entries).

virtual super team (VST): a team that functions as a de facto small business and manages itself as a value center. It can be organized along business, product, process, or technology lines and requires excellent lateral teaming skills and constant reshaping.

vision: a statement that explains in measurable terms what the company wants to become and what it hopes to achieve.

vital few, useful many: a term used by J. M. Juran to describe his use of the Pareto principle, which he first defined in 1950. (The principle was used much earlier in economics and inventory control methodologies.) The principle suggests that most effects come from relatively few causes; that is, 80 percent of the effects come from 20 percent of the possible causes. The 20 percent of the possible causes are referred to as the "vital few"; the remaining causes are referred to as the "useful many." When Juran first defined this principle, he referred to the remaining causes as the "trivial many," but realizing that no problems are trivial in quality assurance, he changed it to "useful many."

voice of the customer: a company's efforts to provide products and services that truly reflect customer needs and expectations ("voice").

W

work breakdown structure (WBS): a project management technique by which a project is divided into tasks, subtasks, and units of work to be performed.

work group: a group composed of people from one functional area who work together on a daily basis and whose goal is to improve the processes of their function.

world-class quality: a term used to indicate a standard of excellence: best of the best.

X

X- chart: average chart

Z

zero defects: a performance standard developed by Philip B. Crosby to address a dual attitude in the workplace: People are willing to accept imperfection in some areas, while, in other areas, they expect the number of defects to be zero. This dual attitude had developed because of the conditioning that people are human and humans make mistakes. However, the zero-defects methodology states that if people commit themselves to watching details and avoiding errors, they can move closer to the goal of zero.

Index

❖❖

❖❖